AF544804

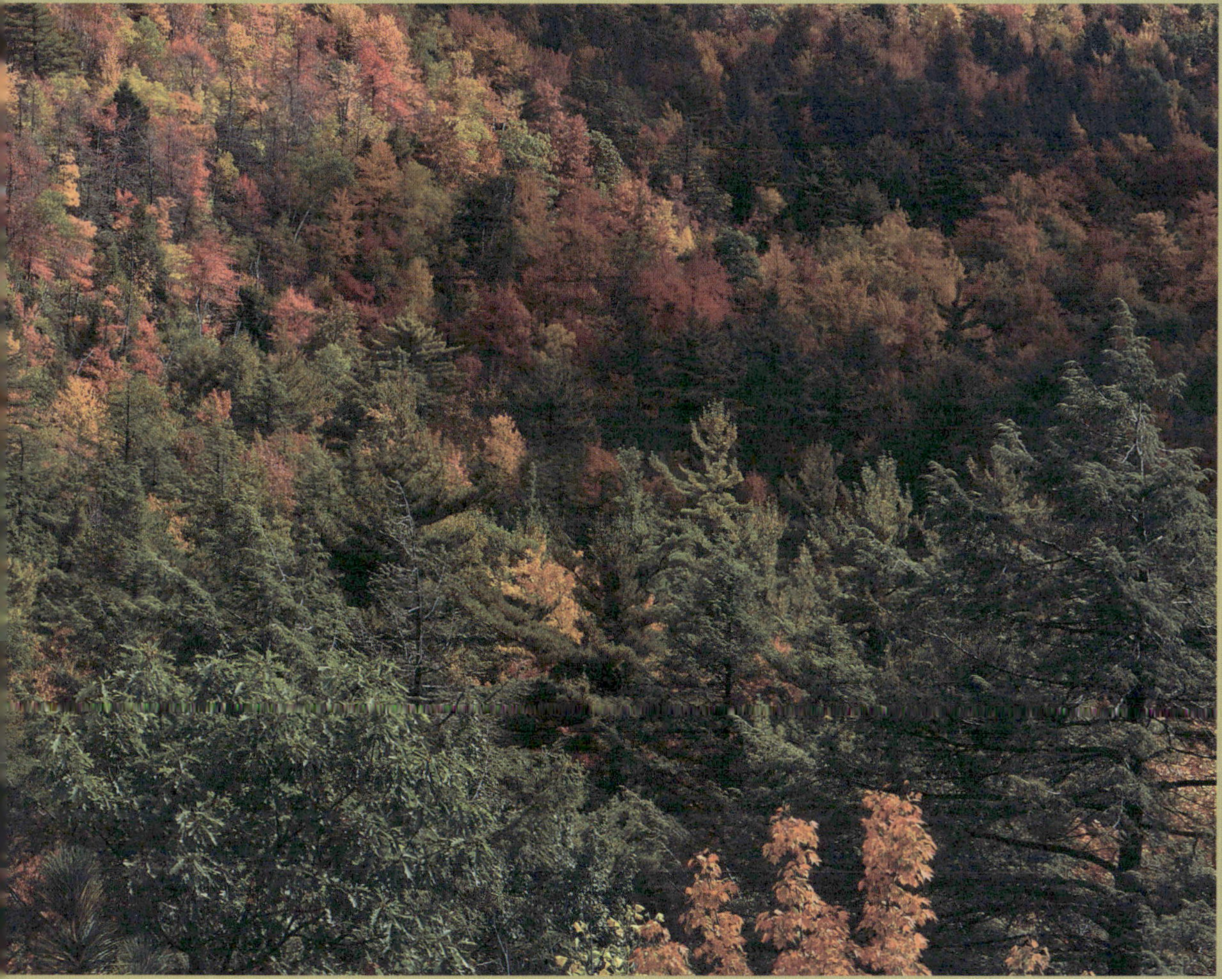

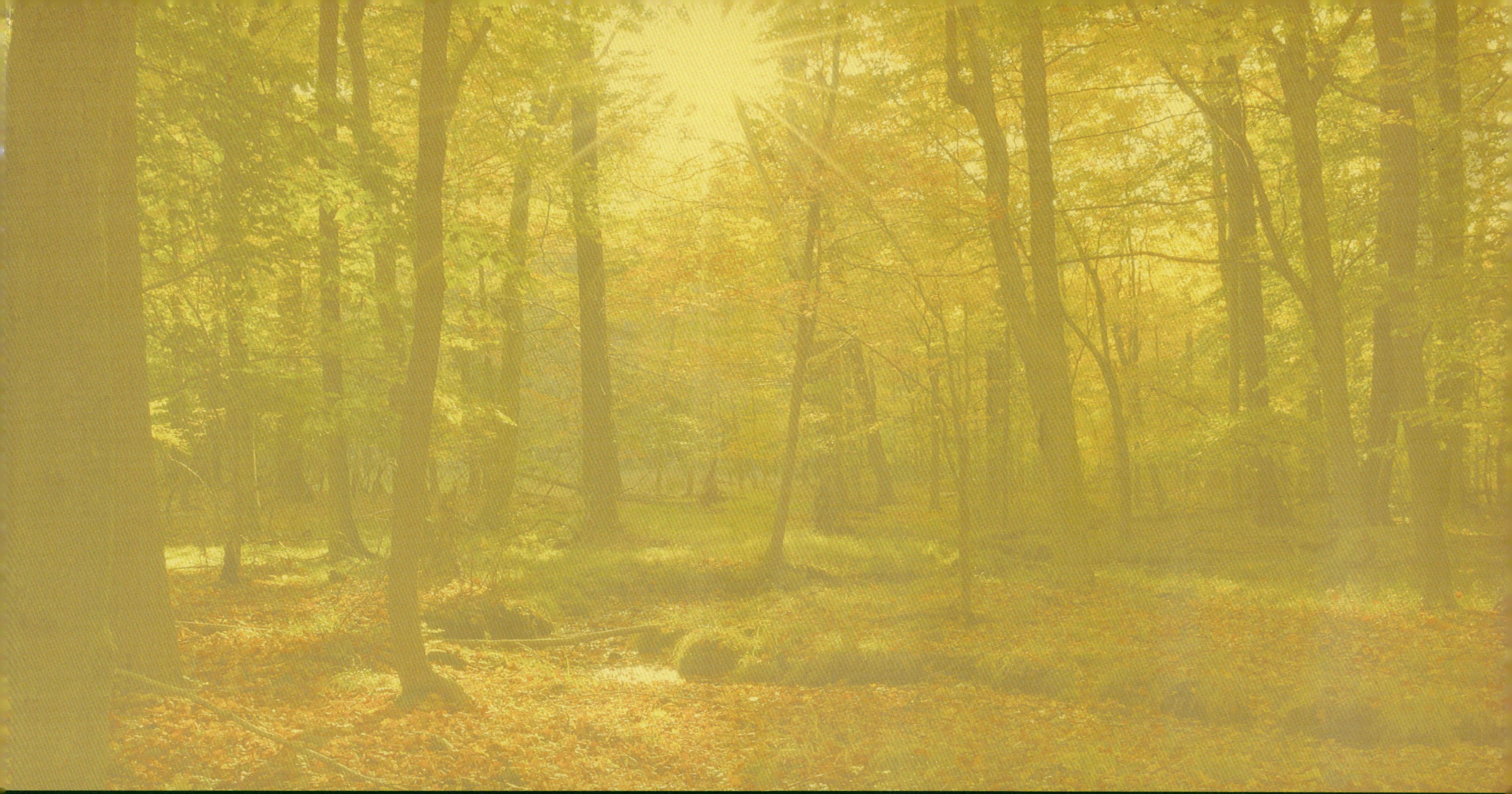

Michael Adamovic

Hudson Valley Reflections

ILLUSTRATED TRAVEL AND FIELD GUIDE

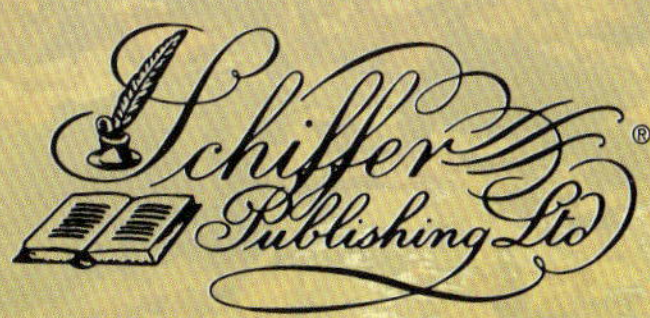

4880 Lower Valley Road • Atglen, PA 19310

Other Schiffer Books on Related Subjects:

Pinelands: New Jersey's Suburban Wilderness, Albert D. Horner, ISBN 978-0-7643-4881-5

Lighthouses of New York, Rick Tuers, ISBN 978-0-7643-2692-9

365 Things to Do in Ithaca, New York: Complete Insider's Guide to All Things Ithaca, Laurel Guy, ISBN 978-0-7643-5257-7

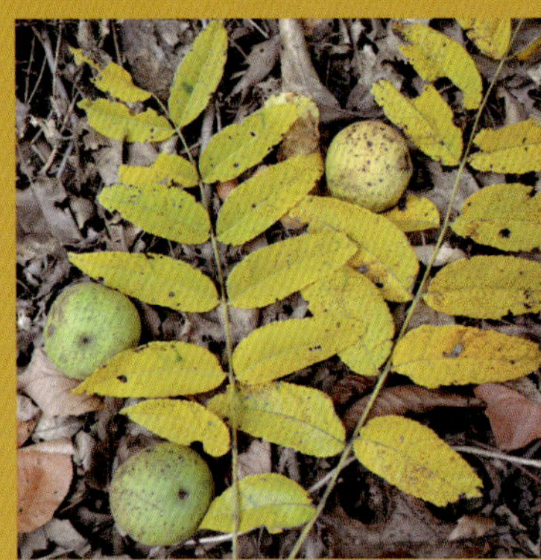

Library of Congress Control Number: 2017934985

Designed by RoS
Cover design by RoS
Type set in Amplitude/Chaparral Pro

ISBN: 978-0-7643-5346-8
Printed in China

Published by Schiffer Publishing, Ltd.
4880 Lower Valley Road
Atglen, PA 19310
Phone: (610) 593-1777; Fax: (610) 593-2002
E-mail: Info@schifferbooks.com
Web: www.schifferbooks.com

For our complete selection of fine books on this and related subjects, please visit our website at www.schifferbooks.com. You may also write for a free catalog.

Schiffer Publishing's titles are available at special discounts for bulk purchases for sales promotions or premiums. Special editions, including personalized covers, corporate imprints, and excerpts, can be created in large quantities for special needs. For more information, contact the publisher.

We are always looking for people to write books on new and related subjects. If you have an idea for a book, please contact us at proposals@schifferbooks.com.

For Meagan—My inspiration & love

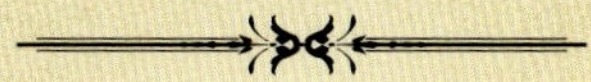

"I thank God I was born on the banks of the Hudson!
I think it an invaluable advantage to be born and
brought up in the neighborhood of some grand
and noble object in nature: a river, a lake,
or a mountain."

—Washington Irving

CONTENTS

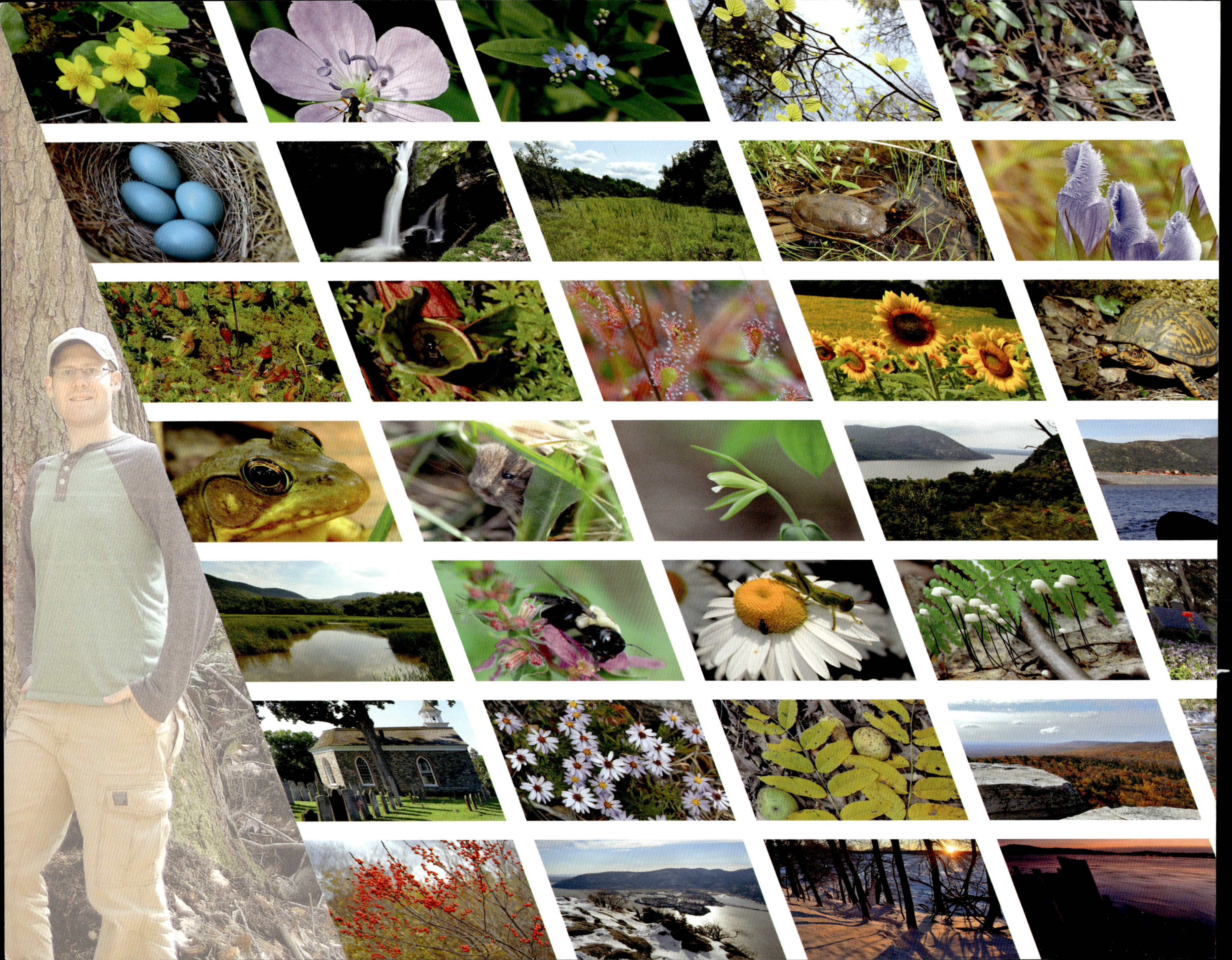

INTRODUCTION

It's been said that had the country been settled in reverse, from the shores of the Pacific eastward to the Atlantic, much of the land now lying within the bounds of the Hudson Valley would have most certainly been set aside, given a protective status, and incorporated into a national park. While this idea may seem odd at first, given the fact that we're accustomed to seeing the land around us being heedlessly razed and developed, having its resources stripped and exploited, and landmarks erased like they hold little importance, if we look upon what remains with a new set of eyes and envision the glory of what once was, it becomes easier to imagine such a proposition. The land is far from mundane. A cursory search of art and literature attests to this—just take a look at Washington Irving's tales of the supernatural, or the innumerable paintings by notable Hudson River School artists such as Thomas Cole and Frederic Church. These people understood the power of the landscape and gained nourishment from it as a muse, ultimately creating profound works that continue to amaze and inspire. These elements still exist.

Anyone who has ever walked among the eclectic wonders of the Hudson Valley would surely agree that some of its aspects are as grand and magnificent as Yosemite, Yellowstone, and yes, even the mighty Grand Canyon. The Hudson itself in certain sections is rather like a canyon, or, as the proper term would be, fjord, like those of Norway. The last ice age carved it, and as the massive ice sheets slowly started melting around 21,000 years ago, its base was filled in with gravelly sediments of glacial outwash several hundred feet thick, before finally being submerged beneath the placid surface of the Hudson's murky waters. Near the promontory of West Point, the Hudson's narrowest and deepest stretch, the river plummets 216 feet. Here, among the craggy mountains of the Highlands that jettison upward from the shores on both sides, the land takes on a primeval appearance, as awe-inspiring from the water's surface as from the summit of one the mountains with such piquant names as Crow's Nest, Storm King, and Breakneck Ridge. Climbing atop one of these peaks, immersed in the sun-dry climate of the region, walking among balds of little-bluestem grass, native prickly-pear cactus, sweet fern, and low-bush blueberry, or rambling among forests of stunted trees composed mainly of various oaks, hickories, maples, and dense groves of black birches, our minds become intoxicated with the sights and smells wholly unique to this enchanted land. Scenes from legendary tales materialize before us.

On misty, stormy days at the southern gate of the Highlands, one fancies hearing traces of a mischievous imp's trumpet, which he supposedly blows at the summit of Dunderberg Mountain to arouse the unkind elements to harass sailors and other passersby who fail to pay homage to him by bowing their heads on approach. On the precipitous slopes of Crow's Nest, one senses the presence of Dolph Heyliger, a Dutch lad in one of Irving's tales, who after being thrown overboard from a sloop heading north to Albany, swam to shore, and ascended the wild mountain's steep sides, rife with rattlesnakes and tangles of vines and unruly catbriars, before fortuitously stumbling across a hunting party that put him back on track to securing his fortune and destiny. As one proceeds further up river, the massive set of mountains looming at the northern entrance of the Highlands brings to mind a Native American legend. Two imposing mountains, Storm King on the western shore, and Breakneck opposite, were said in ancient times to be locked together to form a massive stone dam spanning where the Hudson now flows. Behind the dam lay a lake of massive proportions that harbored vast quantities of fish and other wildlife—a bona fide cornucopia of wealth—that fed the native people well. Local tribes eventually became greedy, killing and taking more than was necessary, which angered Manitou, the Great Creator. In punishment, he destroyed the dam so that its life-giving waters might flow forth to others who would better appreciate the precious gifts. And so, the Hudson was born.

It's easy to become enraptured by the surroundings. Adrien Van der Donck, an early Dutch colonizer, fell under the spell of the Hudson Valley, ultimately becoming one of its greatest admirers and proponents for settlement. In his 1655 treatise, *A Description of New Netherland*, he meticulously detailed everything unique about his adopted homeland, from its diverse plant and animal communities to the rich abundance of natural resources, going so far as to document the lives and customs of its aboriginal inhabitants. This is among the finest and most descriptive records of the Hudson Valley before Europeans changed it forever. What he describes is nothing less than astounding.

New Netherland was a land of plenty, a veritable paradise whose treats could be plucked with ease. Unlike the deforested environs of Europe, the New World possessed a cloak of "fine species of trees in such measure that they cover[ed] almost the whole country." To someone unaccustomed to this rich abundance the scene appeared almost "too plentiful." The land, the waters, and even the sky teemed with a quantity of life so high that Van der Donck doubted whether his vivid descriptions would be believed by those reading his book back home. In salty stretches of the southern Hudson vast reefs of oysters choked the river in places and contained oysters a "foot long and correspondingly wide." Waterfowl flocks were so large that one hunter was recorded to have "shot and bagged sixteen geese with one shot." This paled in comparison to the tremendous flocks of the now-extinct passenger pigeon that swarmed in such prodigious numbers as to "resemble clouds in the sky" that shrouded the "earth in shade." In 1647, two whales, "one white and one brown," swam a remarkable 145 miles up the narrowing river until "one beached itself" near the site of present-day Albany. Gleeful settlers scrambled to extract the valuable oil of the "quite blubbery" creature. Practically tossed at their feet, this precious leviathan was almost certainly taken as a sign that Providence was pleased with their work and was blessing them for it. From this belief, and surrounded by the necessary ingredients, the foundations for an Empire State were laid.

While what remains today is still spectacular, what an Eden it must have been 400 years ago! We owe the landscape's remaining grandeur to the numerous environmental organizations and coalitions, who have fought long battles both in the public arena and in court to secure, preserve, and restore our priceless natural wonders. New York leads the nation in environmental protection. By creating parkland among the most beautiful and biologically significant of habitats, and by stopping polluters from muddying the Hudson and other waterways, we have embraced our heritage, even at a financial cost. The idea that health, recreation, and aesthetics are more important to the human spirit than economic expansion has finally been recognized. The area has not stagnated, as some predicted. Rather, like the ever-flowing Hudson, we continue steadfast on our journey.

Those priorities were neglected and ignored until recent decades. Over the years, the river became an all-too-convenient place to dump everything from paint and cadmium to raw sewage and industrial insulators like PCBs. The Hudson is no longer the sewer it once was. The dumping of waste and chemicals has come to a halt, and swimming and kayaking are in full force. Oysters and other aquatic creatures sensitive to water quality are returning, and with the removal of toxins such as PCBs from the riverbed, wildlife contamination is slowly decreasing. Fishermen are less fearful about consuming the river's bounty. In short, the river is returning to a quality that hasn't been witnessed for well over a century. These advances have led to a new golden age, one dominated by environmental conscientiousness and stewardship that extends well beyond the water's edge.

The Hudson Valley's terrestrial ecosystems also support an unparalleled diversity of life. A lucky visitor venturing into the depths of the lush woods of Orange County in mid-May might stumble across small whorled pogonia, one of the most imperiled orchids in the nation, gracing thick arrays of interrupted ferns. In rockier locales, such as the Highlands and Shawangunks, threatened rattlesnakes wiggle through tight crevices and roam the landscape in search of their next meal. An engaged hiker may be startled to hear the characteristic rattle emanating from a patch of huckleberry bushes just off the trail. Cool mountain streams and lowland rivers contain numerous fishes, including sizable specimens of brook, rainbow, and brown trout, which keep dedicated anglers busy in the spring and throughout the languid summer months. The smooth surfaces of murky marshes and crystalline lakes in Sterling Forest may be interrupted by serpentine ripples as a beaver or muskrat sets off in quest of new building material for a snug wooden hut. Overhead, gliding on gentle breezes, eagles and various species of hawk keep a watchful eye on their domains, scanning every inch of water and ground for a momentary disturbance by their unmindful prey.

Habitats more altered by man, namely the open fields that lend immense pastoral beauty, also foster a diverse array of valuable organisms. Fields not dominated by agricultural crops support hardy and whimsical wildflower species that in late summer and fall blaze out in a quilt-like color pattern. Asters and goldenrods are ubiquitous across the Hudson Valley and add copious blues, whites, and tints of yellow-gold to the breeze-blown fields. In *Henry Hudson, the Navigator* (G. M. Asher, 1860), a member of Hudson's crew wrote that these aggregations of "Grasse and Flowers" permeated the air with "very sweet smells." Uncommon to rare plants may also thrive here—the most exquisite being the amethyst-hued fringed gentian and New England blazing star, both of which prefer the alkaline soils common to parts of Dutchess County. And in a tiny percentage of moist meadows that are underpinned by limestone or have limy seeps among them, the endangered bog turtle hides atop sun-dappled tussocks or buries itself in cool, nutrient-rich mud for incomprehensibly long periods. Important insect pollinators make a feast of these colorful oases.

The region's human population takes advantage of the valley's unparalleled natural beauty by incorporating it into daily routine and recreation. Nature and human culture no longer clash as they once did. Instead, they are blended together to produce a harmony few other regions of the country are capable of achieving. We have realized that there are other ways to profit from the environment than by ruthlessly subjugating it. An example is the city of Beacon, which has been described as the new Brooklyn. Though it is densely populated, residents have the advantage of escaping into the wilderness, unlike Brooklynites. Beacon abuts the aptly named Mt. Beacon, the highest prominence in the Hudson Highland mountain chain. An easily accessible Scenic Hudson park that sits at the base attracts scores of visitors daily, relishing a chance to unwind on the rugged trails that give way to breathtaking views. People no longer clamor to the top to gamble at a casino that once stood at the summit, accessible by means of a cog railway, but now ascend to priceless vistas that can be achieved in a half-hour hike. And the larger city of Poughkeepsie turned an old railroad trestle spanning the Hudson into the pedestrian-friendly Walkway Over the Hudson. Walkers, joggers, and bikers can now enjoy their regimen away from the dangers of roads and the stale environment of gyms. We've changed our priorities and have gained more from doing so.

Just as the first people to settle among the Hudson Valley depended on what the Lenape called the Muhheakantuck, or "river that flows both ways," we owe our success to the river. Annual events celebrating the Hudson are proliferating. The Clearwater Festival, one of the first to arise, is by far the largest. Held in June on Croton Point, a lengthy peninsula jutting into Haverstraw Bay, the widest part of the entire river, the two-day music-fueled jubilee attracts thousands. It offers innumerable booths and educational sloops centered on a common theme: the Hudson's revival. First organized in the 1960s, this festival was initially created to bring to light the many problems besetting the then-neglected river. The festival now draws approximately 15,000 people a year. Another event, the Hudson River Valley Ramble, celebrates the region's history, culture, and trails with numerous events scattered across the valley during the month of September. These events, among many others, strive to help us appreciate our natural and cultural surroundings. Only in this way is it possible to foster a society that will fight to protect our heritage.

The Hudson River Valley stretches approximately from New York City northward past Albany, east to the Taconic Mountains, and west to the Shawangunk Ridge and Catskills, although the exact borders have long been hotly debated. Specifics aren't important. To understand the Hudson Valley, one must regard it simply as a book. The Hudson River is the supporting spine, and on either side, flowing east and west to the nebulous horizons, are the pages that give the region its unique flavor and essence. The river is the launching point into the interior, or heart of the landscape, in which adventures have been had, discoveries made, and dreams fulfilled.

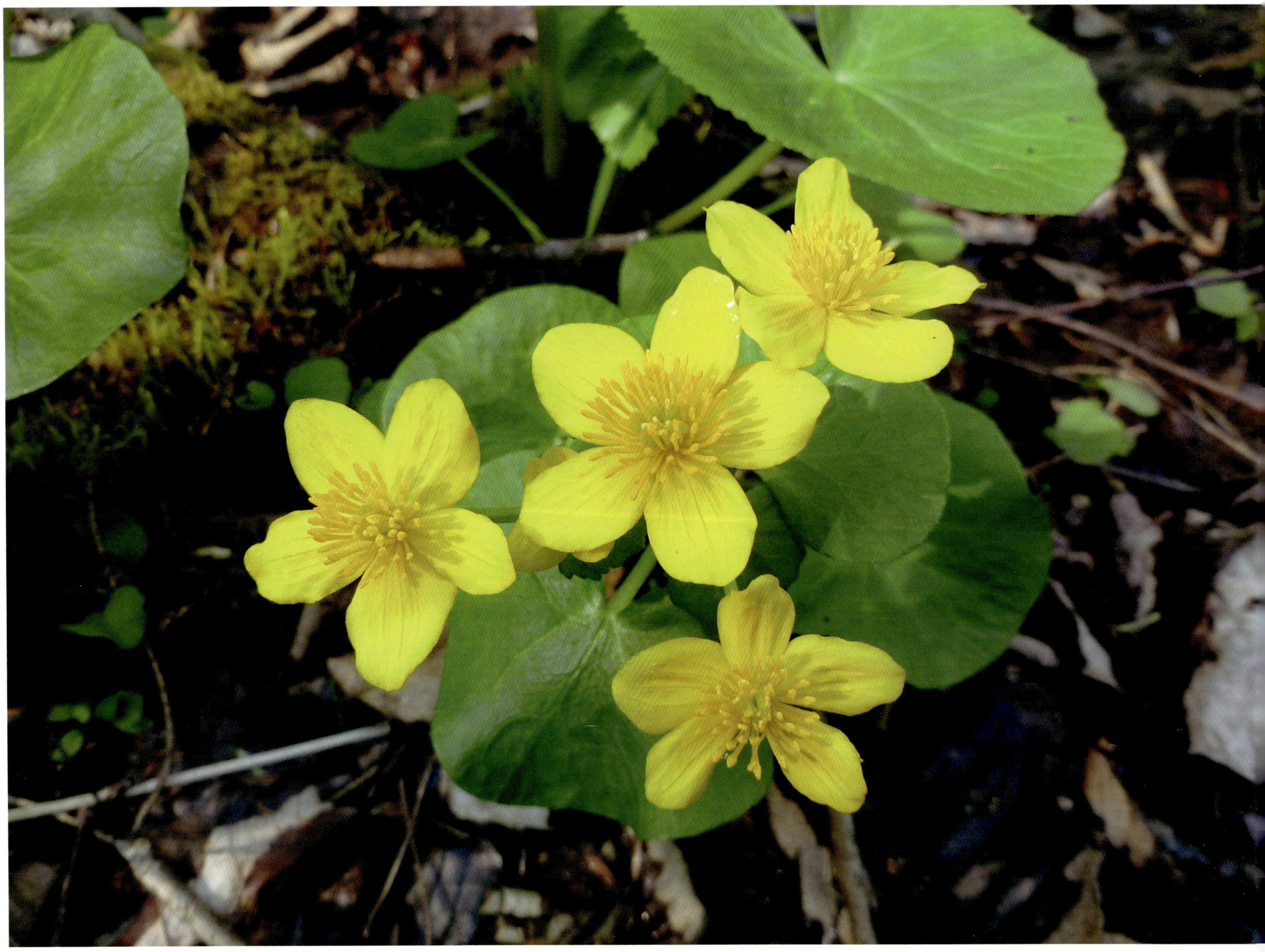

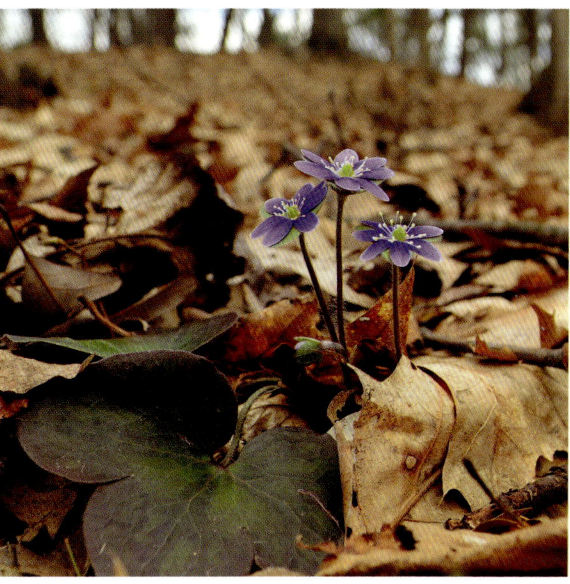

SPRING

In spring the lifeless ground swells, transforming the sober forests into a vibrant patchwork of spring ephemeral wildflowers. As their name implies, spring ephemerals have fleeting lives, blooming at most for a handful of weeks before they disappear until the following year. While unusual weather patterns can delay or accelerate growth, the plants always follow a regimented blooming pattern. Hepatica and coltsfoot arrive first, then trailing arbutus and saxifrage, followed by a succession too lengthy to mention here. By June, most of the spring ephemerals have come and gone, giving way to the lush greenness of summer. At higher elevations, however, some of these plants continue to bloom long after their valley brethren have disappeared.

This page:
Blunt-lobed hepatica
(RamsHorn-Livingston Sanctuary)

Opposite page:
Marsh marigold
(Great Swamp, Pawling)

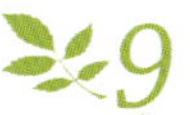

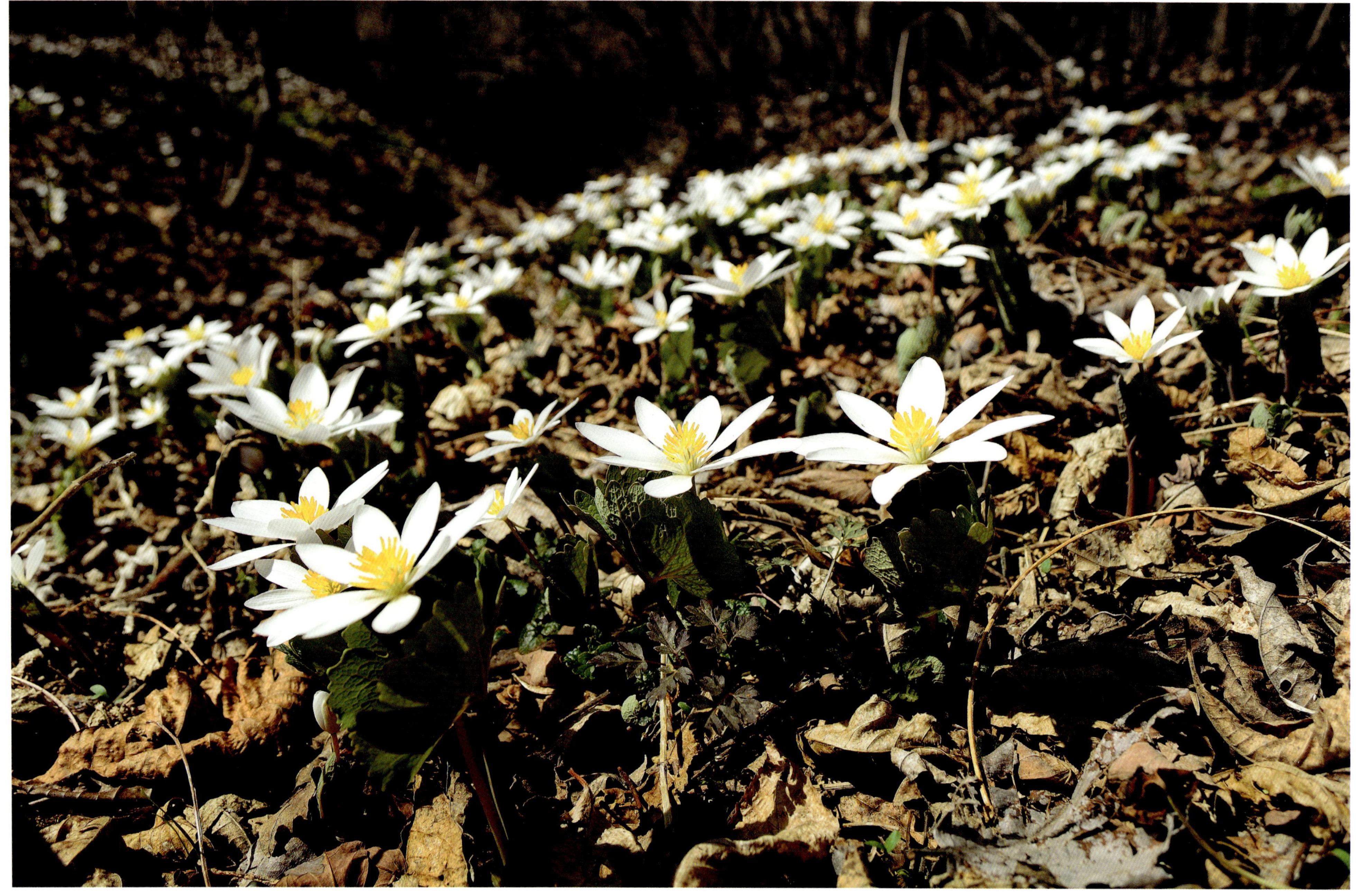

Bloodroot (Tivoli Bays Wildlife Management Area)

Bloodroot is as uncommon as it is beautiful. Bloodroot blooms mid-April through early May, but its flowers last only a day or two before the wind or rain strips the petals away.

Bloodroot gets its name from the bright red liquid that oozes from a broken stem or root. Its stains readily, and Native Americans and colonists used it as a dye.

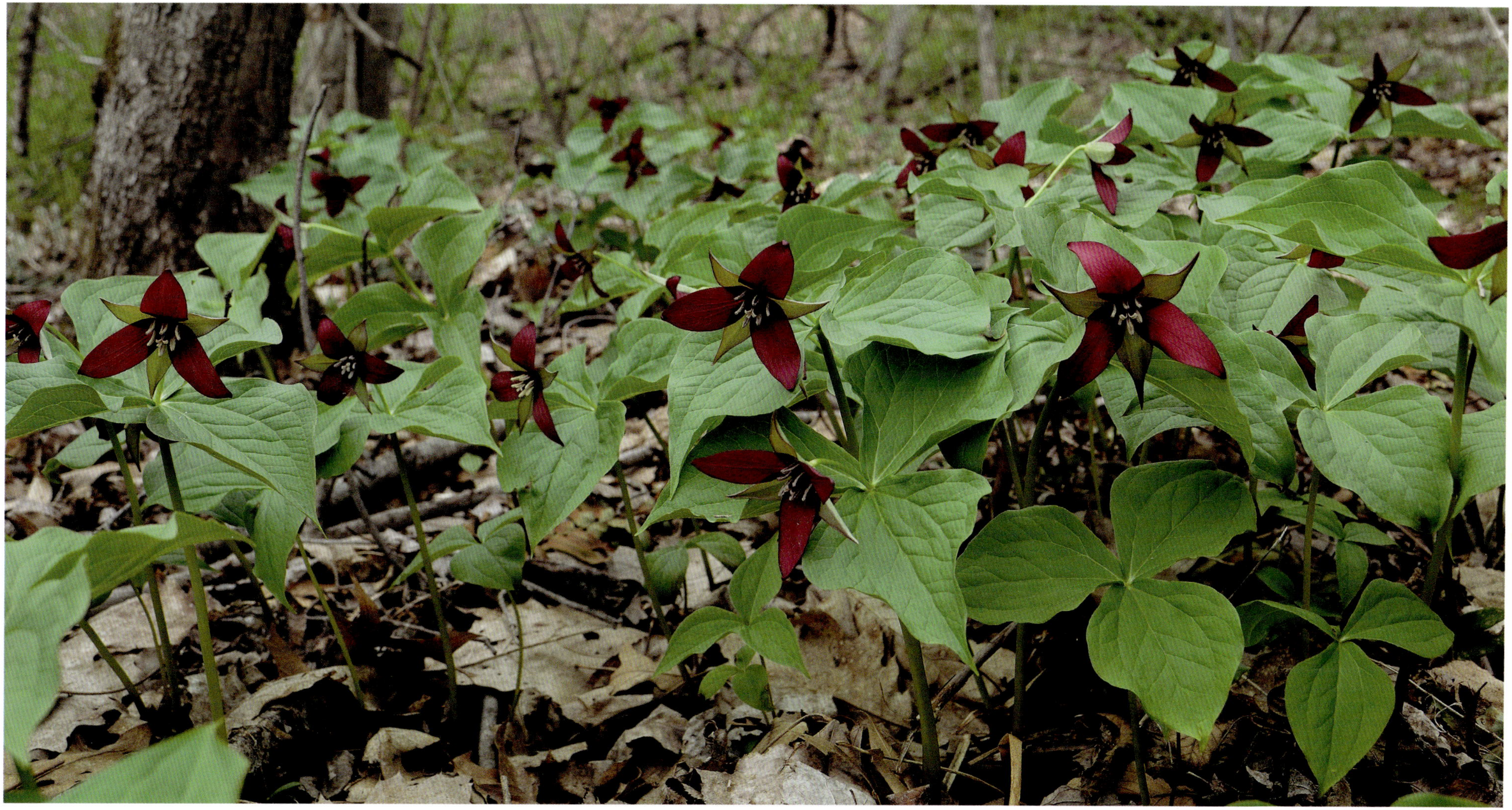

Red trillium (Tivoli Bays Wildlife Management Area)

The name of this flower derives from the plants' speckled leaves that resemble the mottling of trout. Some dense colonies can live to be 300 years old. Only plants with two leaves will produce flowers.

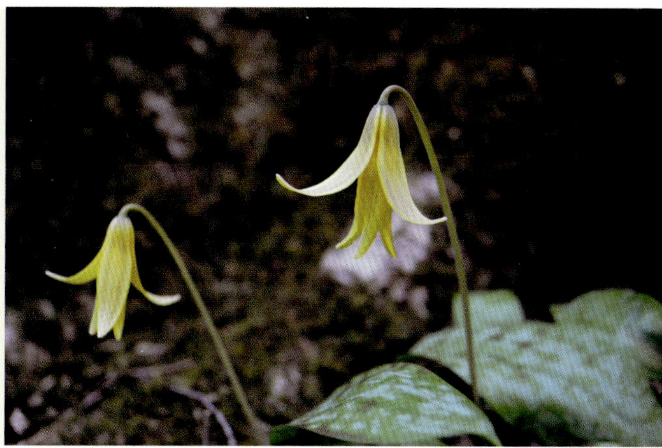

Trout lily (RamsHorn-Livingston Sanctuary)

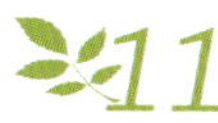

Unlike American ginseng, prized for its stimulant qualities and medicinal use, dwarf ginseng thrives in moist forest woodlands. Some colonies produce hundreds to thousands of plants. It's especially common around streams and low-lying areas where water pools. Because of its diminutive size and less potent chemical properties, it has never suffered from over-collection, which has resulted in the severe decline, and in some areas, disappearance of American ginseng. The plants bloom from April to June.

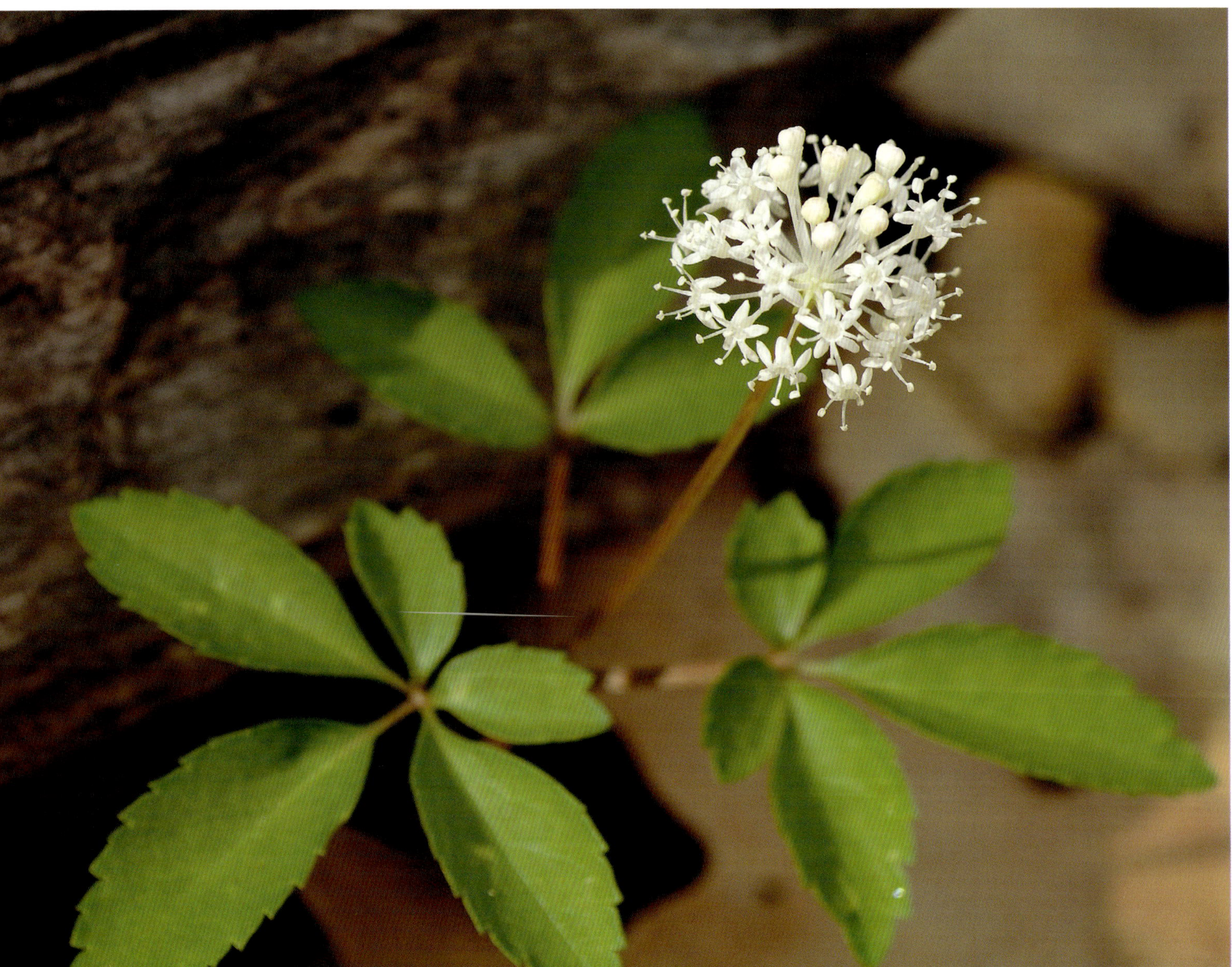

Dwarf ginseng (Schunnemunk State Park)

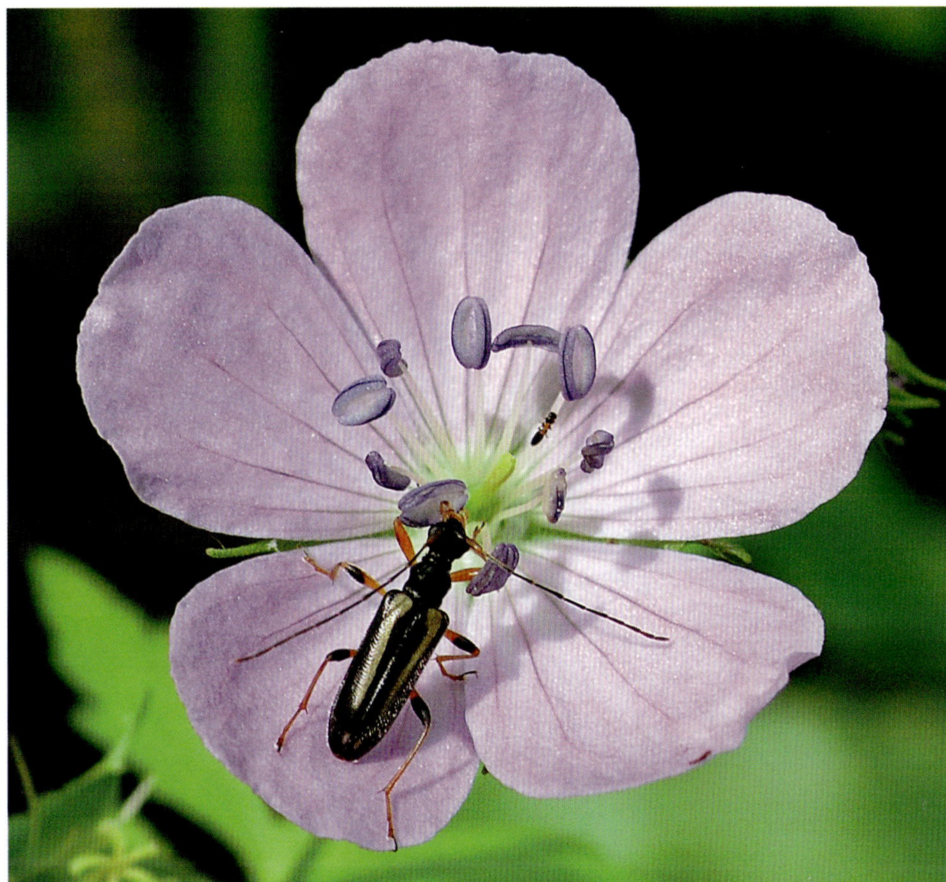

Flower longhorn beetle on wild geranium (Tivoli Bays Wildlife Management Area)

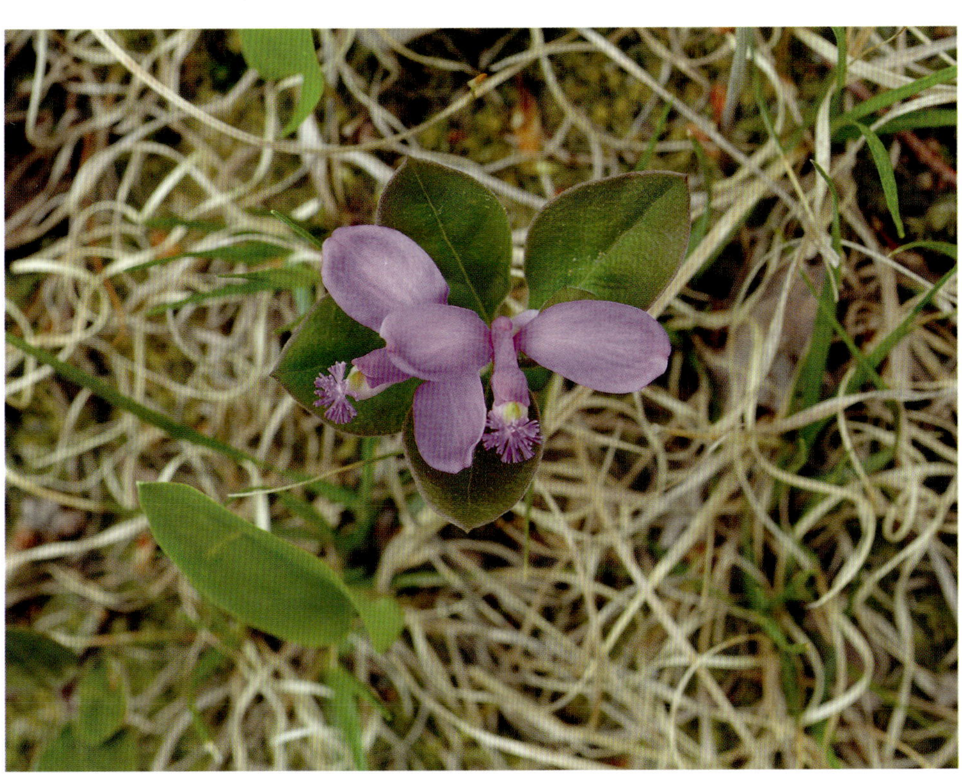

Fringed polygala (Shaupeneak Ridge)

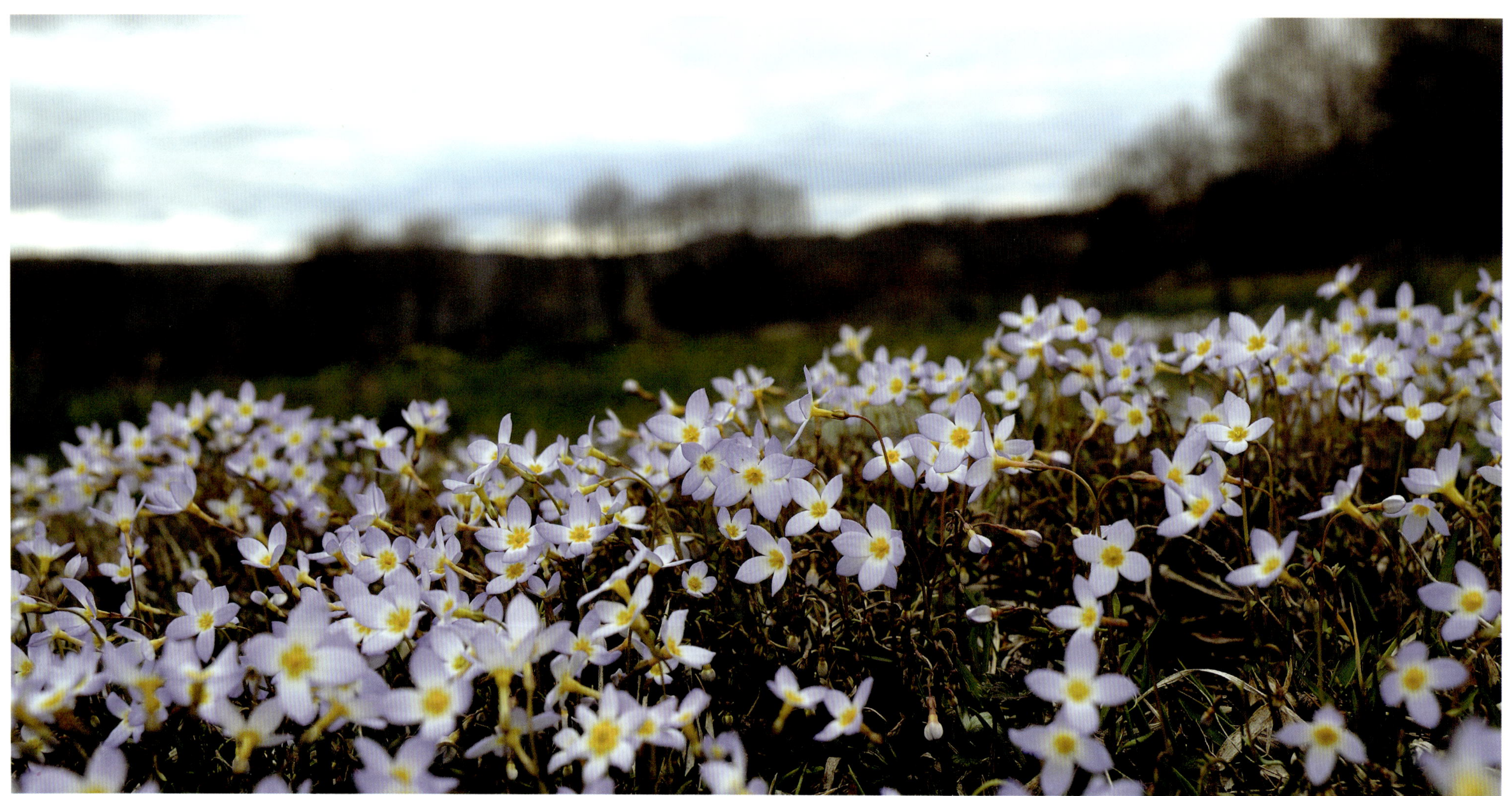

Bluets atop Corbin Hill (Appalachian Trail, Pawling)

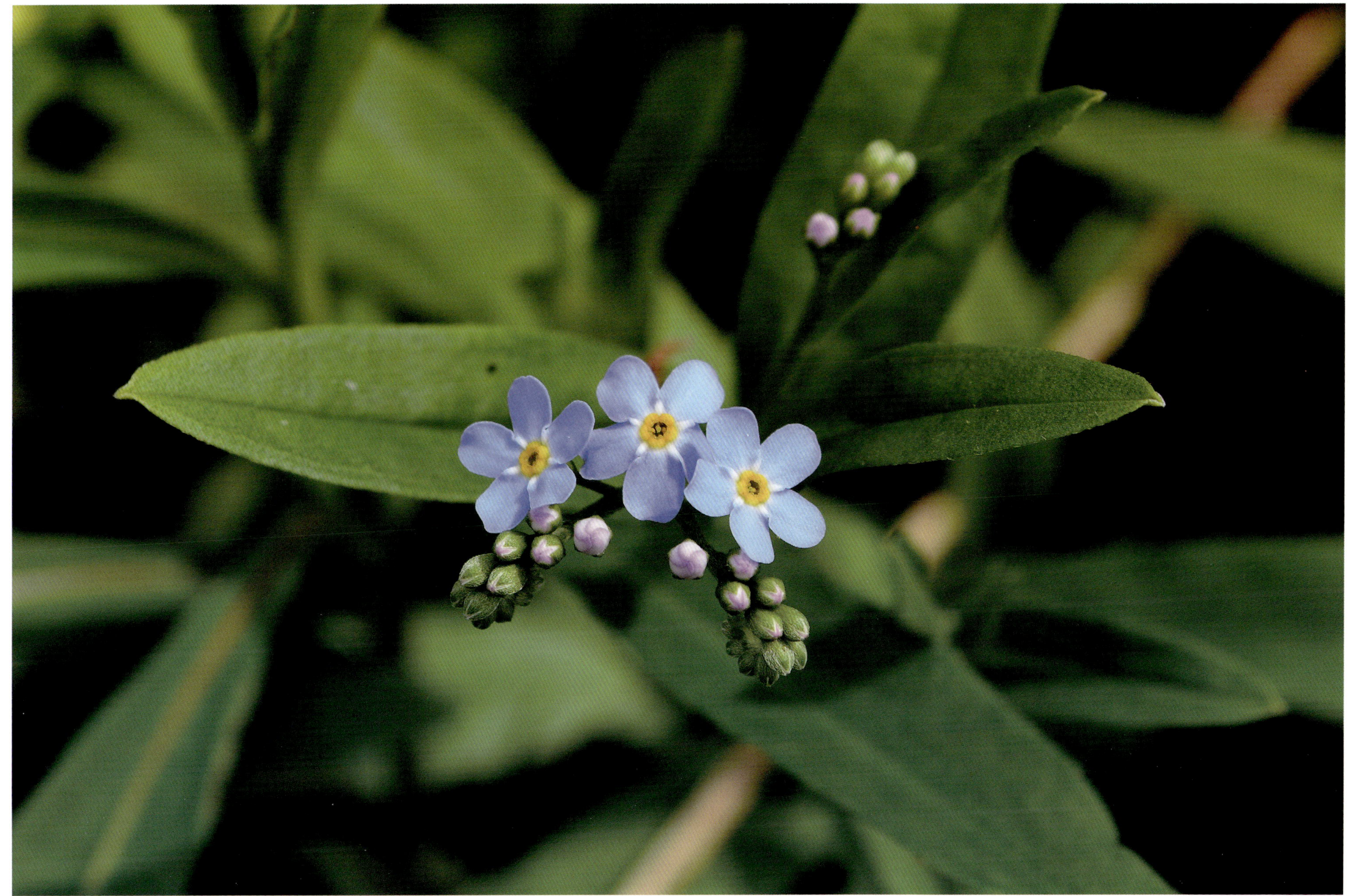

Forget-me-nots (Schodack Island State Park)

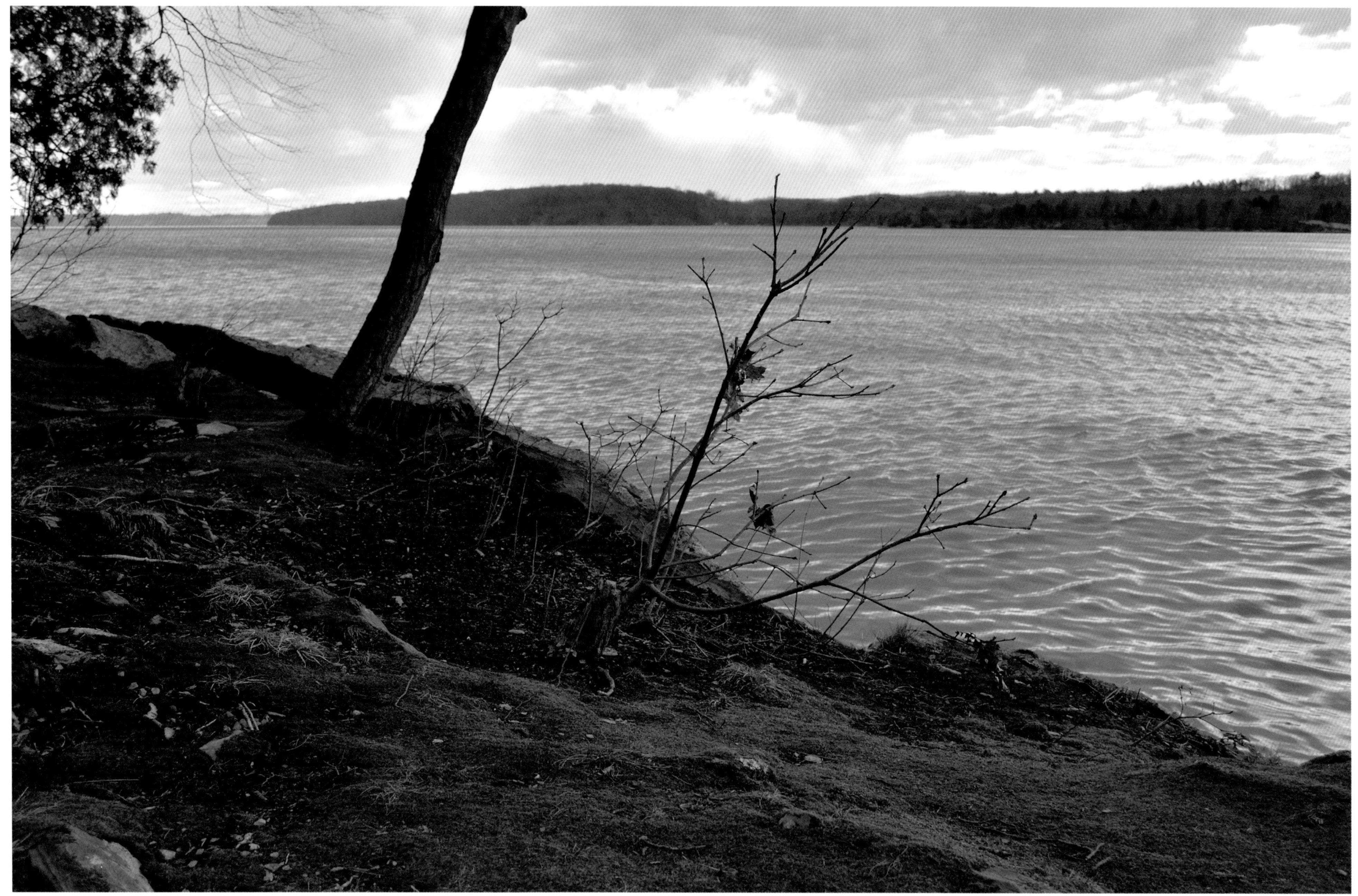

Early spring on the Hudson (Black Creek Preserve)

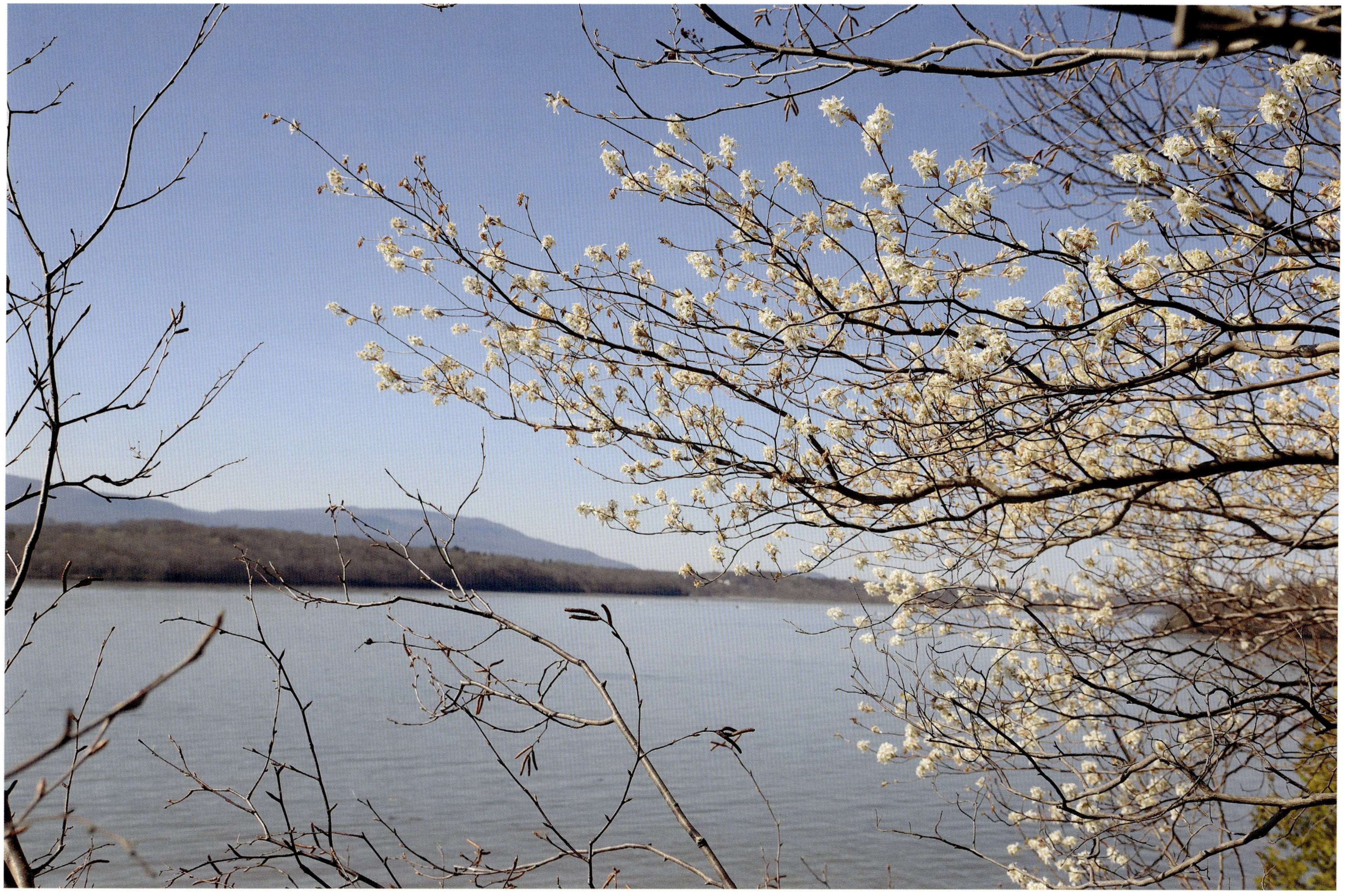

Blooming shadbush (Tivoli Bays Wildlife Management Area)

Native Americans gave shadbush its name. This highly visible, well-distributed tree served as an important temporal marker, as its blooming coincides with the yearly spring arrival of shad in regional estuaries. The fish were a vital diet staple for the Native Americans, who by then had consumed most of their winter food reserves.

The trees were valued for their maroon to purple fruit that tastes similar to blueberries and ripens in late June. The resilient wood was also supposedly used for making arrow shafts.

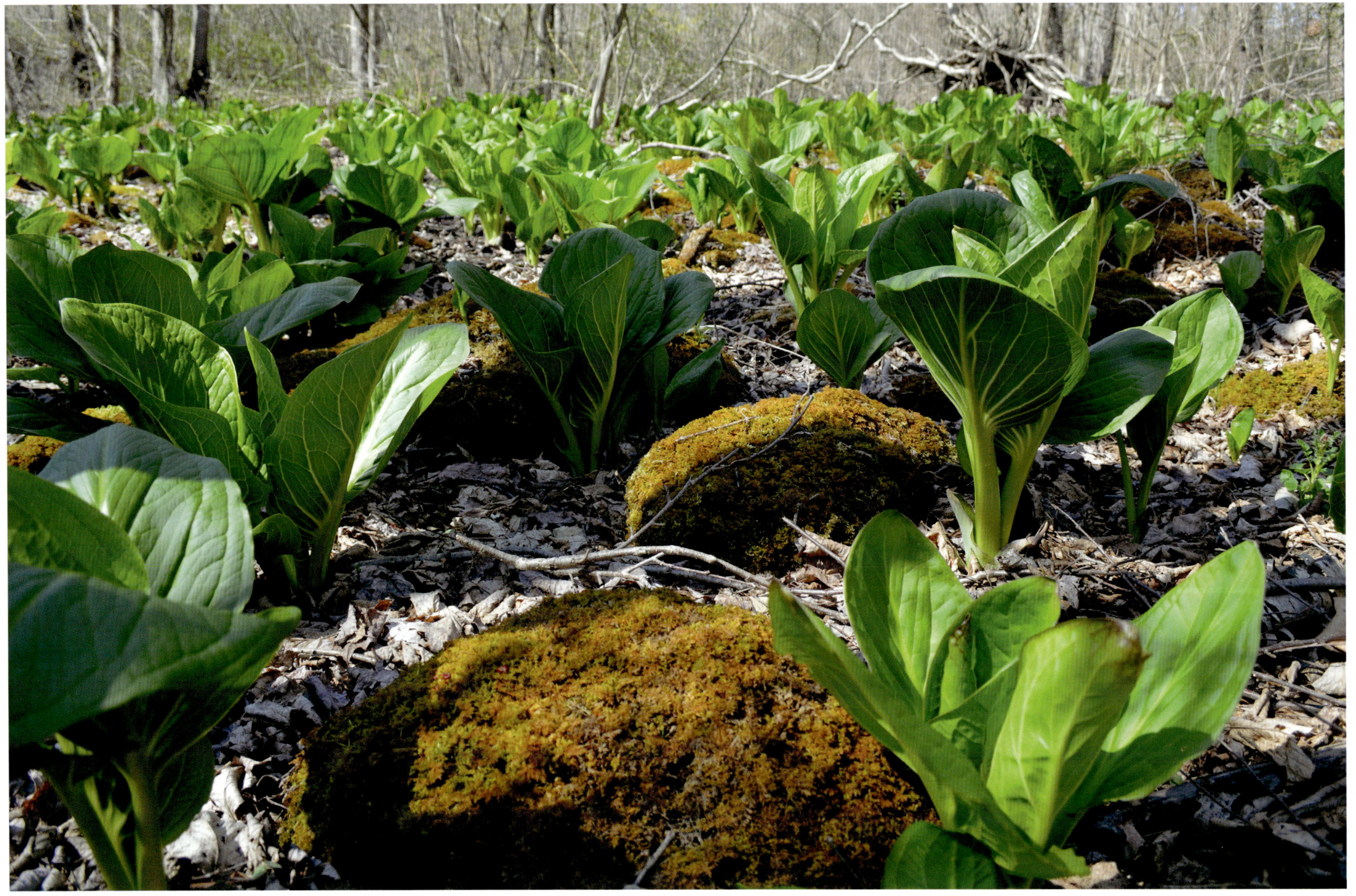

Skunk cabbages (Appalachian Trail, Pawling)

The eastern skunk cabbage is one of the first plants to bloom in spring and frequently begins growing even in late winter. Skunk cabbages exhibit thermogenesis, meaning they generate their own heat—a rare feat. Often they can be observed melting the snow around them, as they are capable of producing temperatures up to ninety degrees even when the ambient air is well below freezing.

Eastern skunk cabbage gets its name from the rancid smell of the leaves when they are damaged. The leaves contain calcium oxalate, which causes an intense burning sensation if tasted. It's interesting to note that calcium oxalate is the main constituent of kidney stones.

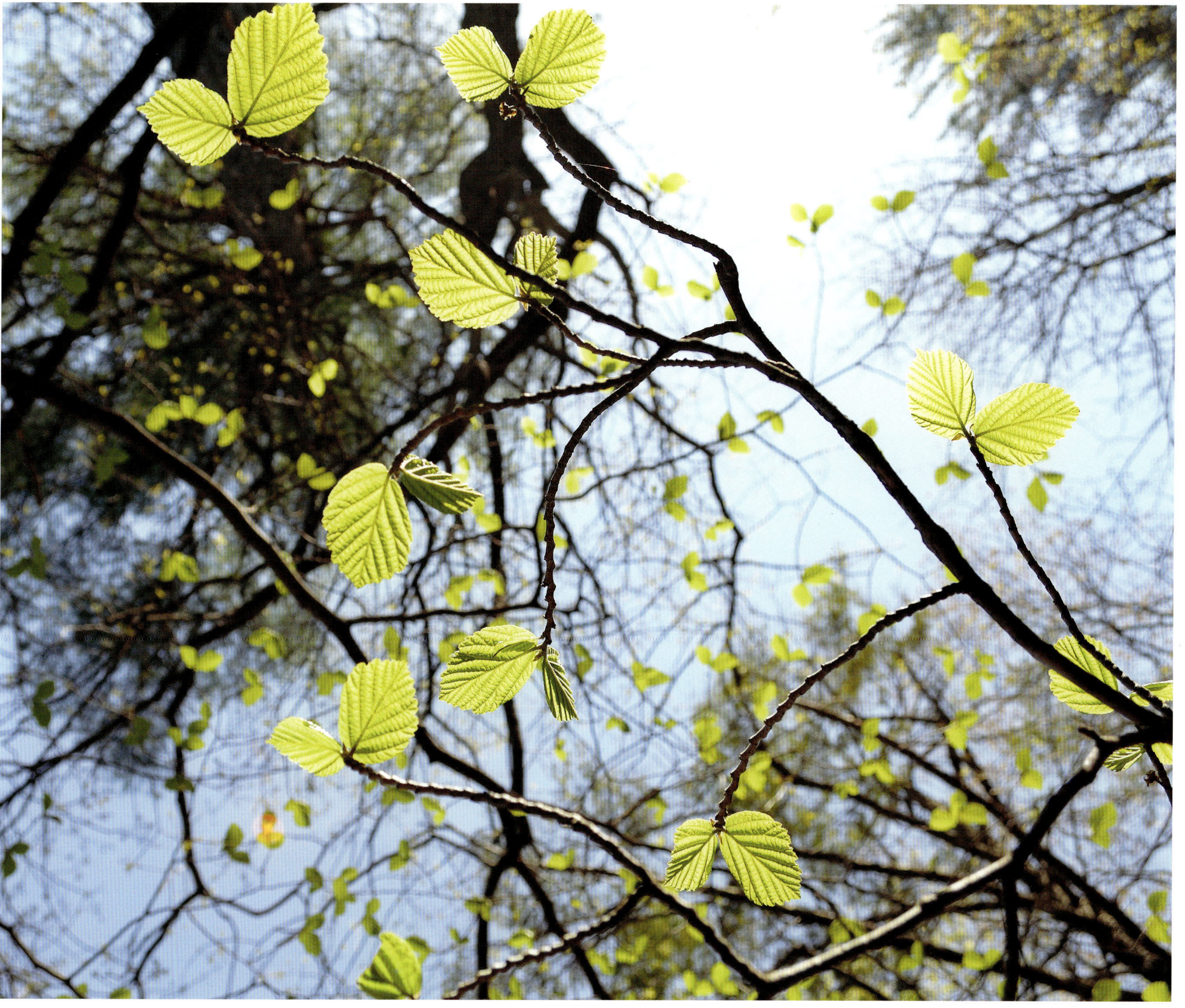

Witch-hazel (Mills-Norrie State Park)

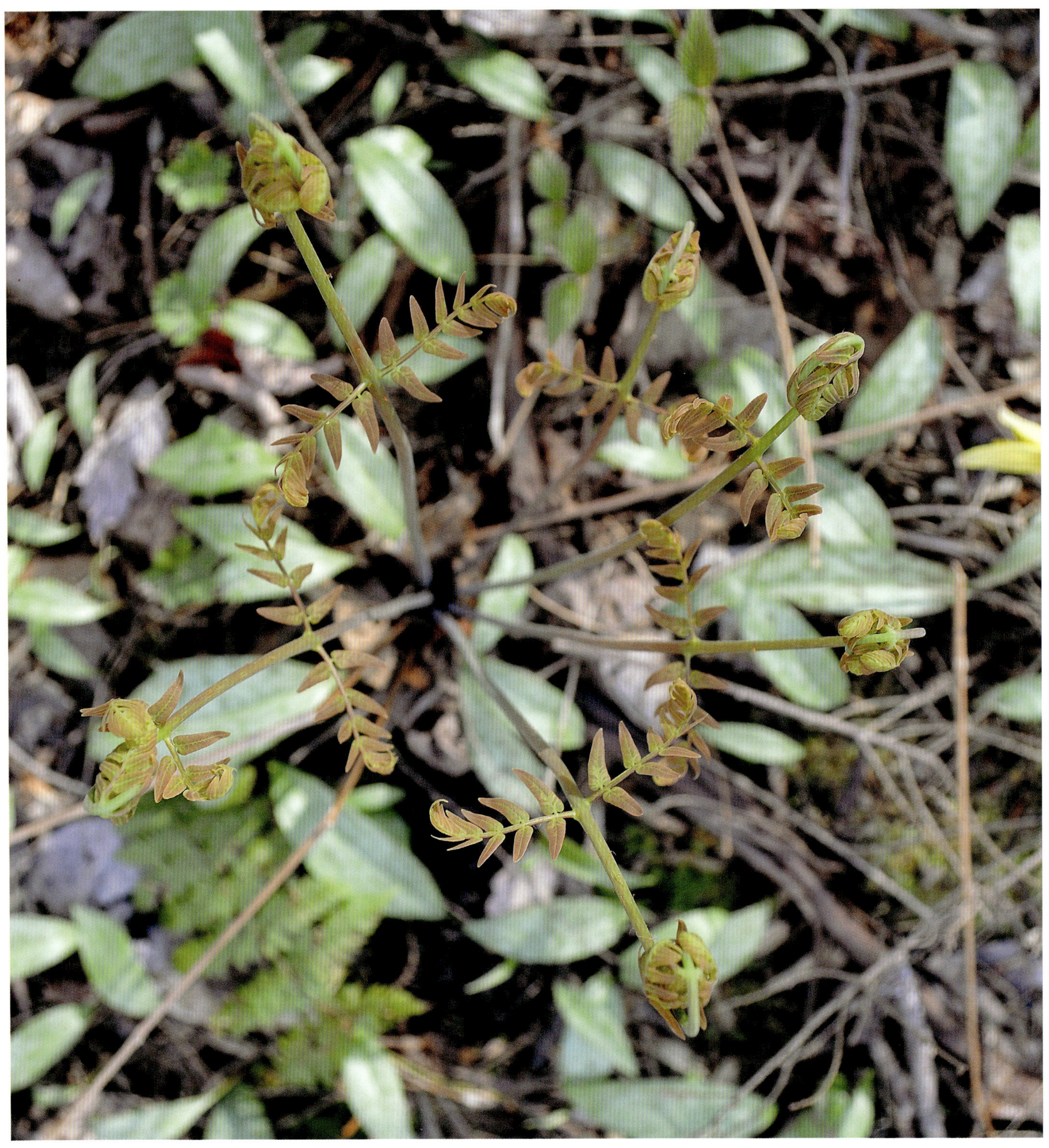

Royal ferns rise above a bed of trout lily leaves
(Stewart State Forest)

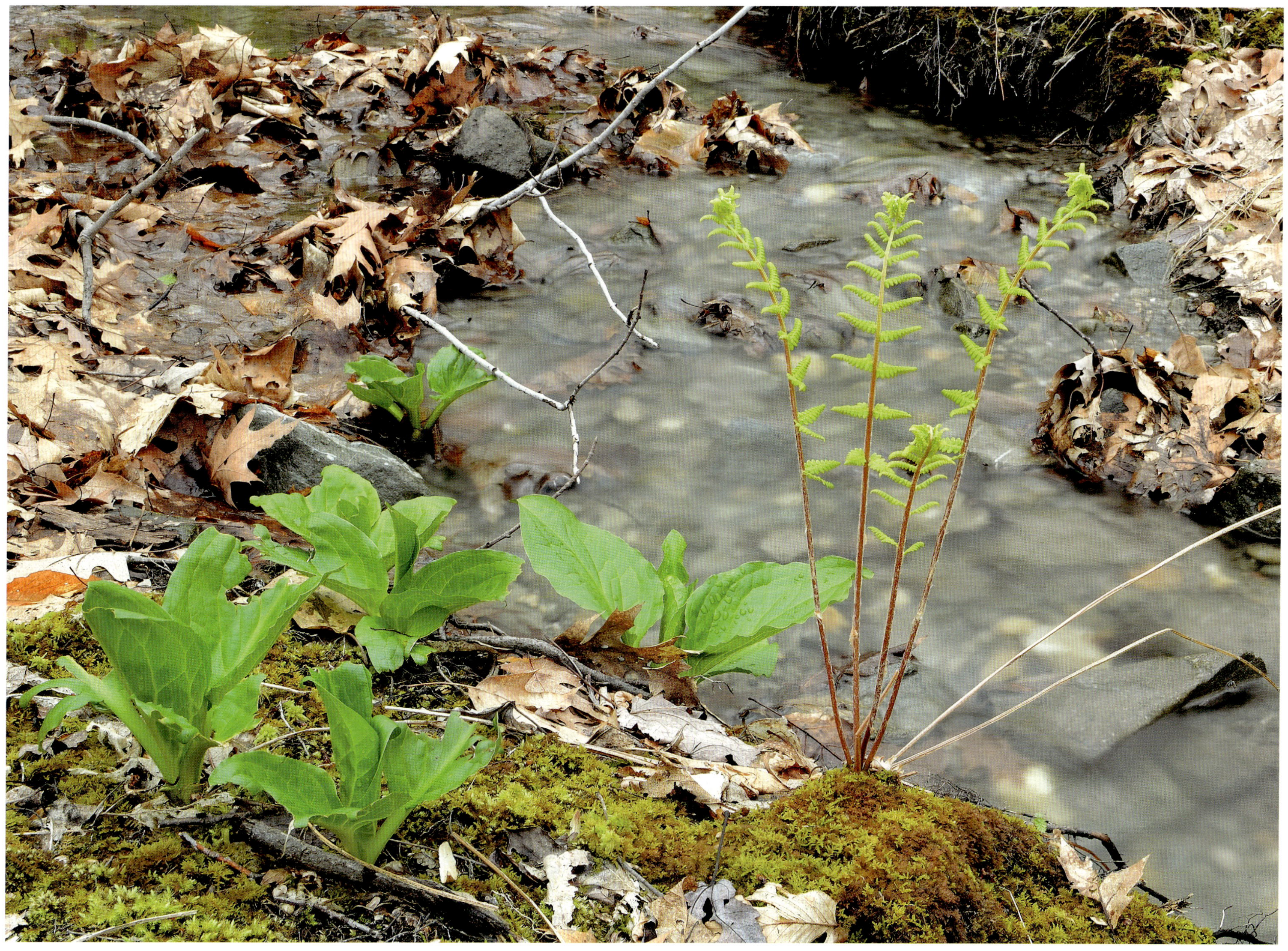

Woodland stream (Schunnemunk State Park)

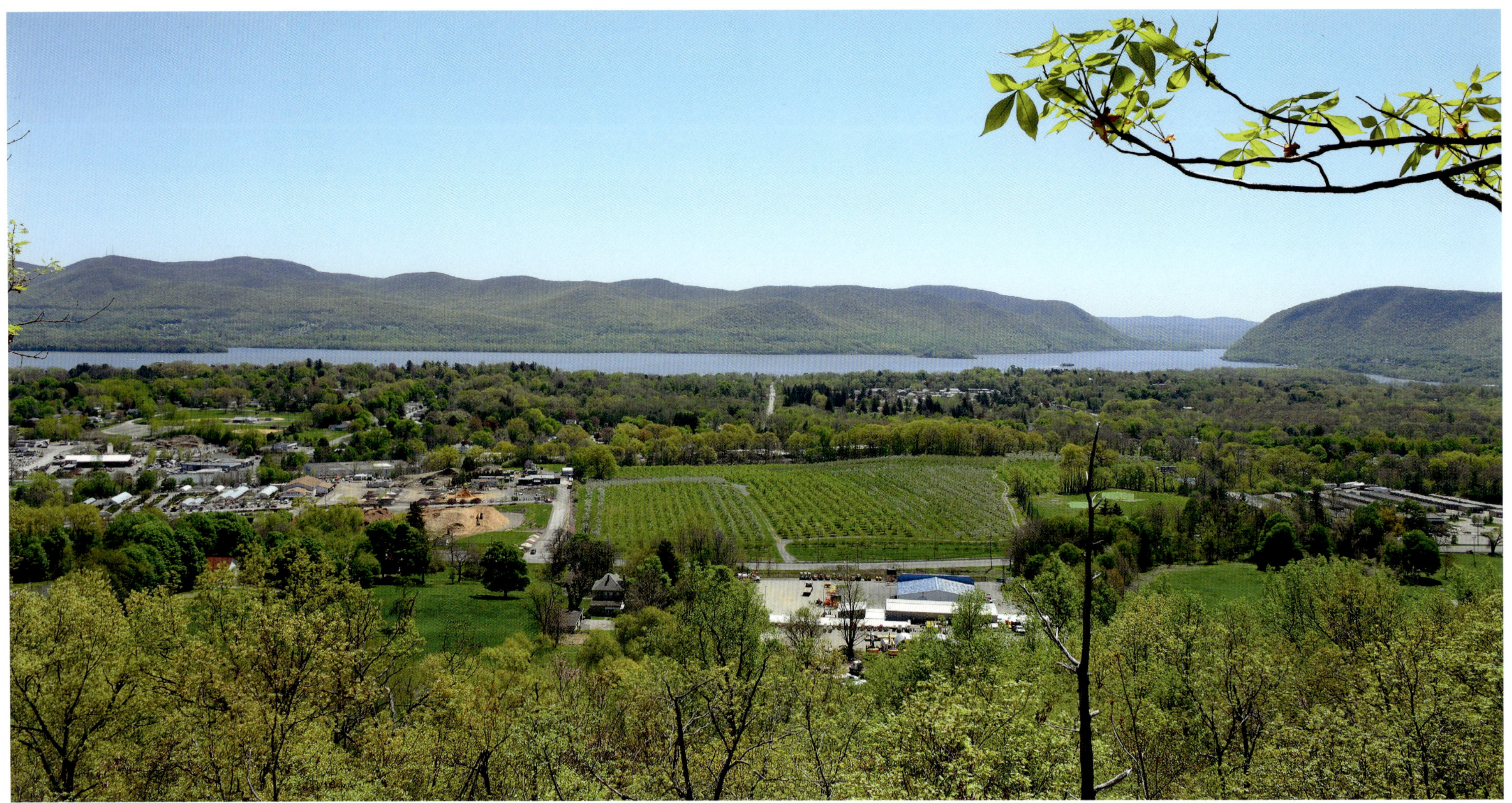

View of New Windsor and the northern Hudson Highlands (Snake Hill)

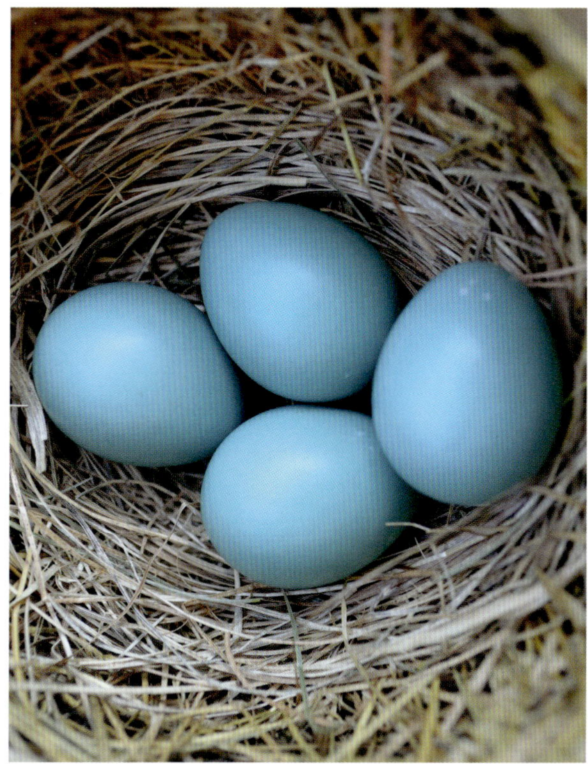

Robin eggs (Franny Reese State Park)

American robins are synonymous with the arrival of spring. As the weather begins to warm they are the first avian species to reappear in the Northeast. They are also the first to begin nesting, which lasts from early April to July. Within this time frame they can have two or three broods. After laying three or four eggs in the nest, females incubate them for around two weeks. After hatching, parental care may continue for an additional six weeks until the young are completely on their own. Sadly, over three-quarters of hatchlings do not live past their first year.

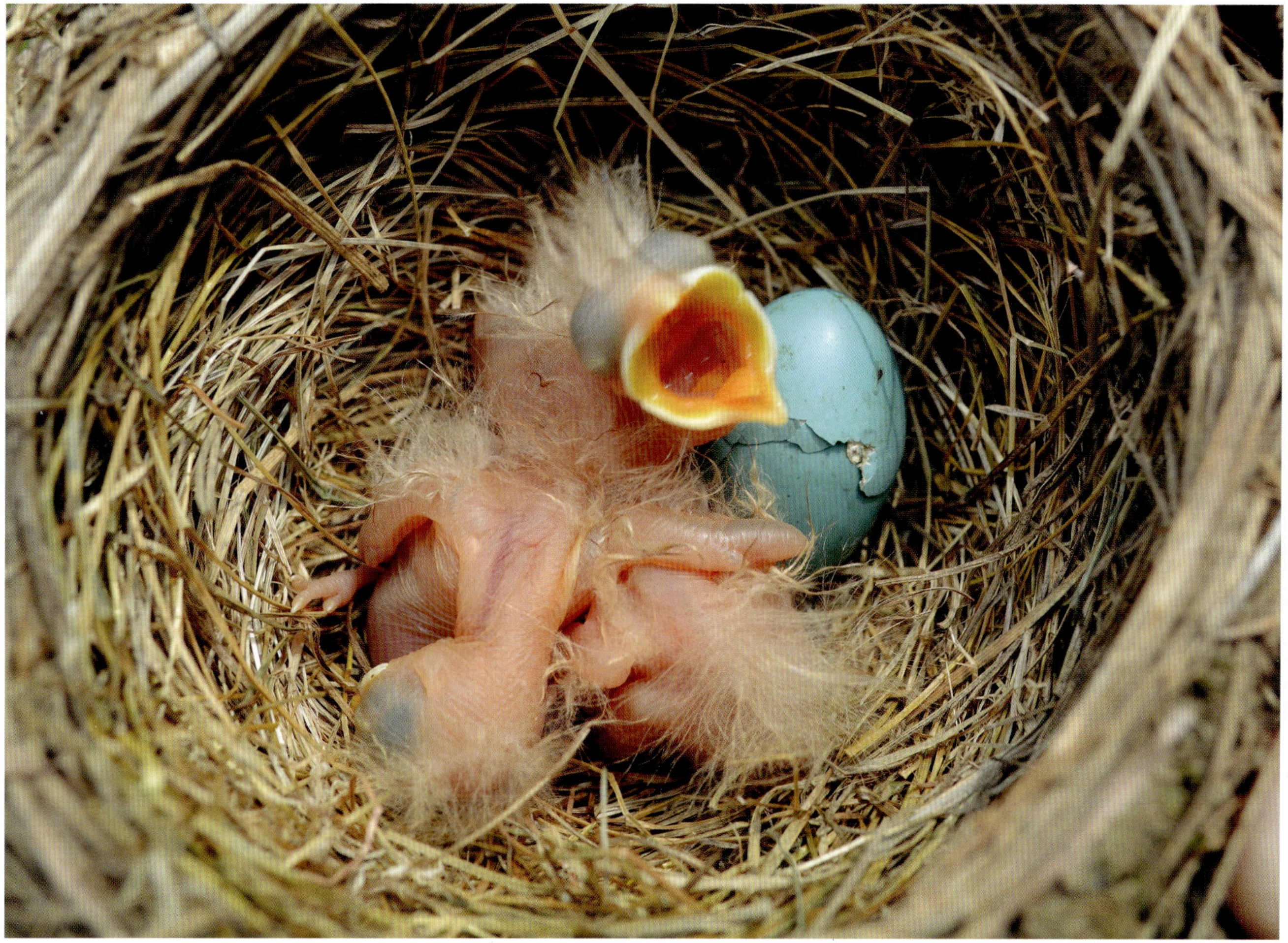

Newly hatched robins (Franny Reese State Park)

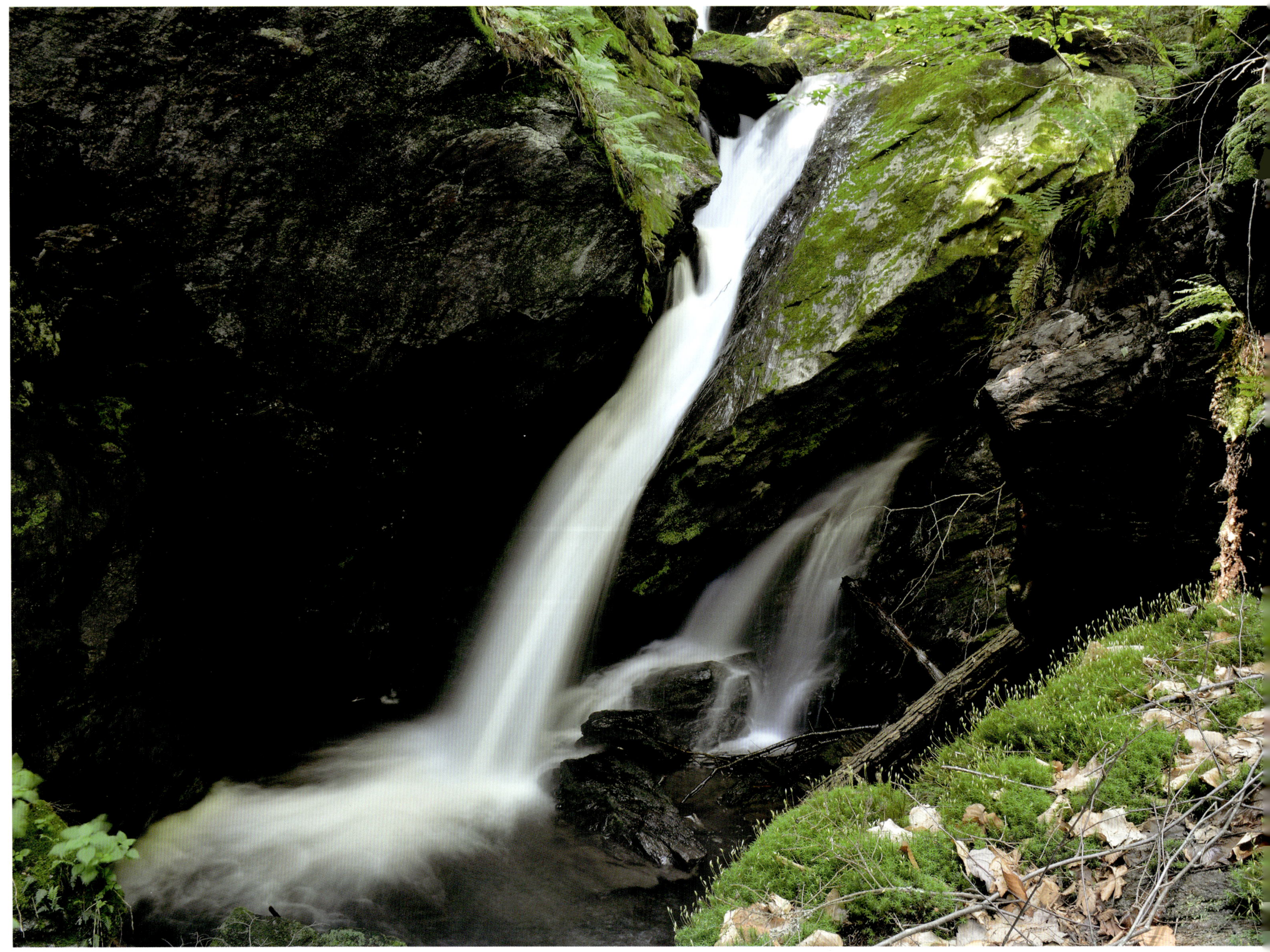

WATERFALLS

There's something deeply captivating about a waterfall. The raw and intense power it wields as it drops its silvery contents headlong to the rocks below produces a roar that from a distance morphs into a gentle, soothing sound. We can't help but revere these natural wonders, not only for their visual and audial thrill, but for the impression they make on the mind. Landscape painter and writer Thomas Cole was referring to waterfalls when he wrote in his essay, "American Scenery," that "in gazing" on these natural artworks, "we feel as though a great void has been filled" so that "our conceptions expand" and "we become a part of what we behold!" (*American Monthly* magazine, January 1836). Apart from the romantic qualities of waterfalls, there's a scientific reason they have a relaxing and rejuvenating effect. Cascading water, as it turns out, is excellent for producing negative ions, which are said to improve mood and increase energy and awareness. Electrons, wrenched from air particles by the force of falling water, form negatively charged ions when they reattach to other molecules in the air. Waterfalls can raise the level of negative ions as much as fifty times.

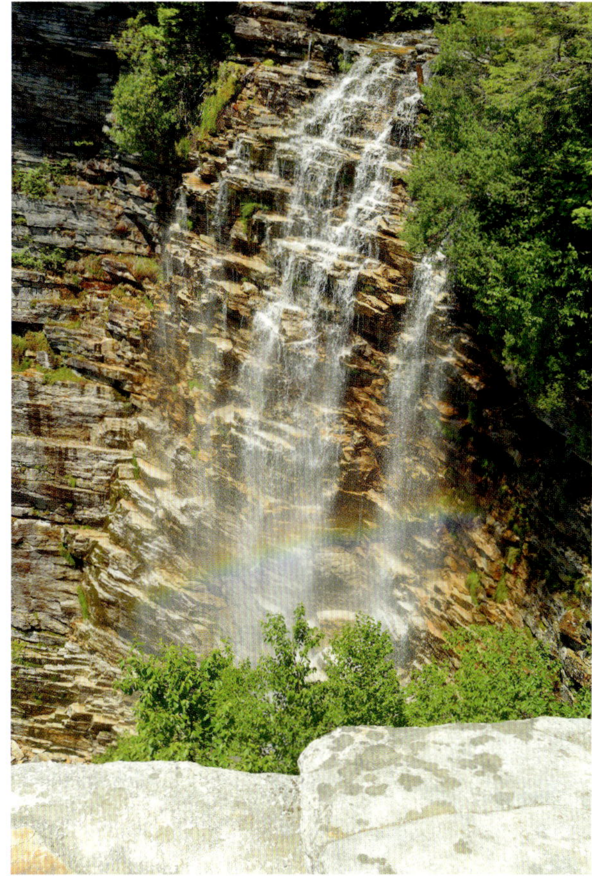

This page:
Verkeerderkill Falls
(Sam's Point Preserve)

Opposite page:
Sassacus Falls
(Dover Stone Church Preserve)

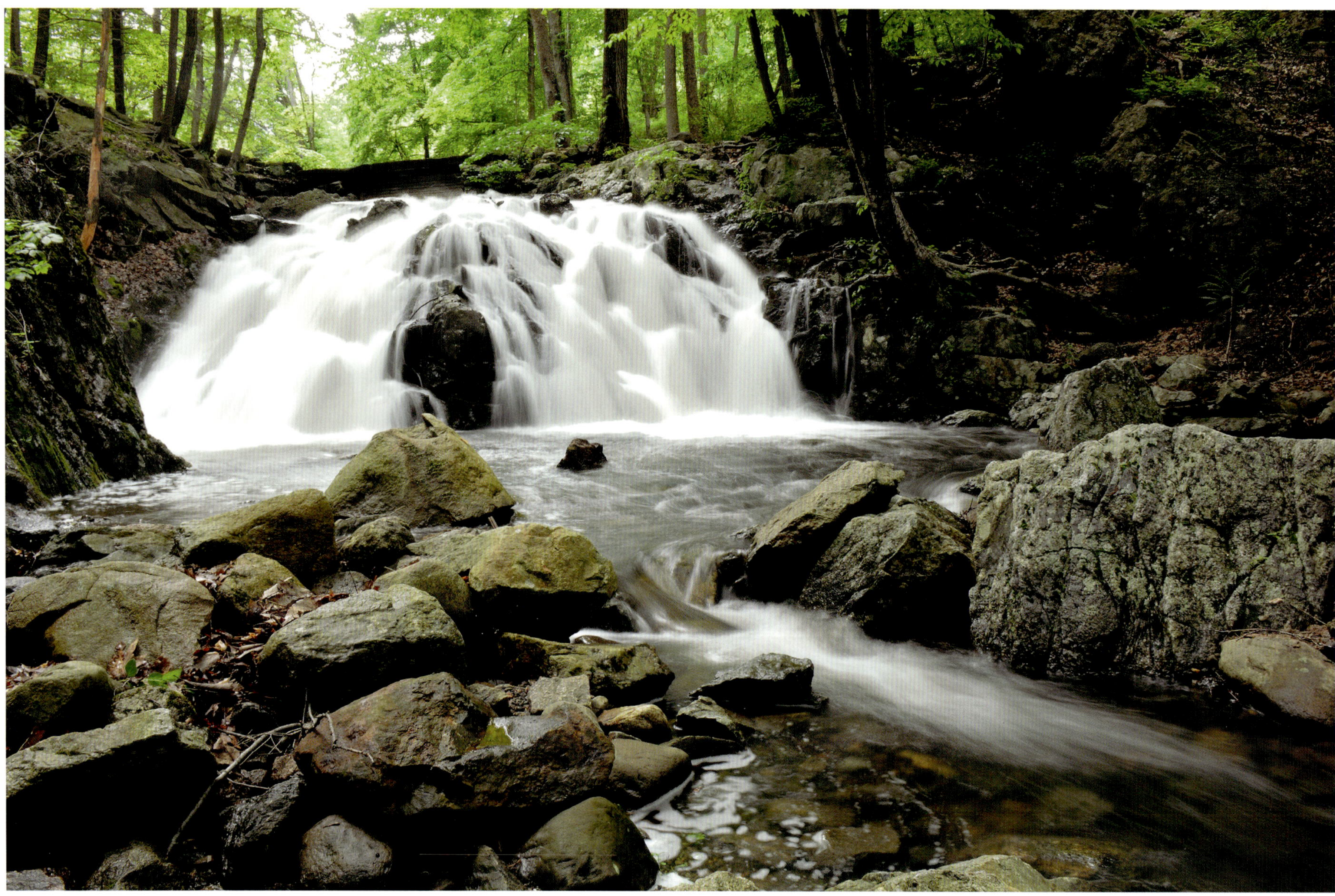

Doodletown Brook Falls (Bear Mountain State Park)

Doodletown residents were once greeted daily with views of this picturesque waterfall as they traversed a bridge across Doodletown Brook just upstream of the falls. While the town was razed in the 1960s to make way for Bear Mountain State Park, visitors can still reach the now-secluded falls and glimpse traces of the surrounding ghost town. Crumbling foundations, ever-narrowing dirt roads, and several overgrown cemeteries are the only remnants of this once-bustling historic river town. They serve as eerie reminders of how quickly nature will reclaim its lost territory once given a chance.

Now, more than ever, Doodletown is a suitable appellation for this defunct settlement. The town was said to be named from the Dutch word for "dead valley," Dooddel.

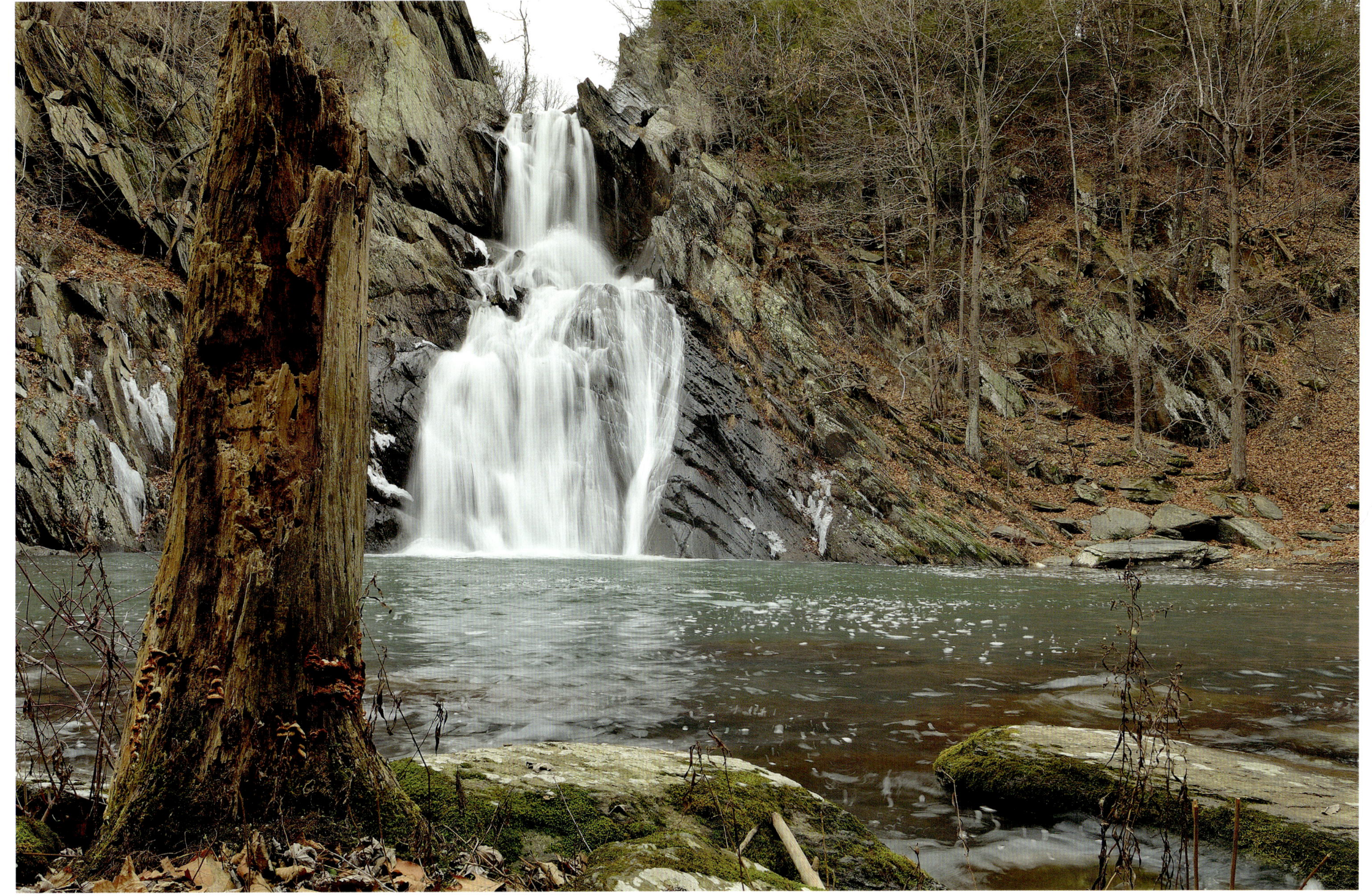

High Falls (High Falls Conservation Area)

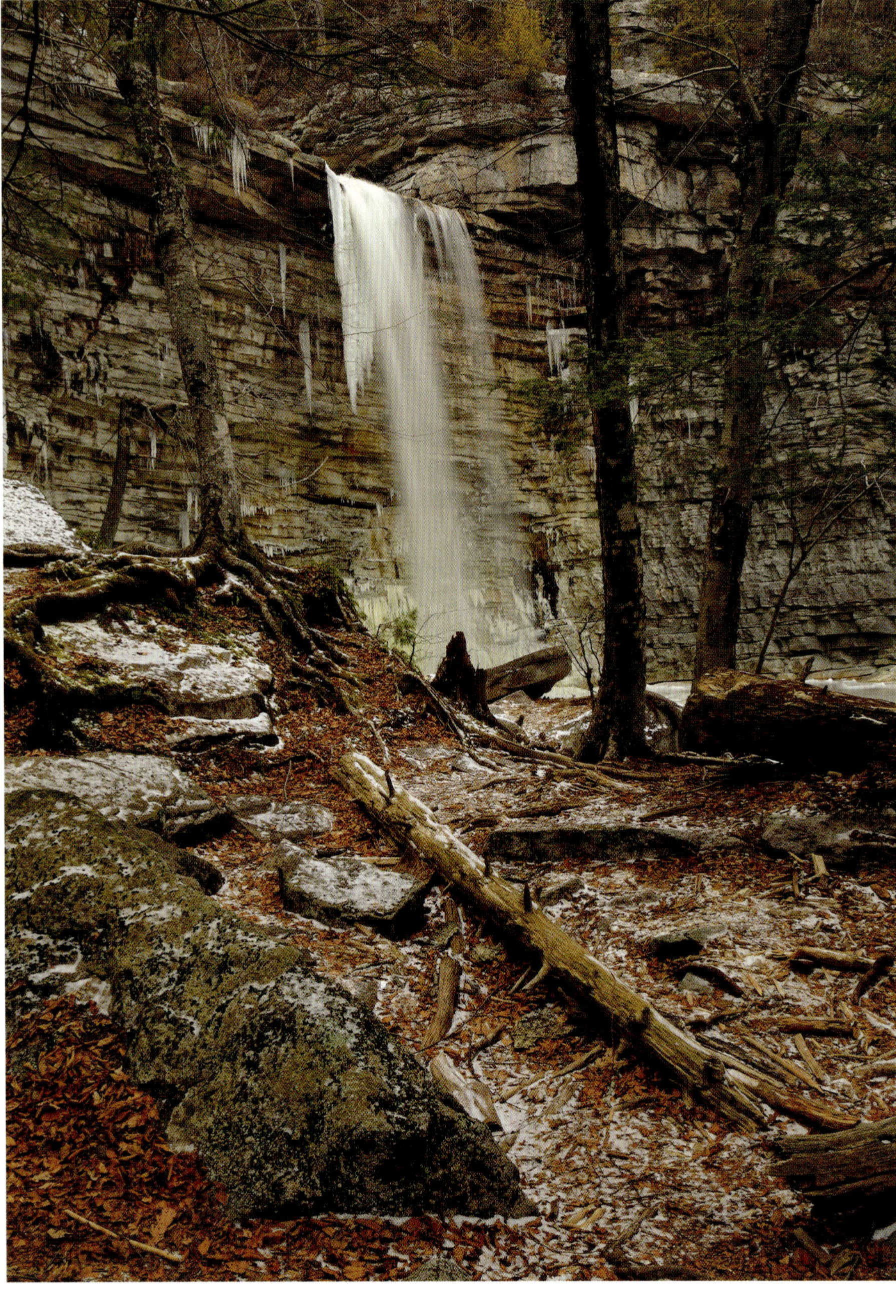

Awosting Falls (Minnewaska State Park)

Legend has it that during Henry Hudson's 1609 expedition, the Half Moon anchored one day near the mouth of Fishkill Creek. On a foray into the countryside, the crew stumbled upon clusters of wild grapes, which they eagerly began collecting, hungry for anything other than a mouthful of stale sea rations. Intent upon the task, they were unaware a group of Indians had arrived and surrounded them. Eventually, a crew member happened to notice something moving in the nearby bushes and walked over to investigate, and a volley of arrows were launched at the intruders. Having left most of their weapons on the ship, there was little to be done except retreat. During the brief skirmish, the Dutchman Jacobus Van Horen was struck by an arrow and promptly captured. Assuming their compatriot was dead, the Europeans sailed on, never to return to such a hostile spot.

Jacobus was transported south and presented to the sachem of the tribe. Intrigued by this strange white man, the first he had ever seen, he instructed his people to properly care for the prisoner. Over time, Jacobus gained their trust and was incorporated into the tribe. Meanwhile, the chief's daughter, Manteo, become enamored with the Dutchman and eventually asked her father's permission to marry him. He happily agreed and a wedding was set for the following summer.

Over the following months Manteo and Jacobus would often meet at a secluded waterfall, sacred to her people, at the bottom of a deep and shaded ravine. Sitting beside the cascading waters that poured into a marshy cove of the Hudson some distance away, Manteo would muse with her lover about their upcoming nuptials and future together. Jacobus smiled and reciprocated the kind words, but inwardly he deeply missed his homeland and secretly prayed for deliverance.

One spring day his prayers were answered. While out on a hunting trip, the deafening report of a gun echoed through the still woodlands. Jacobus dropped everything and ran in the direction of the shot. He eventually came to the shores of the Hudson, and spotted an anchored ship flying a Dutch flag only a few hundred yards away. Jumping into the water, he swam to the vessel and was taken aboard. And from there he disappeared.

Manteo was heartbroken, receiving not so much as a good-bye from the one she thought loved her deeply. Not long after, she, too, disappeared. A few days later her body was discovered at the base of the waterfall where she had spent time with Jacobus. It appeared she had taken her own life.

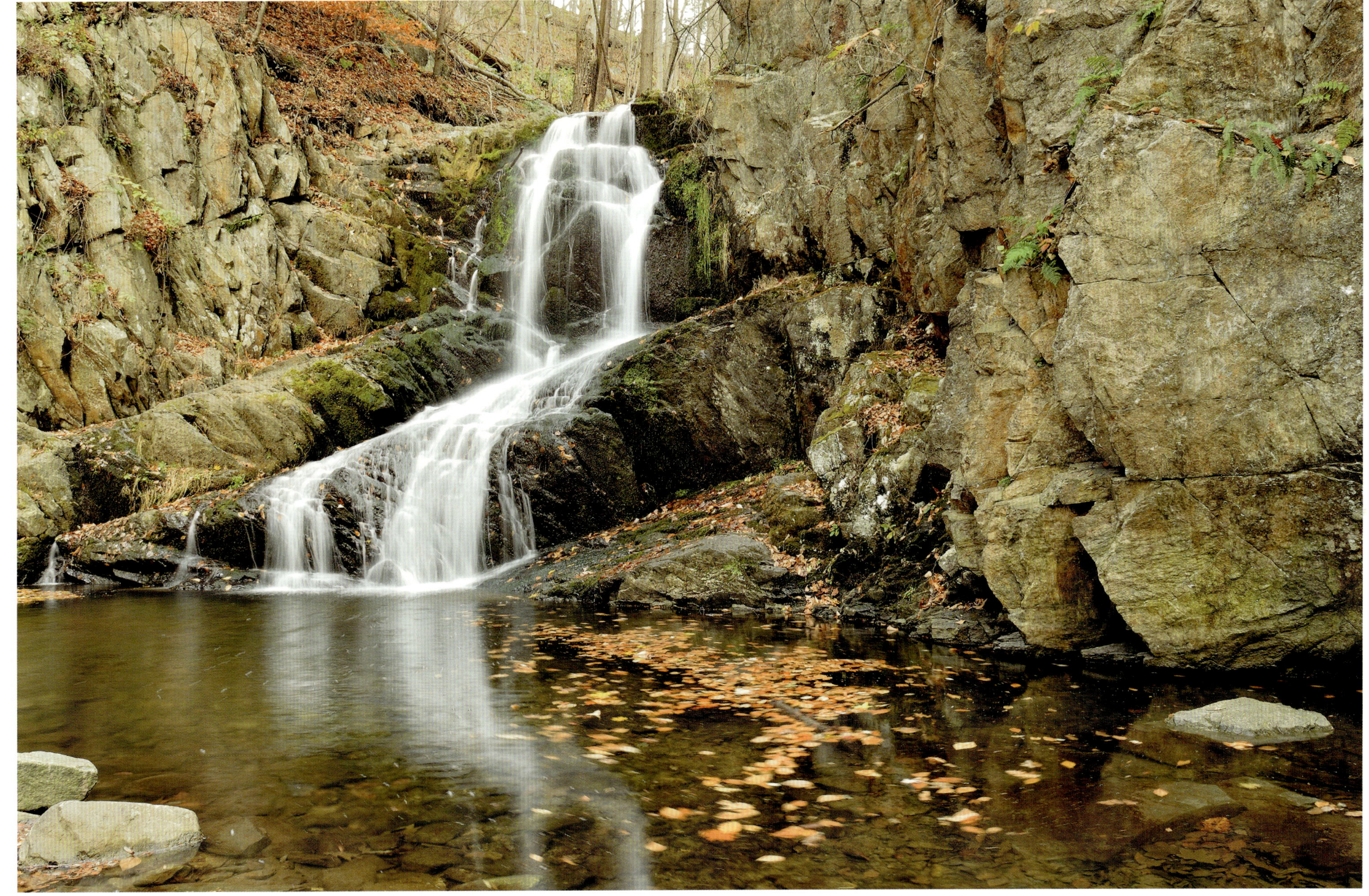

Indian Brook Falls (Garrison)

Likened to a medieval cathedral, the Dover Stone Church is a revered spot that has long inspired pilgrimages. This natural cavern was carved through the millennia by a crystal brook running down the precipitous slopes of West Mountain in Dover Plains. Changing hands various times over the past three centuries, the Stone Church was acquired by the town of Dover in 2002 and promptly transformed into a community park to ensure continued access to this stunning natural curiosity.

The first account of the church dates back to 1637, when it was noted that Sassacus, the sachem, or chief, of the Pequot tribe and his small band of followers hid out in the church. Originally having fled Connecticut to escape the English, and later, a hostile group of natives encountered during their retreat, the Pequots remained sequestered in the cavern and surrounding ravine for a week.

During the nineteenth century, a hotel was constructed close by to house the myriad of annual visitors. An eloquent article in the December 15, 1838 issue of *Poughkeepsie Casket* advertised the benefits of making a pilgrimage to this site, comparing it to a holy temple. The author remarked that the church "is admirably calculated to inspire the contemplative mind with devotional feelings, and to lift the thoughts of the great Architect of the universe, beside whose works the pigmy creations of proud man are merely atoms."

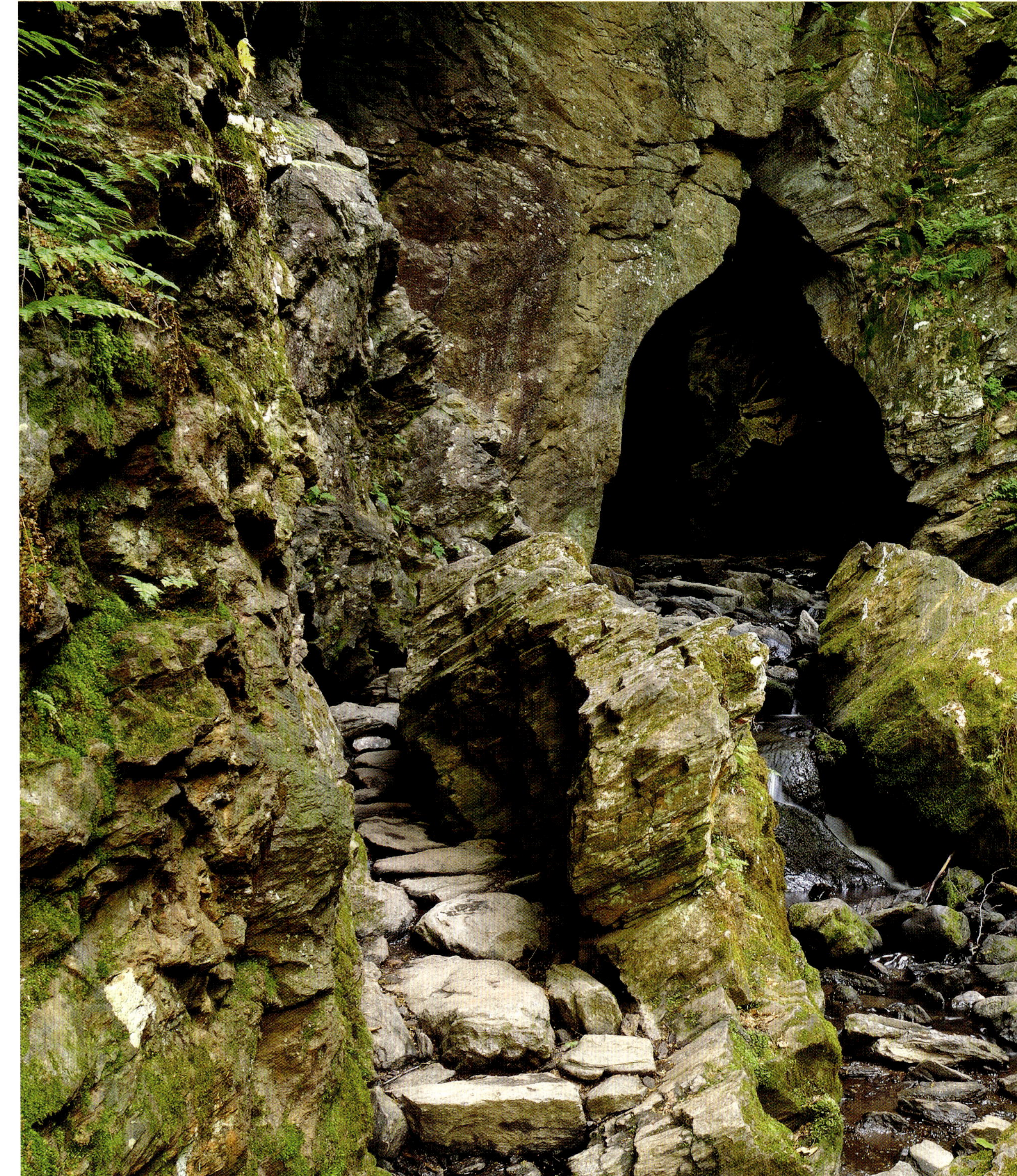

Dover Stone Church (Dover Plains)

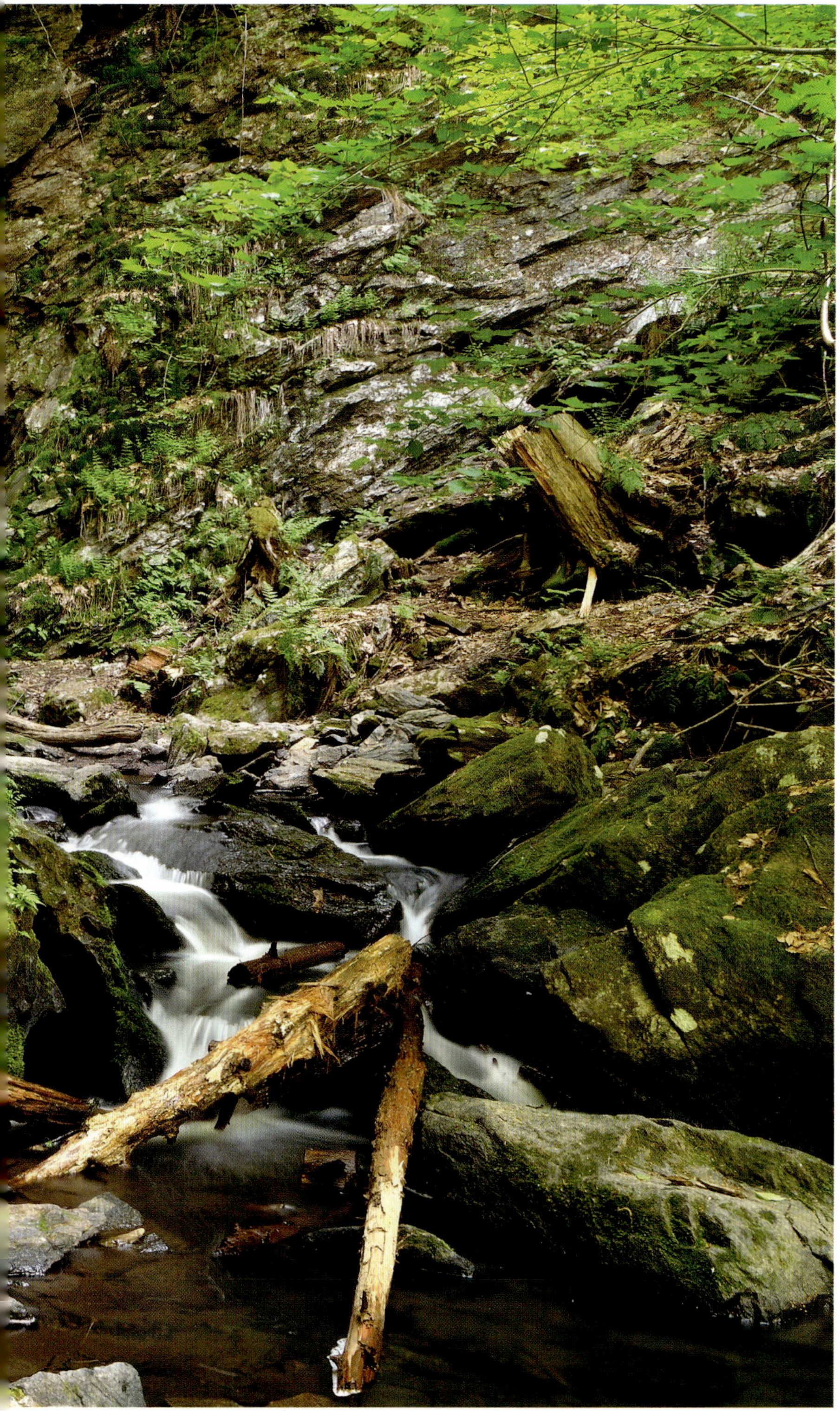

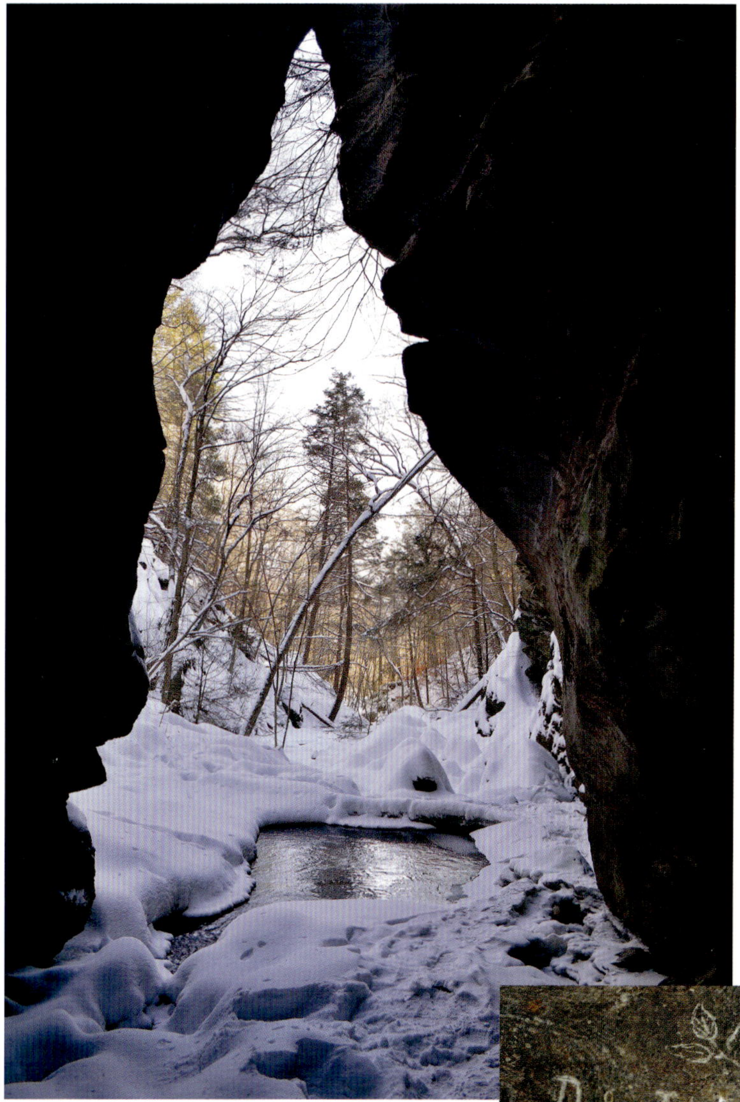

Interior of the Stone Church (Dover Plains)

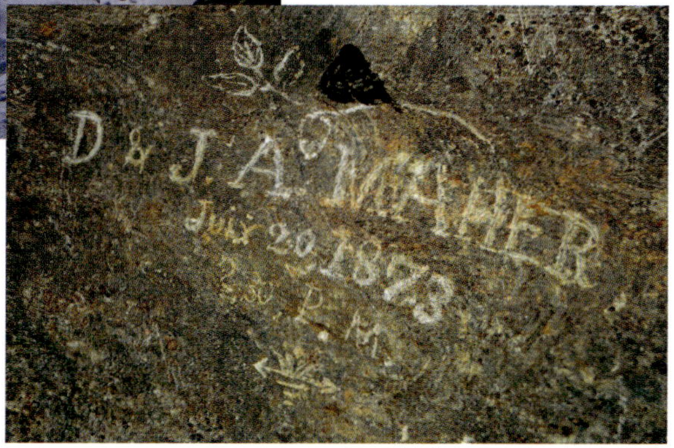

Historical graffiti on the inside of the Stone Church (Dover Plains)

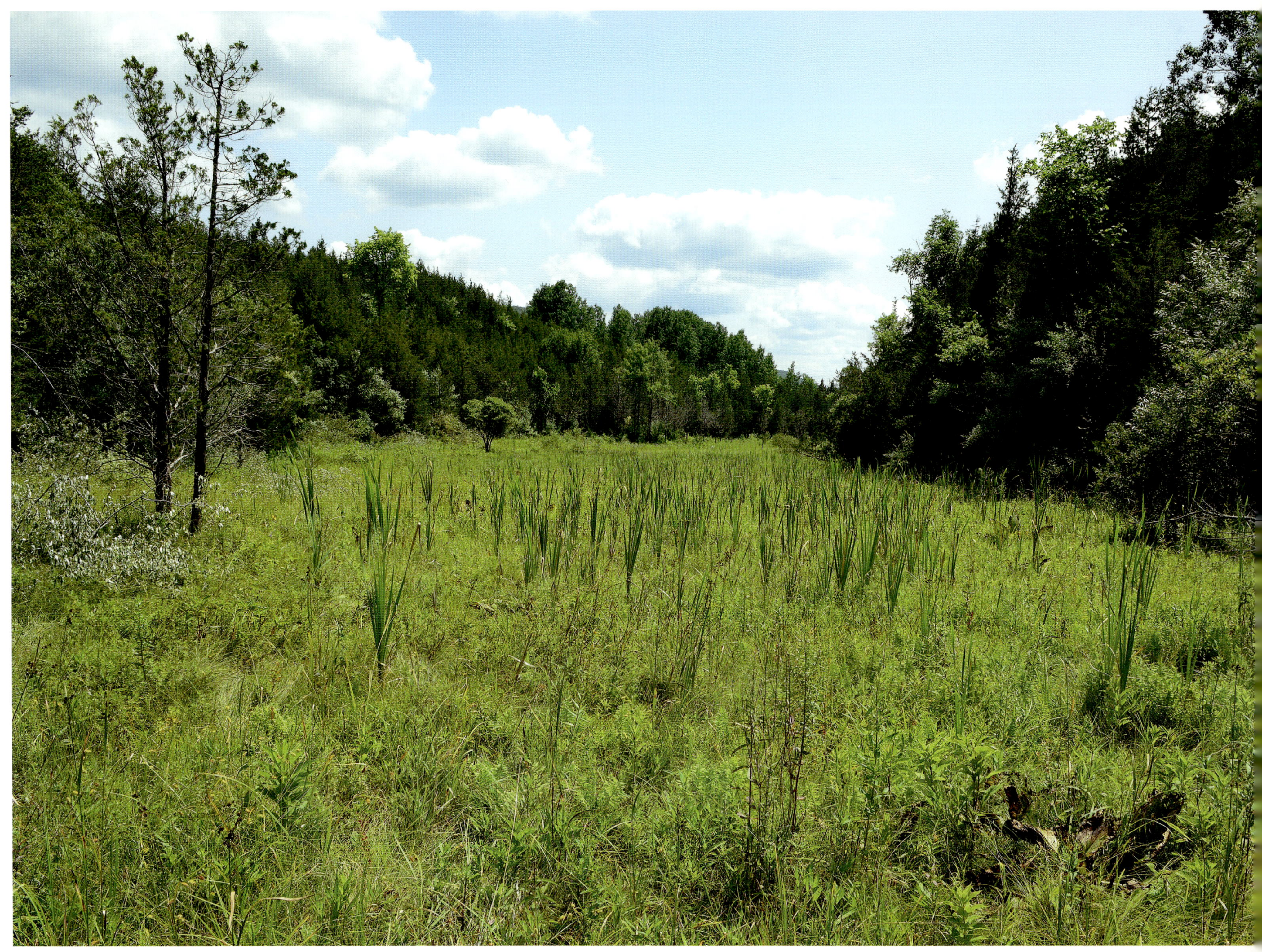

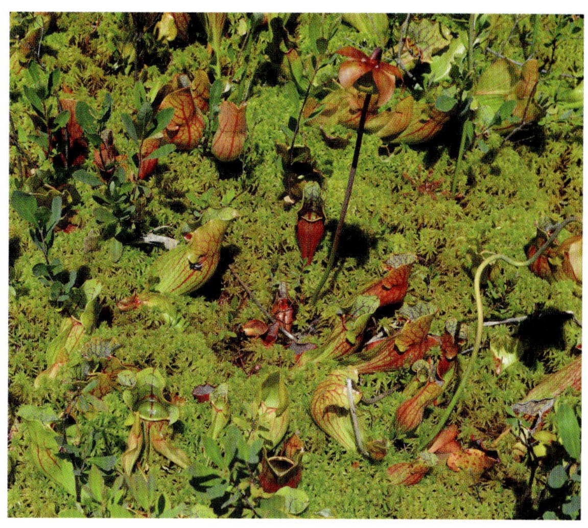

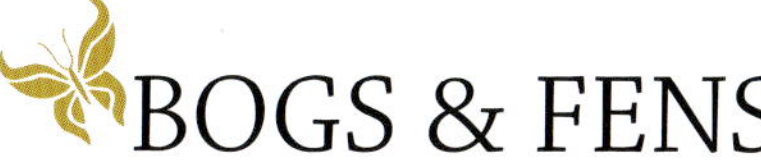

BOGS & FENS

Wetlands take many forms, most commonly lakes, swamps, and soggy riparian areas surrounding streams and rivers. Rarer types include bogs and fens. This latter class comprises only a fraction of wetlands throughout the Hudson Valley. Both are outliers, and if placed on a Bell curve would fall on opposite ends of the spectrum. Bogs contain highly acidic water, while fens have mostly neutral to alkaline conditions. These two types of wetlands have drastically declined over the last few centuries, a result of the myth that they are little more than smelly mosquito breeding grounds. Many were dammed off and transformed into more usable ponds and lakes; others were buried to make way for agriculture and development. These disappearances are a great loss. Bogs and fens contain many one-of-a-kind organisms that are specially adapted to survive in extreme conditions. Despite their typically small size, they contain highly diverse, ecologically important life.

In the Northeast, bogs are more plentiful than their alkaline counterparts. These peaty wetlands, normally occupying glacially scoured depressions, have an unusually low pH by effectively being bottled up and stewing in a broth of humic acid released by the degradation of organic matter. The primary inflow of water is from precipitation. Comparatively small influxes of water, in conjunction with little run-off, results in acidic conditions that inhibit decay. Dead plant matter rapidly accumulates, forming thick layers of peat that keep valuable nutrients imprisoned within. Certain plants have circumvented the nutrient-poor conditions by taking on a

This page:
Bog plants of Pine Swamp
(Harriman State Park)

Opposite page:
Calcareous fen
(Roger Perry Preserve)

feature characteristic of animals—carnivory. Pitcher plants, sundews, and bladderworts have evolved specialized mechanisms to capture and digest insects to obtain key elements like nitrogen and phosphorous. Along with these plant oddities, bogs are dominated by quaking mats of sphagnum mosses and heaths (highbush blueberry, azalea, leatherleaf). Fleeting displays of rare orchids routinely add a touch of vibrancy to the scene, often serving as the highlight of a visit to those lucky enough to encounter them in bloom.

Aside from having a different pH, fens differ from bogs by receiving significant water inputs from groundwater sources as well as precipitation. Upwelling springs and small braided streams supply a bulk of the moisture. Alkaline conditions are imparted to the system from the underlying rock strata, which in the case of our regional calcareous fens is normally limestone. The largest concentrations of these alkaline wetlands occur in Dutchess and Columbia counties. Due to a greater abundance of available nutrients, plant communities here contain a higher number of species than their acidic cousins. Unlike bogs that are clustered with shrubby heaths, the most prominent members of fens are grasses and sedges, making them resemble moist meadows. Several orchid species thrive among the knee-high vegetation, in addition to the "calciphiles," rare plants tolerant of high calcium levels that live almost exclusively in limy soils. The reclusive bog turtle, an endangered species and smallest native turtle in America, also primarily makes its home in places such as these, despite its misleading name. Calcareous fens are one of the rarest natural communities on the continent and normally occupy no more than a handful of acres.

The endangered bog turtle is New York's smallest and rarest turtle. This species' average length is a mere four inches when fully grown. Despite their diminutive size, individuals can live up to twenty or thirty years in the wild. Bog turtles are usually constricted to calcareous wetlands (those with an alkaline pH).

Their endangered status results mainly from habitat destruction, as well as low reproductive rates and the introduction of invasive plants.

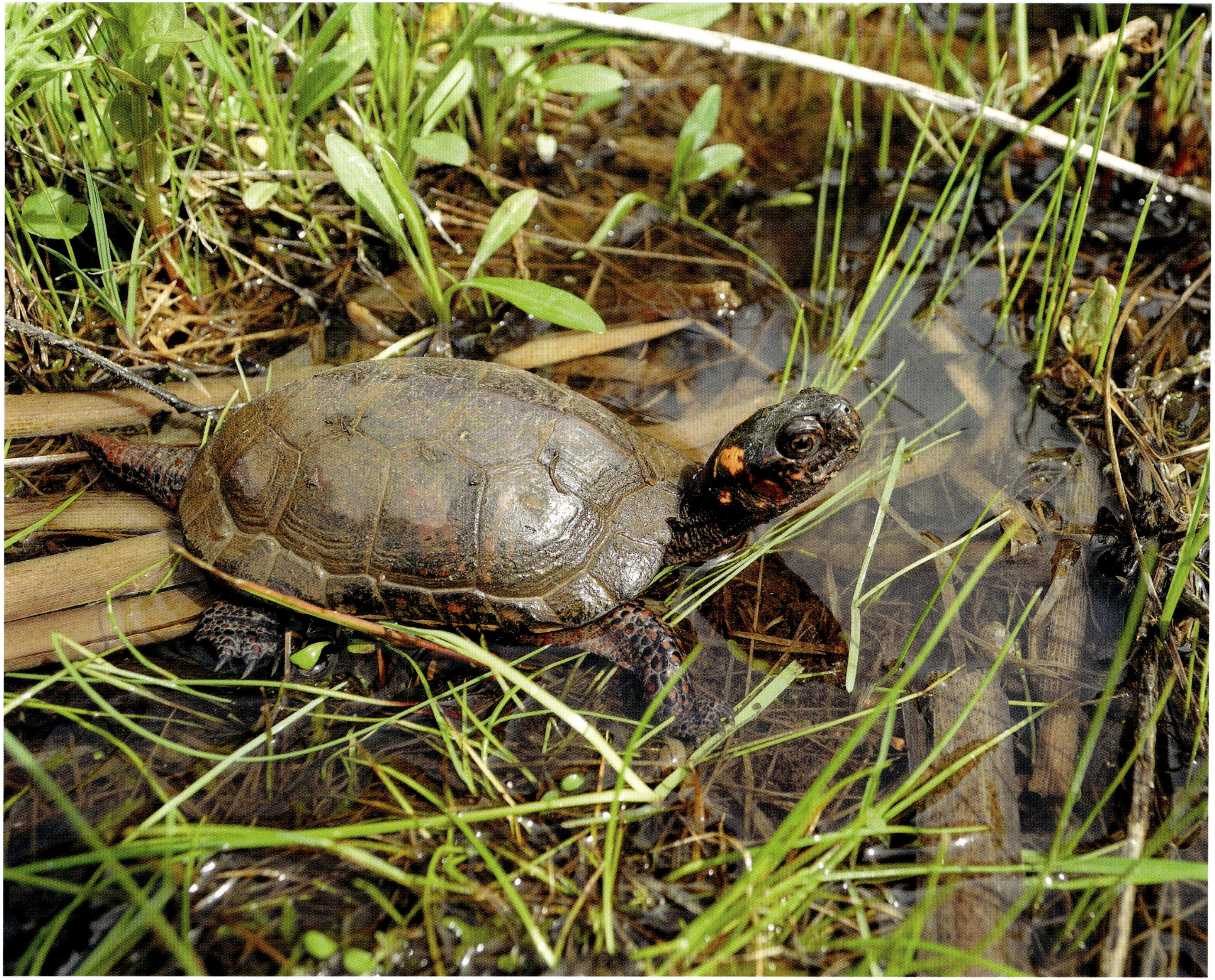

Bog turtle (Dutchess County)

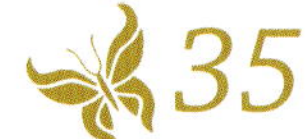

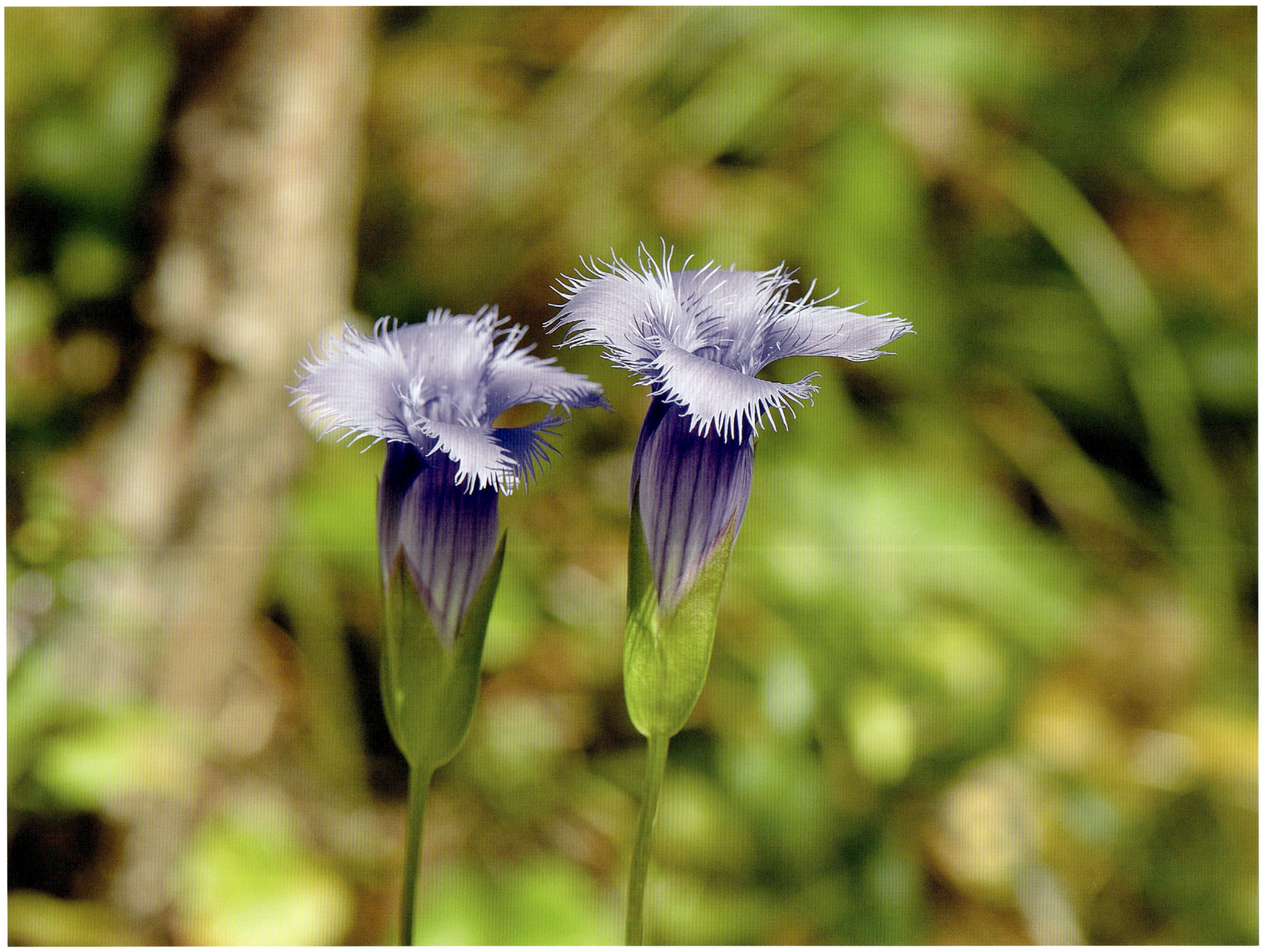

Fringed gentian (Roger Perry Preserve)

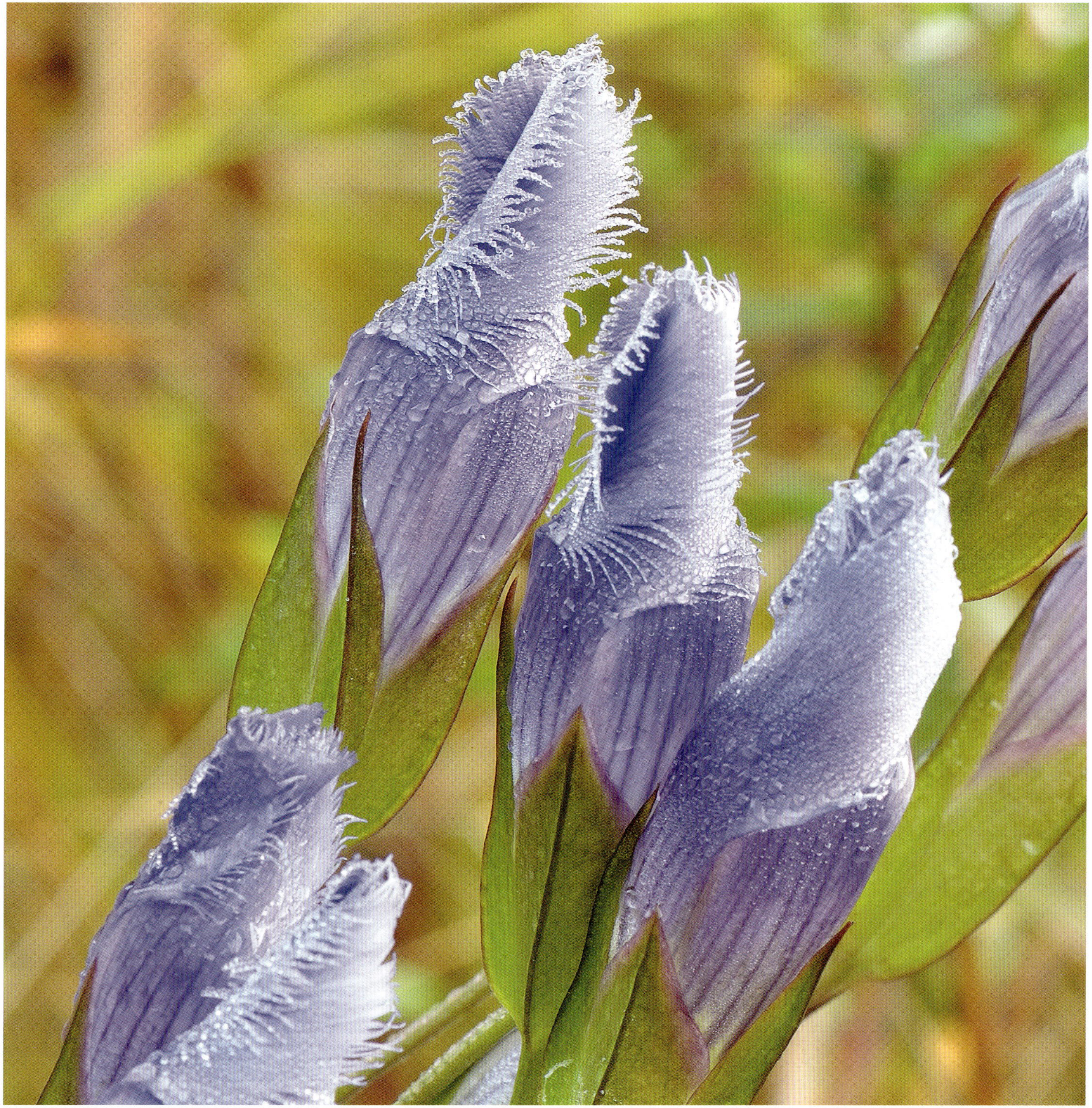

Unopened fringed gentian in the early morning (Roger Perry Preserve)

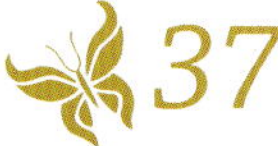

Great blue lobelia (*Lobelia siphilitica*) blooms in late summer and typically grows one to three feet tall. Its preferred habitat is along streams and river banks, but it also thrives in open areas such as meadows and forest edges containing abundant moisture. As evident in the scientific name, this plant was once believed to be a cure for syphilis. Native Americans used the root to treat various venereal diseases. When the first Europeans arrived to the continent they shipped it back to the Old World with high hopes. It was quickly discovered to be ineffectual and fell out of favor.

Native lore holds that this and other lobelia species can be used as a talisman to ward off spirits, and that if dried, crushed, and tossed toward an approaching storm, it will render it benign.

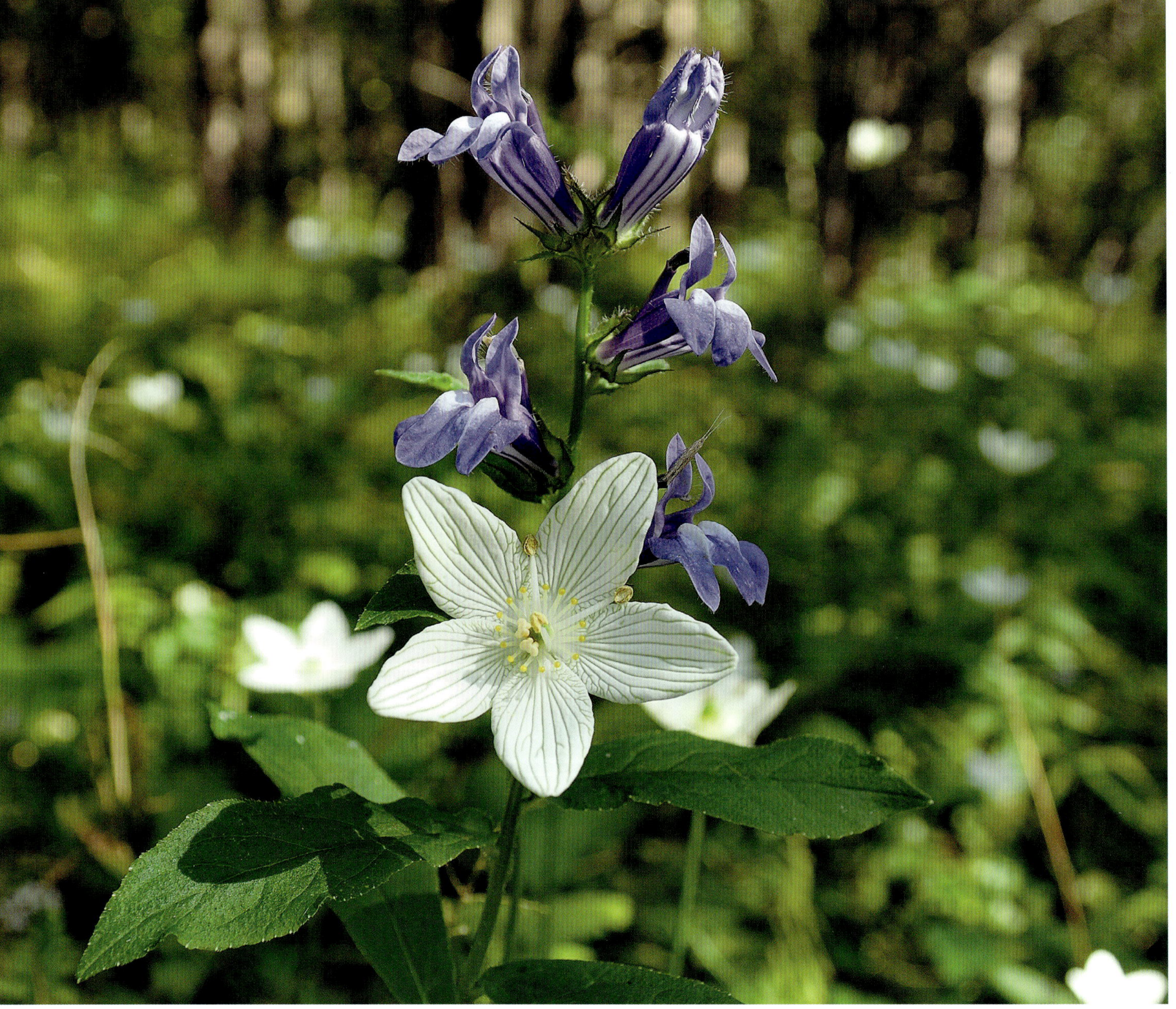

Great blue lobelia and grass-of-Parnassus (Roger Perry Preserve)

Pitcher plants capture their more nimble insect prey by employing several deceptive techniques. First, the openings of the pitchers are crimpled or contorted to vaguely resemble the shape of a large flower. In late summer, similar to the leaves of trees, the pigment anthocyanin develops, adding gaudy splashes of red that further helps the plant achieve its mimicry. A bacteria and enzyme-laced solution at the bottom of the pitcher helps digest previously captured organisms and emits pungent, carrion-like odors that are enticing to certain insects like flies. Once the lured insect makes it to the base of the pitcher and finds nothing of interest, it attempts to escape. Those with wings often get their vital appendages soaked in the liquid, rendering them unable to fly. The inside of the plant is coated with a slick, wax-like substance that makes gripping the walls to climb out nearly impossible. Higher up, recurved or downward-pointing hairs add yet another obstacle. Exhausted insects eventually drown in the pool of liquid and are broken down into a stew of easily absorbable nutrients for the plant.

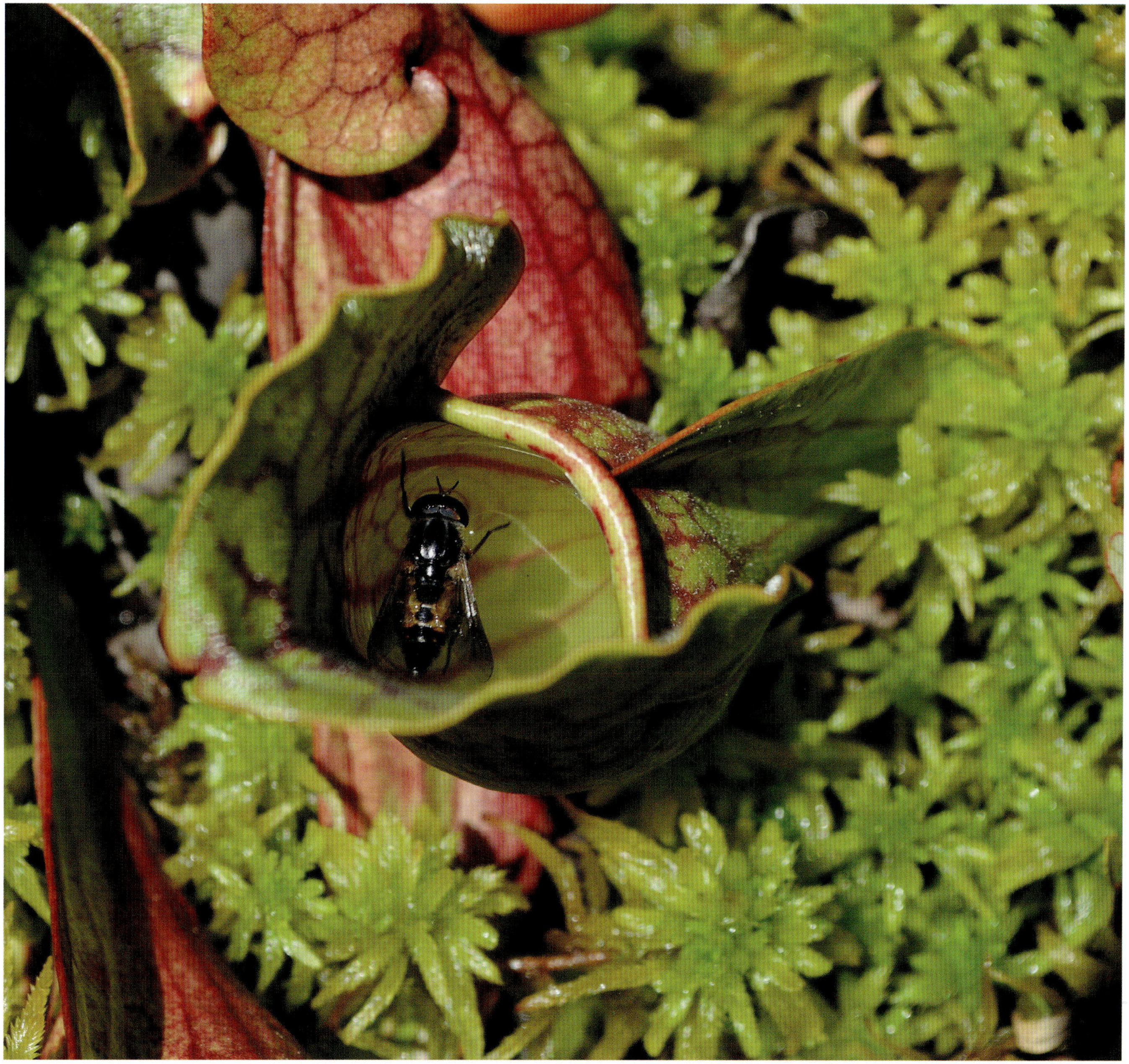

Pitcher plant with captured prey (Pine Swamp)

The strangely beautiful sundews, with their seemingly fragile hairs decked with sticky globs of mucilage resembling glistening morning dew (hence the name), are often quite abundant in bogs and peatlands. Despite their tiny size, collections of these carnivores trap mammoth quantities of insects. A study undertaken in England during the 1970s estimated that a two-acre bog filled with sundews had an average of six million insects trapped at any one time!

Insects attracted by sweet secretions, and also probably by the glistening droplets, become entangled in the tentacle-like hairs upon contact. A chemical anesthetic in the viscid droplets quells the struggles of the newly captured prey. The initial movements of attempted escape act as a stimulus that triggers the leaf to begin wrapping around the insect, ensuring greater surface contact with the body. Digestive enzymes also present in the mucilage begin dissolving flesh; nutrients are absorbed through cells on the leaf's surface.

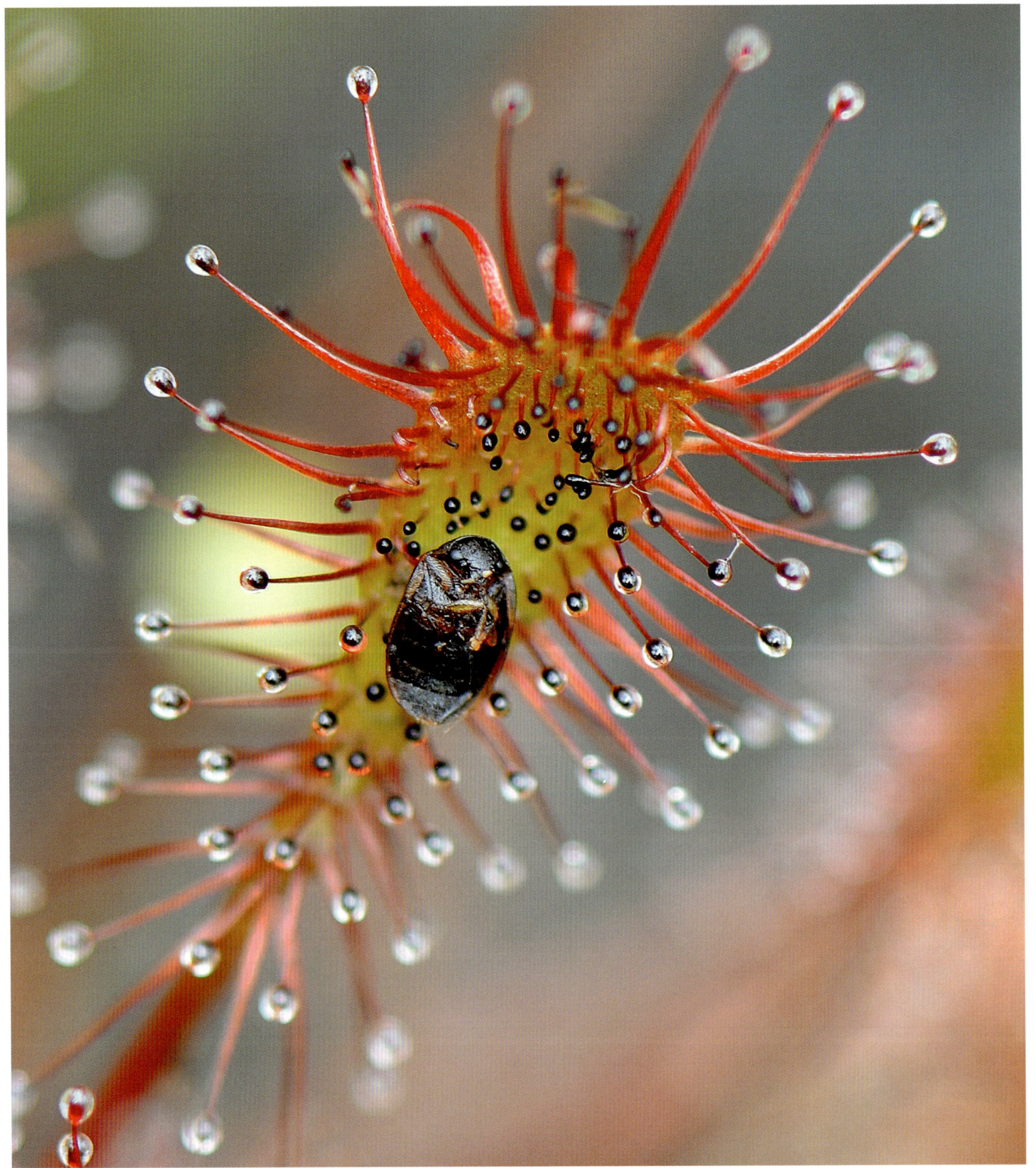

Sundew with captured prey (Pine Swamp)

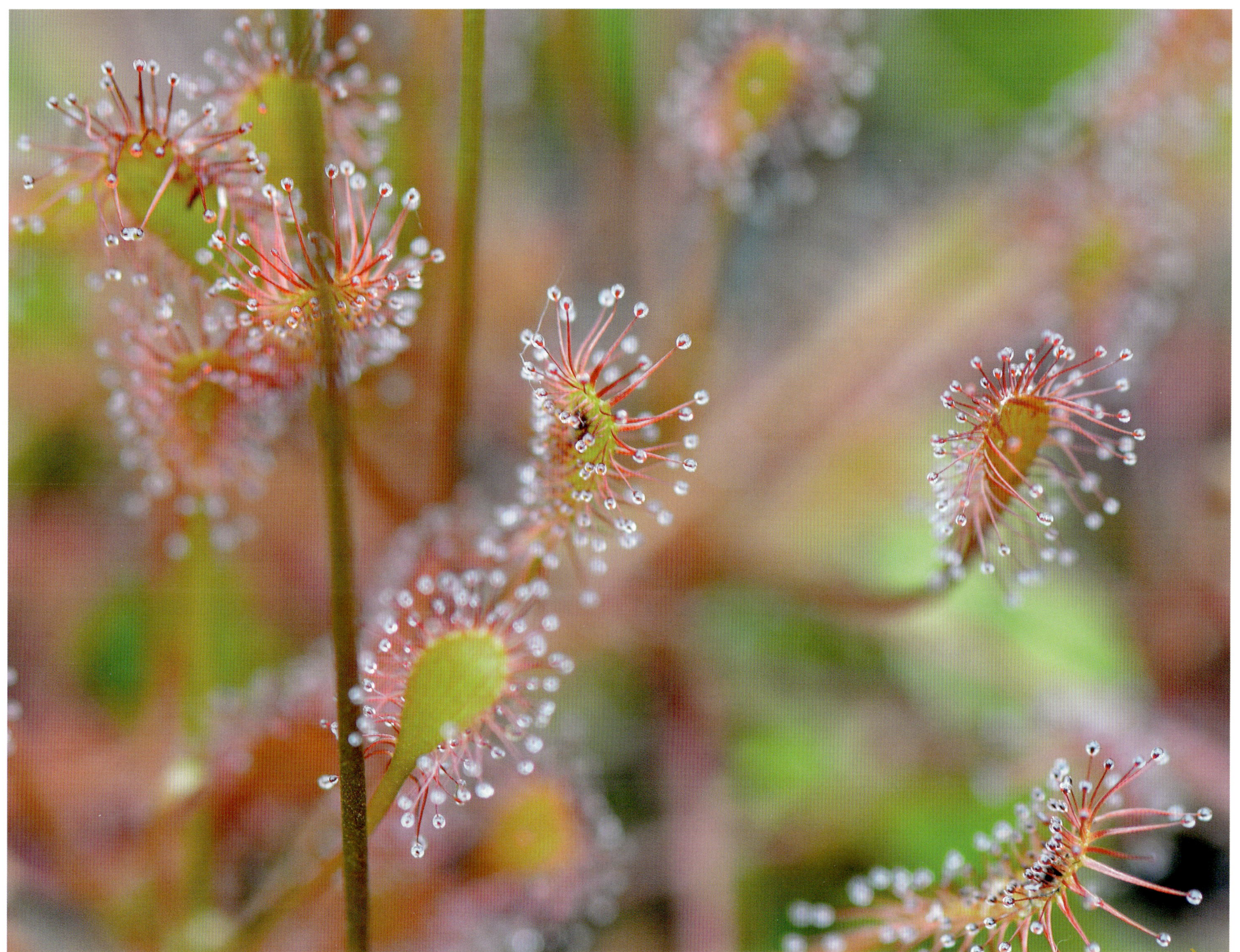

Spatulate-leaved sundew (Pine Swamp)

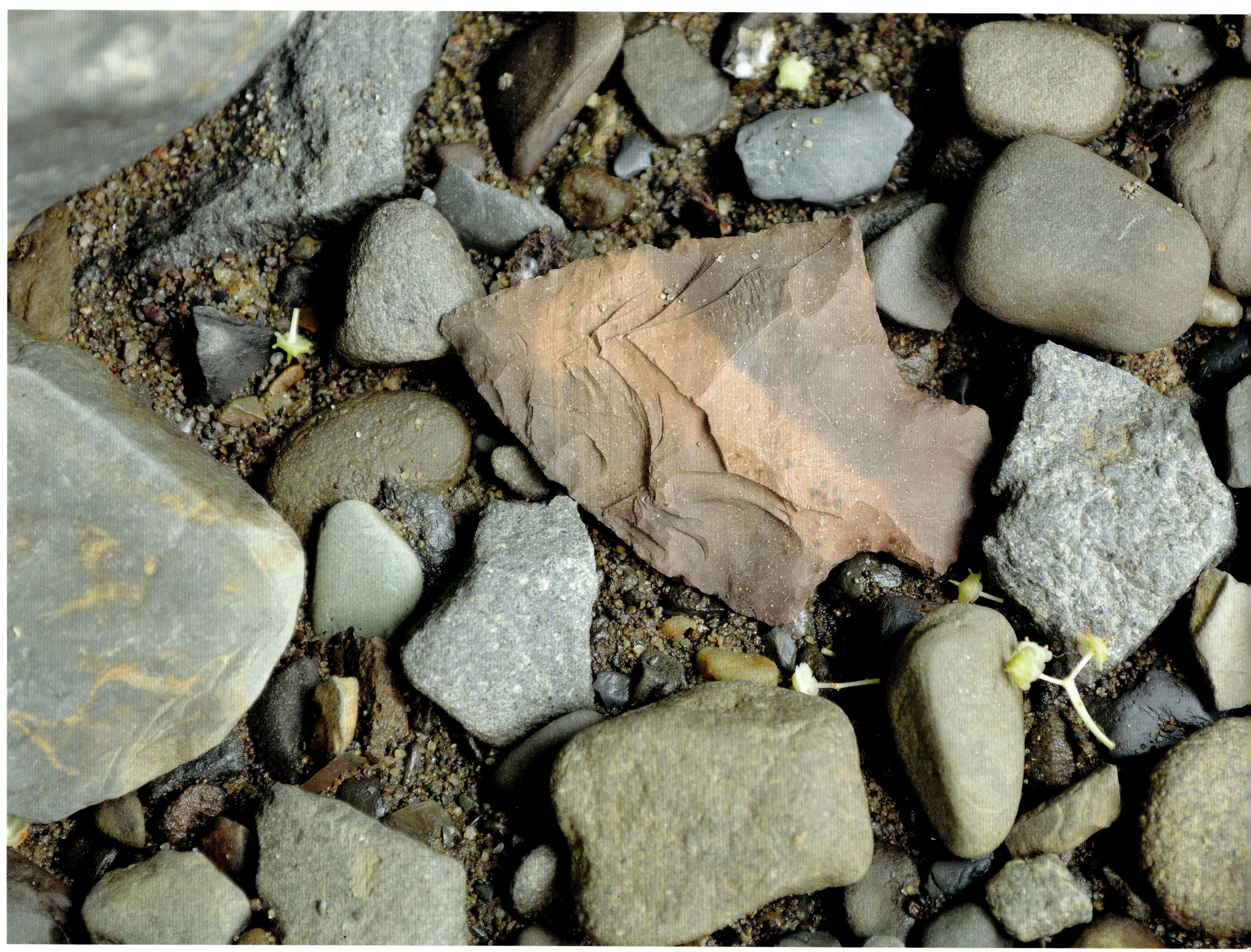

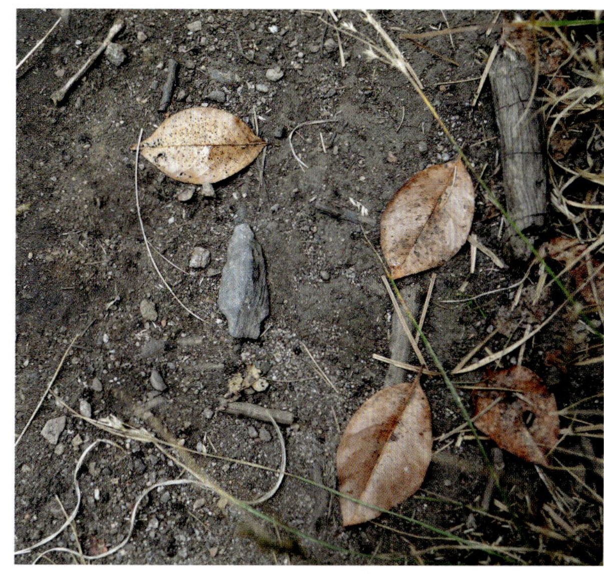

THE PEOPLE

Native Americans began inhabiting the Hudson Valley shortly after the last ice age ended. Fluted spear points and other artifacts recovered from the Dutchess Quarry Mine in southern Orange County are some of the oldest known in the state and indicate a human presence for at least 12,500 years.

The Lenape, or Delaware tribe, held sway over the lower and middle reaches of the Hudson Valley, while to the north, the Mohicans reigned. A majority settled along the shores of the Hudson River. The murky waters teemed with a richness and diversity of life almost unimaginable today, offering sturgeon, herring, shad, and shellfish in seemingly limitless quantities. The surrounding soils were also vastly fertile, and in later years, when agriculture was developed, were ideal for growing crops. As Henry Hudson remarked in September 1609, after visiting a native village while on his maiden voyage up the river that would later bear his name: "The land is the finest for cultivation that I ever in my life set foot upon" (G. M. Asher, 1860). All that remains are tiny pieces of their daily lives. Arrowheads, pottery fragments, and shell middens are occasionally found near village sites or hunting grounds, revealed by the forces of erosion or commissioned archaeological digs.

The Dutch and English, in contrast, left far more indelible marks on the land. New Netherland, which would later be renamed New York after the English seized control

"It is a stone fruit. Each one yields me a thought. I come nearer to the maker of it than if I found his bones."

—Henry David Thoreau

This page:
Projectile point lying atop hiking trail (Putnam County)

Opposite page:
Perkiomen broad point (2000–500 BC) (Orange County)

in 1664, was originally colonized by the Dutch, mainly to partake in the fur trade. The Indians collected pelts, which were bought by enterprising individuals for trinkets and other nominal goods. Beaver, otter, and mink pelts were especially prized and would result in a handsome profit when shipped back to Europe for use in hats and other garments.

As the first Europeans to colonize the region, the Dutch had the luxury of bestowing names to the surrounding natural features and the towns they later constructed. Many of these names survive today—Yonkers, Peekskill, Kinderhook, Claverack, and Catskill, to name a few. Additionally, their architecture is visible throughout the valley. Numerous churches and personal dwellings from the early days still stand and find themselves welcoming a steady stream of curious visitors.

Bare Island projectile point (3000–1000 BC) (Ulster County)

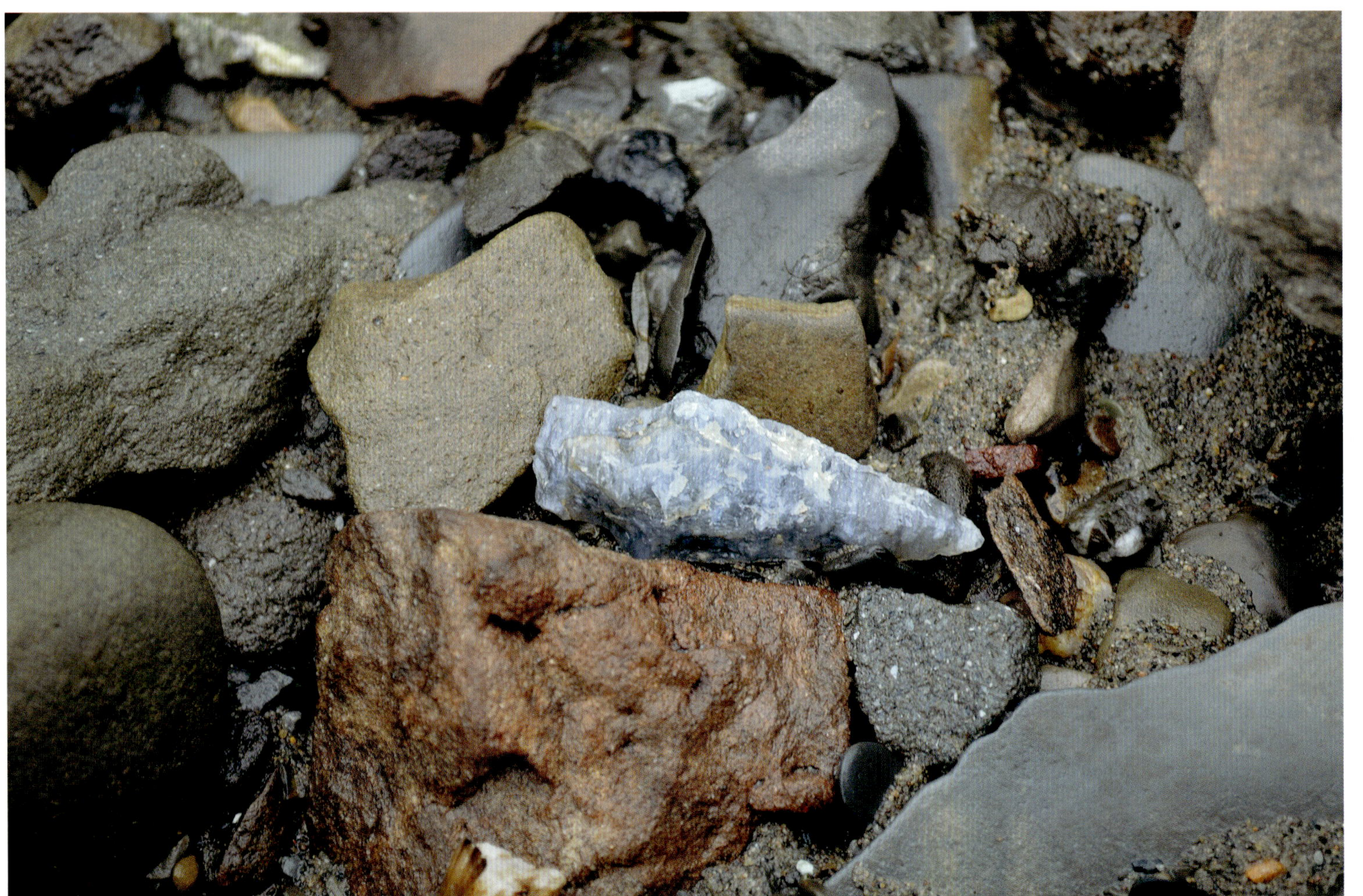

Not an actual arrowhead, this quartz Bare Island projectile point (3000–1000 BC) is an atlatl dart tip. True arrowheads—triangular-shaped points—did not appear until around 700 AD. Prior to the invention of the bow, long darts or spears, sometimes exceeding six feet in length, were used for hunting. These were propelled in excess of ninety miles per hour by use of a simple, yet effective hand-held device called an atlatl, which extended the reach of the forearm, thereby enabling the thrower to add substantial force to the projectile.

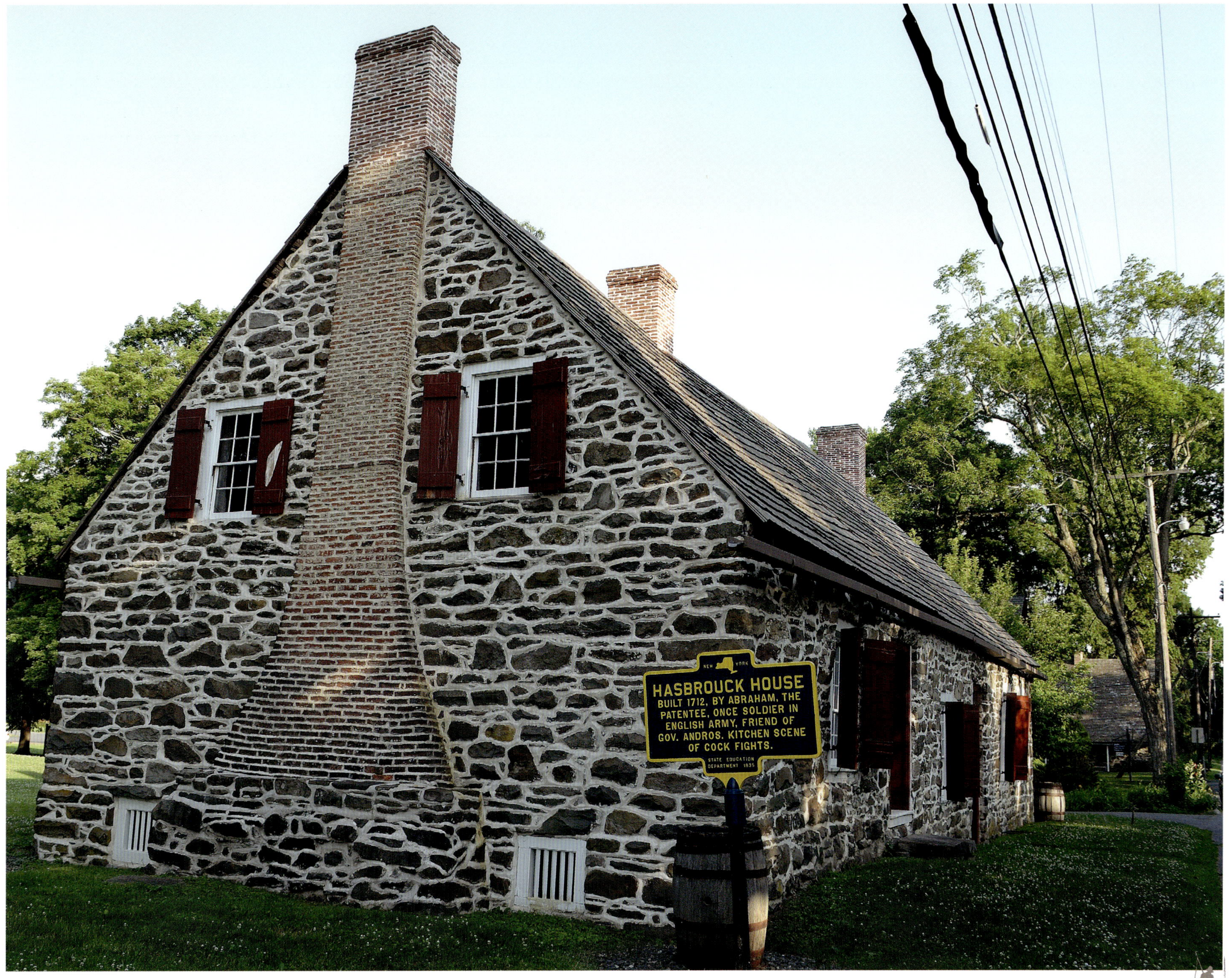

Huguenot Street (New Paltz)

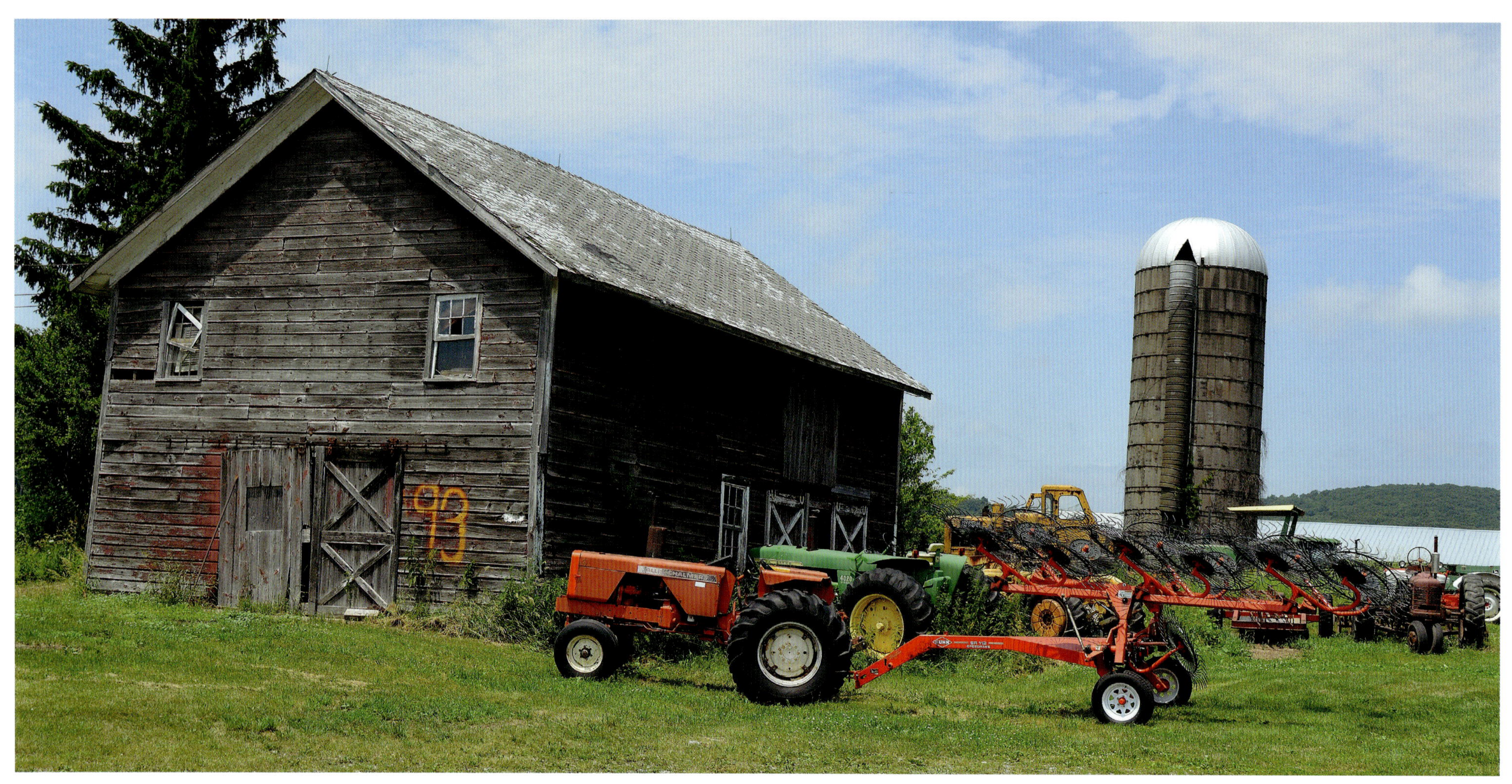

Columbia County farm (Ancram)

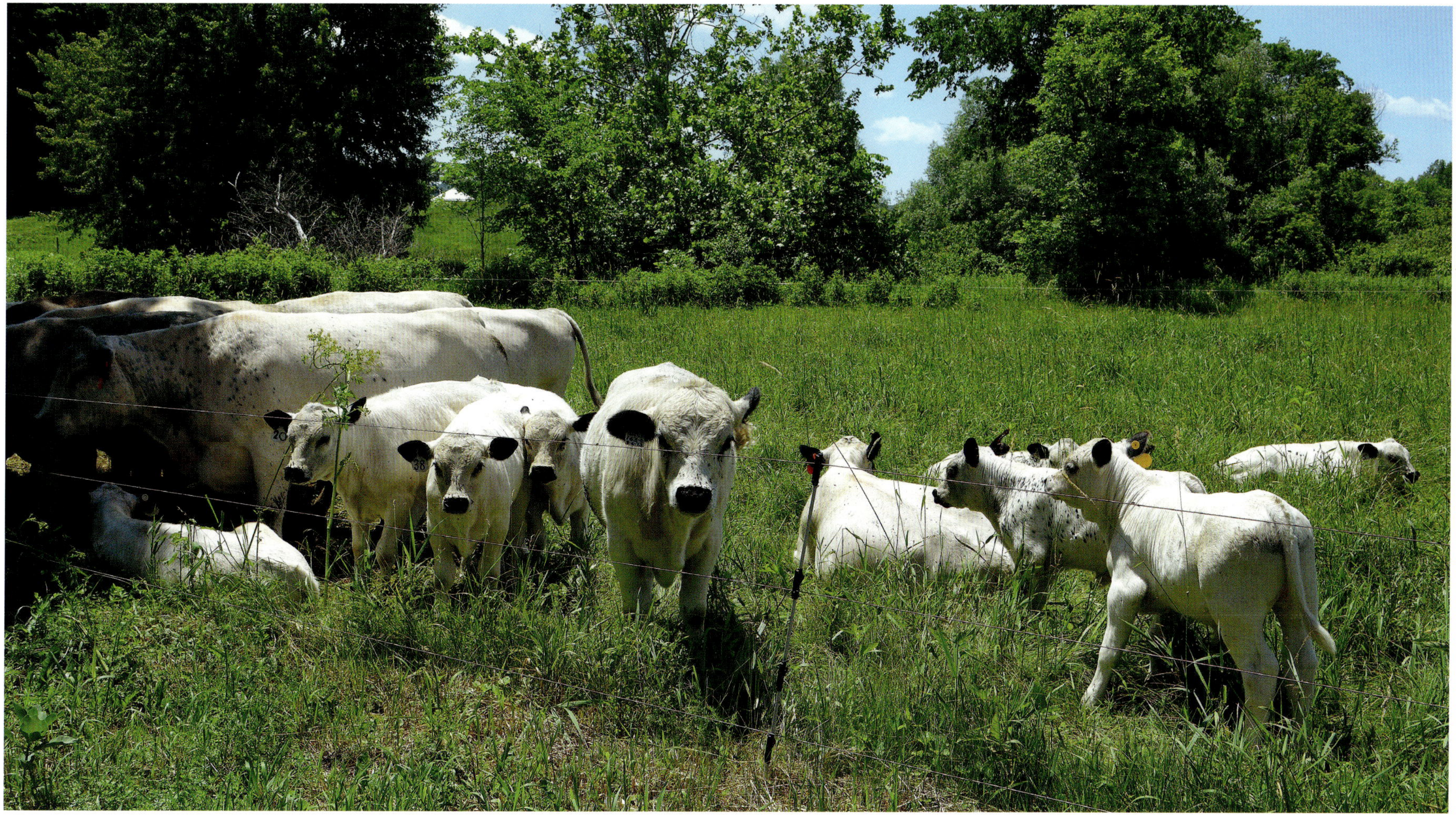

Cow pasture (Ancram)

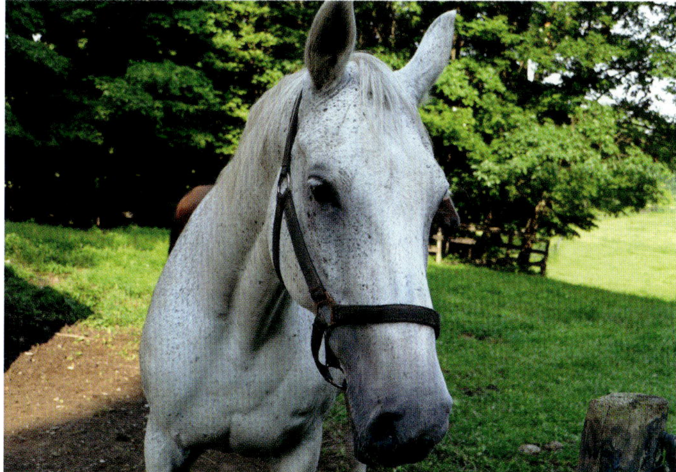

Farm horse (Ancram)

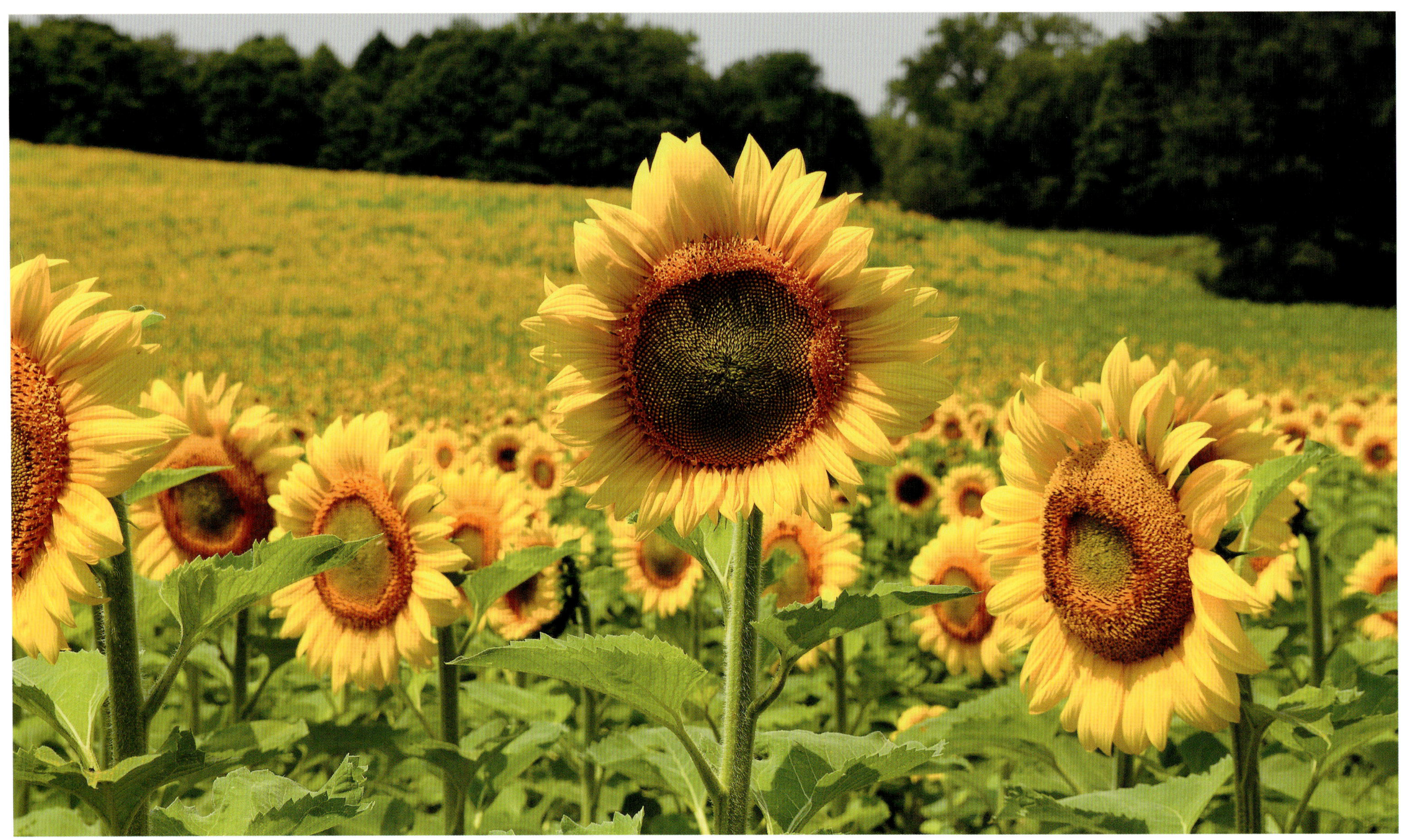

Sunflowers (Ancram)

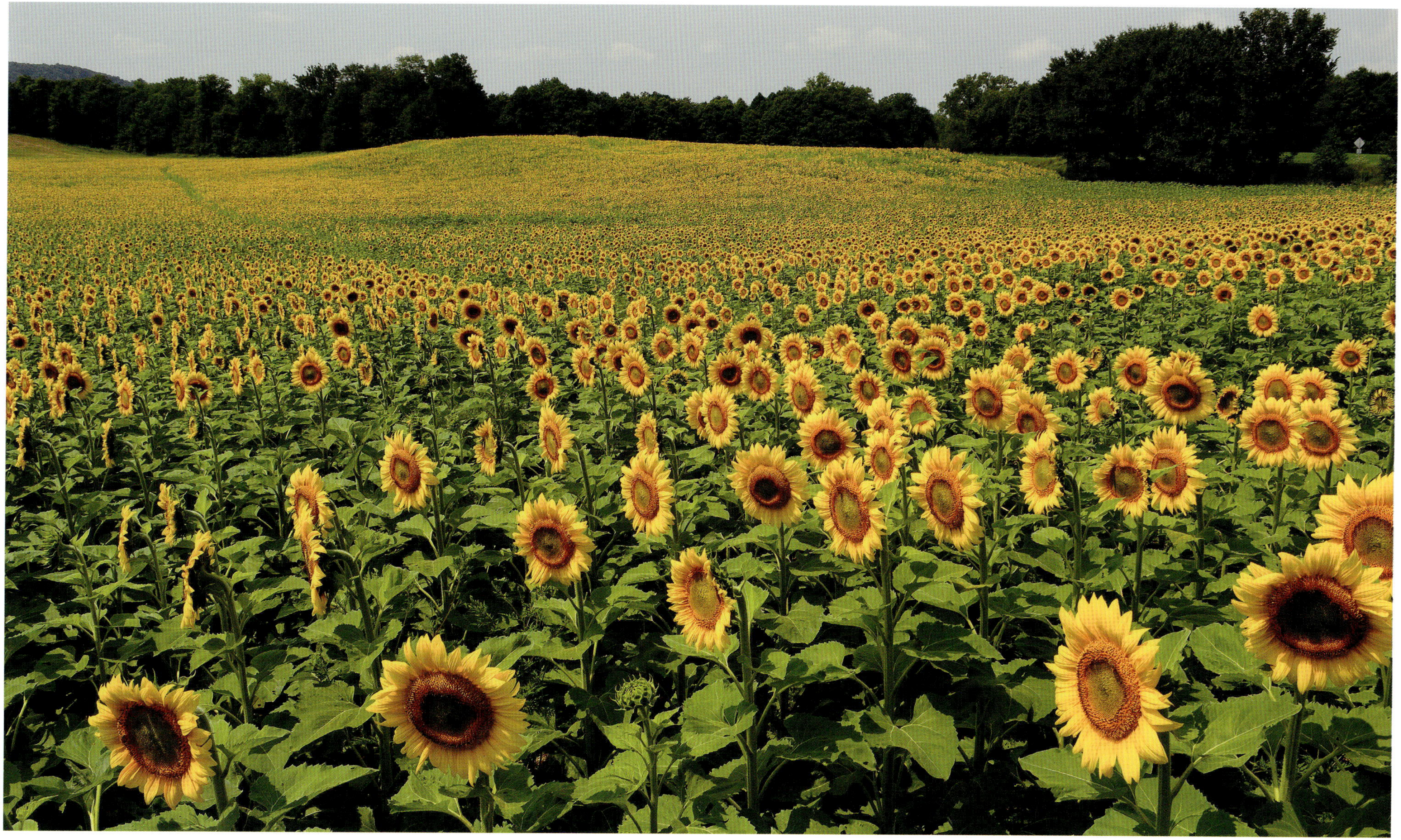

Sunflower crop (Ancram)

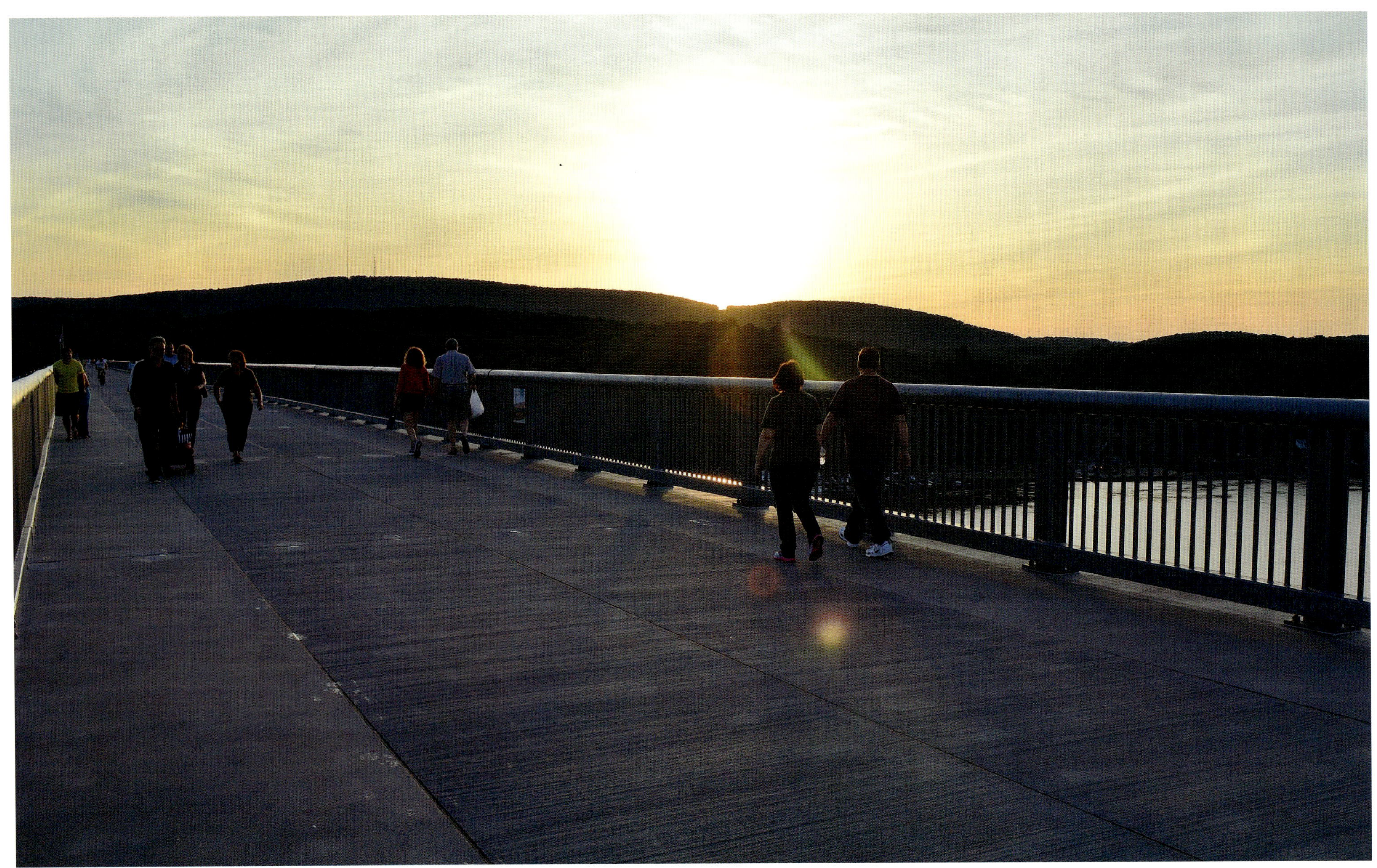

Walkway sunset (Walkway Over the Hudson State Park)

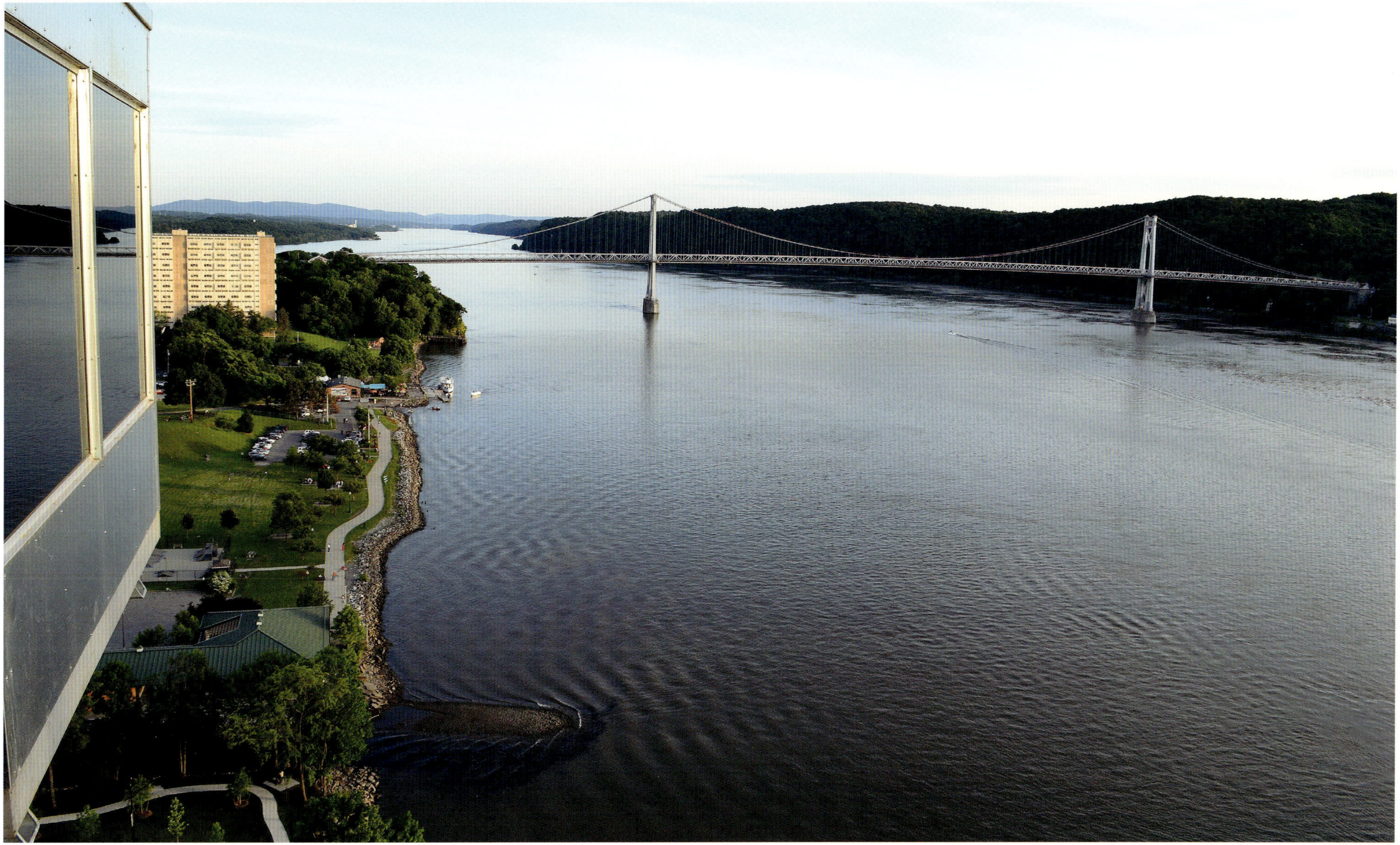

Looking south from the walkway

Constructed atop an abandoned railroad bridge built during the late nineteenth century (the first bridge to ever span the river), the Walkway Over the Hudson rises to 212 feet above the river's surface. At 1.28 miles long, the walkway is the longest elevated pedestrian bridge in the world. It opened in October 2009 for the state's quadricentennial festivities, celebrating the 1609 discovery of the region by Henry Hudson and his crew aboard the *Half Moon*.

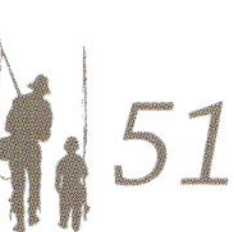

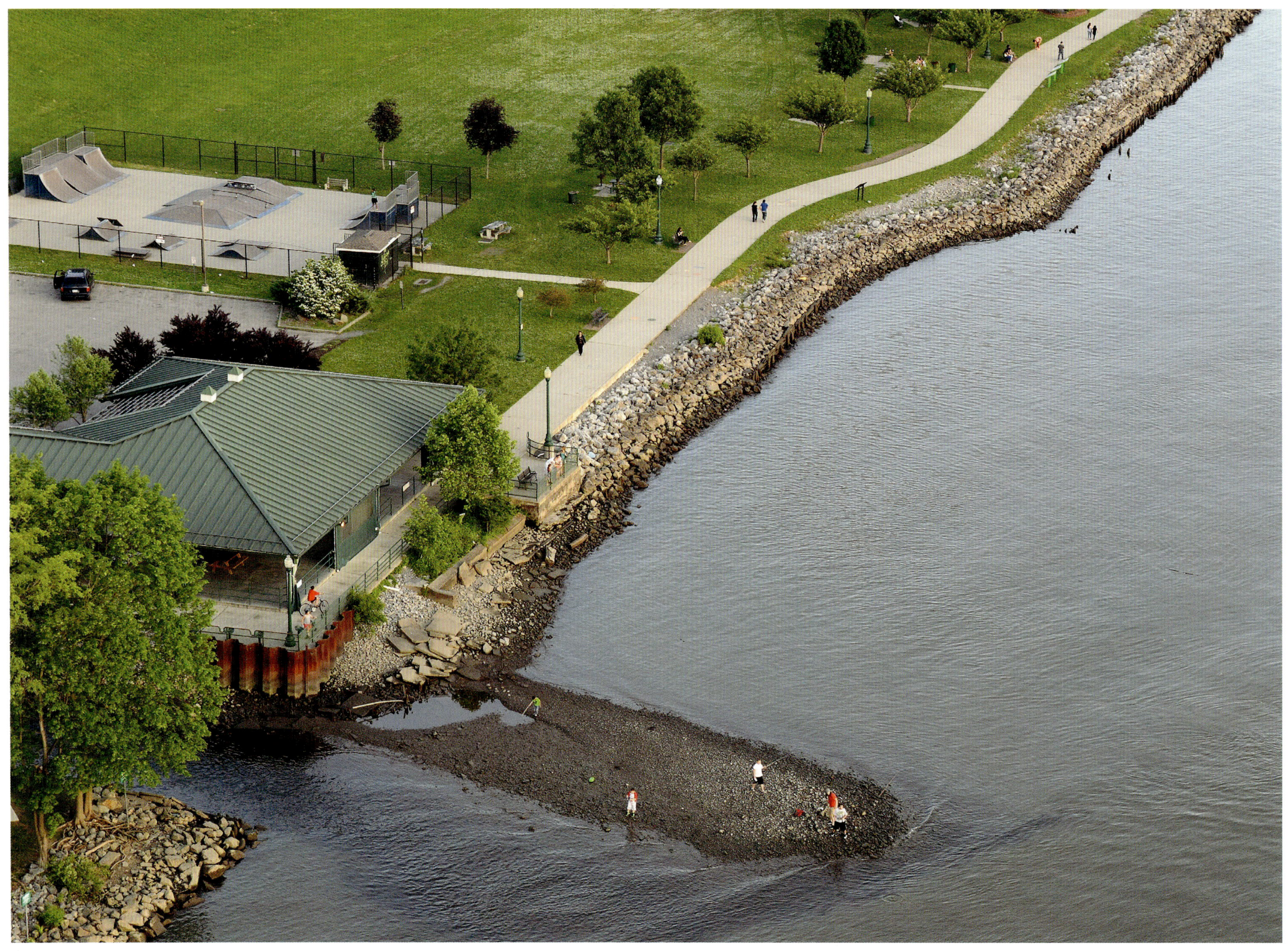

Poughkeepsie shoreline

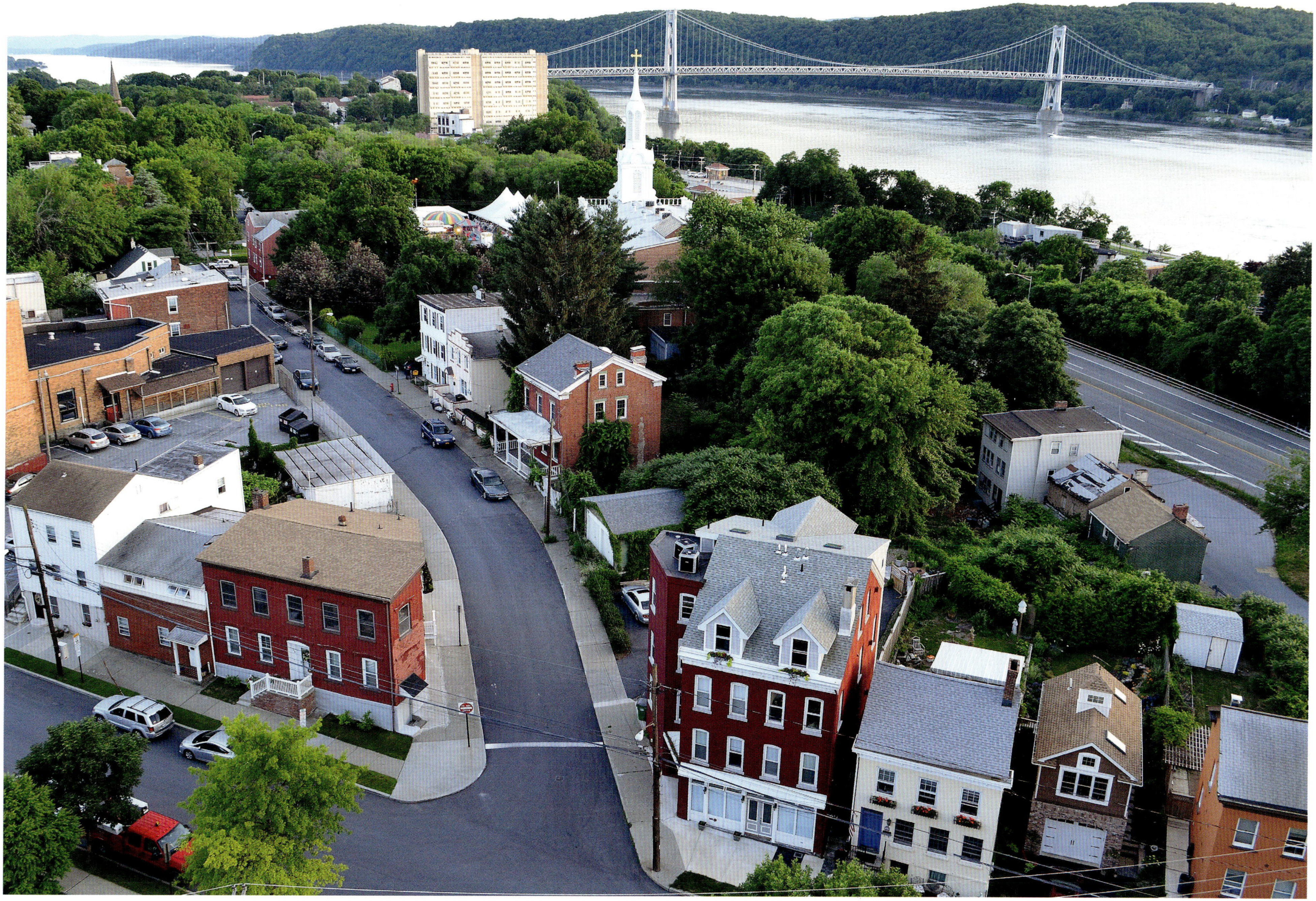

View of Poughkeepsie from the walkway

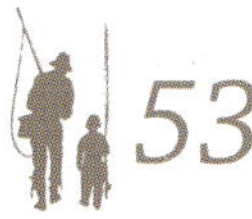

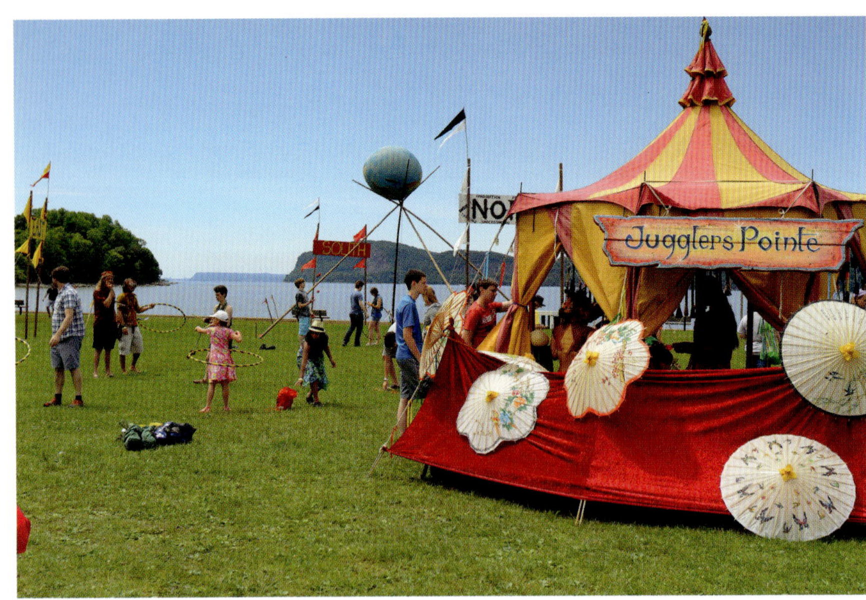

Clearwater Festival booths

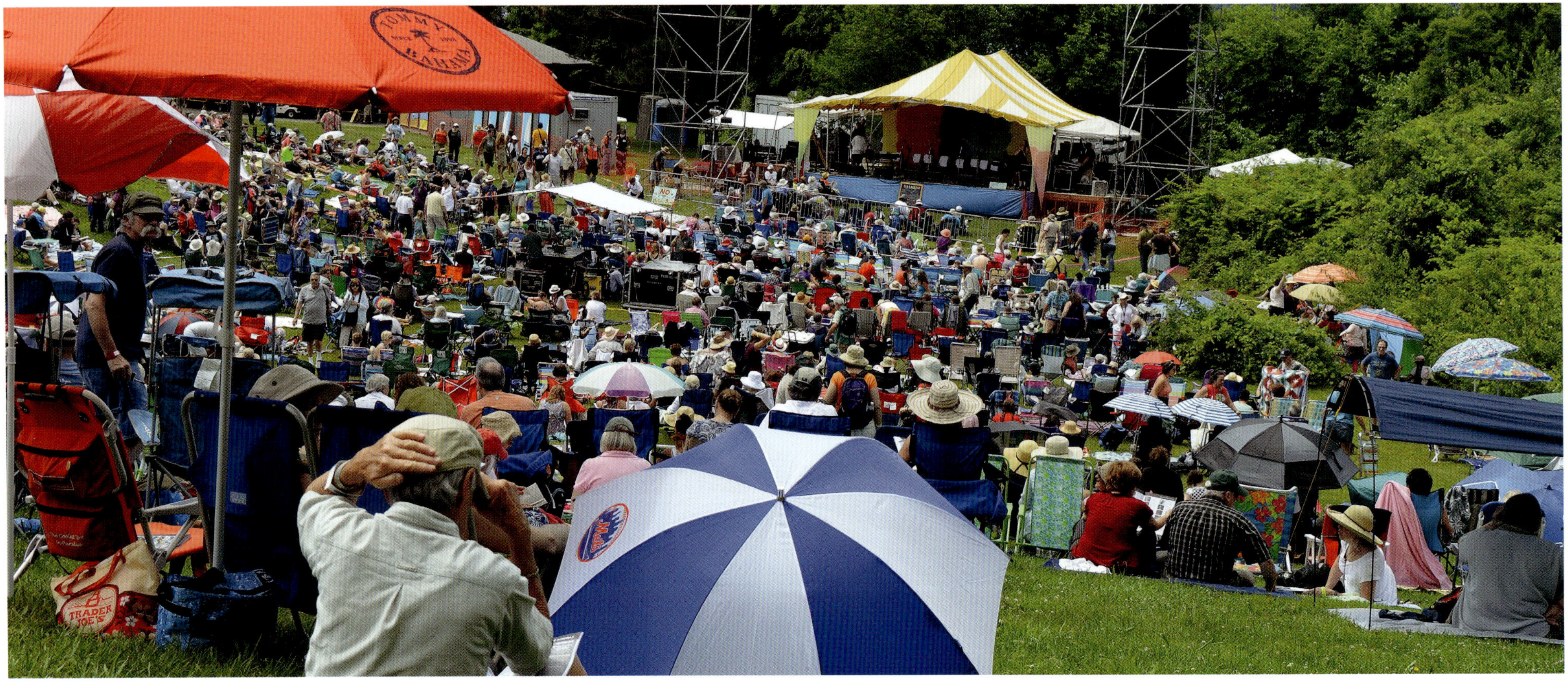

Clearwater Festival (Croton Point)

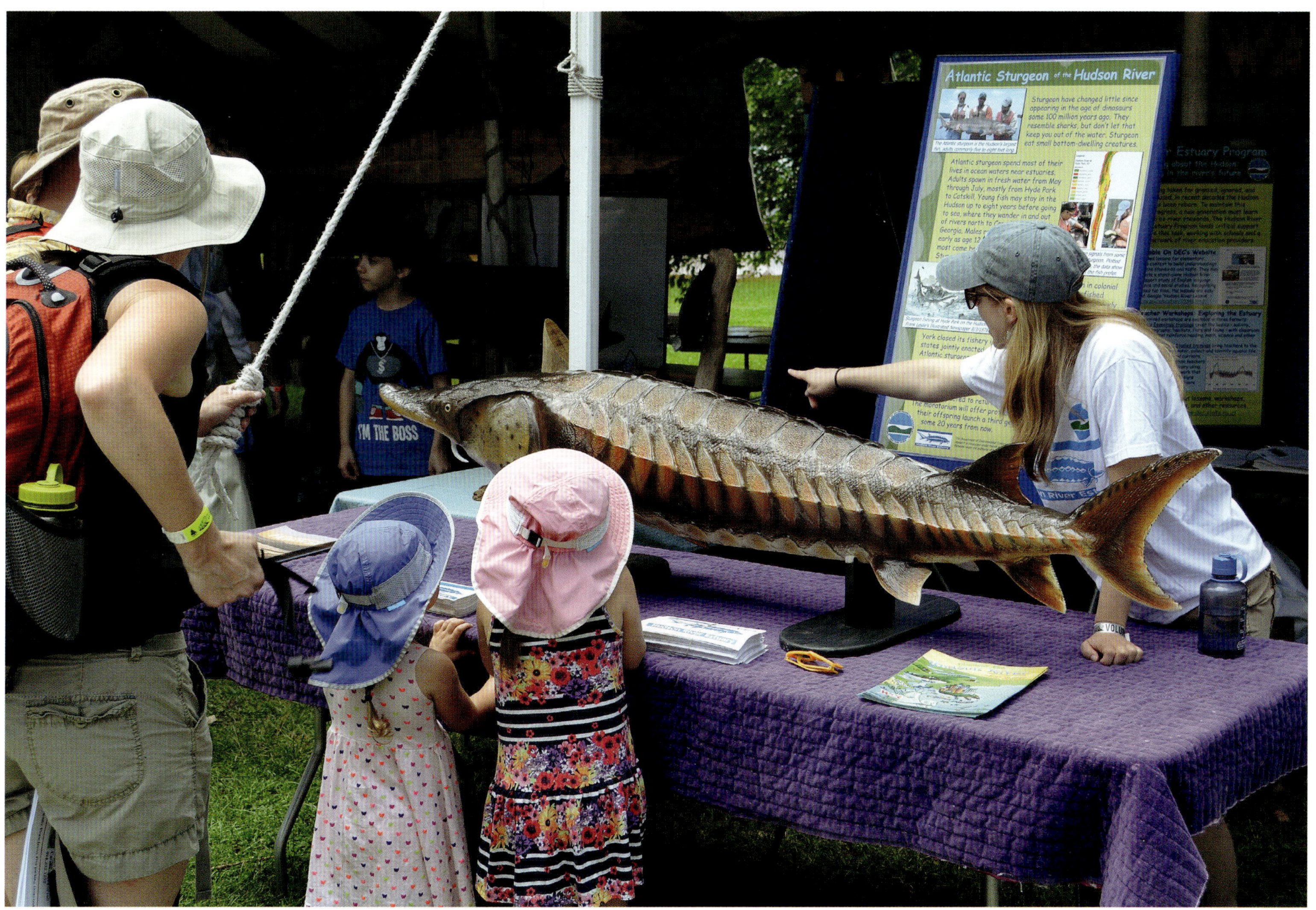

Hudson River Estuary Program (Croton Point)

Tasked with protecting the Hudson River through a variety of means, the program, a part of the state's Department of Environmental Conservation (DEC), was set up in 1987 to address the countless problems affecting the Hudson. Aside from traditional habitat restoration and other direct conservation projects, the Hudson River Estuary Program widely engages in hands-on education approaches. Their most successful programs revolve around "citizen science."

A Day in the Life of the Hudson River occurs once a year during the fall, when school groups assemble at various spots along the entire length of the river and perform scientific testing, ranging from taking water temperature and dissolved oxygen readings to recording the organisms present via haul seining. Another similar project, one designed to attract a wider audience, deals with eel monitoring on several tributaries. Participants not only learn scientific methodology and the finer points of research, but also get to contribute valuable data to an ongoing study that helps assess the state of the Hudson.

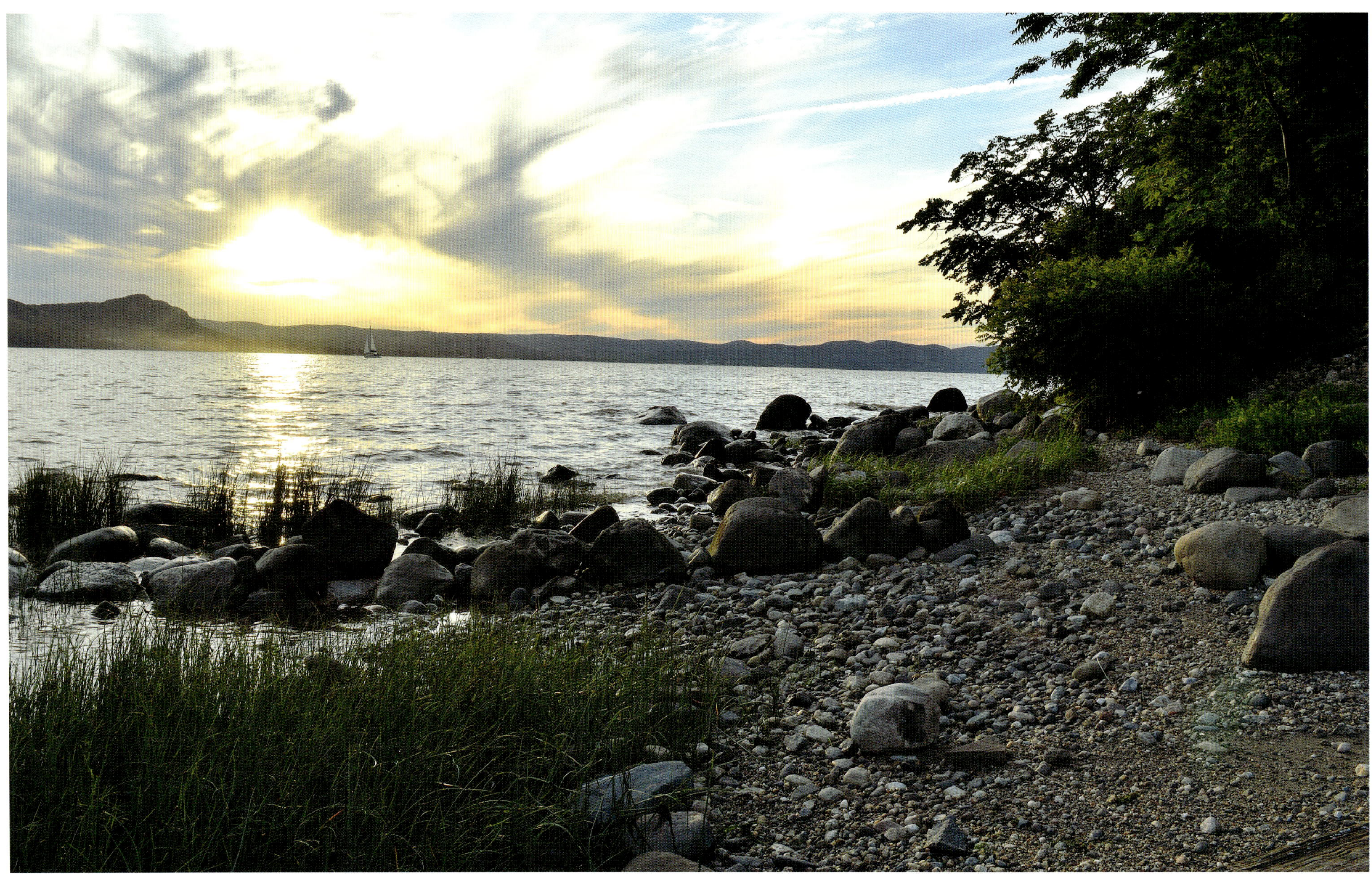

Croton Point sunset

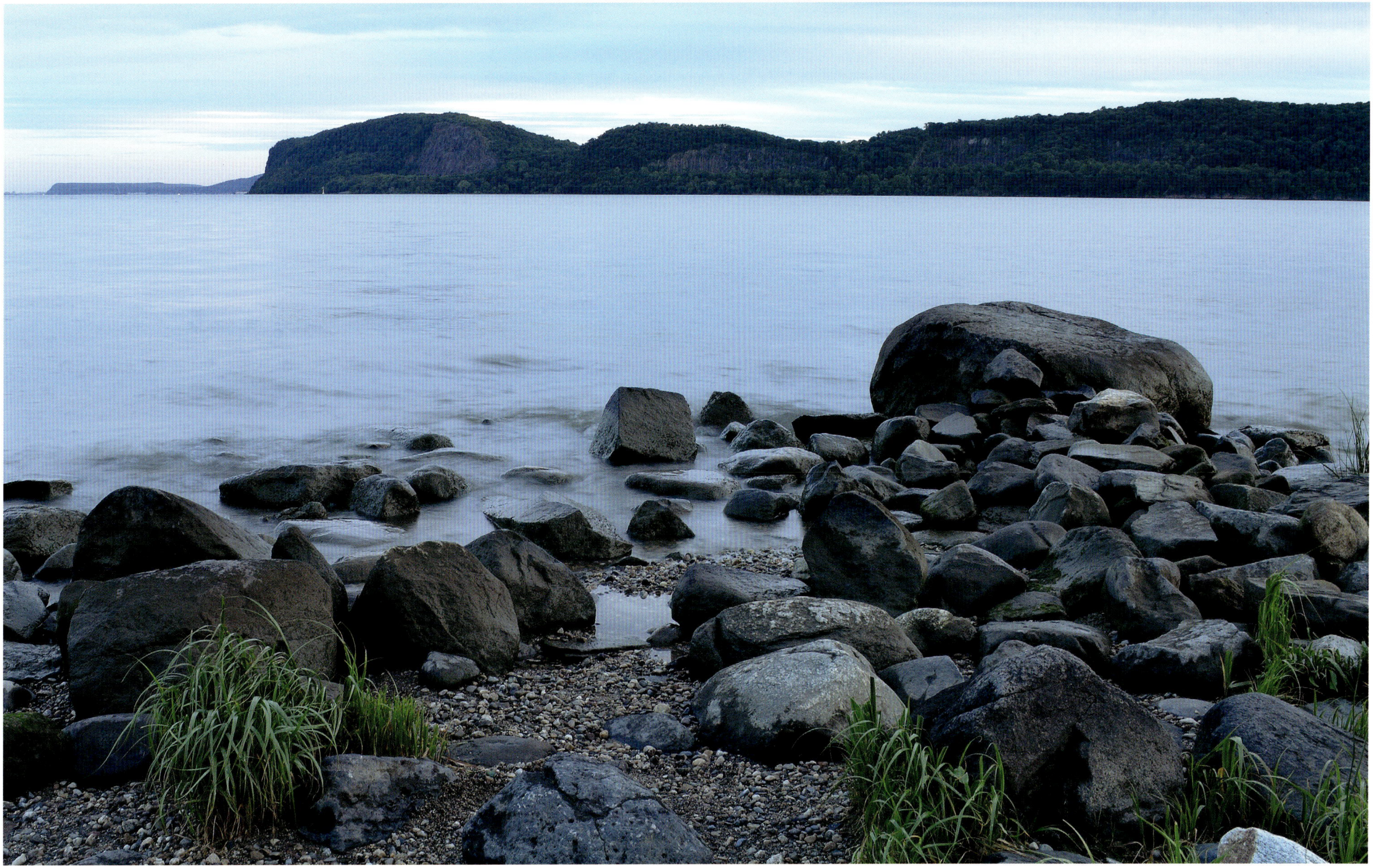

Southern tip of Croton Point

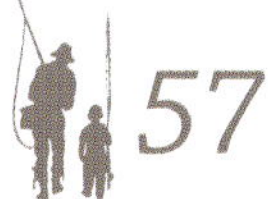

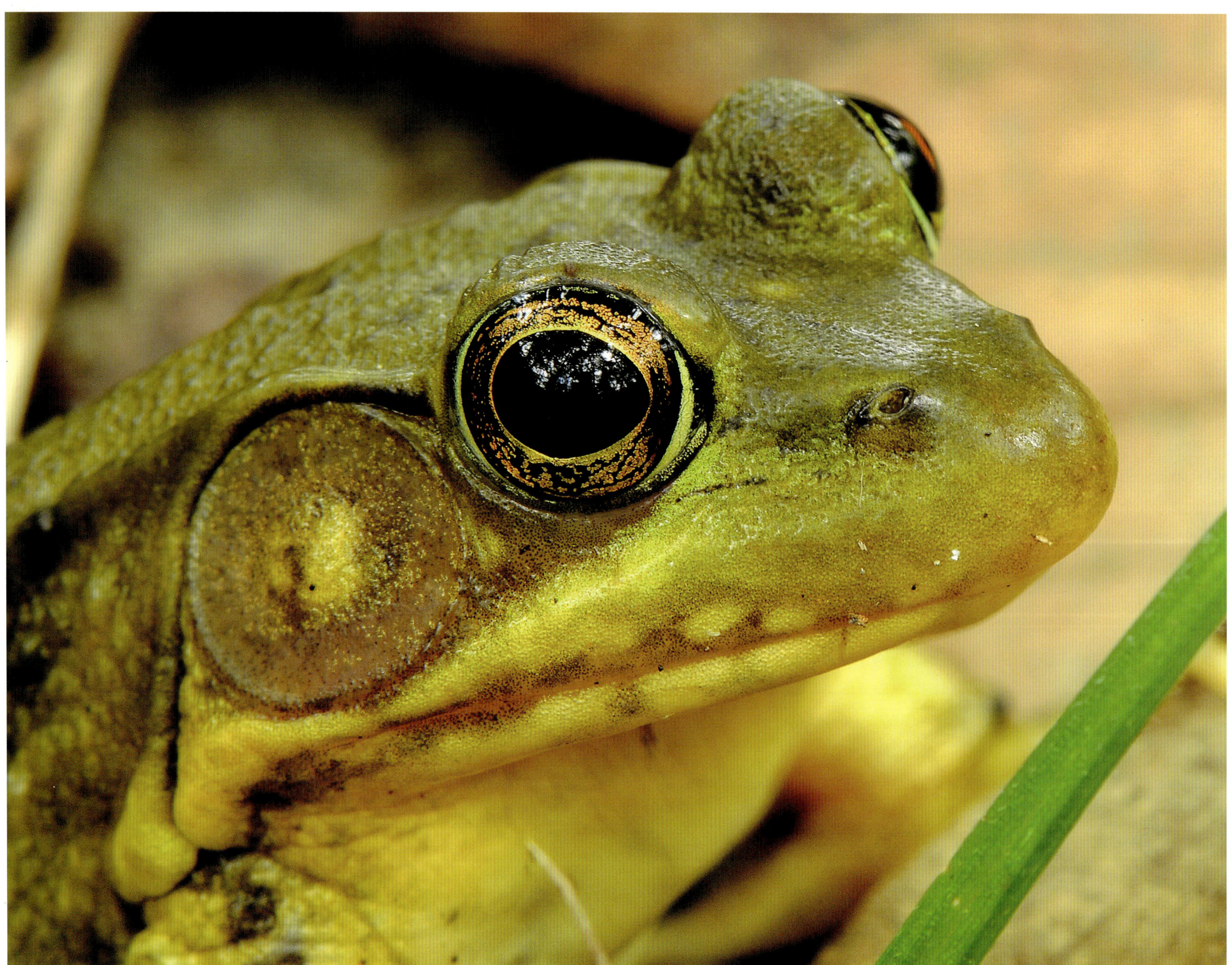

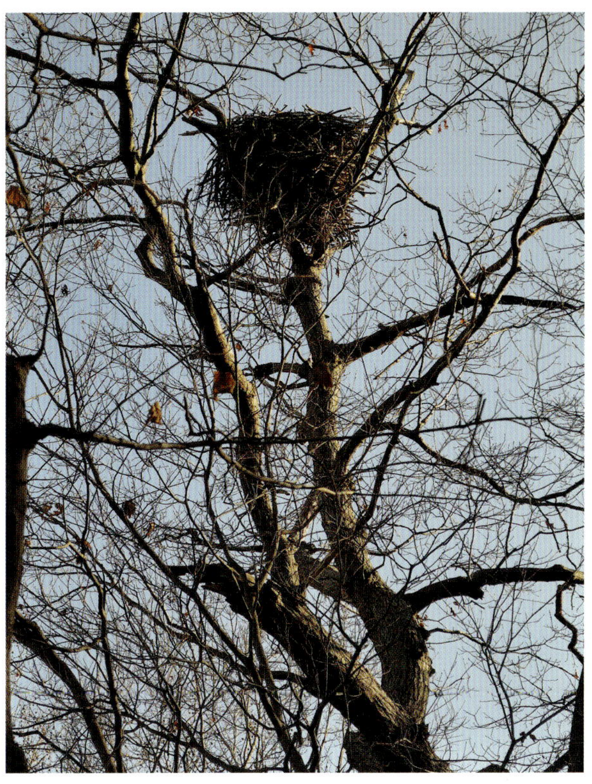

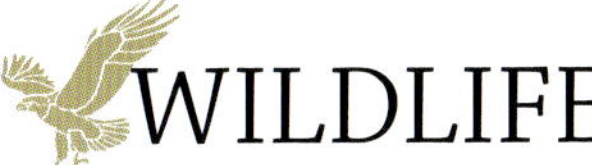

WILDLIFE

Southern New York is dominated by oak-hickory forests, which as the name implies, are primarily composed of members of these two mast-producing genera. Their nuts are an invaluable resource for wildlife, and their presence is the prime reason the forests boast such a prolific and eclectic array of species. Squirrels, of course, feast on them, but so do many other creatures. Turkeys, blue jays, raccoons, rabbits, chipmunks, and deer regularly browse on fallen nuts. Scratch marks and the associated mounds of leaves are evidence that hungry animals have rooted around in the detritus to uncover these meaty morsels. Bears consume the nuts as well, and can be seen in late summer and early fall ascending even the narrowest of trees to strip nut clusters directly from the branches. Seemingly cumbersome and awkward, bears are quite agile and appear to have little difficulty in their acrobatic endeavors. Snakes and raptors benefit indirectly from the nutty profusion by feasting on the hefty rodent population that abounds nearby.

Before an exotic fungus was accidentally introduced to the US in the early 1900s, the American chestnut comprised nearly a quarter of the trees in what was then known as oak-chestnut forests. Tree mortality rate from the resulting blight was nearly one hundred percent. And with this lethal invasive fungus still hanging around on chestnut root re-sprouts, these once lofty trees will probably never return as a canopy species. The loss of the chestnut, which produces far larger and meatier nuts than most trees, was a major blow to wildlife and radically reshaped the composition and

This page:
Eagle nest
(Rockland County)

Opposite page:
Green frog
(Harriman State Park)

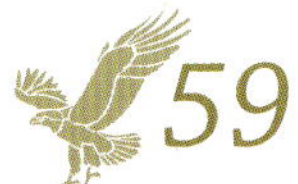

health of our forests. For decades, as the blight swept across the land, trees quickly sickened and toppled like dominoes within several years of infection, turning once robust ecosystems into skeletal versions of their former selves. Forests are still recovering.

Human short-sightedness also nearly caused another cherished feature of America to vanish. Until relatively recently, a bald eagle was a rare sight anywhere in the country. Populations of our national icon began to precipitously decline during the first half of the twentieth century, a result of pesticides containing DDT, which affected the viability of eggs by thinning shells to a fraction of their former thickness. Since DDT was banned in 1972, bald eagle populations have rebounded significantly, and seeing one gliding gracefully overhead or regally perched among the uppermost branches of a riverside tree has become commonplace in some areas.

In February 2013, while participating in an eagle survey along the Hudson, I recall counting slightly over 140 bald eagles in a single evening as they retreated to a roost site on an east-facing mountain slope across the river from Peekskill. Though it is uncommon to have that many eagles in one area, their numbers are plentiful enough that they no longer require protection under the Endangered Species Act.

Though less emblematic than this rebounding raptor, other Hudson Valley wildlife can fill us with a similar awe and respect if watched intently. Far too often we don't care about a species until it becomes rare. We should appreciate and protect our natural resources when they are thriving, not just when they begin to slip away. The damage cannot always be reversed.

The timber rattlesnake is listed as a threatened species in New York. With females reproducing only every two to six years, populations grow slowly and are therefore highly susceptible to extirpation in areas altered by humans.

Despite their aggressive reputation, rattlesnakes are generally docile and frequently give ample warning by using their well-known rattle before striking. As with most creatures, biting will only occur if they are provoked or stepped on. Venom is costly for snakes to make and they will not wantonly waste it. Bites rarely prove fatal if treatment is quickly sought. There hasn't been a confirmed death in New York from a wild snake for the last several decades.

Snakes may possess one of four types of venom. Type A is neurotoxic (harms the nervous system); type B is hemorrhagic and proteolytic (causes bleeding and degrades essential bodily proteins); type AB has traits of both A and B and is an especially dangerous combination; and type C is comparatively weak and causes little damage.

Generally snakes will not live past their early twenties and have a maximum age of about thirty years. One of the oldest on record is a forty-three-year-old snake that was tracked by a biologist over many years in the remote Adirondack wilderness.

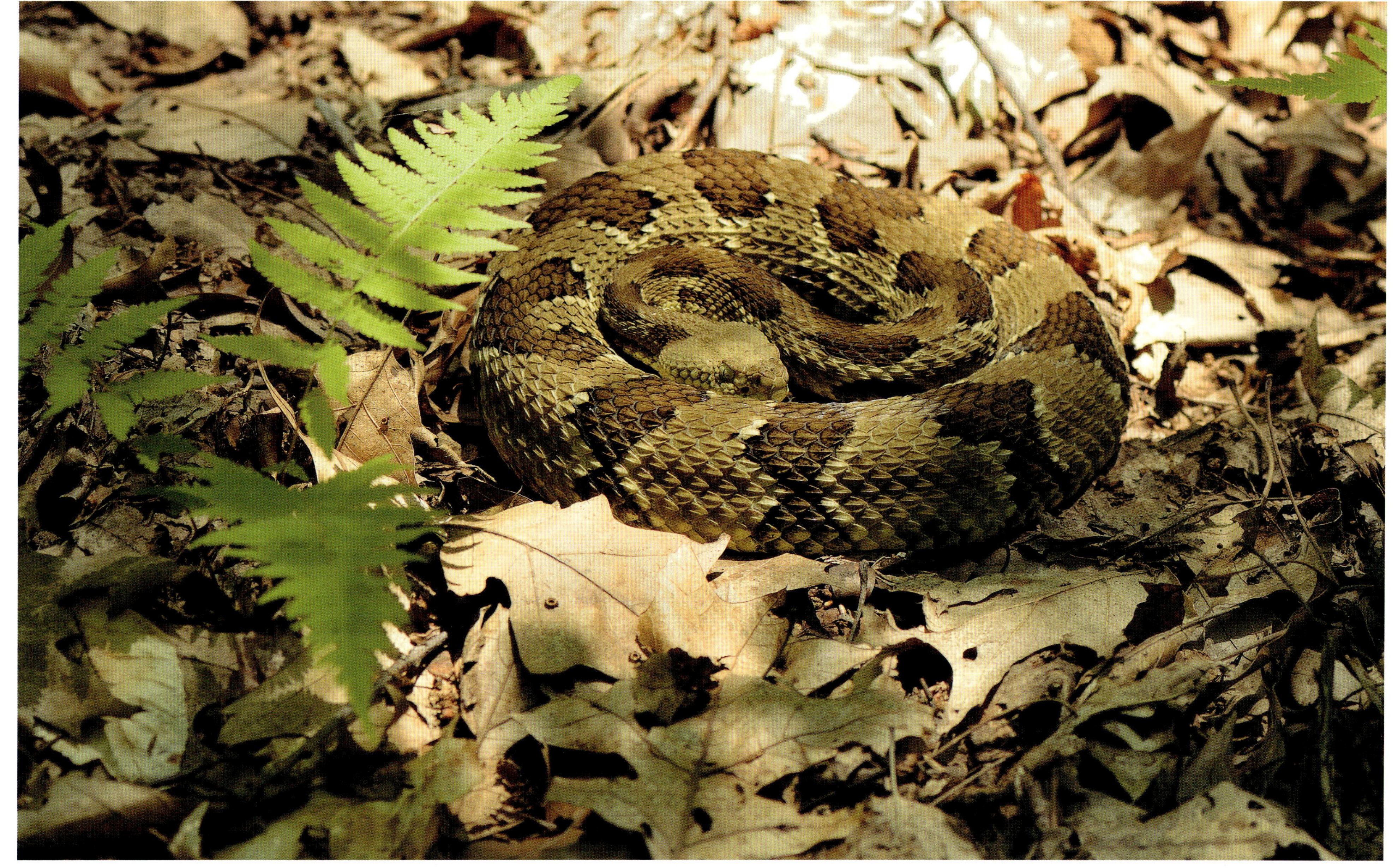

Coiled timber rattlesnake (Schunnemunk State Park)

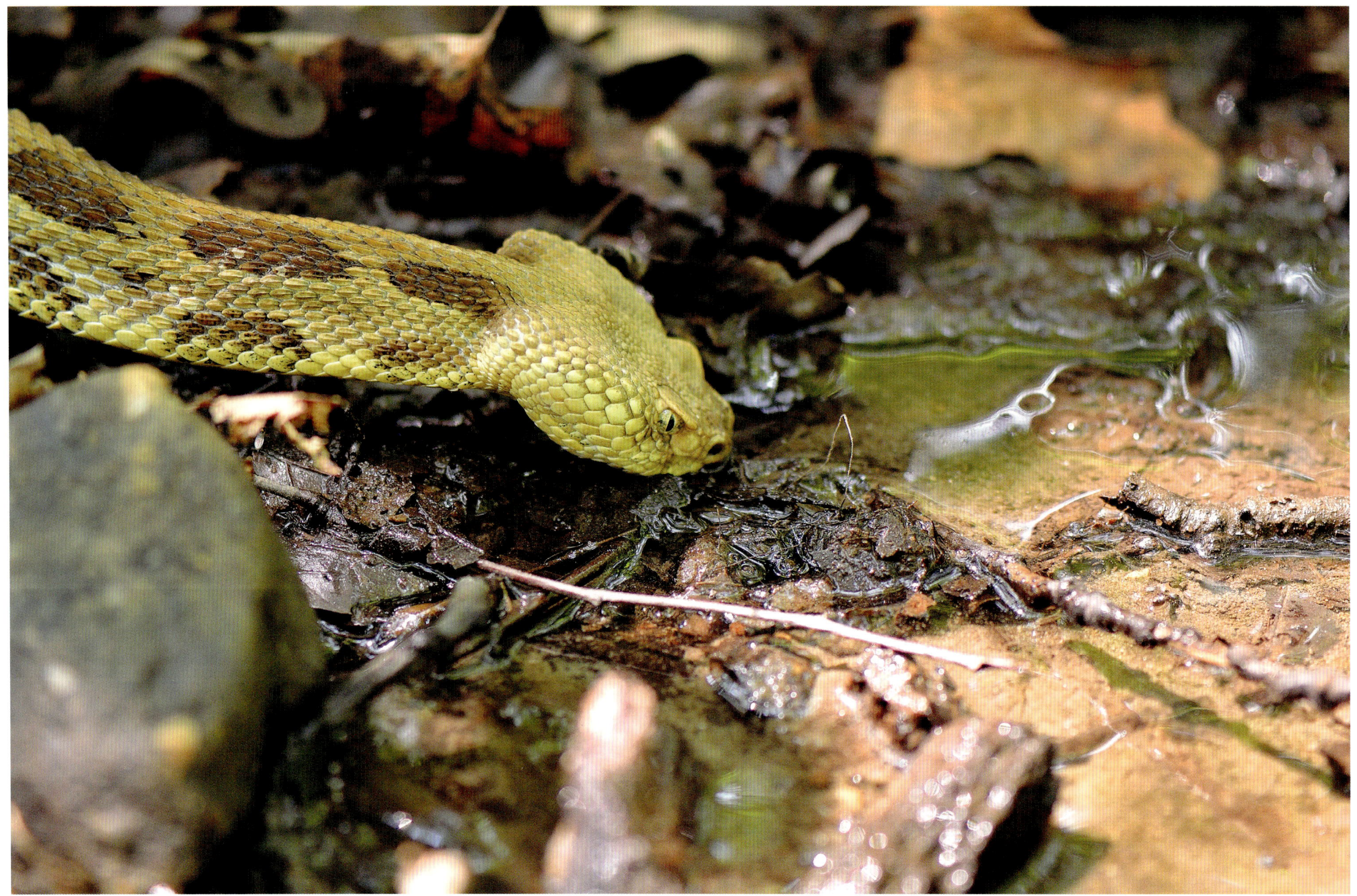

Drinking rattlesnake (Schunnemunk State Park)

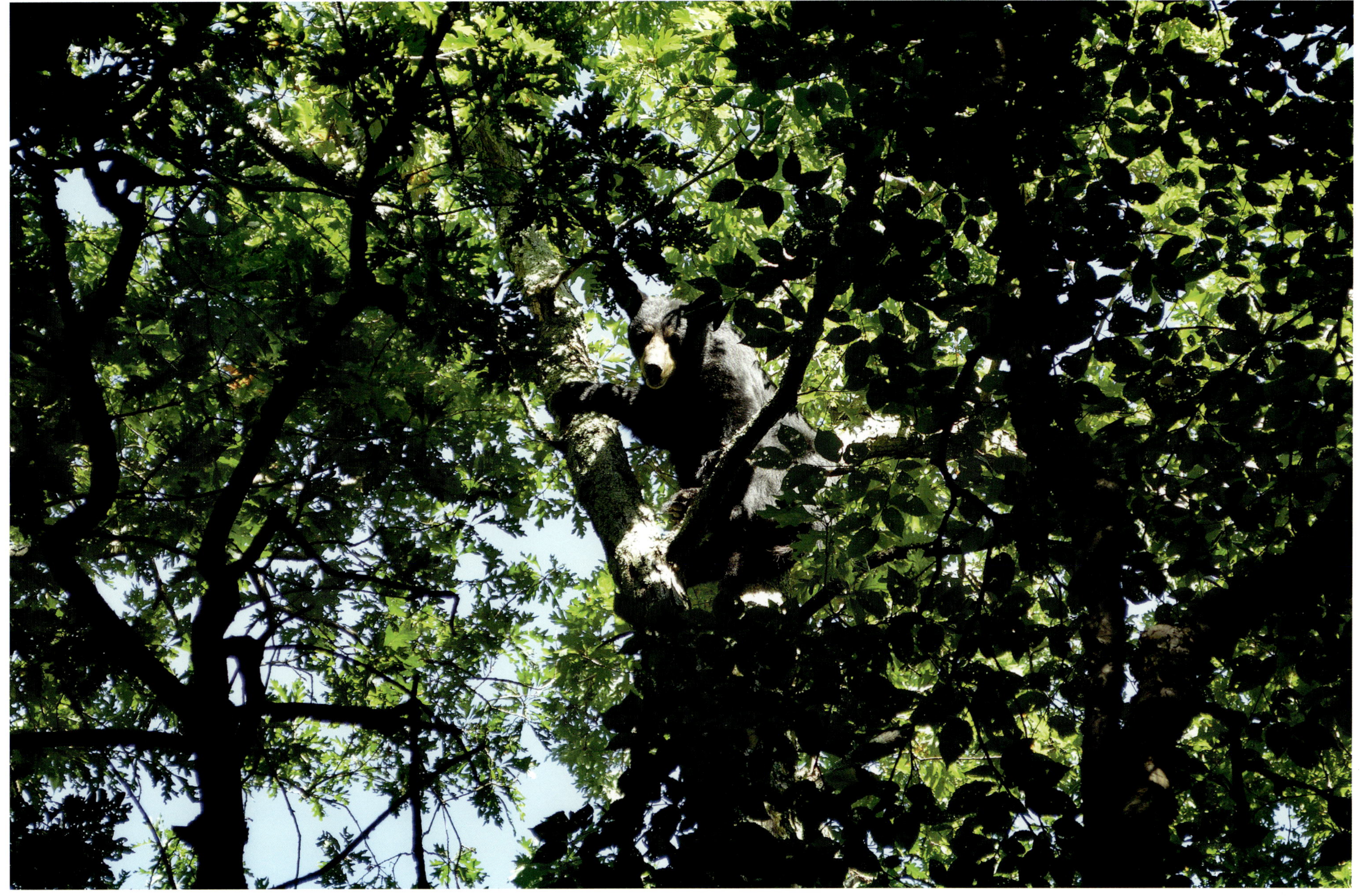

Black bear climbing oak tree (Schunnemunk State Park)

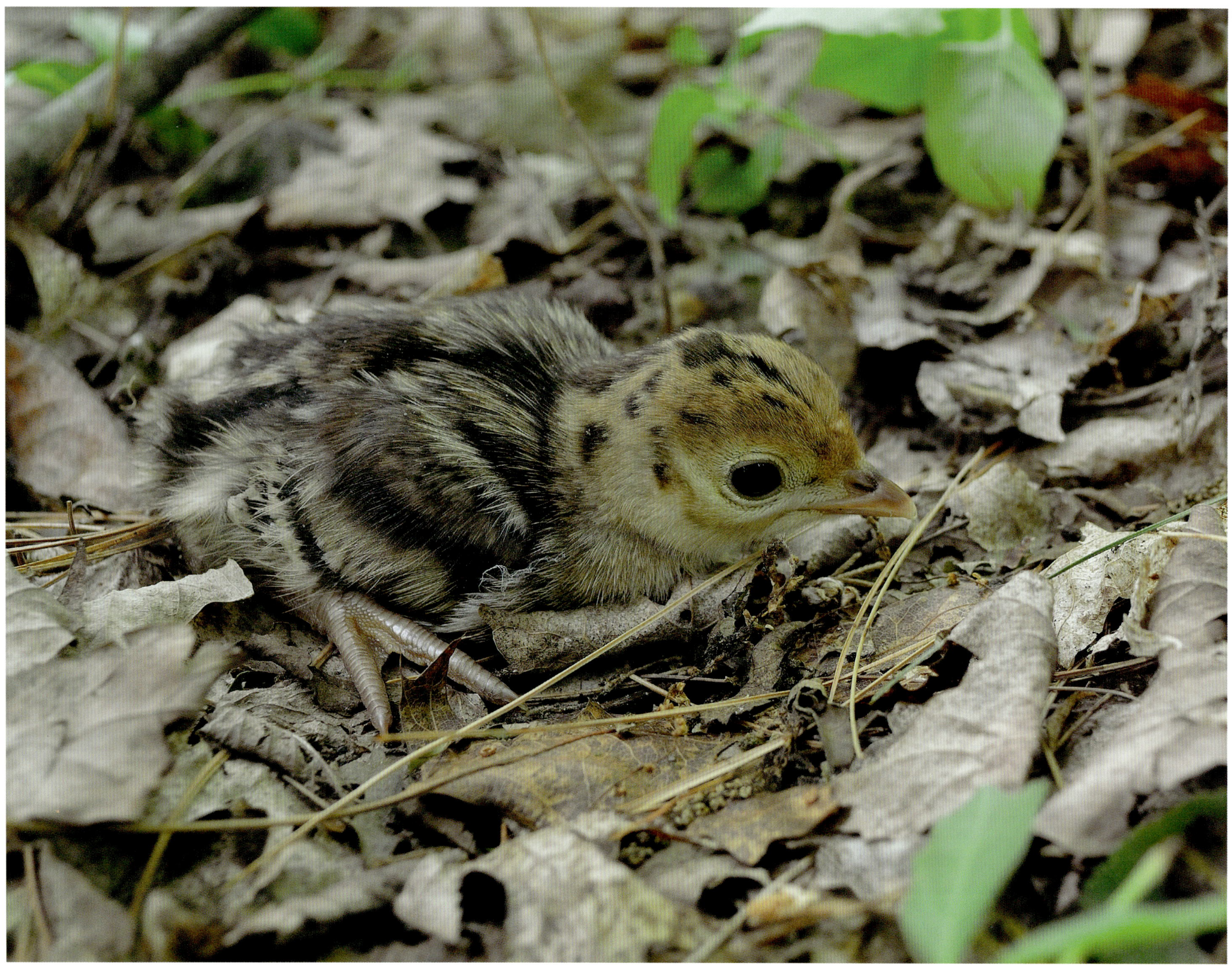

Turkey chick (Illinois Mountain Park)

The average lifespan of a box turtle is fifty years. It's not unusual for some to make it to their one hundredth birthday!

Unlike most other turtle species in the area that are forced to stay close to water, box turtles roam freely throughout rich forest woodlands.

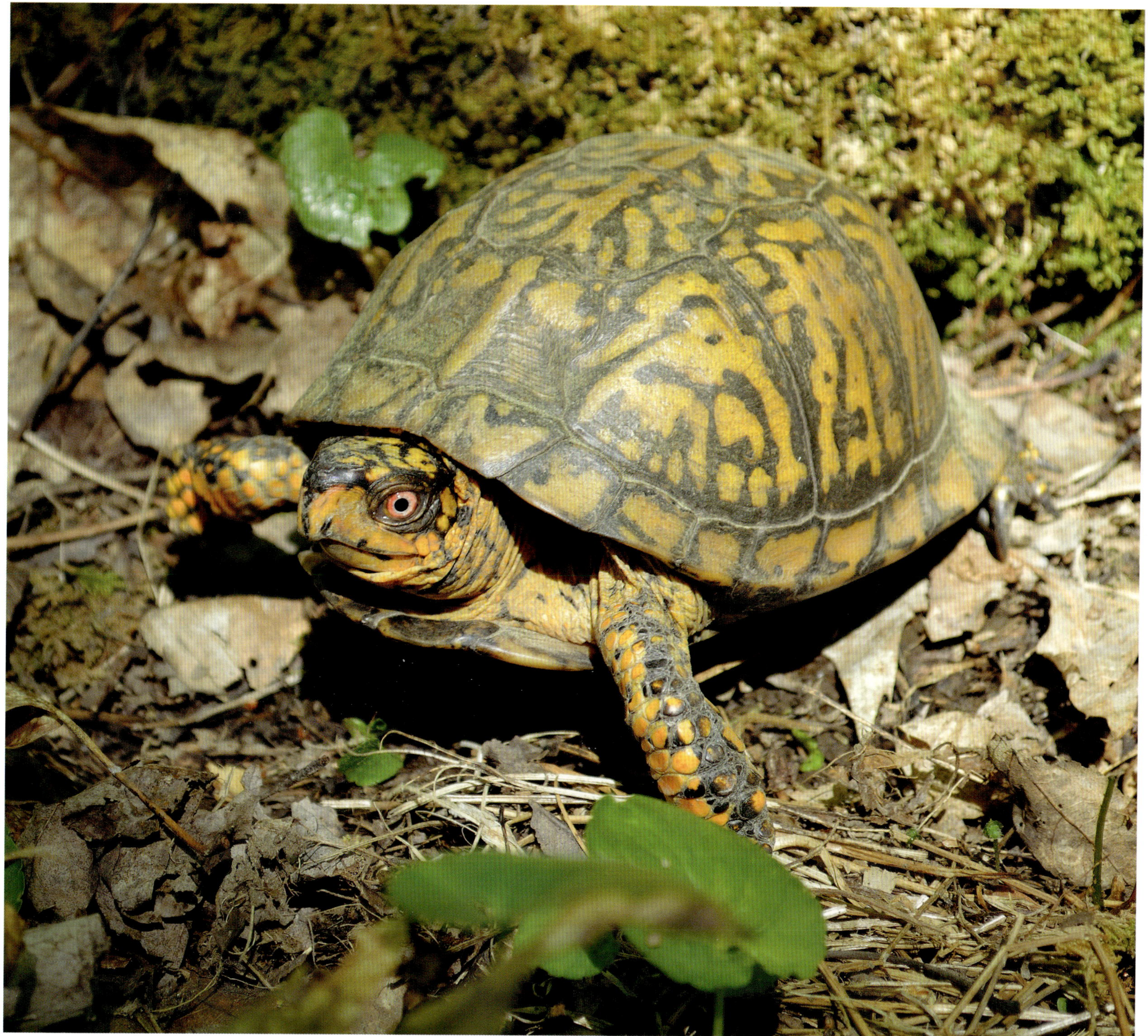

Box turtle (Harriman State Park)

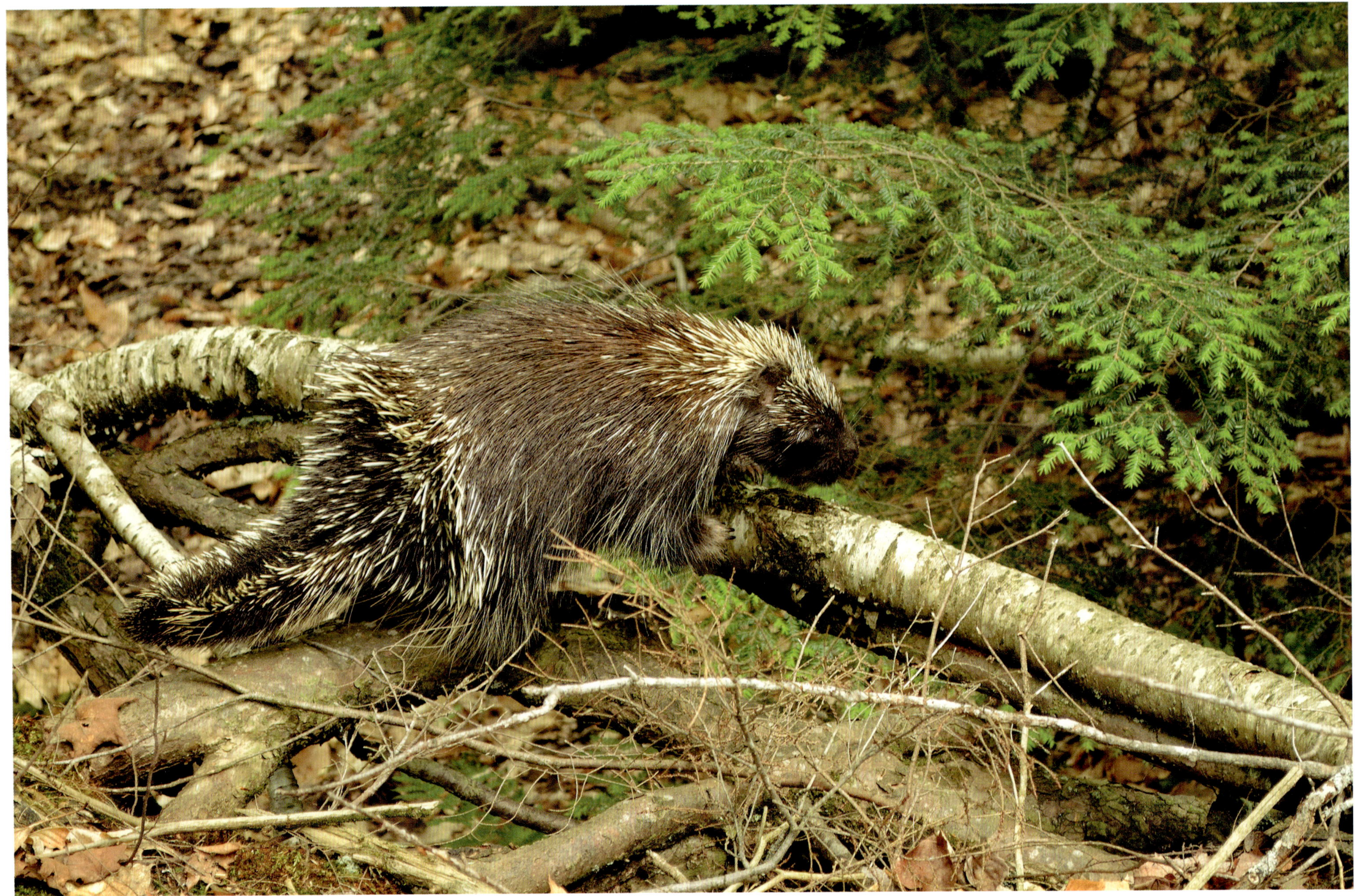

Porcupine (Minnewaska State Park)

Of the three native lizard species in New York, the five-lined skink is the most common in the Hudson Valley, especially in the Hudson Highlands, where it often can be found darting with near-lightning speed from rock to rock as a person nears. The bright blue tail of this species makes them stand out on rock outcroppings.

Skinks have a clever way to evade harm. If a predator happens to get a hold of their tail, they simply shed and regrow it. The vertebrae are very loosely attached and break off in a way similar to the undoing of a zipper. To further keep the predator occupied, the disembodied tail will continue to thrash around, giving the skink ample time to flee. A tail can be lost multiple times, but when it regenerates it will never be quite as long or vibrant as the original. A year or more may pass before it's fully restored.

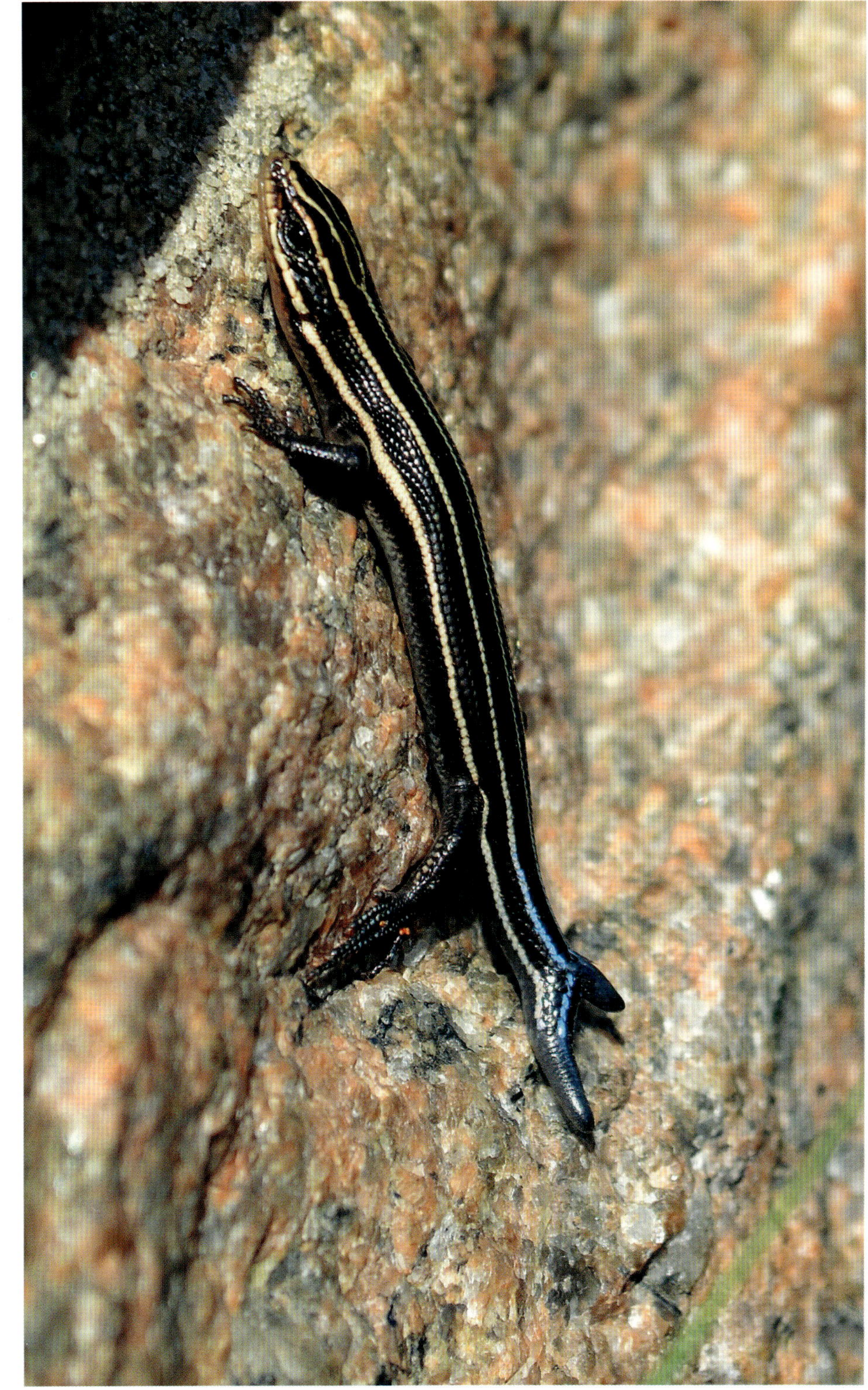

Five-lined skink (Bear Mountain State Park)

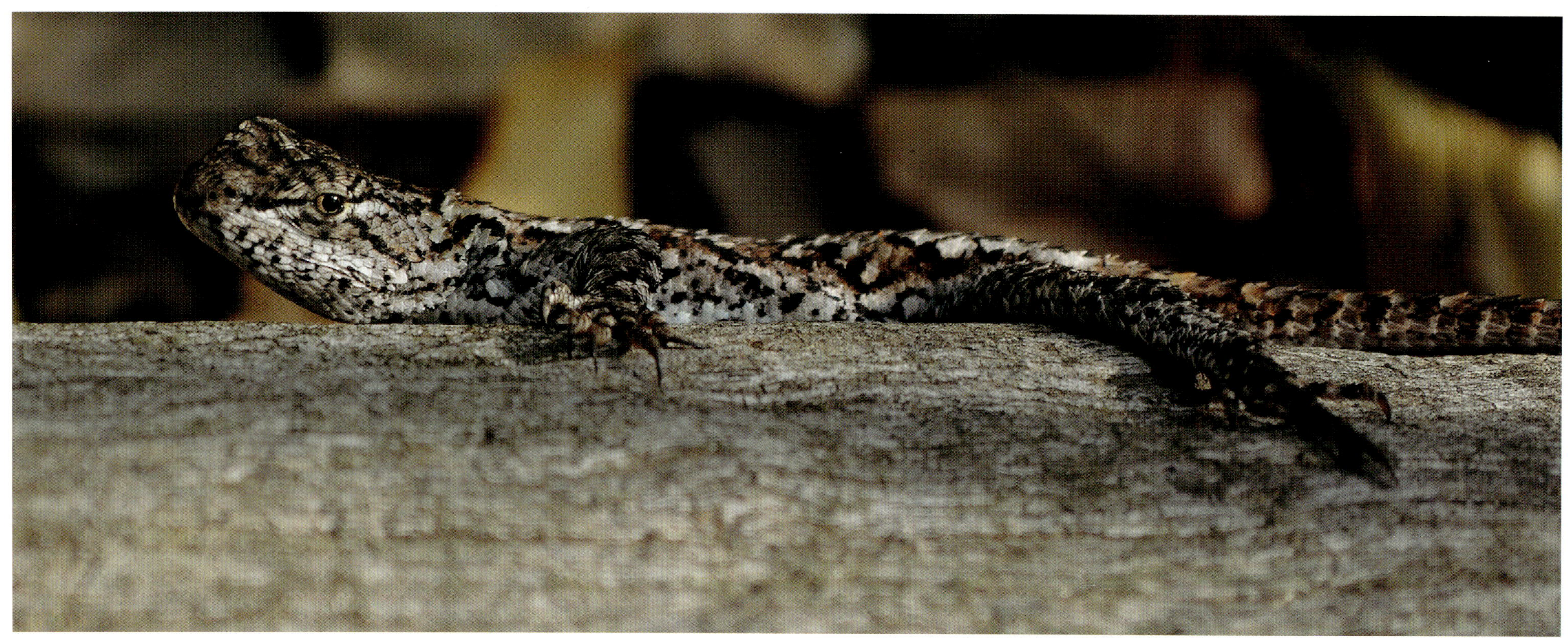

Northern fence lizard (Hudson Highlands State Park)

Naturally occurring populations of the northern fence lizard are confined to Putnam and Westchester counties, with most individuals being found in the eastern sections of the Hudson Highlands, primarily between Anthony's Nose and Breakneck Ridge. It's listed as threatened in New York State but is quite common in most parts of its range, extending from Florida to central New Jersey. New York's disjunct population is the farthest north this creature can be found this side of the Appalachians.

In New York, the northern cricket frog is listed as an endangered species, with populations occurring in scattered locations in the southeastern portion of the state. Relatively widespread before the mid-twentieth century, the use of pesticides containing DDT and other noxious chemicals is widely believed to have been a major factor in this amphibian's precipitous decline in the state. Heavy use of road salt, the introduction of invasive predatory fish, and fungal infections continue to hamper cricket frogs.

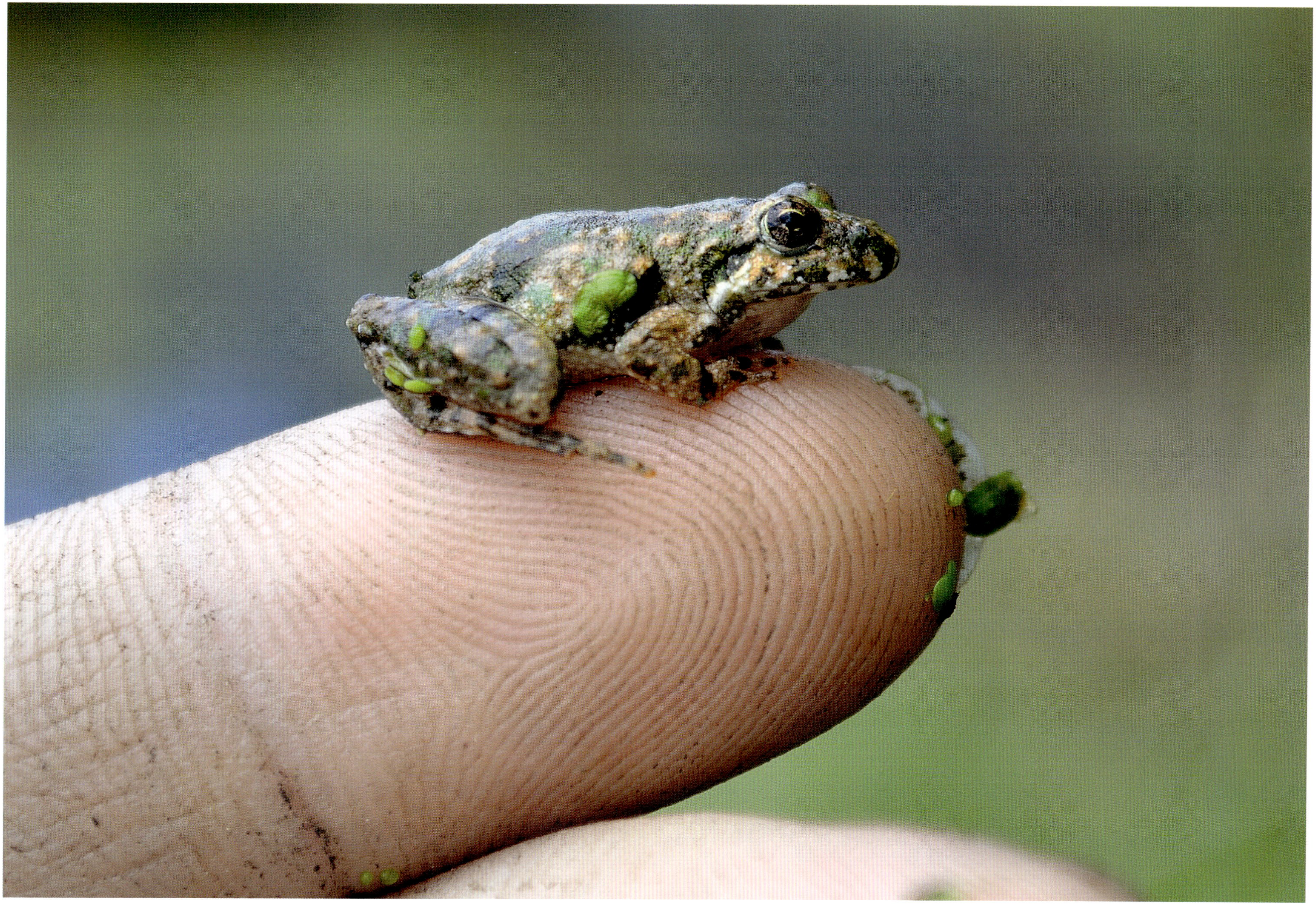

Northern cricket frog (Ulster County)

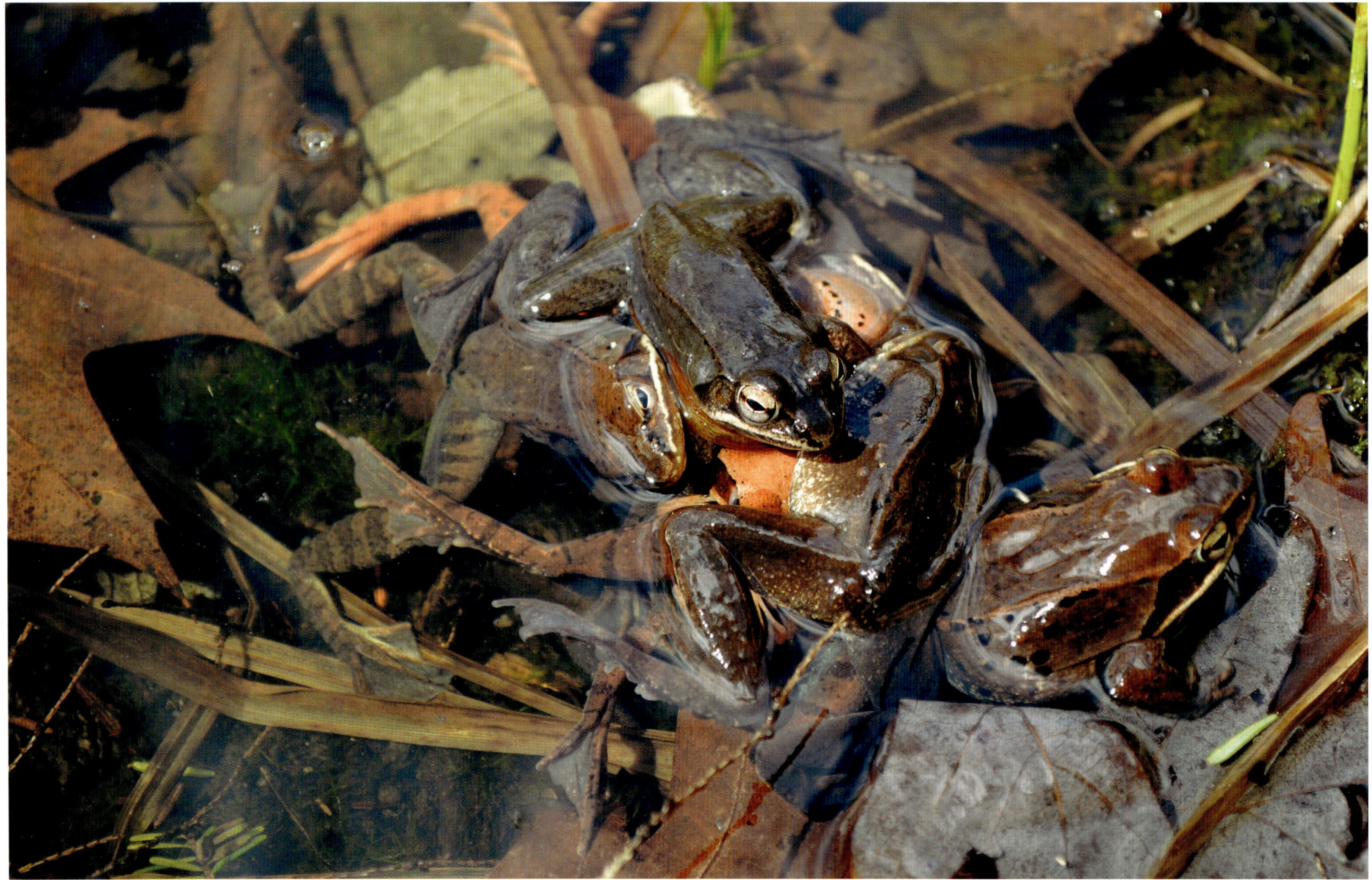

Mating wood frogs (Black Creek Preserve)

The wood frog is the official New York State amphibian. They are typically the first frogs to mate in the spring. Large groups of them gather in vernal pools, transitory ponds that will normally dry up in the summer months. Frenzied mating calls blur together and at a distance sound similar to a flock of noisy ducks.

This species can become partially frozen in the winter with no adverse effects. A compound with antifreeze-like properties in the wood frog's body protects cells from damage so long as no more than sixty-five percent of their internal water freezes.

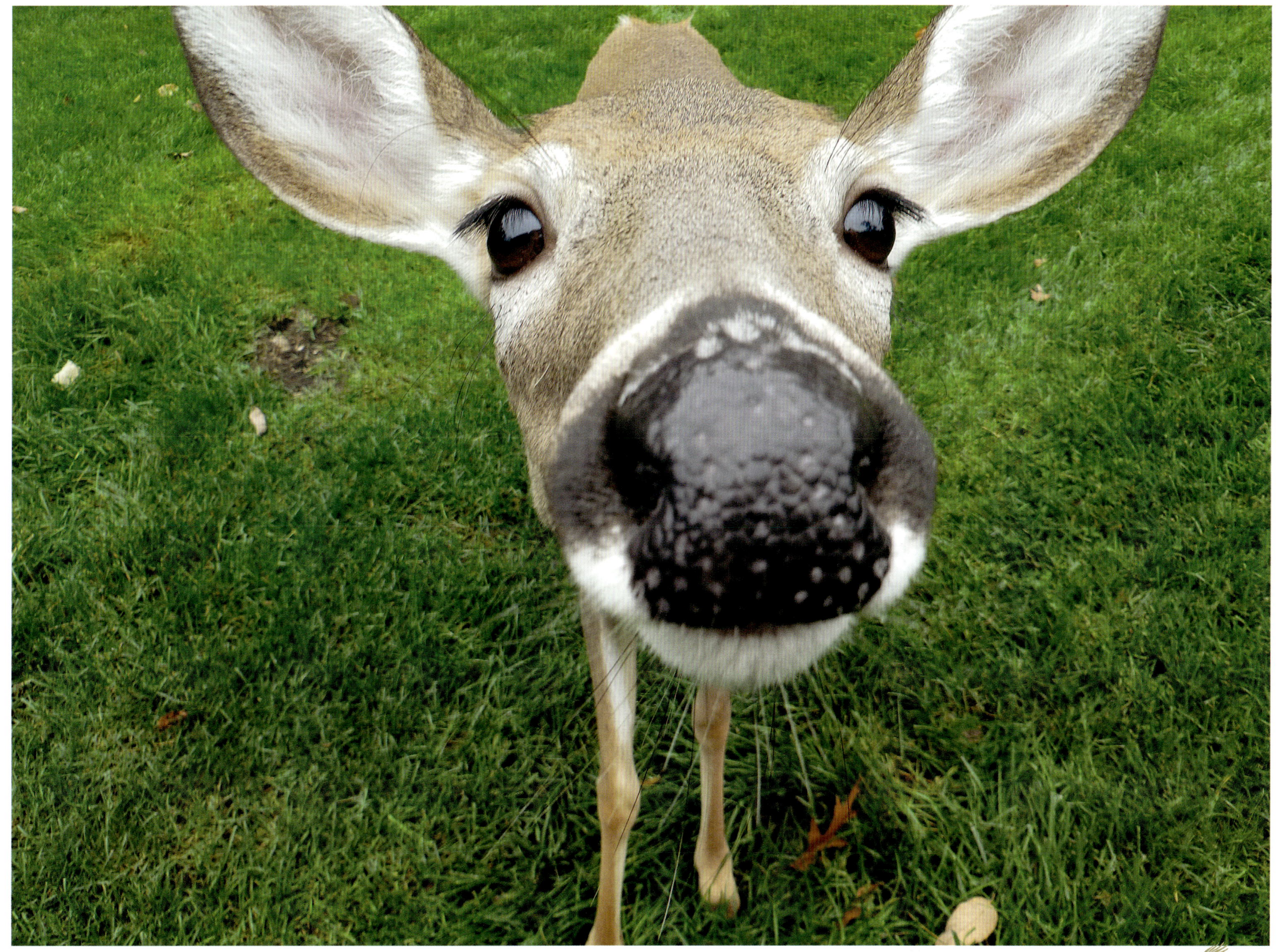

White-tailed deer (Rockefeller State Park)

Bats fluttering across a twilight sky were once a common sight. But since 2007, the year the infectious fungus, *Pseudogymnoascus destructans*, was first reported in the state, populations of nearly every bat species in the region has rapidly declined. Some species have dwindled by as much as ninety percent. The fungus tends to accumulate prominently in patches on the nose, hence the name white-nose syndrome. It's believed the pathogen rouses bats from their winter hibernation, causing a depletion of their fat reserves, and ultimately resulting in a slow death by starvation.

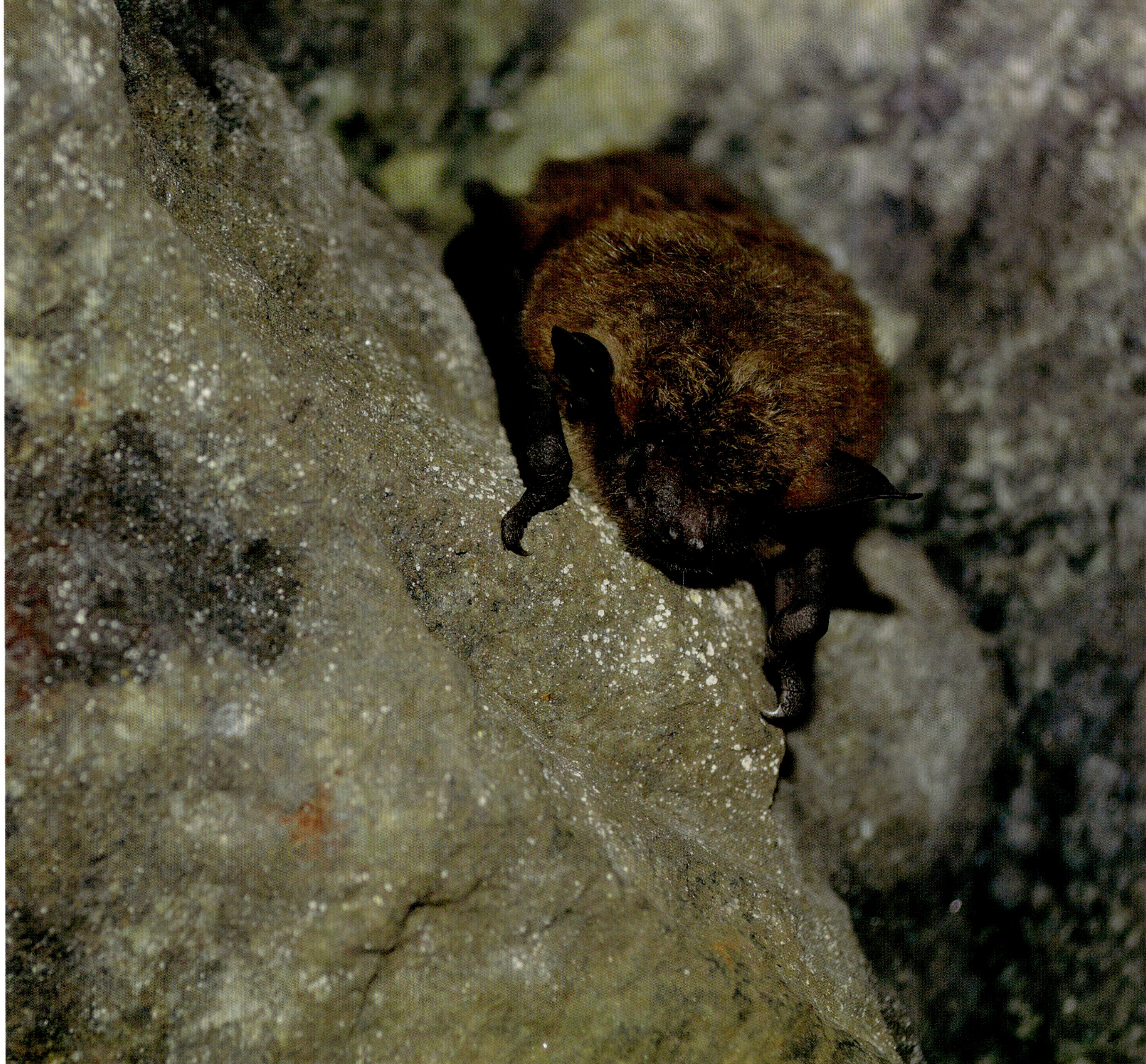

Big brown bat (Harriman State Park)

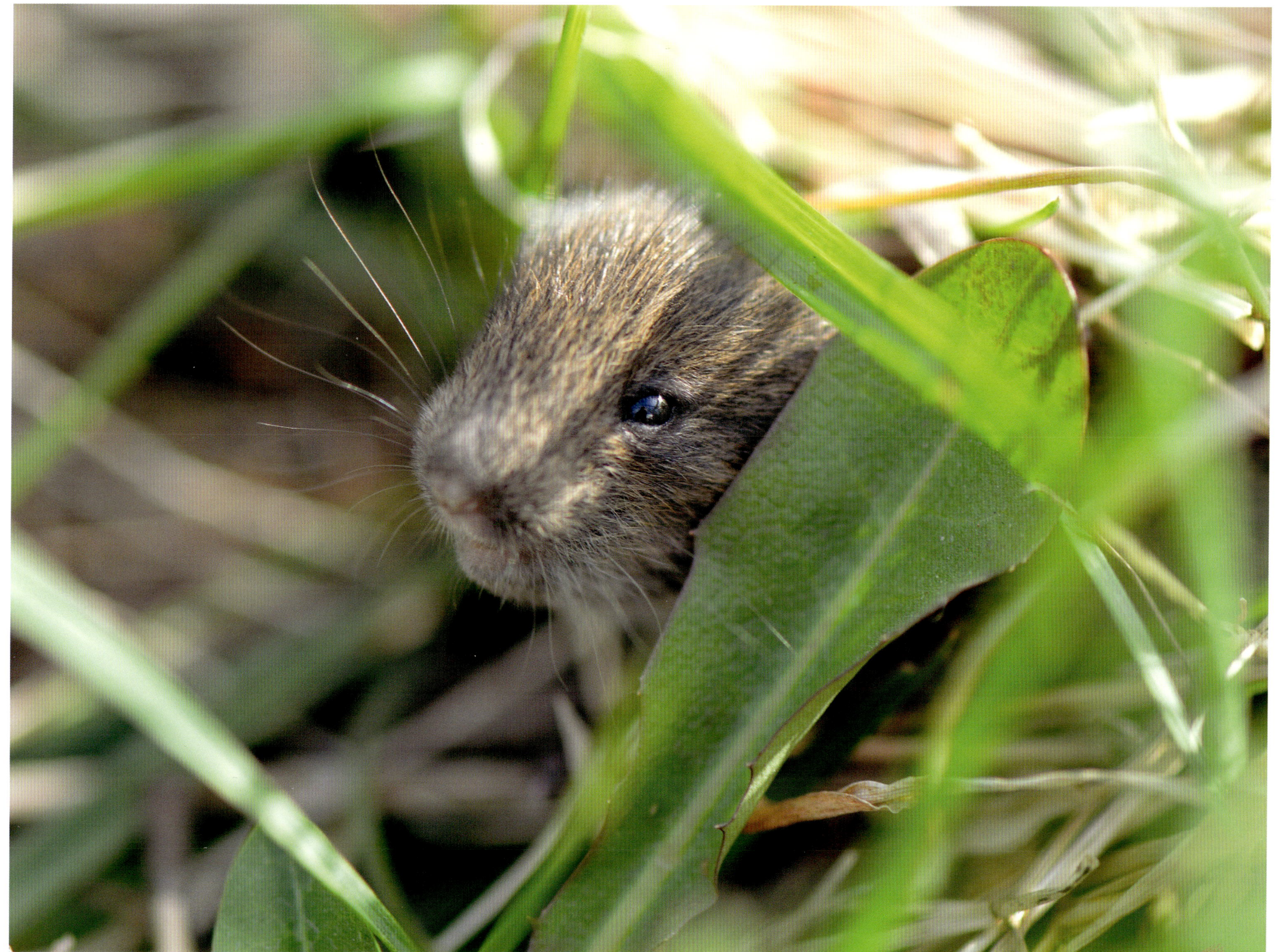

Meadow vole (Bowdoin Park)

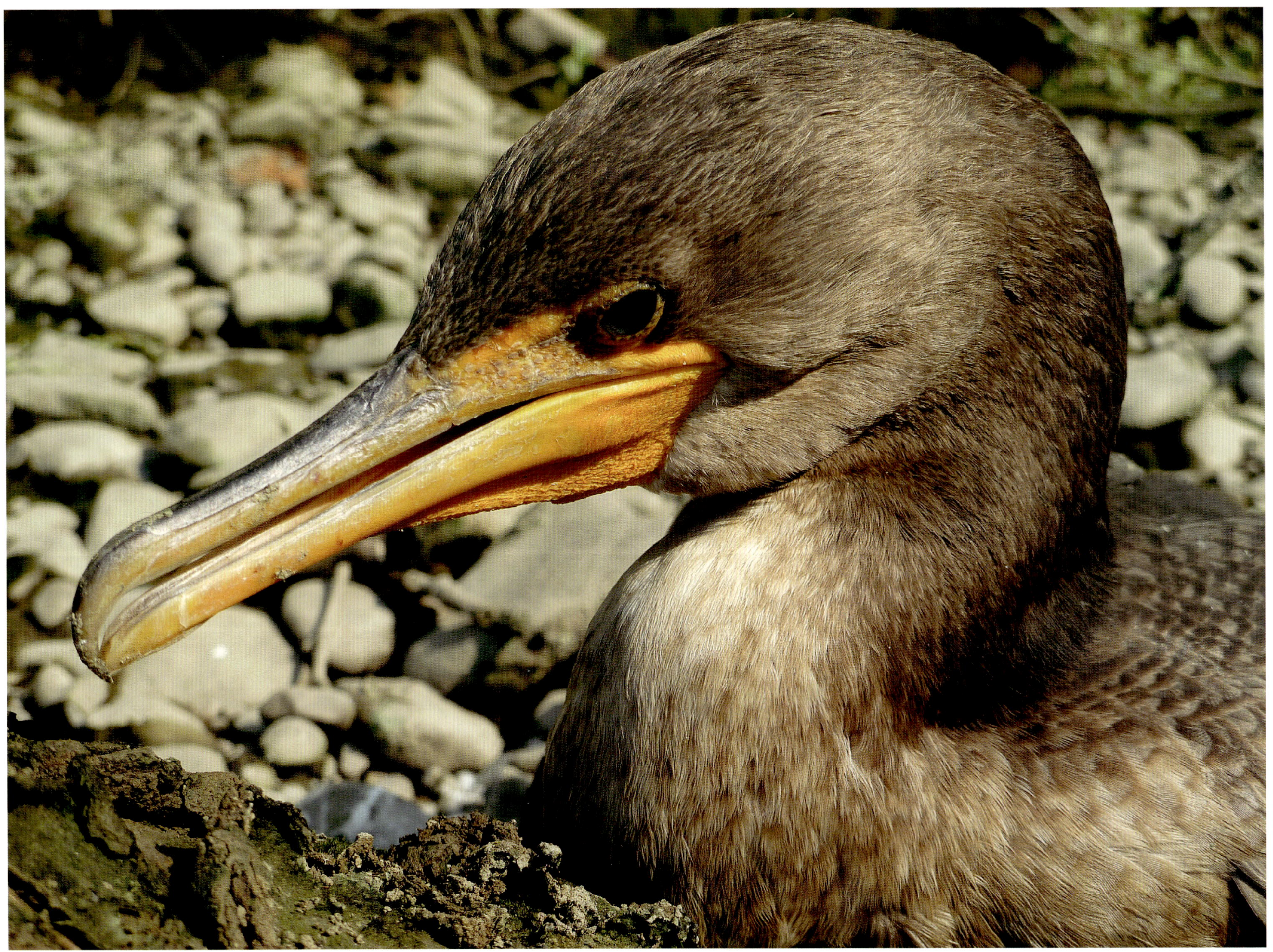

Cormorant (Moodna Creek)

Cormorants are regularly seen along the shores of the Hudson throughout New York. It wasn't always like this, though. These birds were almost placed on the list of federally endangered species in the 1960s as a result of DDT poisoning from pesticides.

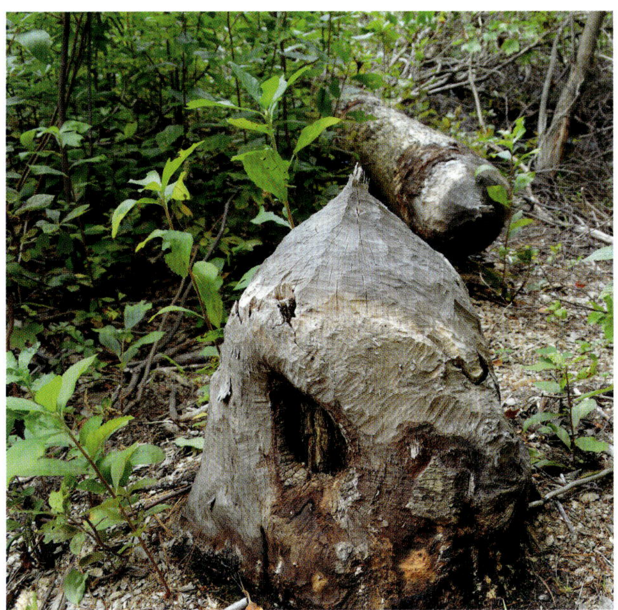

Beaver chewed tree along Sterling Lake (Sterling Forest State Park)

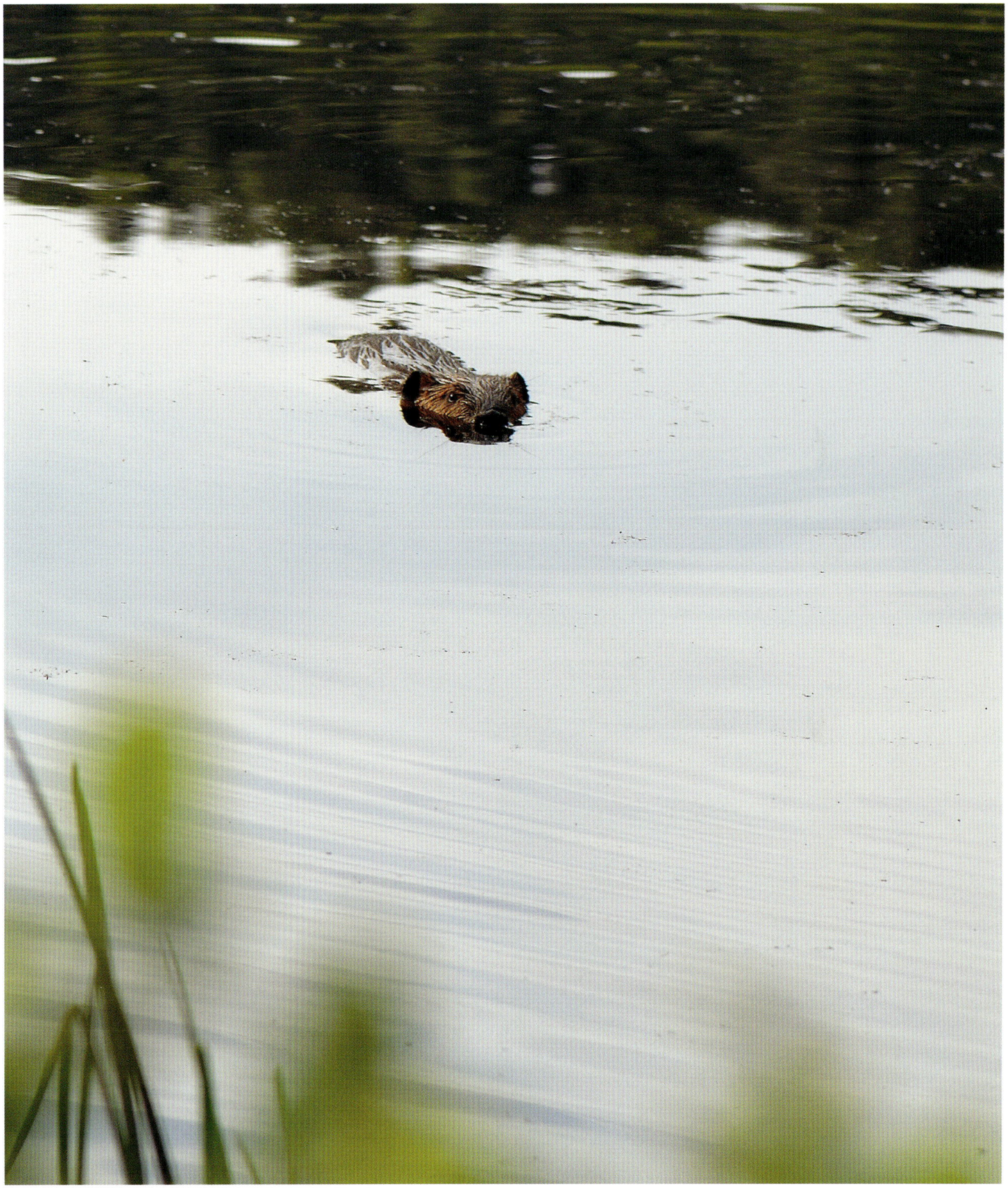

Beaver (Sterling Forest State Park)

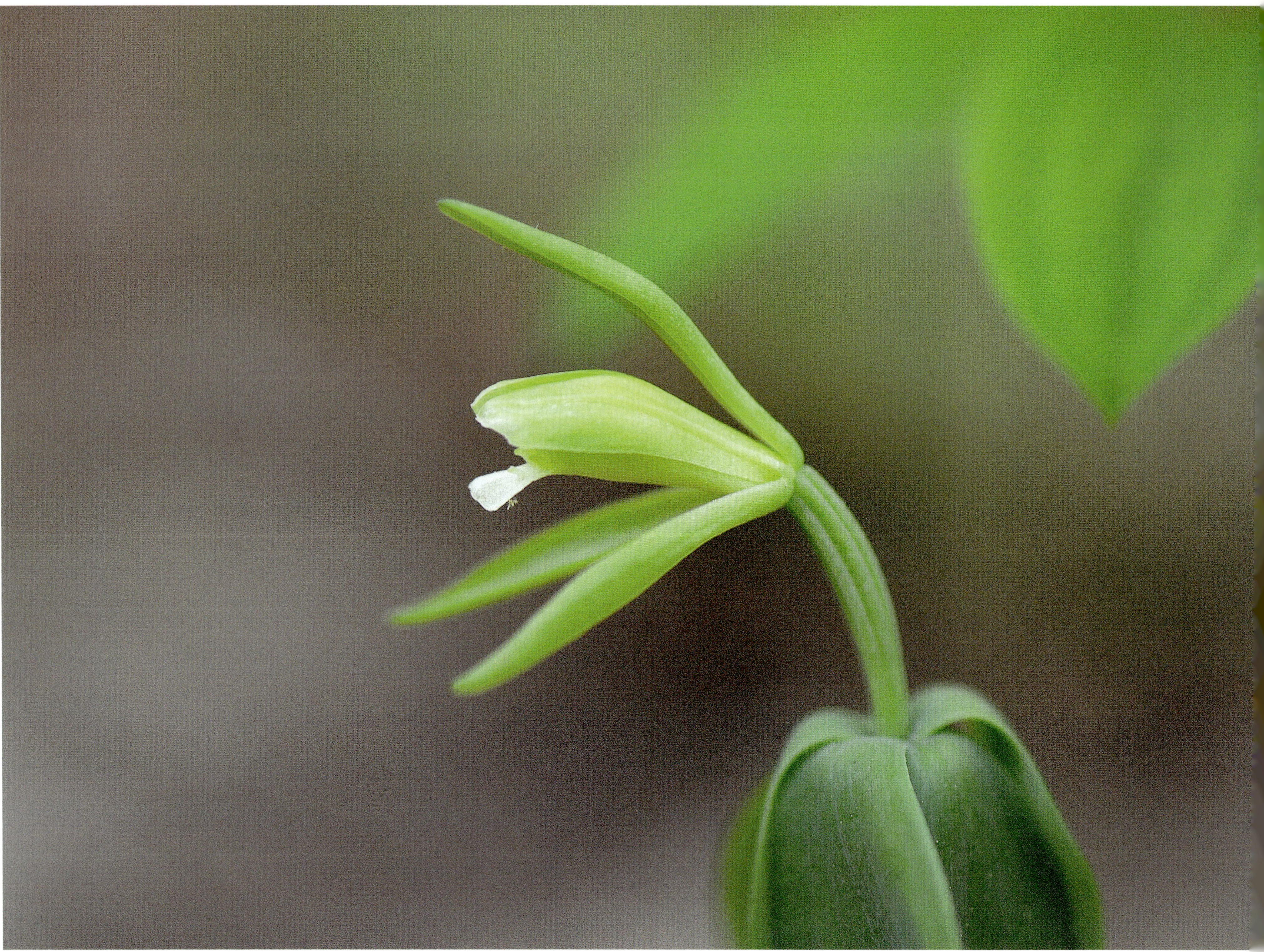

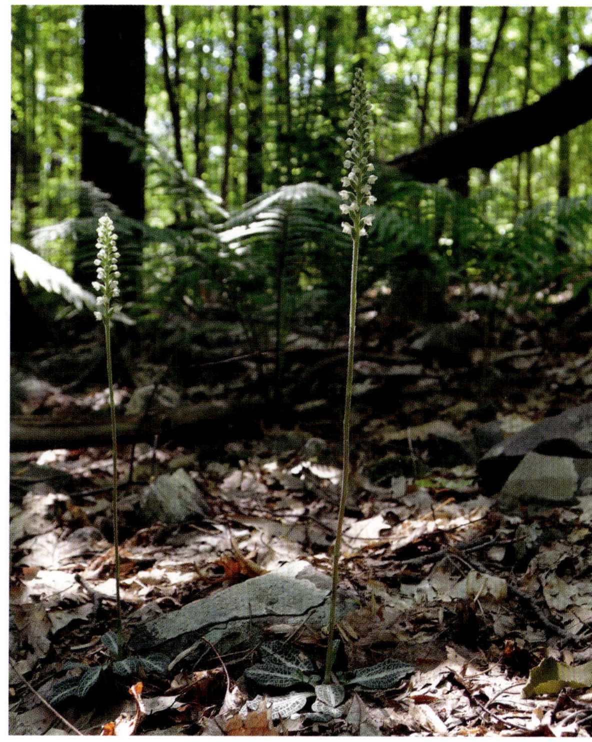

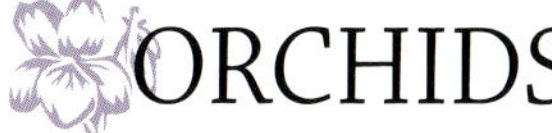

ORCHIDS

Loved for their peerless beauty, delicate sculpture-like form, and seemingly exotic attributes, orchids are often revered above all other wildflowers. Witnessing one thrive in the wild, whether a common or rare species, is an exhilarating experience, especially when one comes to know and appreciate the complex mechanisms at play in their existence.

Orchids are finicky plants, growing only when a narrow set of environmental conditions are met. Any small deviation from their stringent requirements, such as soil type and pH, among other abiotic and biotic factors, will result in failure to grow or disappearance from where they're already established. Every orchid species has different needs, with some inclined to grow in the understory of deeply shaded woodlands, while others call only the most acidic of bogs or other open wetlands home. No matter the habitat type, one thing all orchids require at some point in their life is a fungal partner.

Unlike most other plants, whose seeds are provided with an energy-rich food source to help nourish them upon germination, the dust-like seeds of orchids lack this crucial medium. Instead, orchid seeds form a mutualistic association with soil fungi to gain the necessary nutrition for propagation. Fungi, in return, are able to siphon off additional nutrients when the plants mature. Many species will retain this symbiosis for the rest of their lives. To make matters even more complex, usually not

This page:
Rattlesnake plantain
(Fahnestock State Park)

Opposite page:
Small whorled pogonia
(Schunnemunk State Park)

just any particular fungus will do, but rather fungi from a particular genus, or even a single species. As most soils do not contain the correct variety, orchids are almost impossible to successfully transplant. Therefore they are best left in the wild.

The Hudson Valley is home to numerous native orchids, along with several non-natives. Nearly every habitat type is sure to harbor at least a few varieties. Like the spring ephemerals, these flowers often have fleeting lives.

Our greatest claim to fame resides deep in the understory of a regenerating forest in Orange County, where lies a tiny population of what has been called "the rarest orchid east of the Mississippi." Until its rediscovery in 2010, small whorled pogonia (*Isotria medeoloides*) was believed to have disappeared in the state. The last known orchid specimens had last been seen in Onondaga County in the 1970s.

The Hudson Valley population consists of a mere six plants and the number fluctuates constantly. Not every orchid plant emerges each year. Often they will lay dormant due to poor environmental conditions, needing to recuperate from a previous year's energy-intensive blooming, or an unknown stress. Small whorled pogonia is exceedingly rare throughout its range and has been listed as a federally threatened species.

The pink lady's slipper, or Indian moccasin, is one of the most common orchids in the Northeast. Plants are exceedingly long-lived and can survive for over a century, although average lifespans hover at around twenty years. Moreover, maturation takes a good deal of time—at least a decade—for a seed to transition into a fertile, blossom-producing adult.

The production of flowers and seeds is exceptionally costly in terms of resources. Plants may require up to four years to build up sufficient energy and nutrient reserves between flowering periods.

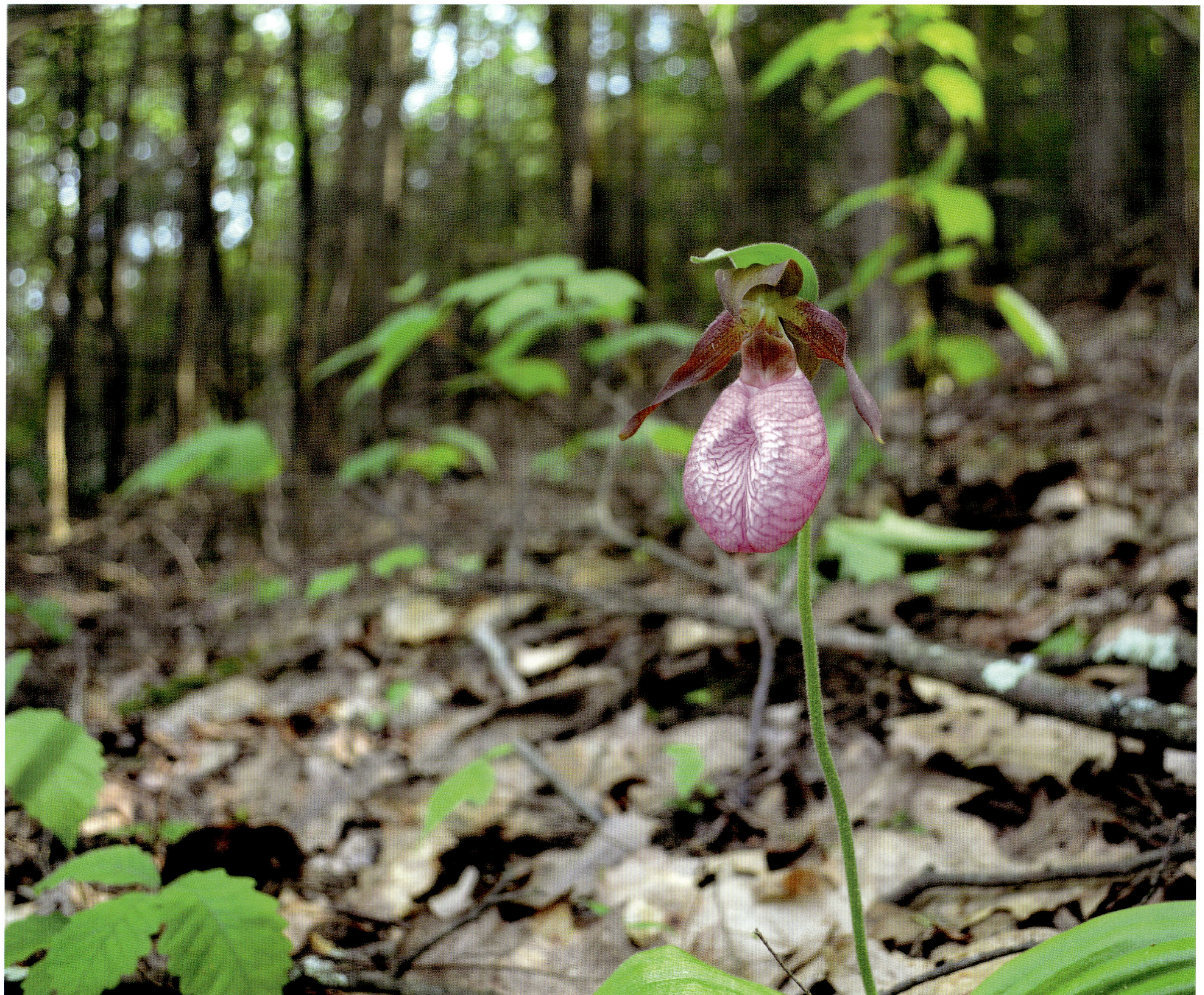

Pink lady's slipper (Fahnestock State Park)

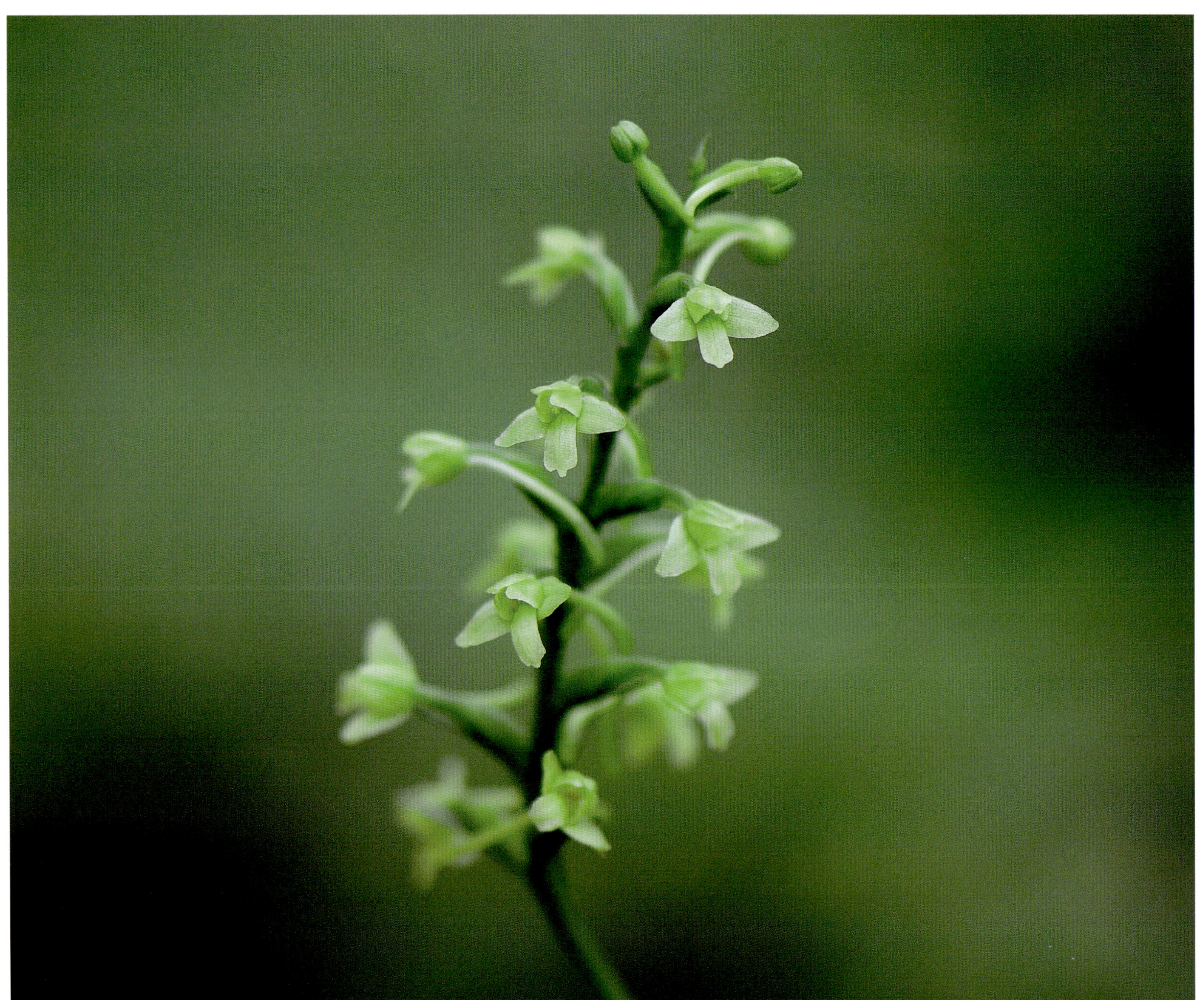

Little club-spur orchid (Schunnemunk State Park)

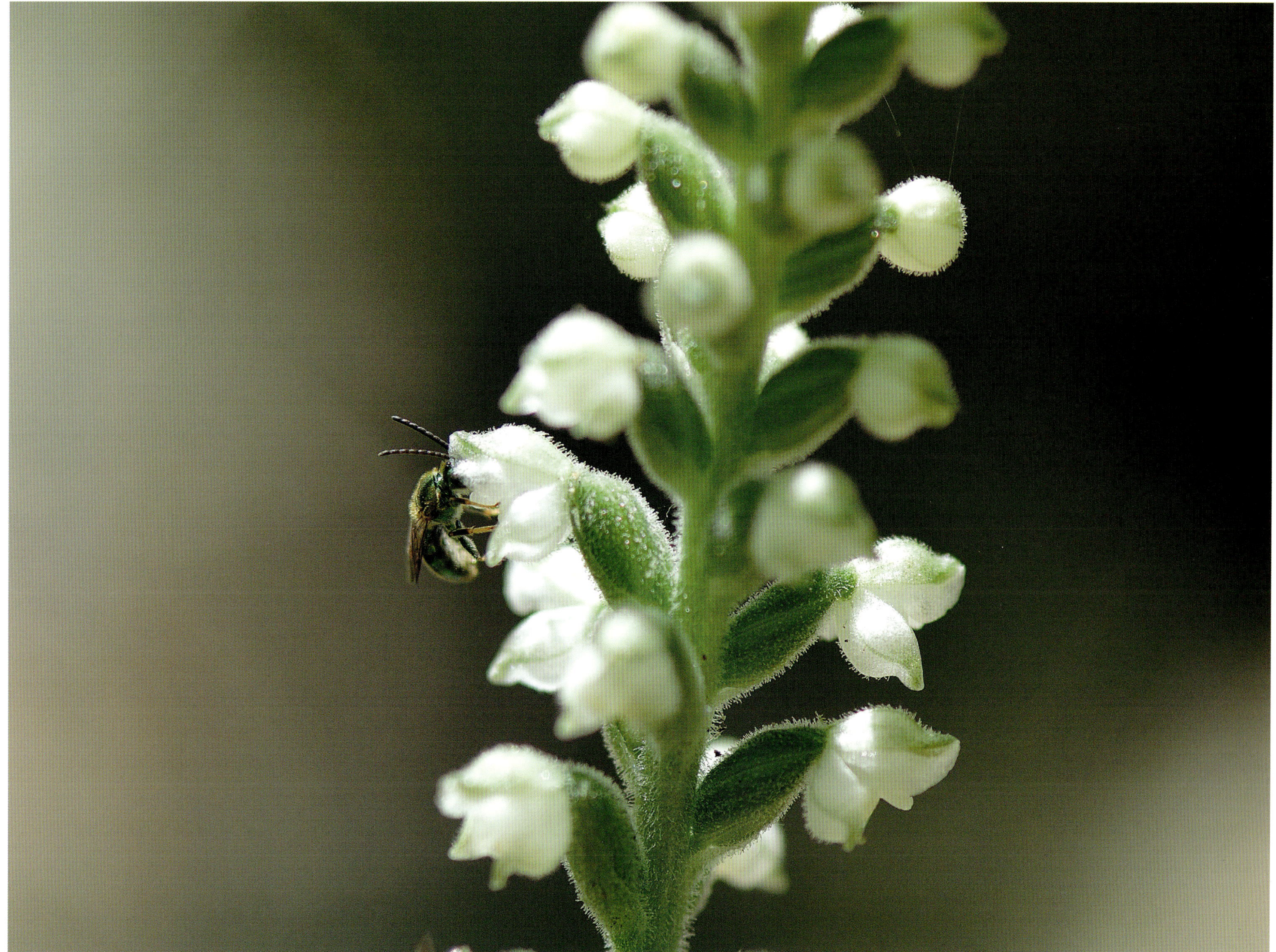

Rattlesnake plantain pollinator (Fahnestock State Park)

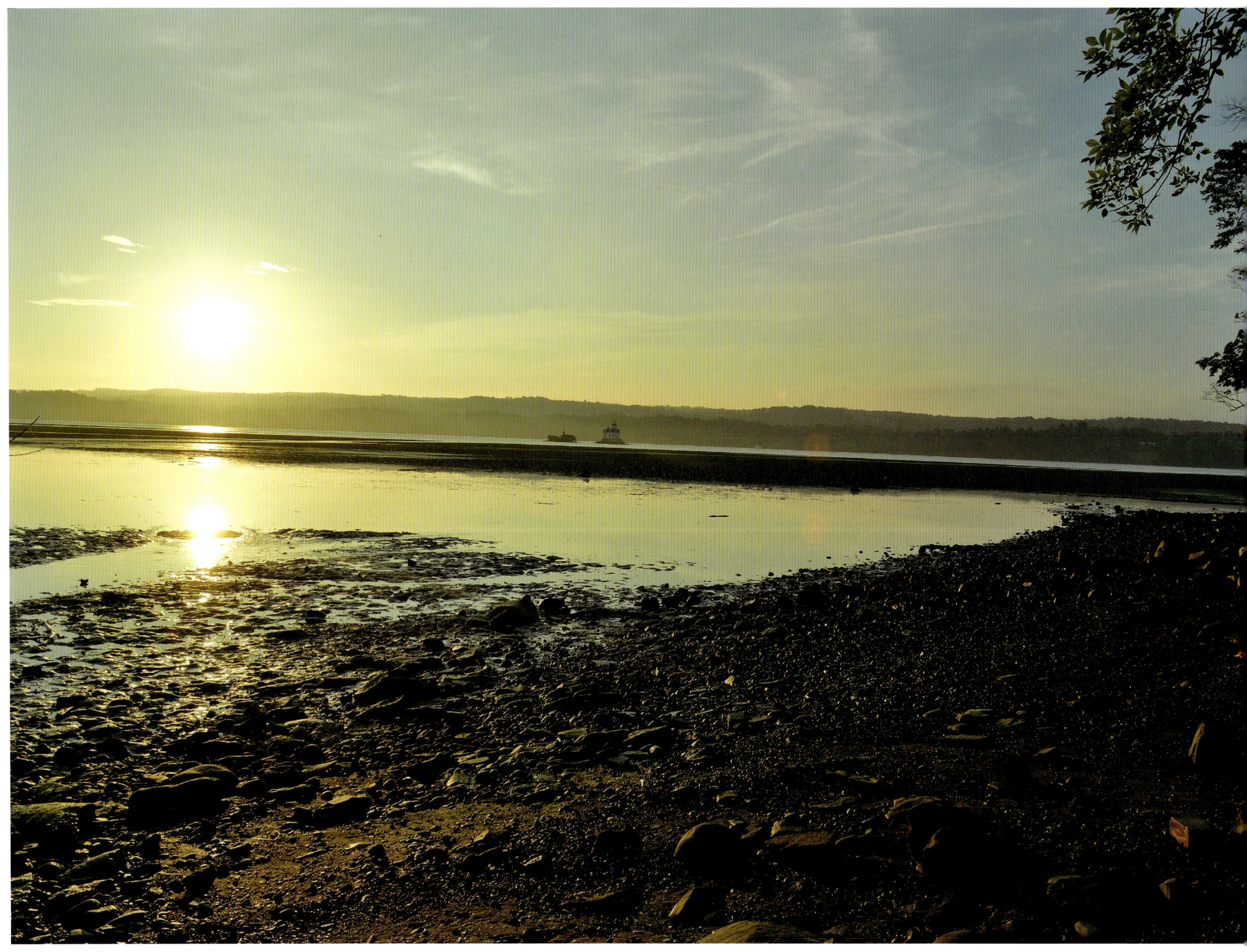

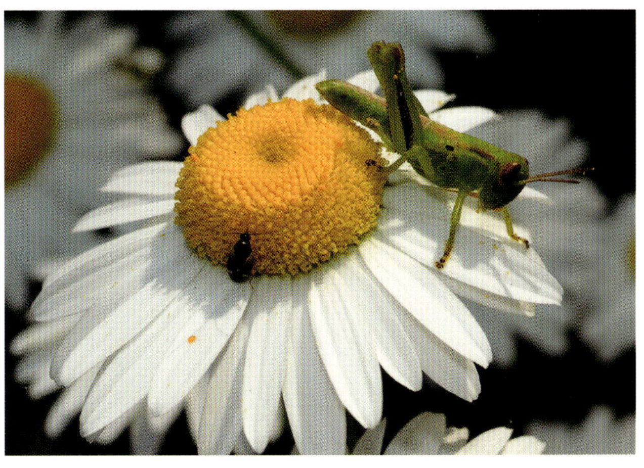

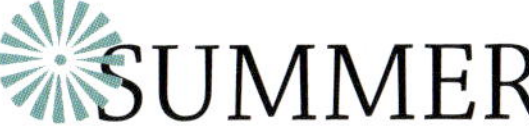

SUMMER

As the languorous heat of summer gradually descends on the Hudson Valley, residents seek respite in the mountains and on lakes and rivers. Some head to the naturally refrigerated ice caves unique to the Shawangunk Ridge, while others hit the trails to pick ripening blueberries that thrive in the thin soils and fresh mountain air. Along the Hudson, swimmers amass on the clean public beaches of Croton Point and elsewhere. Kayakers compete with leviathan-like barges for control of the river, and fishermen sit in patches of dappled shade on the piers, waiting to land some lunker of a catfish or eel. Commercial crabbing is at its peak, with long days devoted to catching delectable blue claw crabs of a size and abundance worthy of being shipped, ironically, to Maryland.

This page:
Ox-eye daisy with grasshopper & minute pirate bug
(Ward Pound Ridge Reservation)

Opposite page:
Sunrise on the Hudson
(Esopus Meadows Preserve)

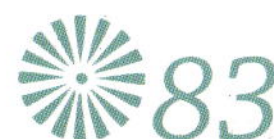

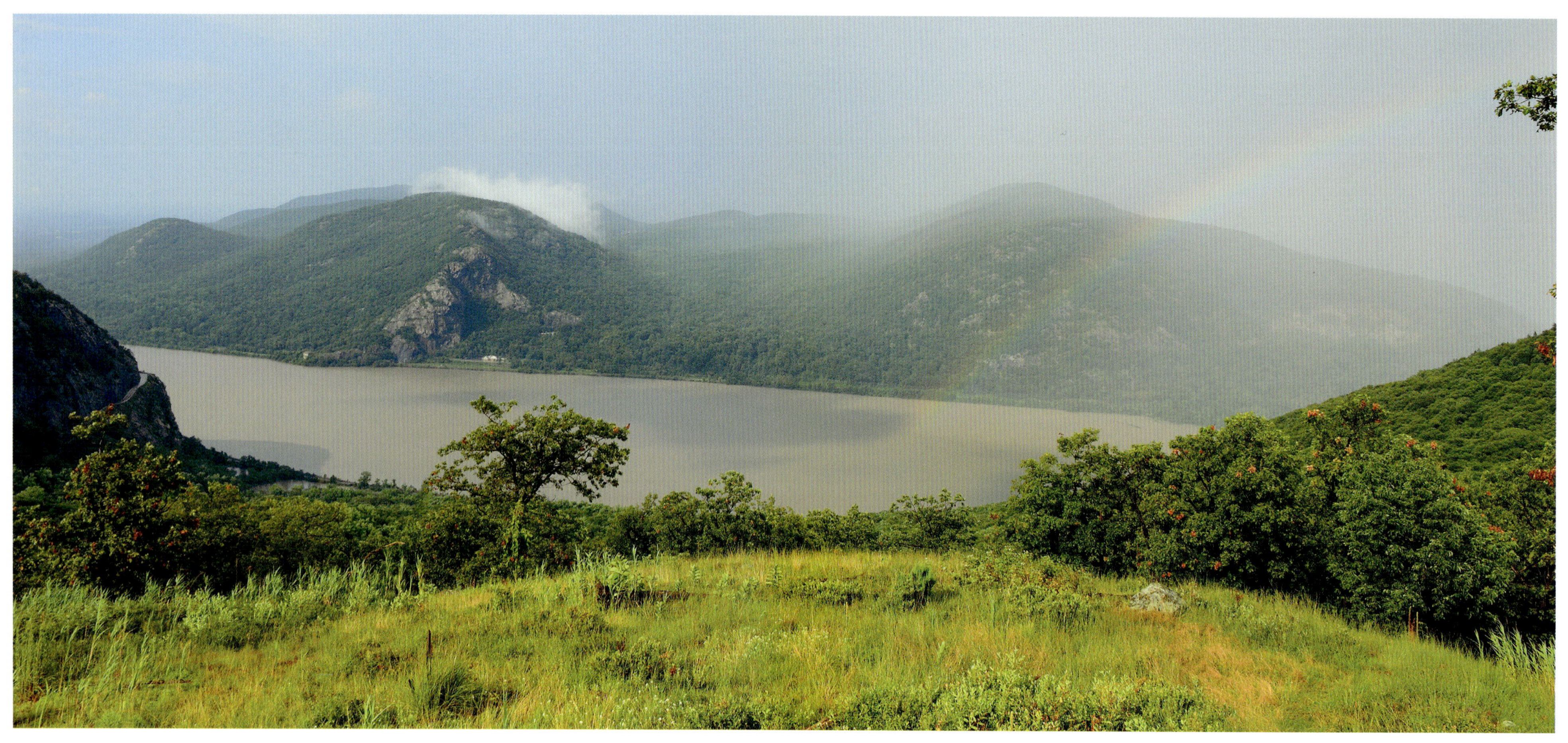

North Point summit (Storm King State Park)

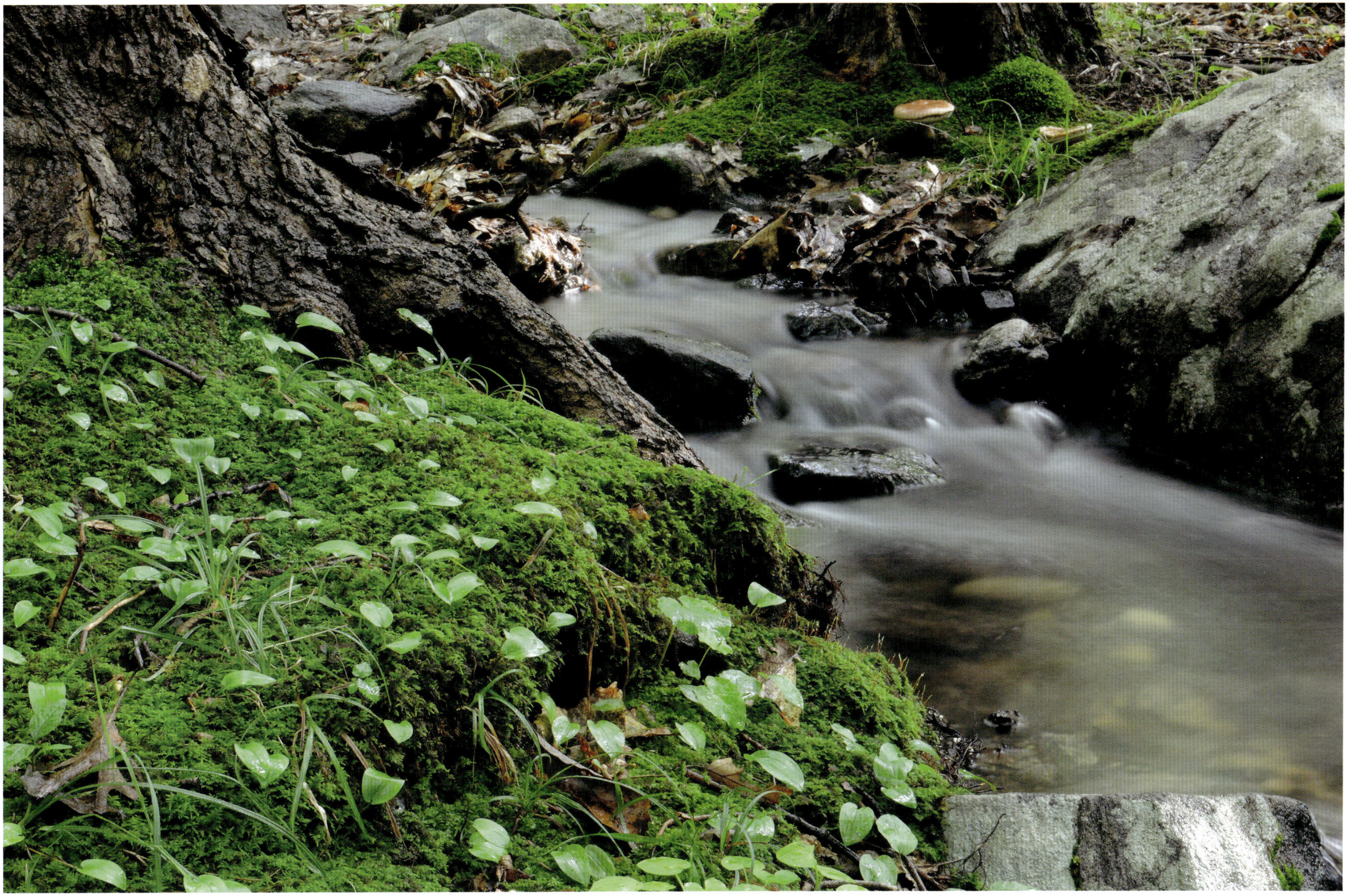

Summer rivulet atop North Point

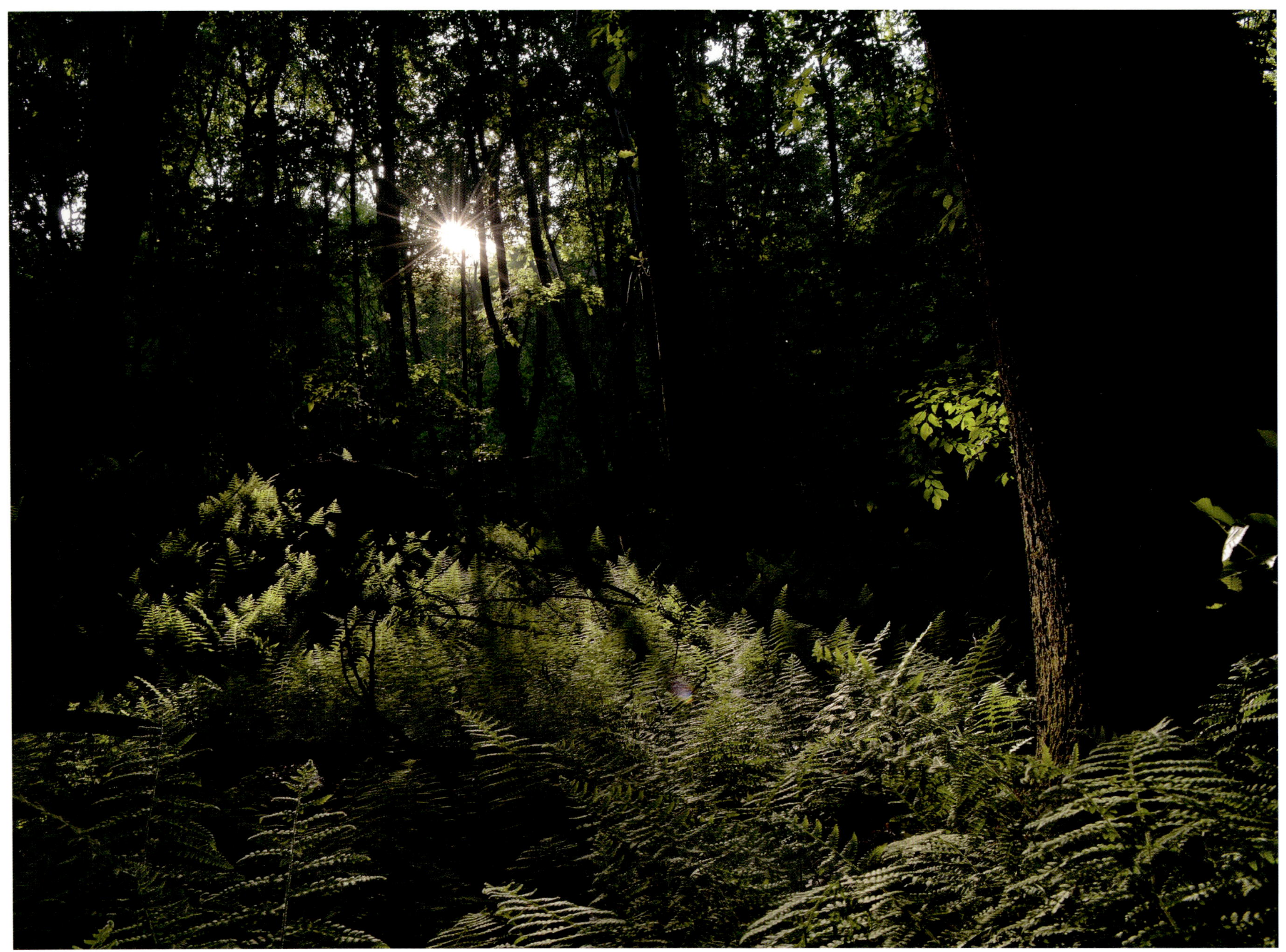

Hay-scented fern glade along the Appalachian Trail (Pawling)

In older forests that are relatively free of invasives or other brush in the understory, it's a common sight to see large glades of hay-scented ferns while hiking. This fern is easy to identify by visual inspection, but even easier to discern by its distinctive aroma alone. As the name implies, it somewhat smells like newly cut hay, but with a stronger and sweeter odor.

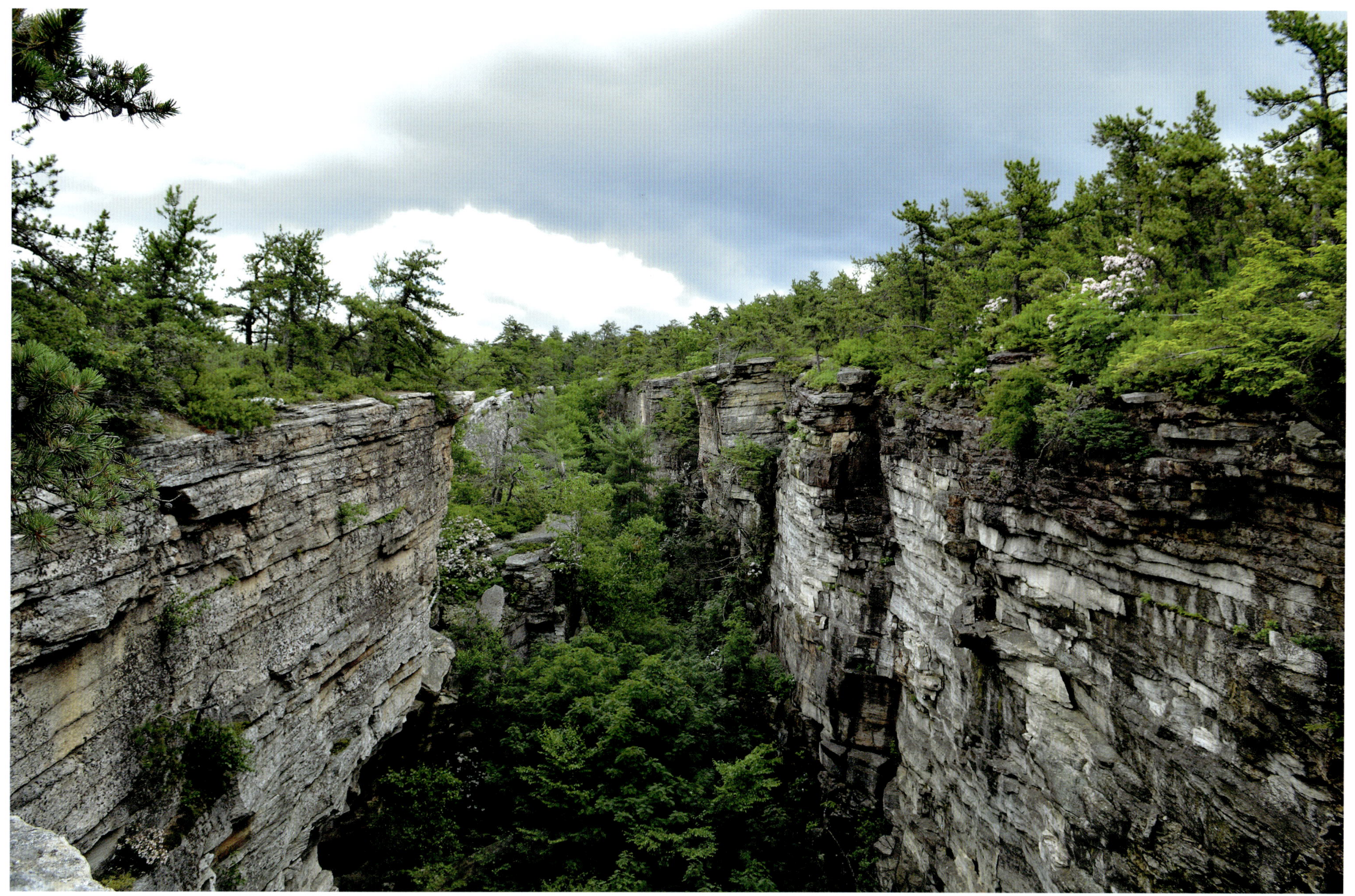

“Grand Canyon” of the Ellenville Ice Caves (Sam’s Point Preserve)

Unique to the Shawangunk Mountains, the Ellenville ice caves are part of an open fault line system, the largest in the United States. Snow and ice that fall into the deep and sheltered crevasses during the winter often remain until early July. The year-round cool temperatures create special microclimates that support more northerly species that are typically found in only the high peaks of the Catskills and Adirondacks.

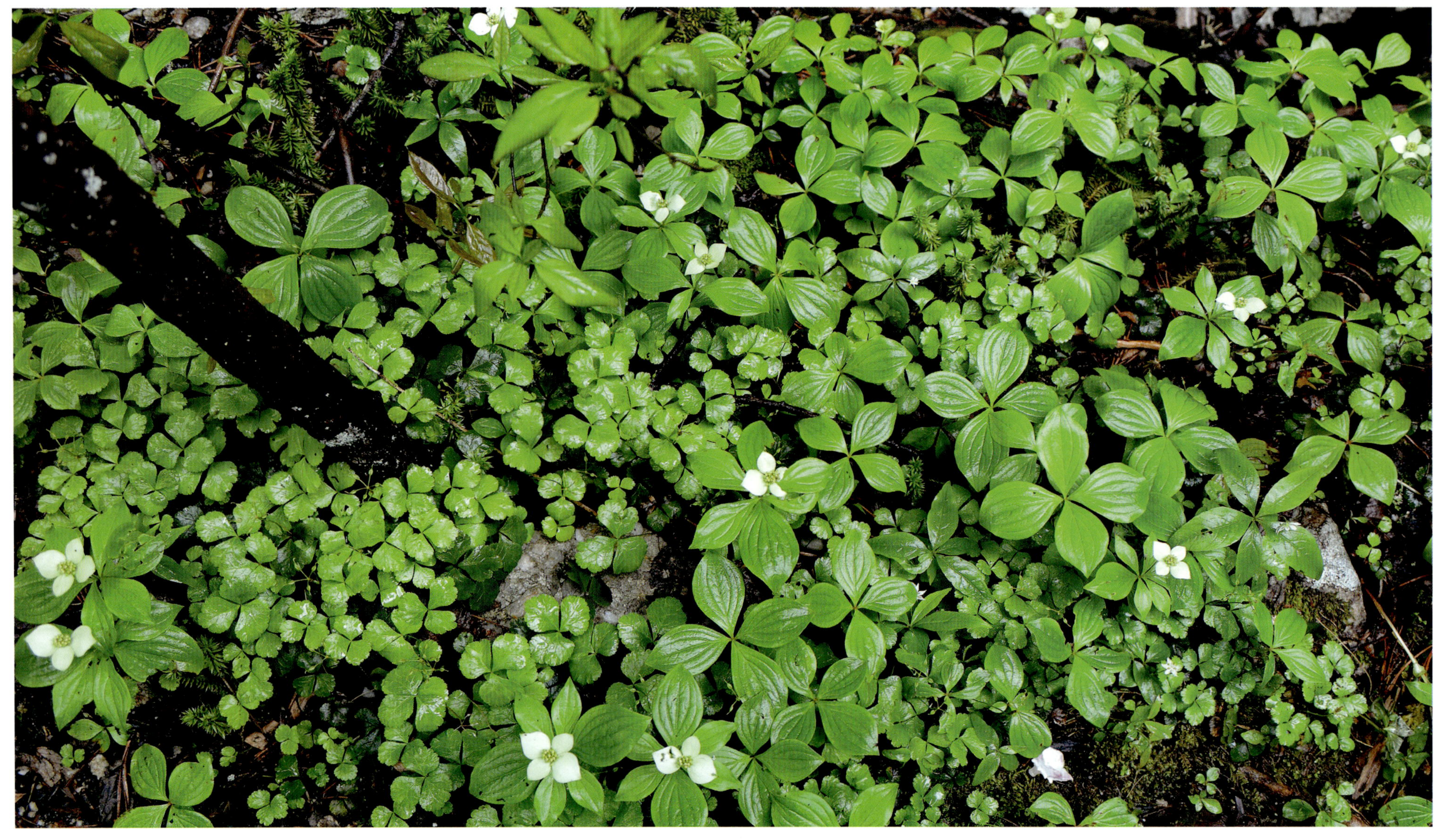

Bunchberry at the bottom of the "Grand Canyon"

Bunchberry, American mountain ash, hemlock, various spruces, and a wide spread of bryophytes—many of which are rare—can be found throughout some of the larger ice caves. The "Grand Canyon" is especially diverse due to its immense size.

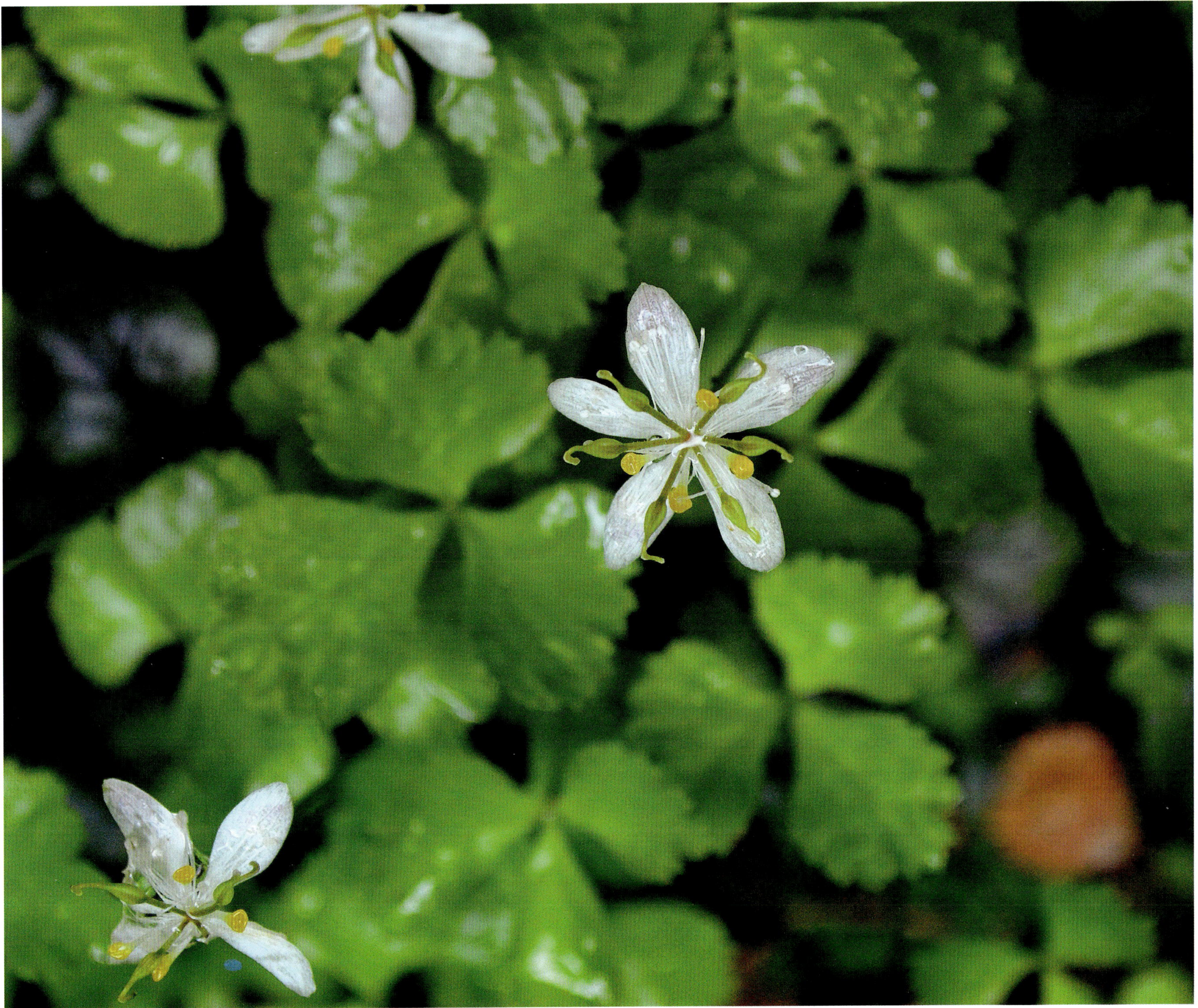

Goldthread (Sam's Point Preserve)

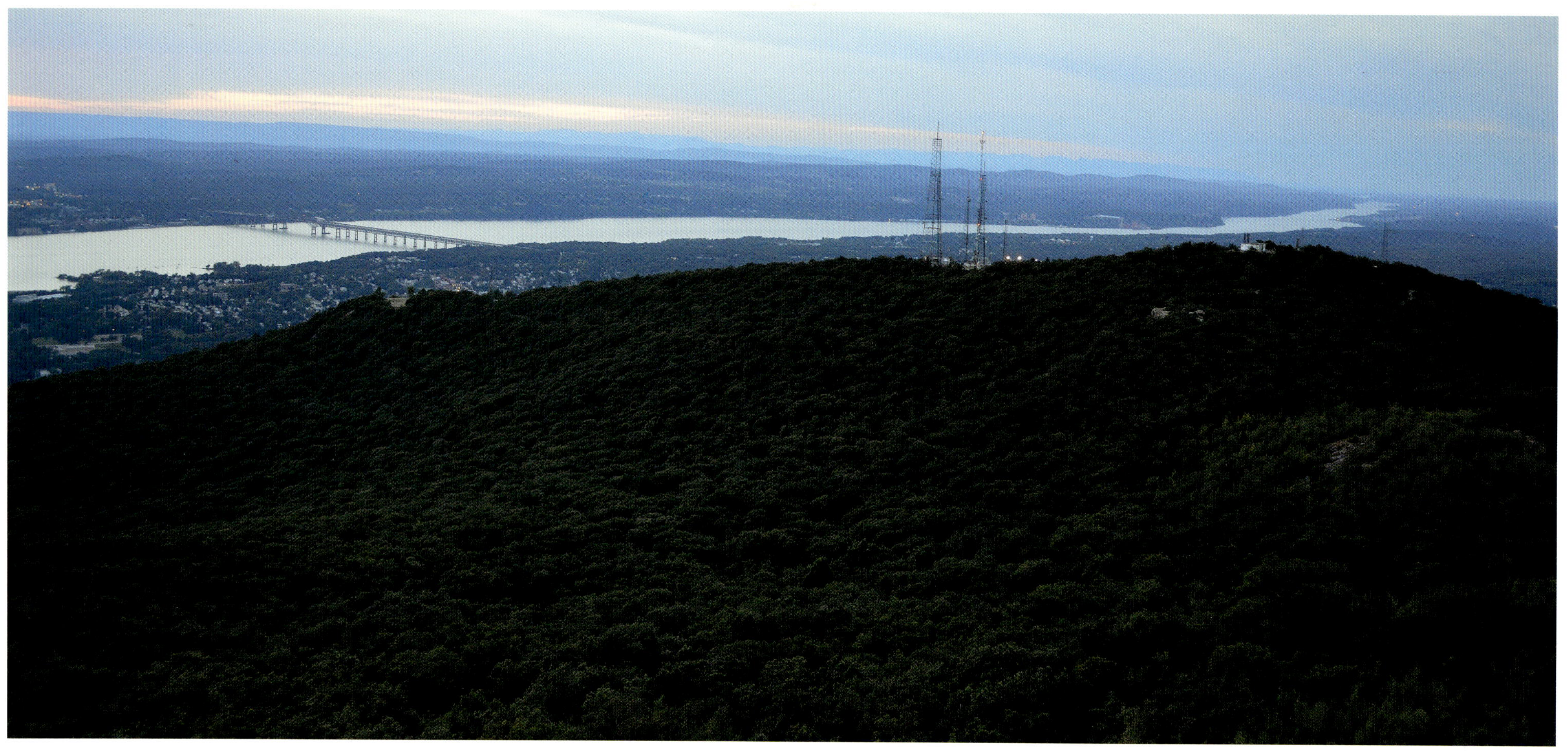

Mt. Beacon (Hudson Highlands State Park)

Steeped in legend dating back to the era of colonization and continuing well into the American Revolution, Mount Beacon, the dual summited mountain that towers above surrounding peaks at an altitude of 1,610 feet, marks the northern boundary of the Hudson Highlands. Of all the mountains in the Hudson Valley, no other has been associated with such an eclectic array of legends over the last four centuries.

One well-known legend relates to Francis Rombout and the Wappinger Indians. Rombout, a typical Englishman of colonial times, desired to increase his social standing by purchasing large tracts of land, which during this era, was the chief commodity in which to invest. In 1683, he made an agreement with the natives to purchase "as much land as he could see." They were, of course, referring to the land he could observe at ground level, but failed to explicitly mention it. A cunning man, he implemented his scheme by leading the natives to the highest point on Mount Beacon, and there, with an expansive view before him, declared himself proprietor of all that he beheld, resulting in a gain of approximately 85,000 acres.

Mount Beacon would receive its name during the Revolutionary War, when American forces lit signal fires at the summit to alert their comrades of the enemy's movements.

In 1902, construction of an incline railway was completed that transported visitors to a casino at the northern summit. The railway was the steepest in the world and ran until 1978 when financial issues forced it to close. Today, all that can be seen are the casino's concrete foundations, as the rest burned down a few years after its doors closed.

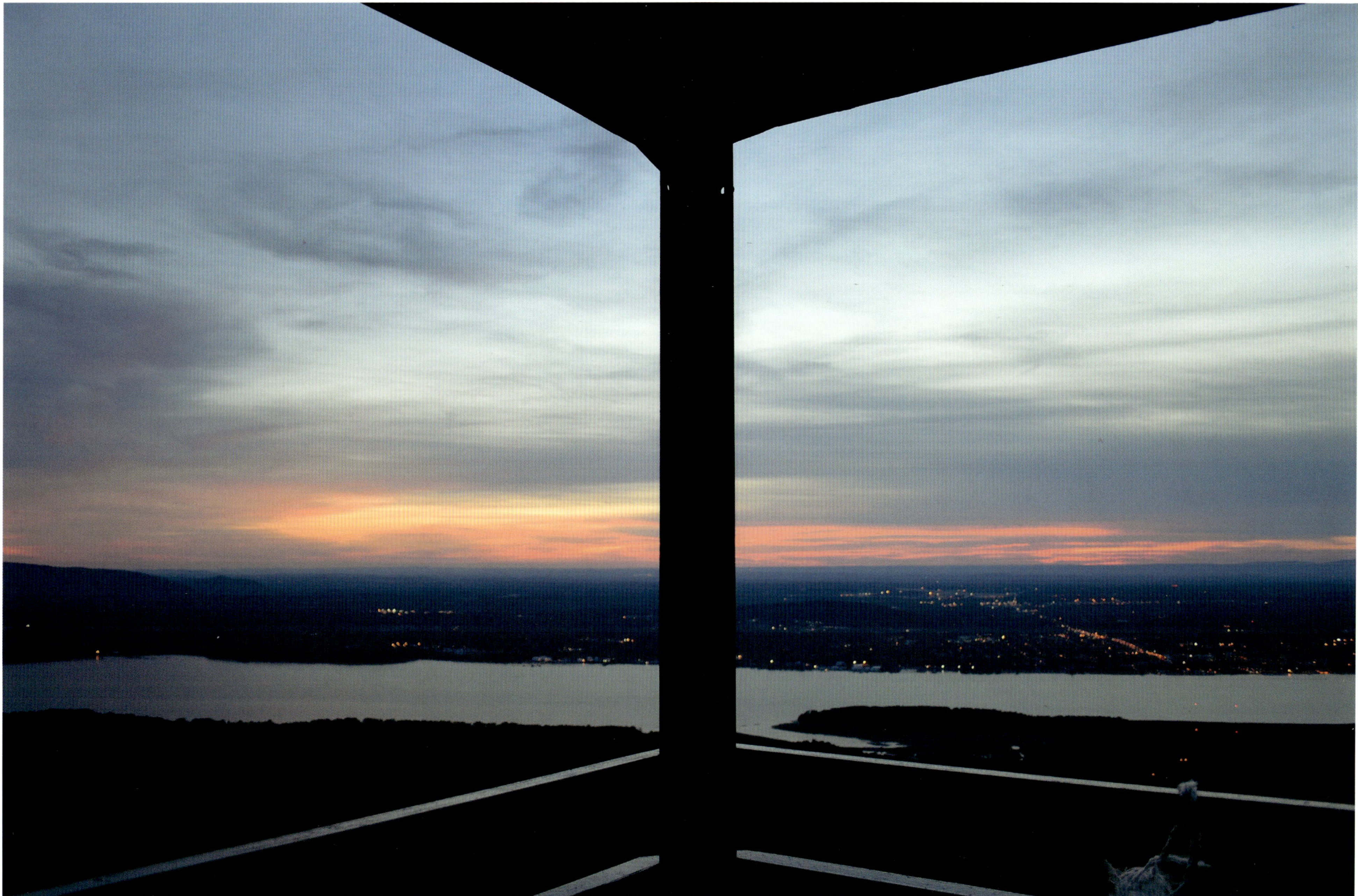

Mt. Beacon firetower

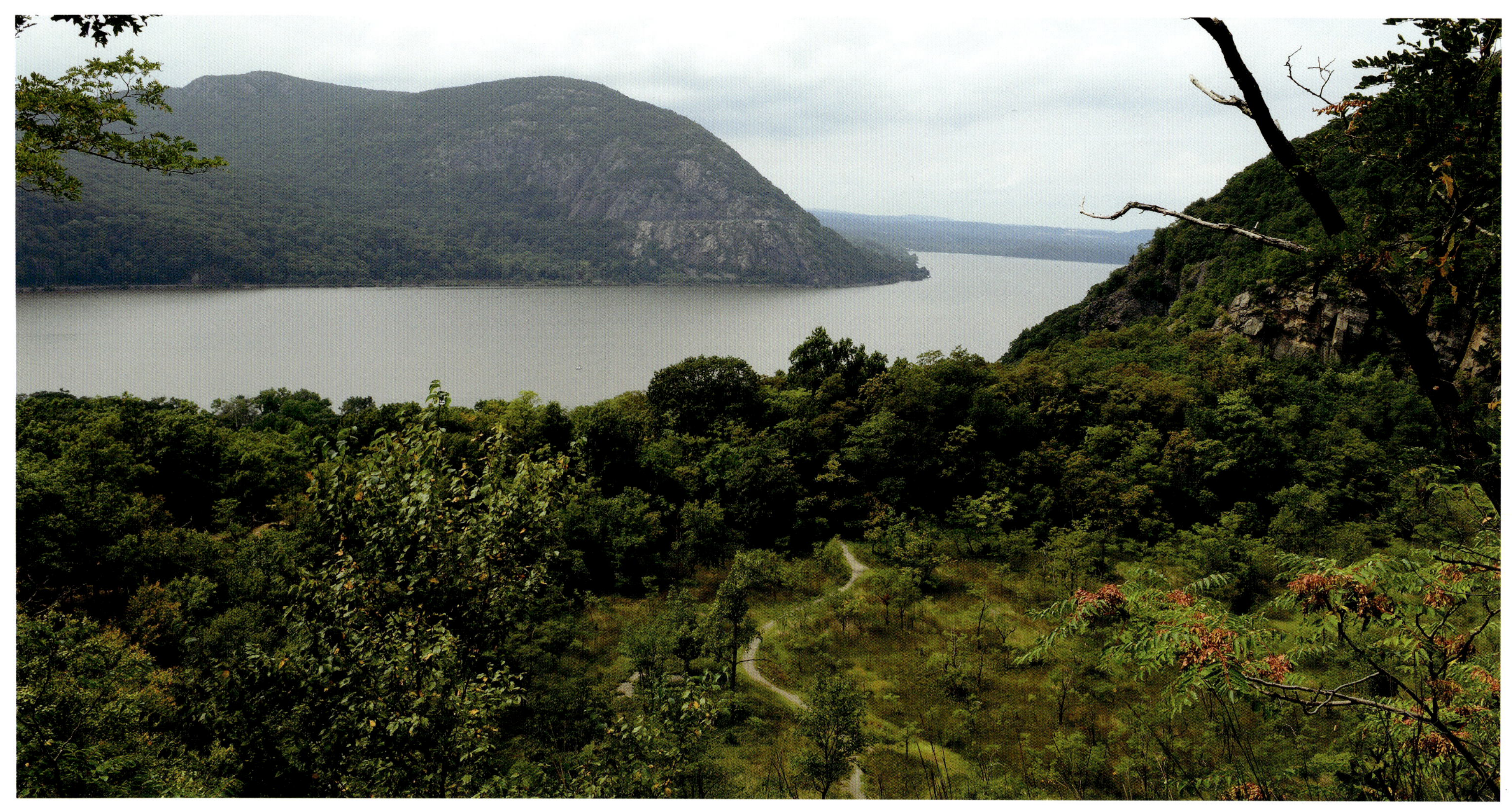

Bull Hill (Hudson Highlands State Park)

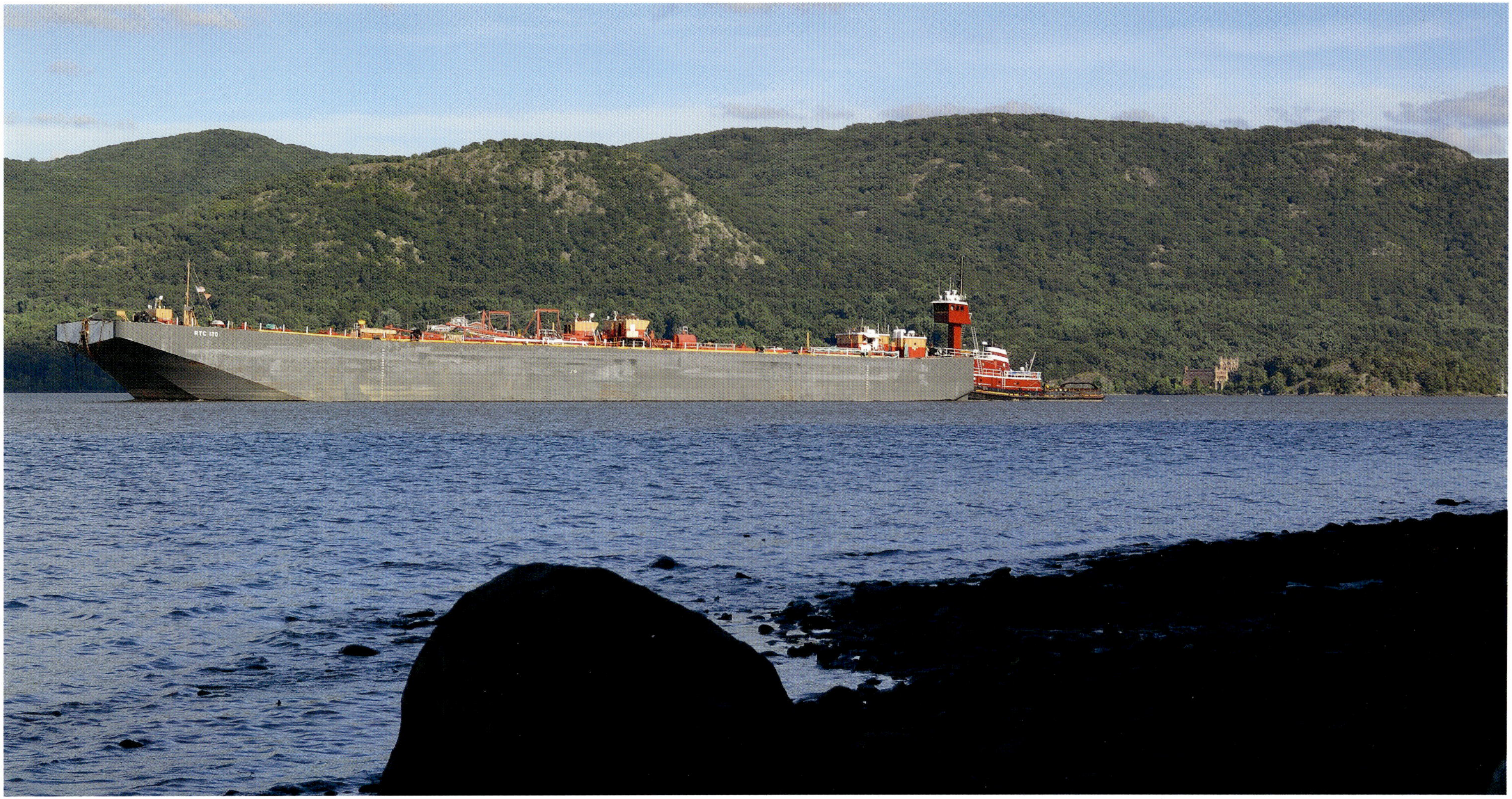

Barge on the Hudson (Plum Point)

The Hudson has always been the state's chief channel of commerce, and many barges still ply the river today. First serving as a route to extract furs (mainly beaver) from the remote interior during the days of Dutch rule, it became rich from trade and was the envy of Europe. Its success was the downfall of the Dutch colonizers, as the British usurped control in 1664. Peter Stuyvesant, the director-general of the colony, surrendered without firing a single shot, knowing he could not possibly defeat an armada of British warships that swarmed New York harbor with his limited men and munitions.

New York would truly see success when the steamboat debuted in 1807, an invention of Robert Fulton. He and his partner, the wealthy investor Robert Livingston, held a monopoly on the waters of the Hudson for many years. Sloop owners who were angered by their loss of business would frequently ram their ships into the steamboats, hoping to disable them. The damage was but a minor inconvenience that could not stop the ushering in of a new era. This time change would come through technological innovation instead of political conflict and war.

When the Erie Canal opened in 1825, it provided the state with an additional trade bounty that would cement New York's status as one of the most prosperous states in the Union.

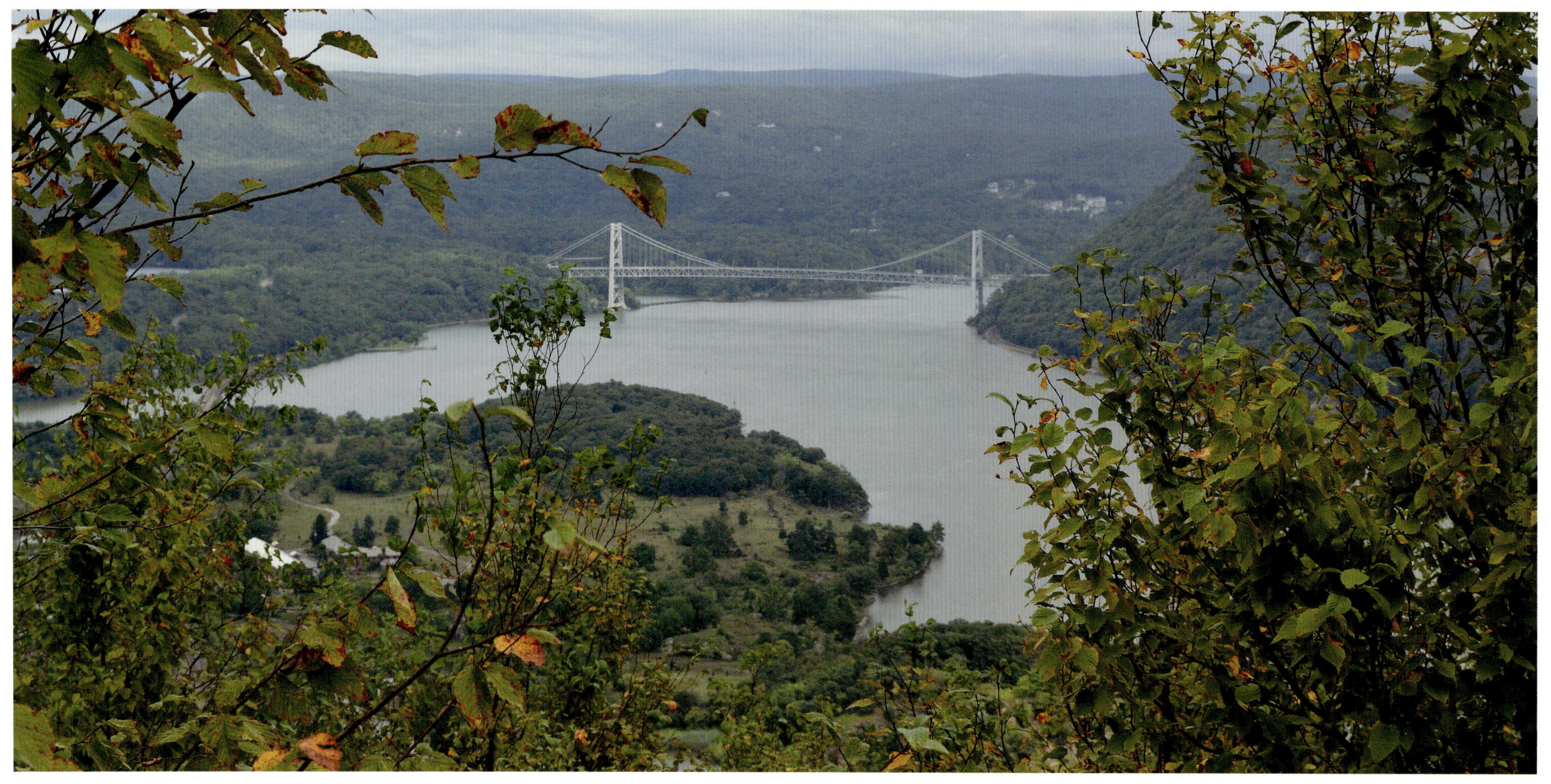

View of Bear Mountain Bridge from Dunderberg Mountain (Bear Mountain State Park)

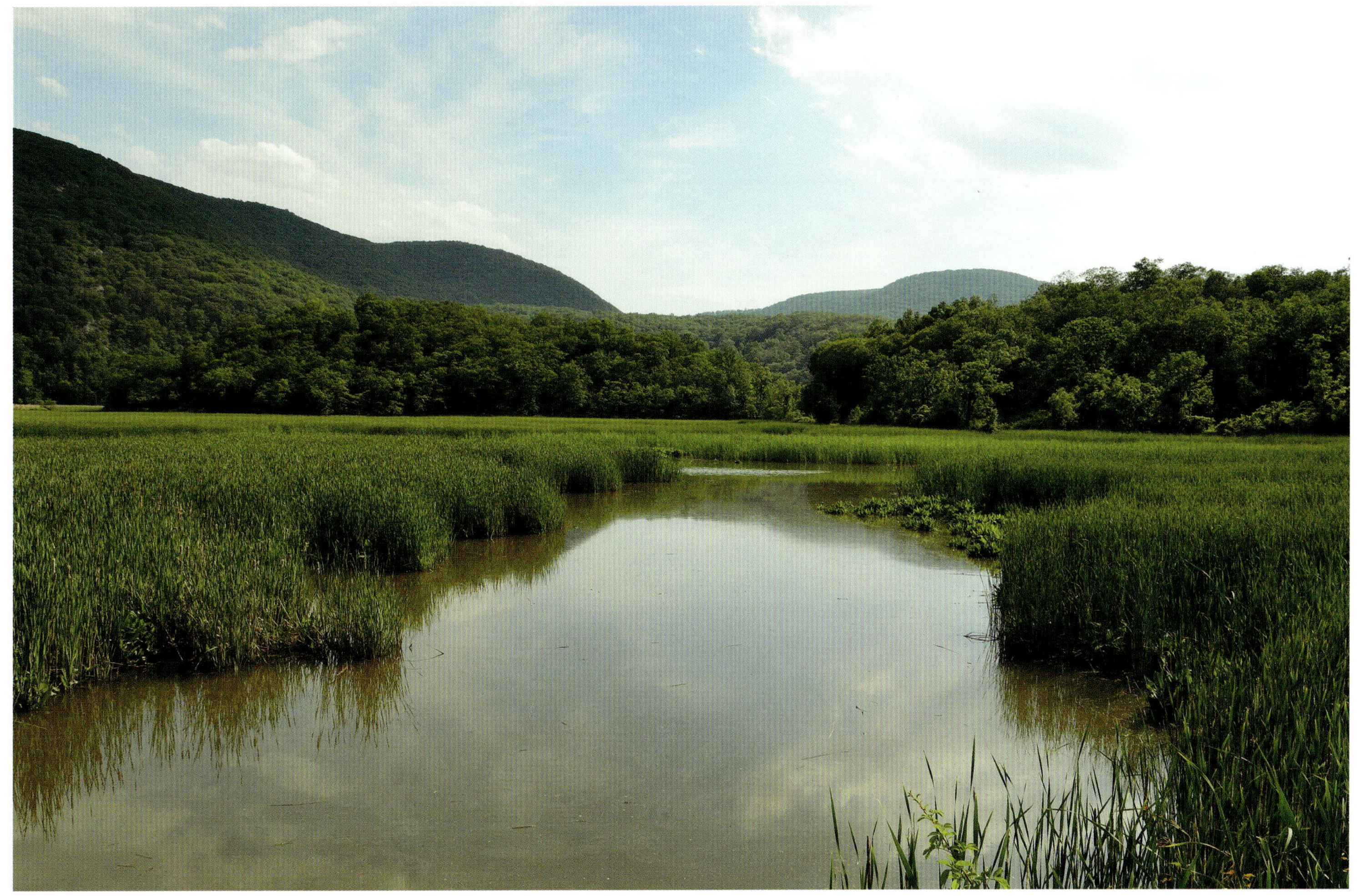

Iona Island marsh
(Bear Mountain State Park)

Under siege from phragmites, an invasive reed, the marsh's density is increasing, to the detriment of many species. The NYS Park System and Palisades Interstate Park Commission are now beginning to fight back and are developing plans to remove the reed.

In the era of the Native Americans, oysters as large as an outstretched hand were routinely found in the marsh—none are left, but traces of them have been uncovered in archeological sites surrounding the island. Needham's skimmer, a state-listed rare dragonfly, can be found in substantial numbers throughout the area, requiring the optimal estuarine conditions that Iona Marsh generously offers.

The 556-acre Iona Island, which lies in the lower highland amphitheater, originally served as an orchard and vineyard in the mid-1800s. The island received its name from the Iona grapes first planted there by the Grant family. These are still grown throughout the Hudson Valley, although they weren't popular enough at the time to save the Grant farm from being foreclosed.

The island would later serve as a significant tourist destination, complete with an amusement park and hotel. In 1900, it served as a naval storage depot that operated until several years after the close of World War II. After the Palisades Interstate Park Commission acquired the property in 1965, the island began reverting back to a wilder state. Today, most of the island is off-limits to the public, as it serves as a wintering site for bald eagles and a research station for investigating the dynamics of invasive plants.

Swamp rose mallow (pink), cardinal flower (red), and common sneezeweed (yellow) begin blooming in early August.

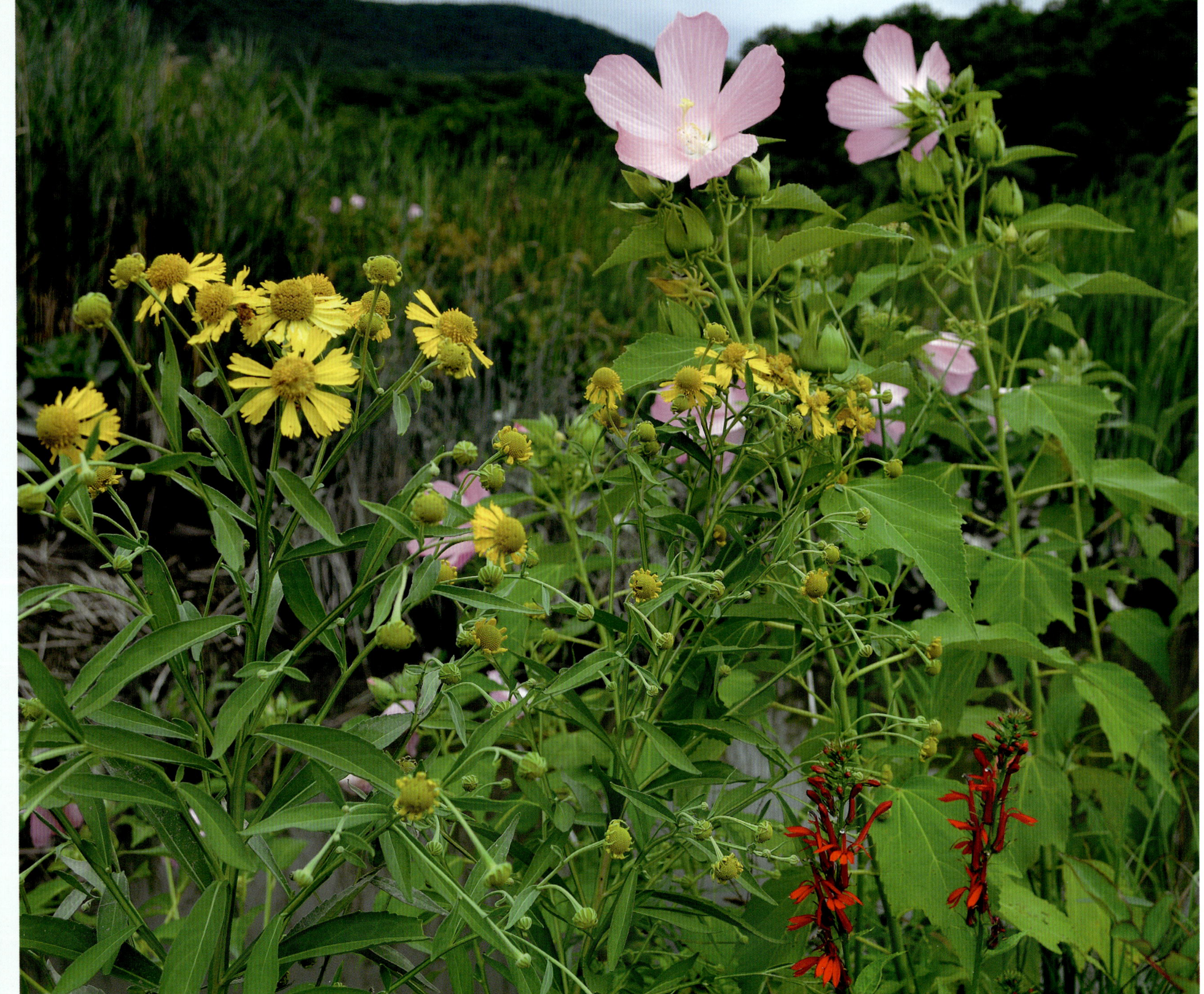

Iona Island wildflowers

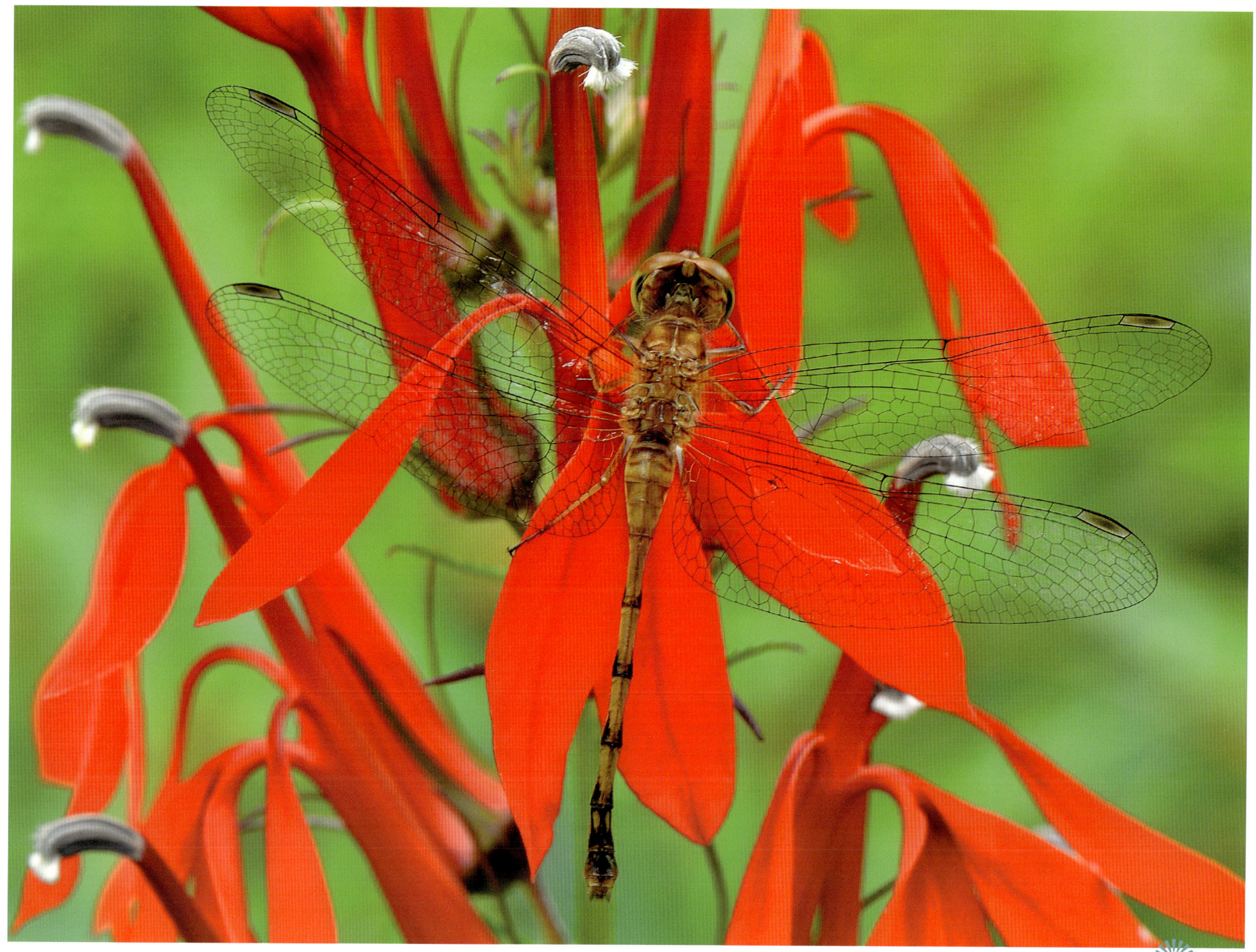

Dragonfly on cardinal flower (Sterling Forest State Park)

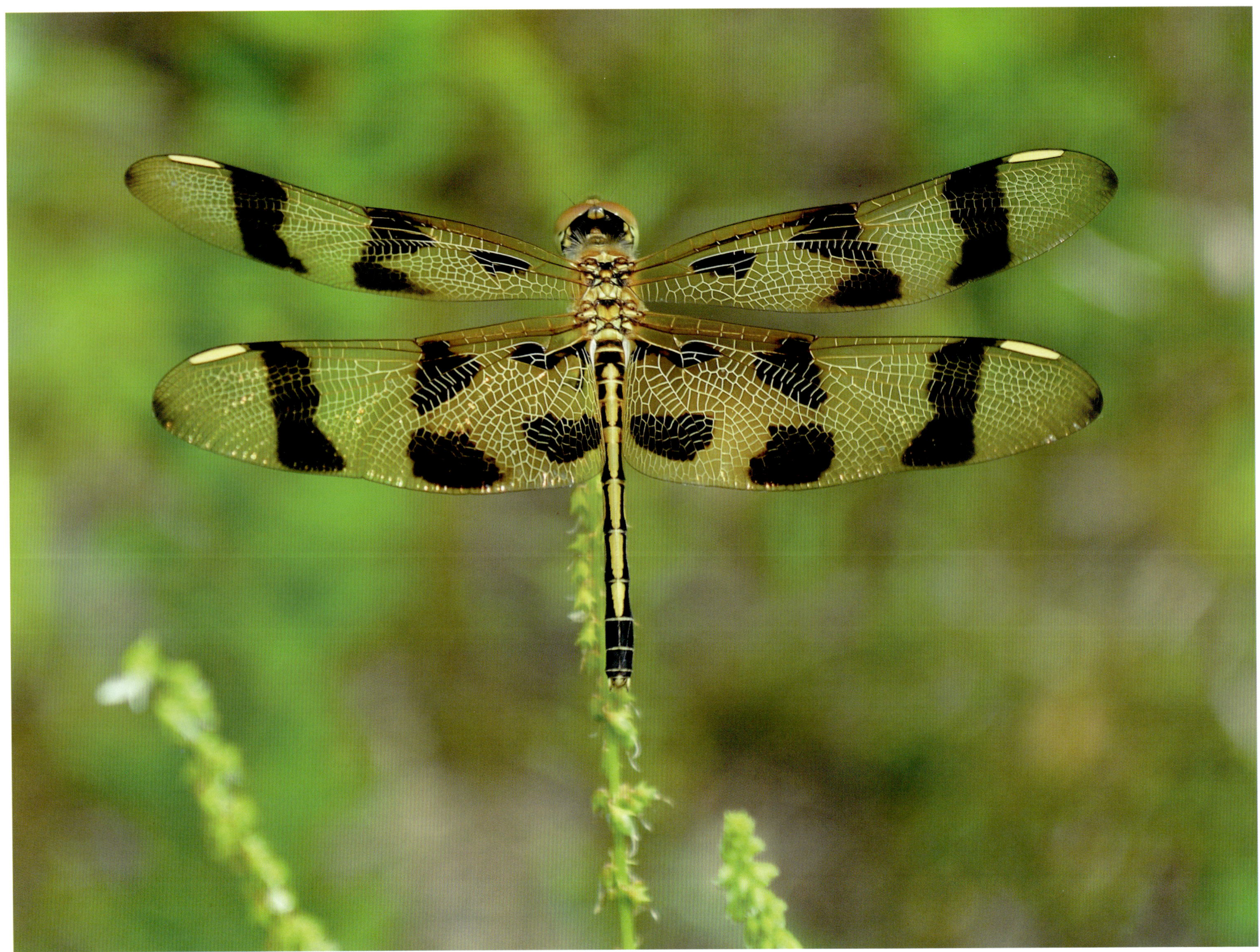

Halloween pennant (Hook Mountain State Park)

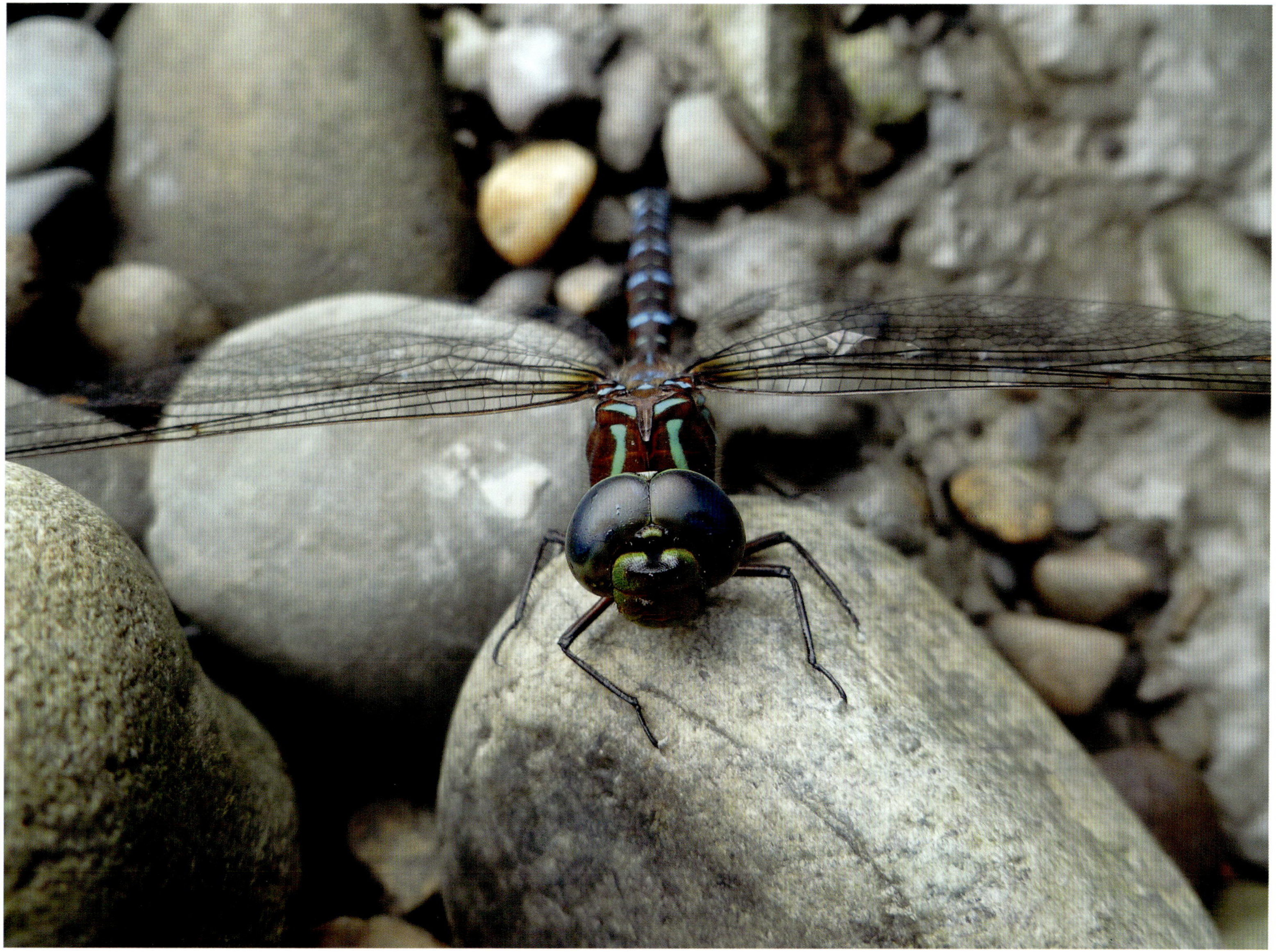

Southern New York has approximately 128 dragonfly and fifty-five damselfly species. Many of these inhabit the environs of the Hudson River and some are intimately tied to it, utilizing brackish wetlands for mating and ovipositing (egg laying). Habitat destruction along the Hudson has caused serious declines in certain species. The larval stage of some can last up to five years. Since larvae spend most of their time near riverine sediment, they are prone to PCB contamination. After emerging as adults, the chemicals are capable of transferring to terrestrial environments if the insects are consumed by birds or other animals.

Black-tipped darner (Moodna Creek)

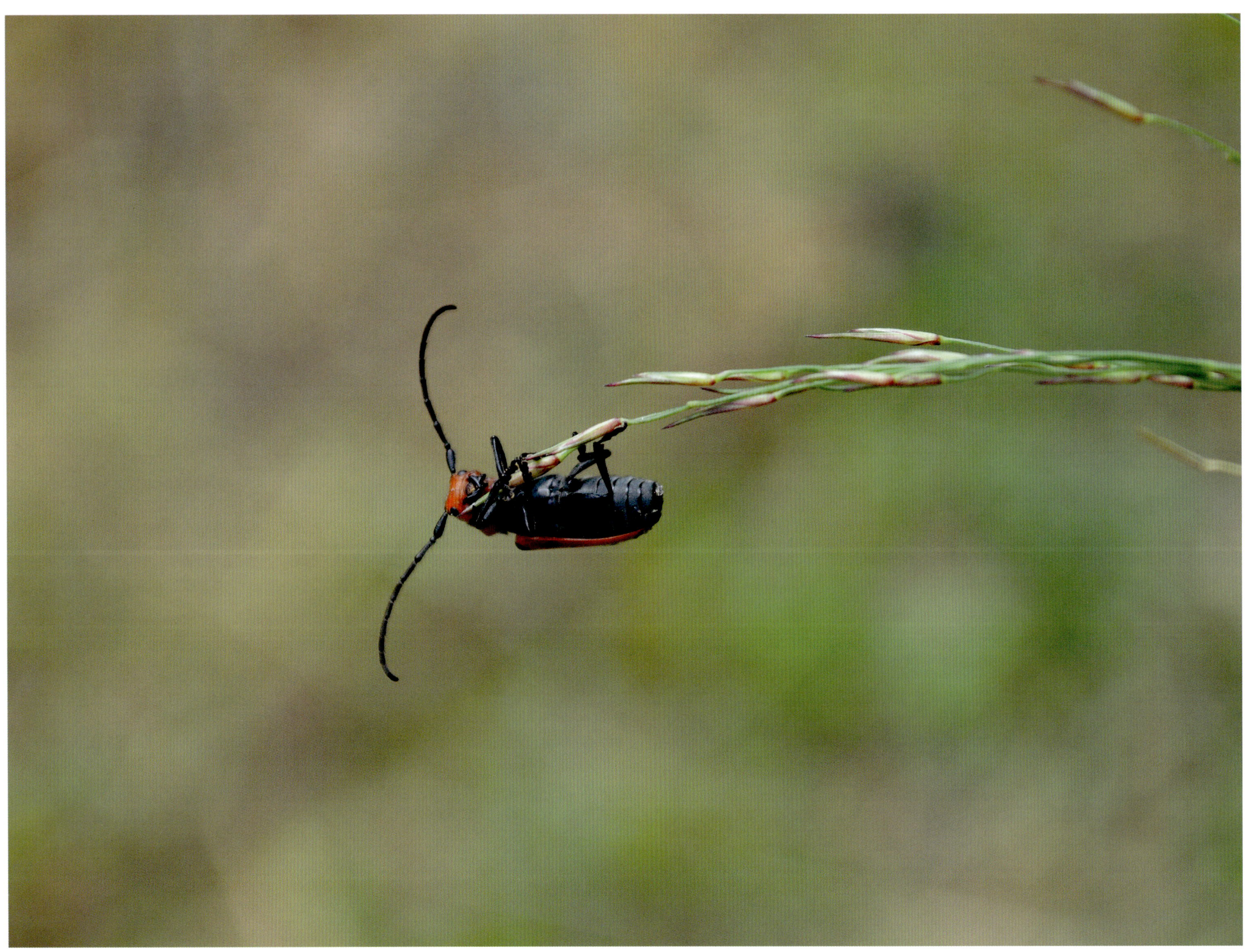

Red milkweed beetle (Esopus Meadows Preserve)

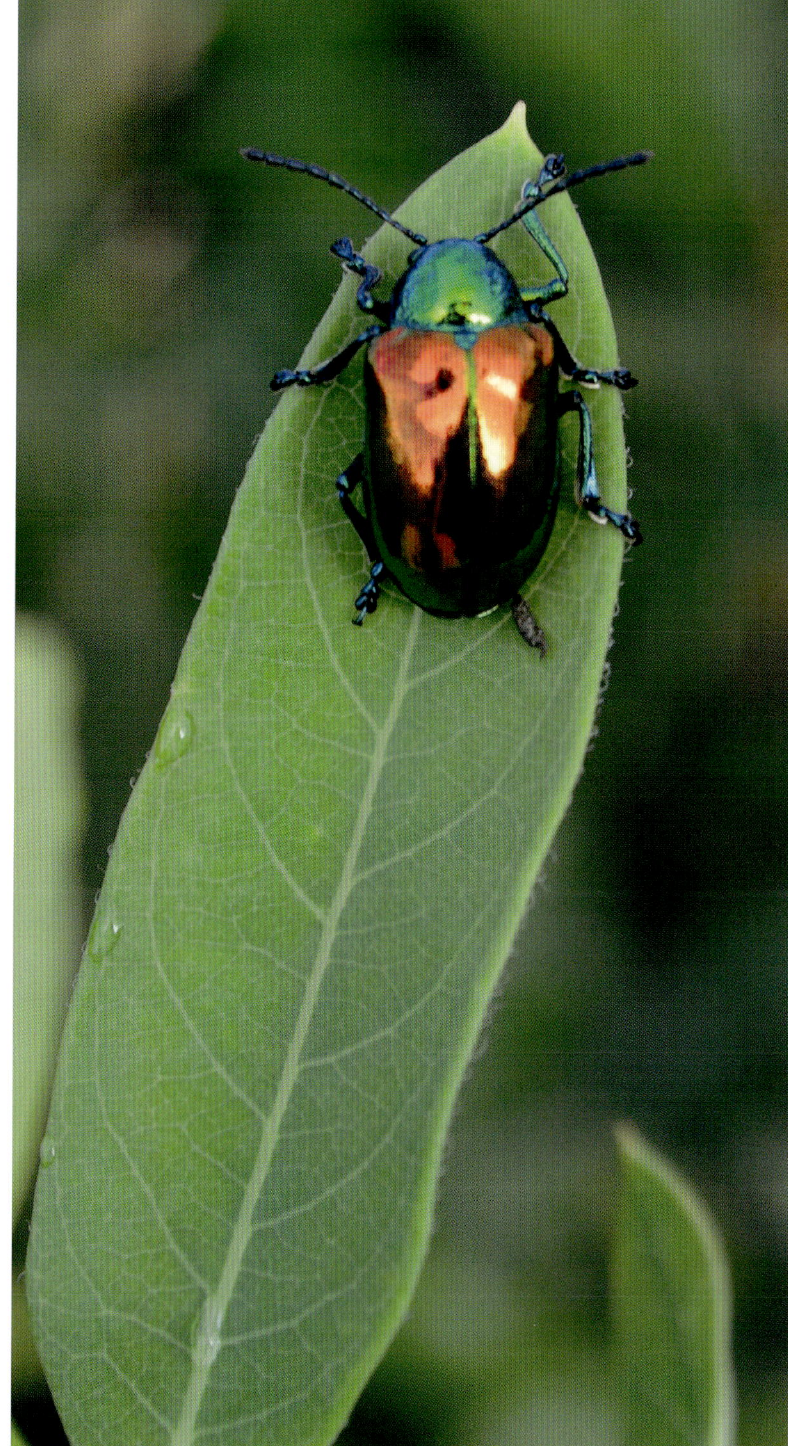

Dogbane beetle (Storm King State Park)

Dogbane beetles exhibit iridescence, which means the colors of their shell appear to change when the angle of the insect or viewer changes. This shift in color is caused by sloping, plate-like structures in the insect's exoskeleton that reflect light either from the surface of the structures or from beneath where the pigment lies. Differing angles of light striking these plates causes the light to travel at different speeds, which results in the light waves becoming congested, creating the wavy patterns and changing the colors we see.

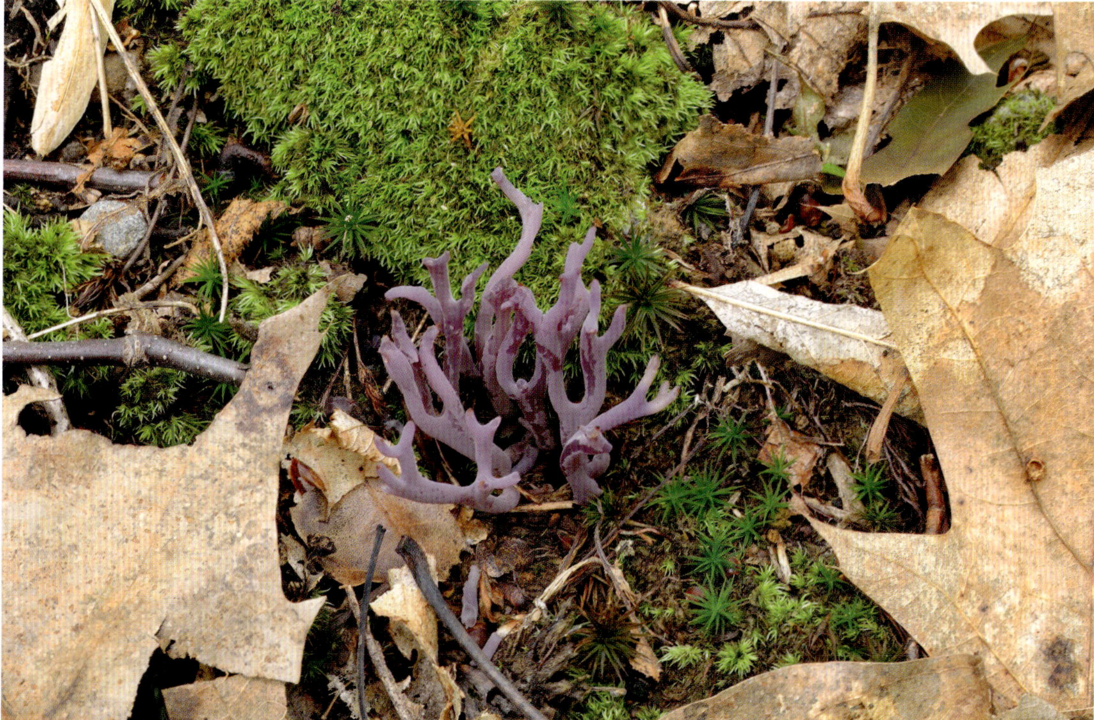

Violet coral mushroom (Blauvelt State Park)

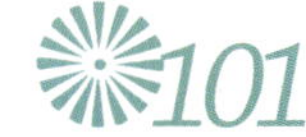

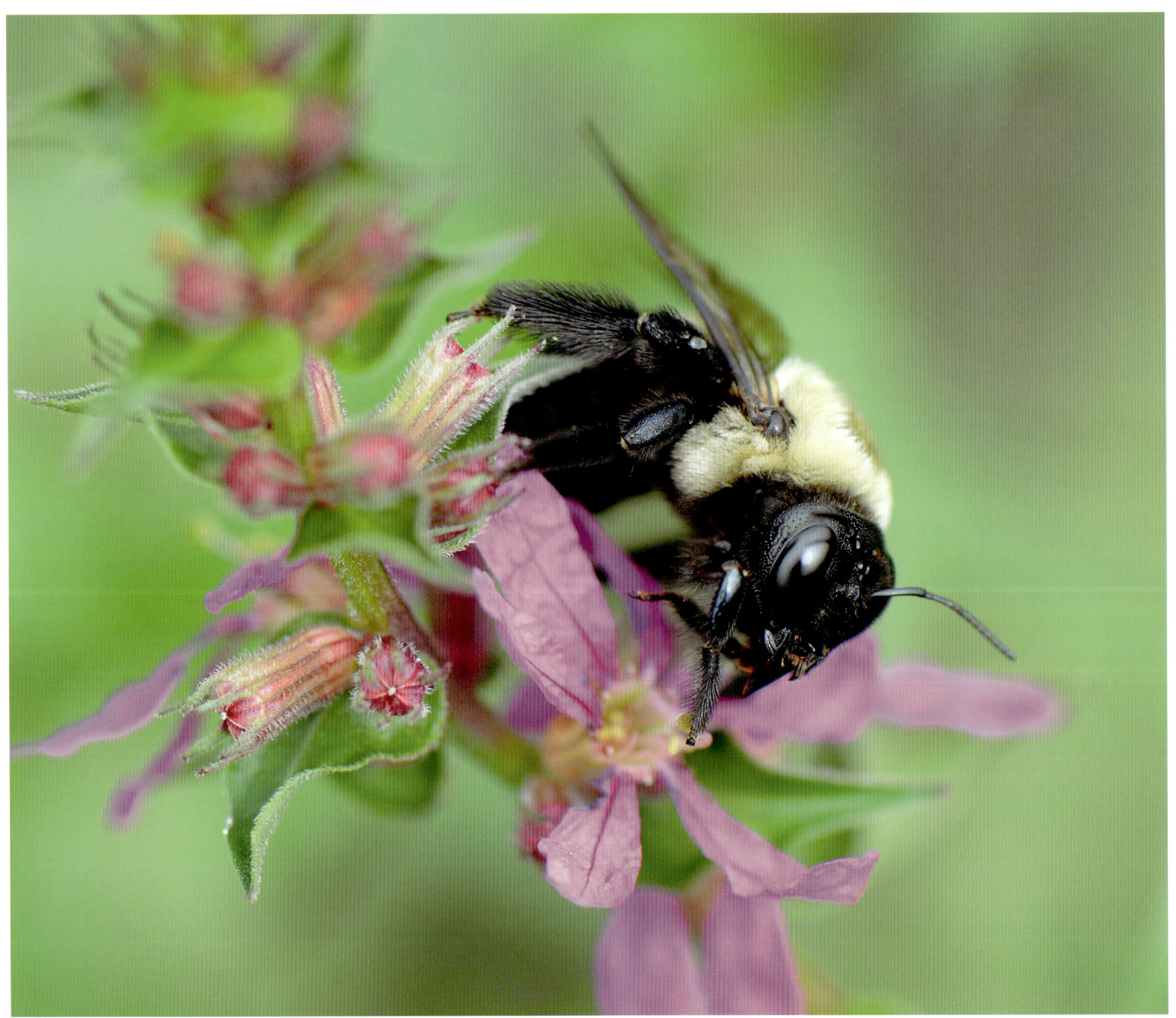

Bumblebee on purple loosestrife (Rockefeller State Park)

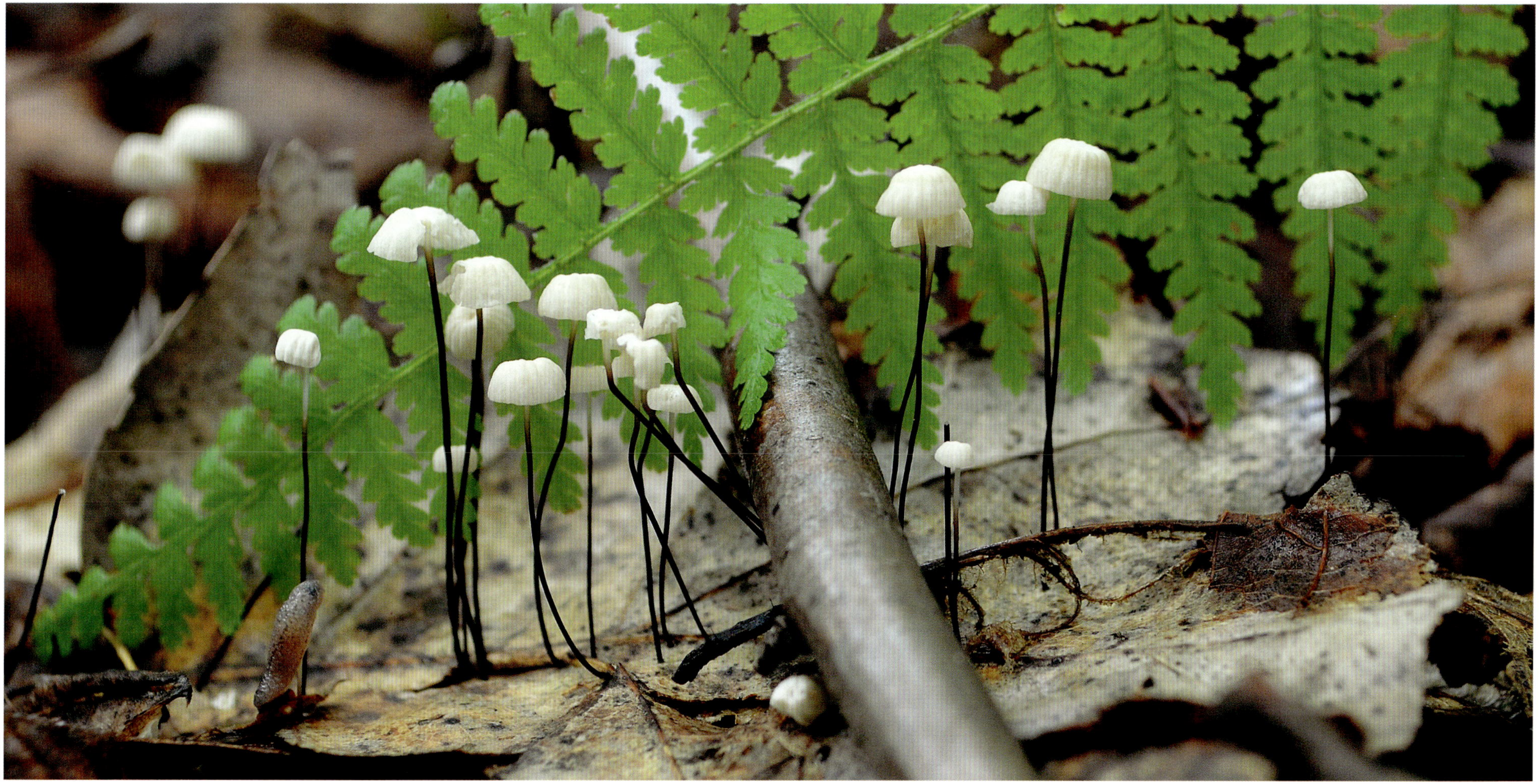

Pinwheel mushrooms (Bear Mountain State Park)

Pinwheel mushrooms can be found growing on a wide array of decomposing woody matter, but especially favor beech trees. Despite not being reported as poisonous, this mushroom should probably not be tasted, as it has the potential to absorb high concentrations of the heavy metal cadmium.

This fungus depends on rain for spore release, unlike many other mushrooms that release based on a circadian rhythm cycle, or internal clock. In dry conditions they desiccate and shrivel up until sufficient moisture returns and resurrects them, at which time they can continue to release spores for several more weeks. An enzyme recently isolated from this species is being researched for use as a biosensor for certain compounds and may be used for drug monitoring in the future.

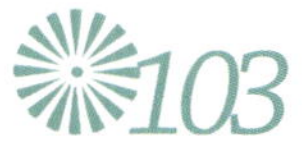

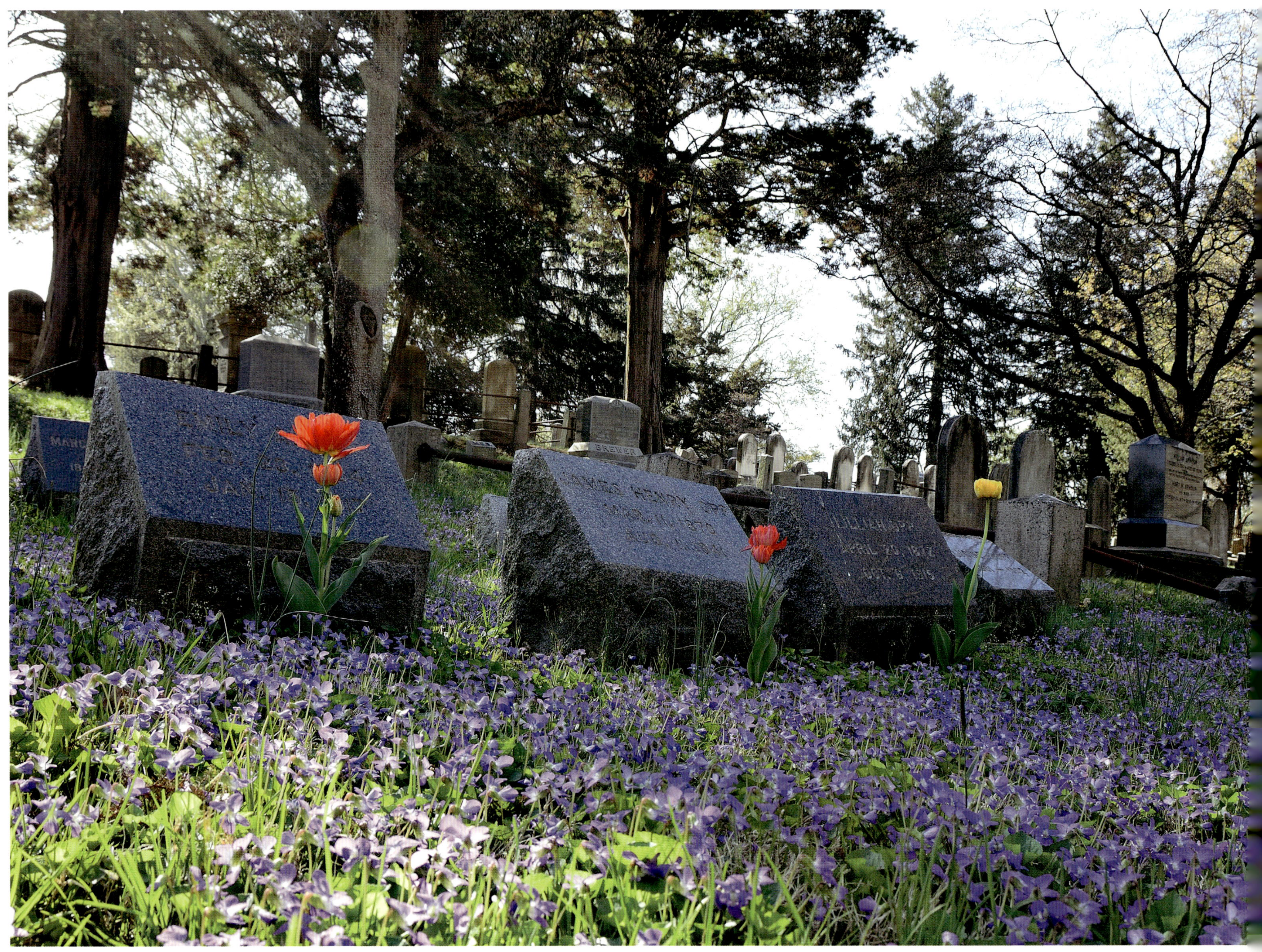

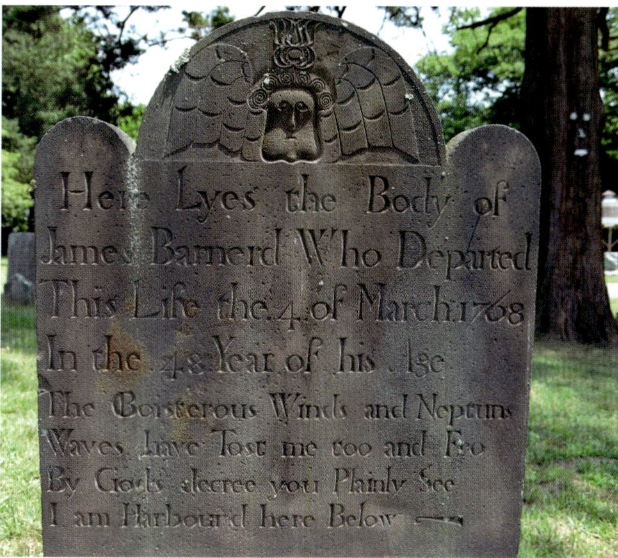

HISTORY & LORE

During the American Revolution, Westchester County was wedged between British-occupied New York City and land held by American forces to the north in upstate New York. This so-called "neutral ground" was anything but, and was subjected to many hostile interactions between the opposing forces. Battles were fought and skirmishes ceaselessly raged between guerilla-fighting bands of loyalist "cowboys" and patriot "skinners," spies for both sides plied their deceptive trade, and the most infamous treasonous plot in American history—Benedict Arnold's plan to give up West Point—was uncovered in this strife-filled border zone. A long and encompassing war, in addition to the fact that Westchester was settled early and heavily by the Dutch, suffused the region with a higher quantity of legends and lore than any other part of the Hudson Valley.

We owe much of this lore-laden remembrance to Washington Irving. A romantic-style writer, one who glorified the region's culture and history with lavishly descriptive tales set among real places, Irving made his native land famous the world over. *The Legend of Sleepy Hollow*, *Rip Van Winkle*, and *Dolph Heyliger* portrayed southern New York as imbued with something even more captivating than its pretty features. Overrun by ghosts, mischievous imps, and nine-pin playing gnomes, and bewitched by Indian shamans, he showed that this haunted land is not so much cursed as it is gifted. Irving directly set the stage for the ubiquitous phantom-themed celebrations that now arise every year around Halloween and give us the fright we delight in.

"The poetry of the earth is never dead."

—John Keats

This page:
Old Dutch Burying Ground

Opposite page:
Sleepy Hollow Cemetery in May

The Great Jack O'Lantern Blaze held at Van Cortland Manor in Croton-on-Hudson, a colonial-era estate decorated with over 7,000 carved pumpkins arranged in numerous spooky displays, is one of the most widely attended events of the fall season. In Ulster County, the Headless Horseman Hayrides, which takes its name from one of Irving's most iconic apparitions, has dominated the competition to become the most popular haunted hayride in America. And more recently, tours of the Sleepy Hollow Cemetery have begun offering visitors the opportunity to wander at night among graves of several high-profile individuals scattered across American history, from Irving himself to the landscape painter Jasper Cropsey to industrialists like Rockefeller and Carnegie. Several different lantern tours that specialize in themes such as "Murder and Mayhem" and "The Good, the Bad, and the Unusual" provide the history buff or supernaturally inclined a chance to hear ghost stories and legends of more recent origin on property abutting the Old Dutch Church, a landmark that played a prominent role in *The Legend of Sleepy Hollow*.

The Old Dutch Church of Sleepy Hollow and its burial ground made famous by Irving still both manage to hold the same rustic charm as when they were penned into his work almost two centuries ago. While the surrounding towns and cities have exploded in size and population, this historic site, along with many others he detailed, have been preserved, and only the closest inspection reveals traces of the current century. As Irving noted, "the great torrent of migration and improvement, which is making such incessant changes in other parts of this restless country, sweeps by . . . unobserved." His description is still mostly accurate, at least when it comes to the "bewitched" and "haunted" land of the churchyard and its deeply forested environs.

The Old Dutch Church of Sleepy Hollow is the oldest extant church in New York State, construction having commenced in 1685. Frederick Philipse, a wealthy New Netherland landowner and merchant, is credited with the church's creation, building it only a couple hundred yards from a nearby mill he owned and operated. Philipse acquired a vast fortune during his lifetime and ranked as one of the wealthiest men in the province. The church was built, at least partially, by his slaves.

The land on which the church now sits was used by the Dutch settlers as a cemetery perhaps as far back as 1645, although the earliest readable gravestone dates to 1755. Many of the first burials had wooden markers that have long since rotted away. Numerous stones are richly ornamented with whimsical designs; most notable are the soul effigies. Several gravestones are inscribed in Dutch.

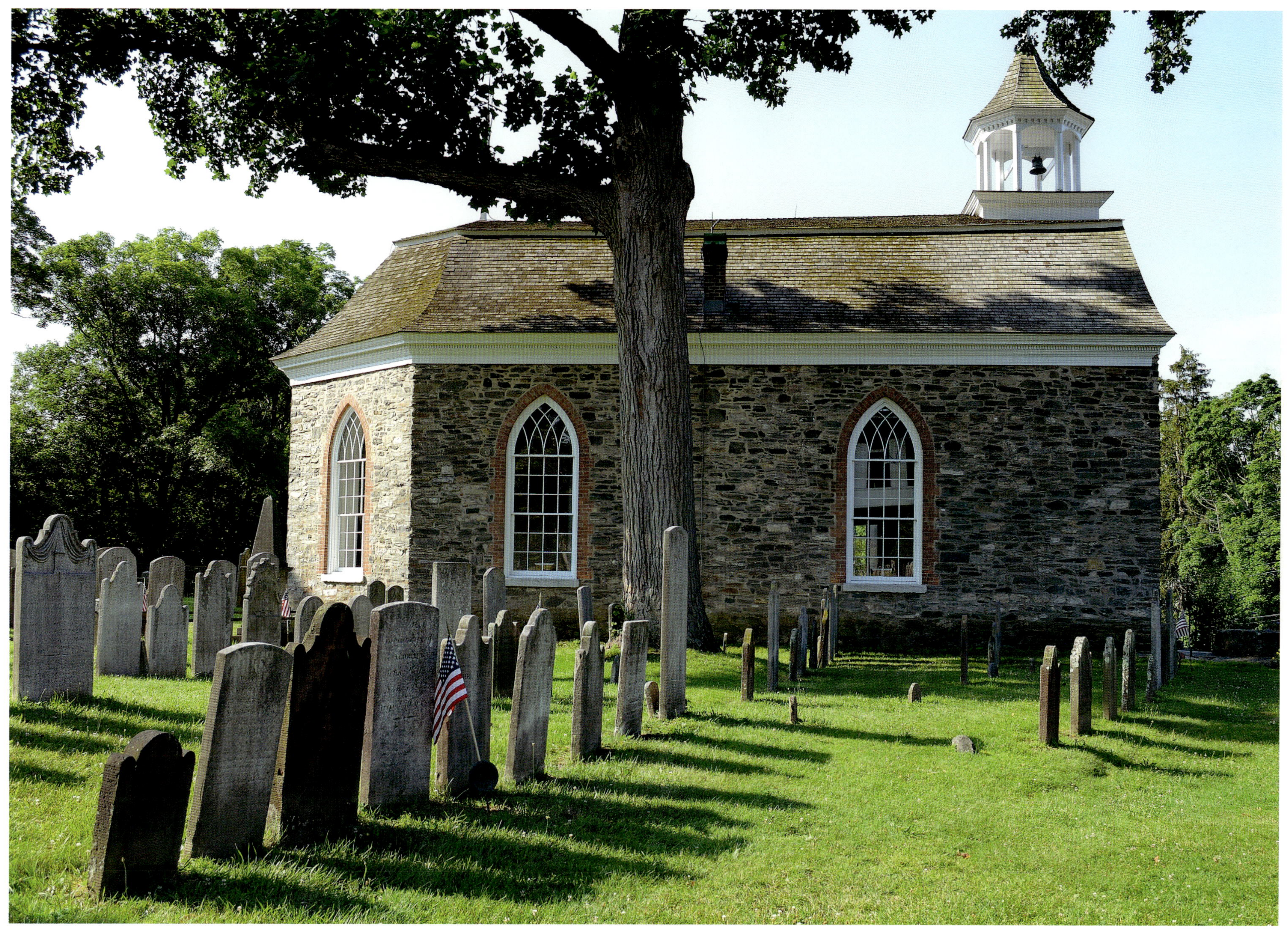

Old Dutch Church (Sleepy Hollow)

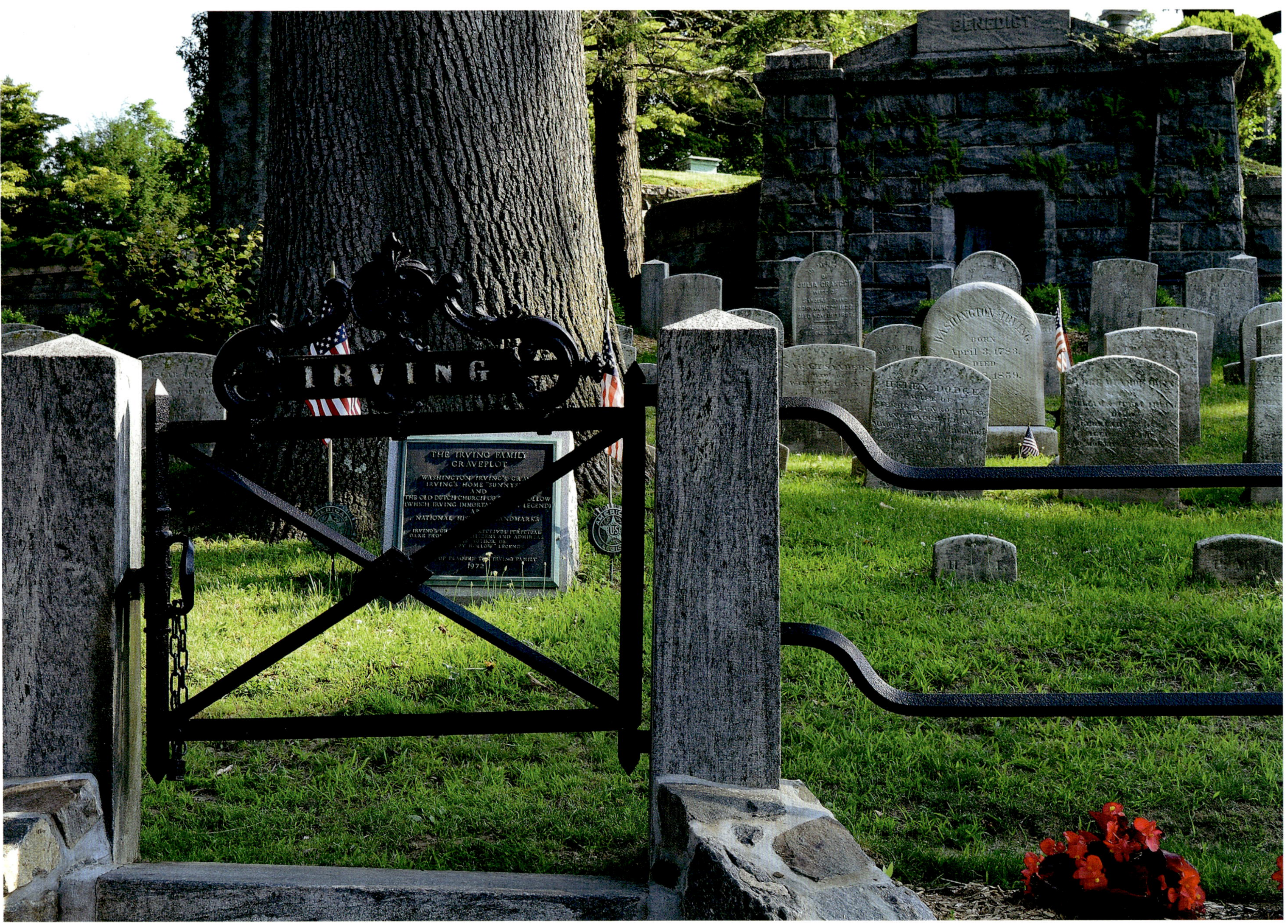

Washington Irving's Grave (Sleepy Hollow Cemetery)

Irving himself picked his burial plot in the Sleepy Hollow Cemetery and purportedly planted the massive oak seen behind the gate. His grave overlooks the Old Dutch Church, accompanying burial ground, and several other features he memorialized in his timeless tale, *The Legend of Sleepy Hollow*.

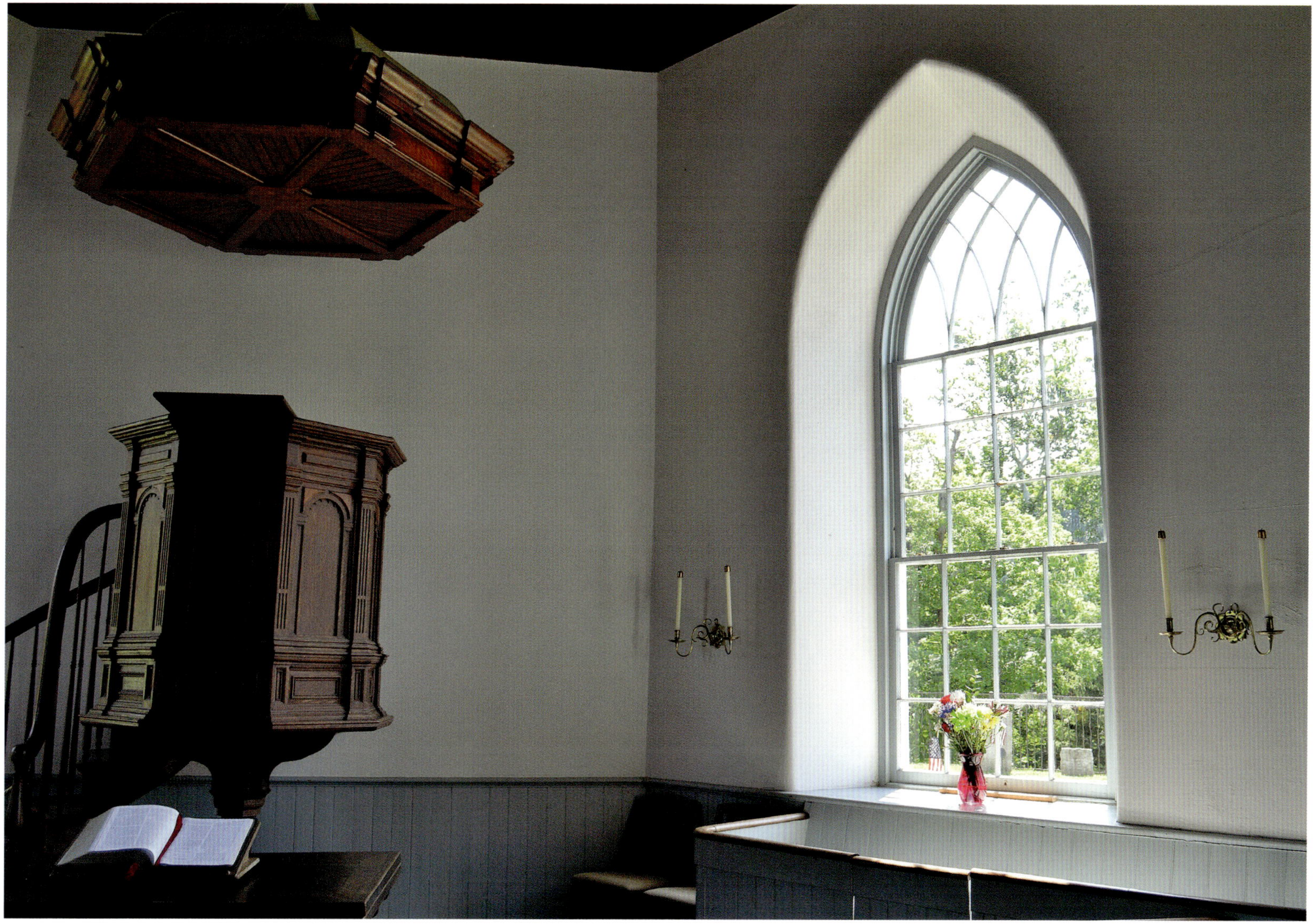

Old Dutch Church interior

Apart from renovations in 1837, in which the entrance was moved from the south wall to the west, and rectangular box windows traded in for wide Gothic arches, the church still possesses the same features it did throughout the colonial era. Many of the furnishings are original, or at the very least nearly identical reproductions, such as the preacher's pulpit. The black oak and ebony inlay communion table produced in Holland during the seventeenth century continues to grace the interior, willed to the church by Philipse's wife upon her death. In the front of the church, beneath the table lies a crypt in which numerous members of the Philipse family repose. The bell in the steeple is also original. Cast in 1685, it bears, in Latin, the motto: "If God be for us, who can be against us?" Behind it, a patinaed copper weathervane incised with Frederick Philipse's brand mark shows the motion of the wind. Although the church now resembles a museum, services are still held there throughout the summer and on select holidays.

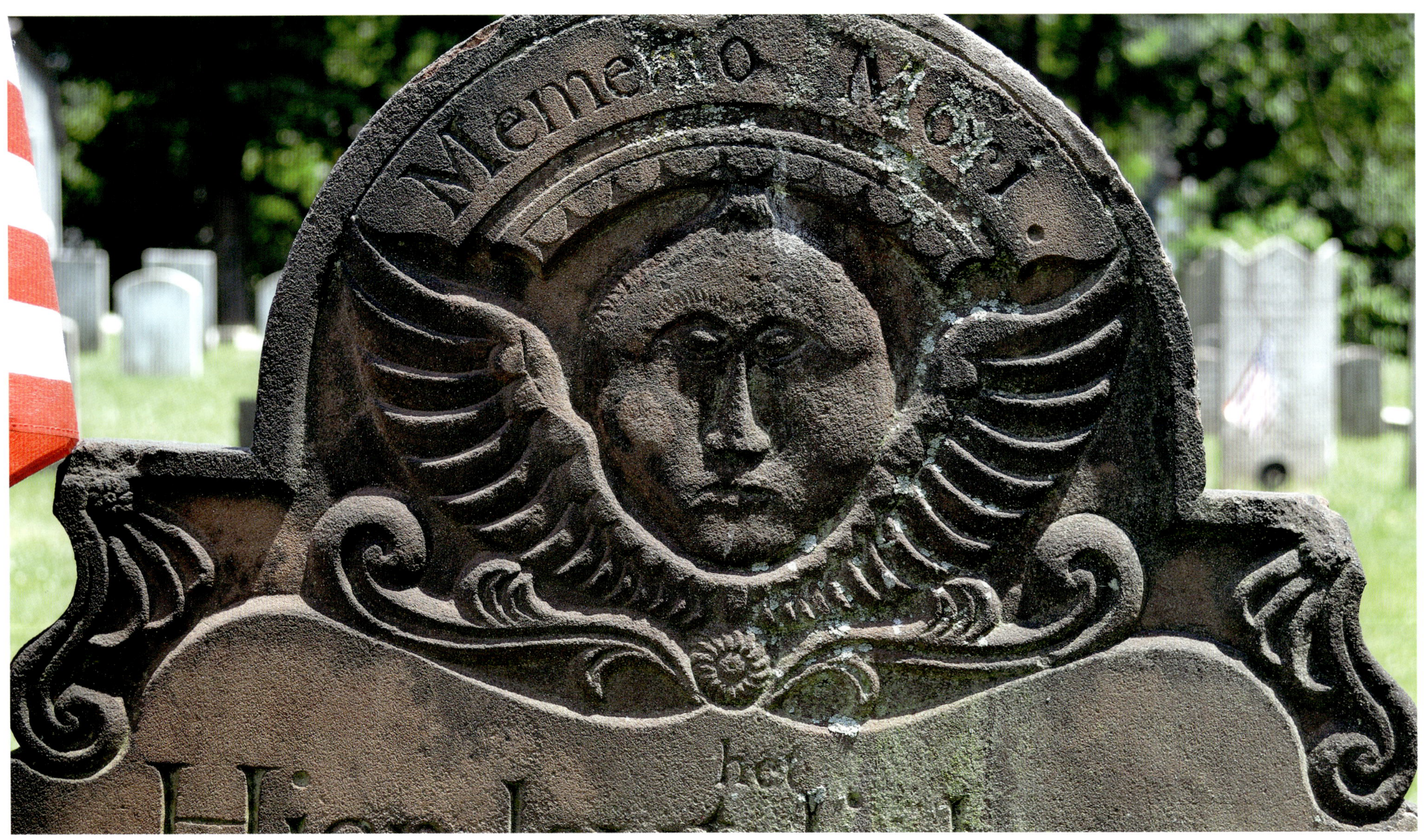

Gravestone soul effigy (Old Dutch Burying Ground)

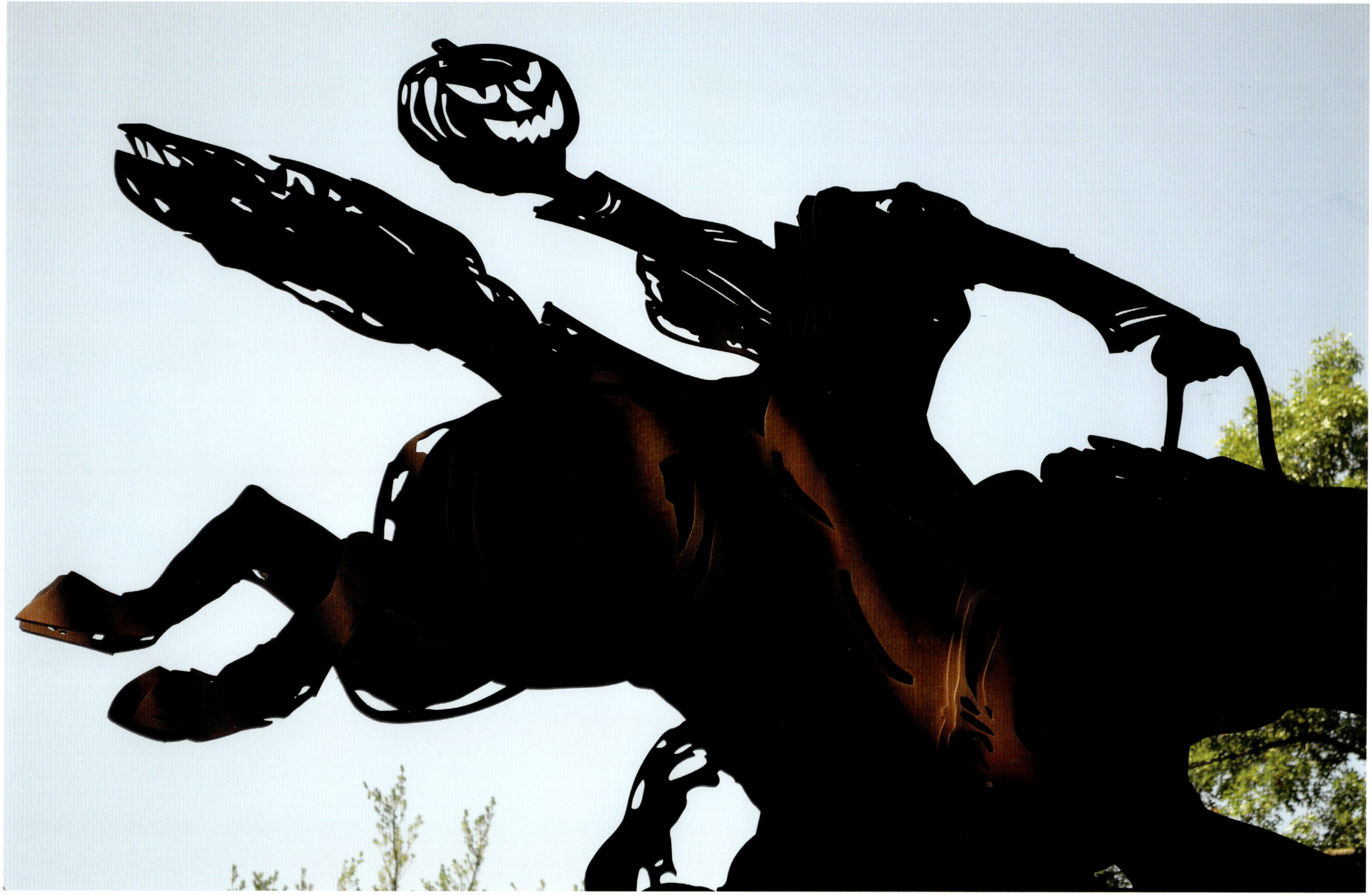

Headless Horseman along Broadway (Sleepy Hollow)

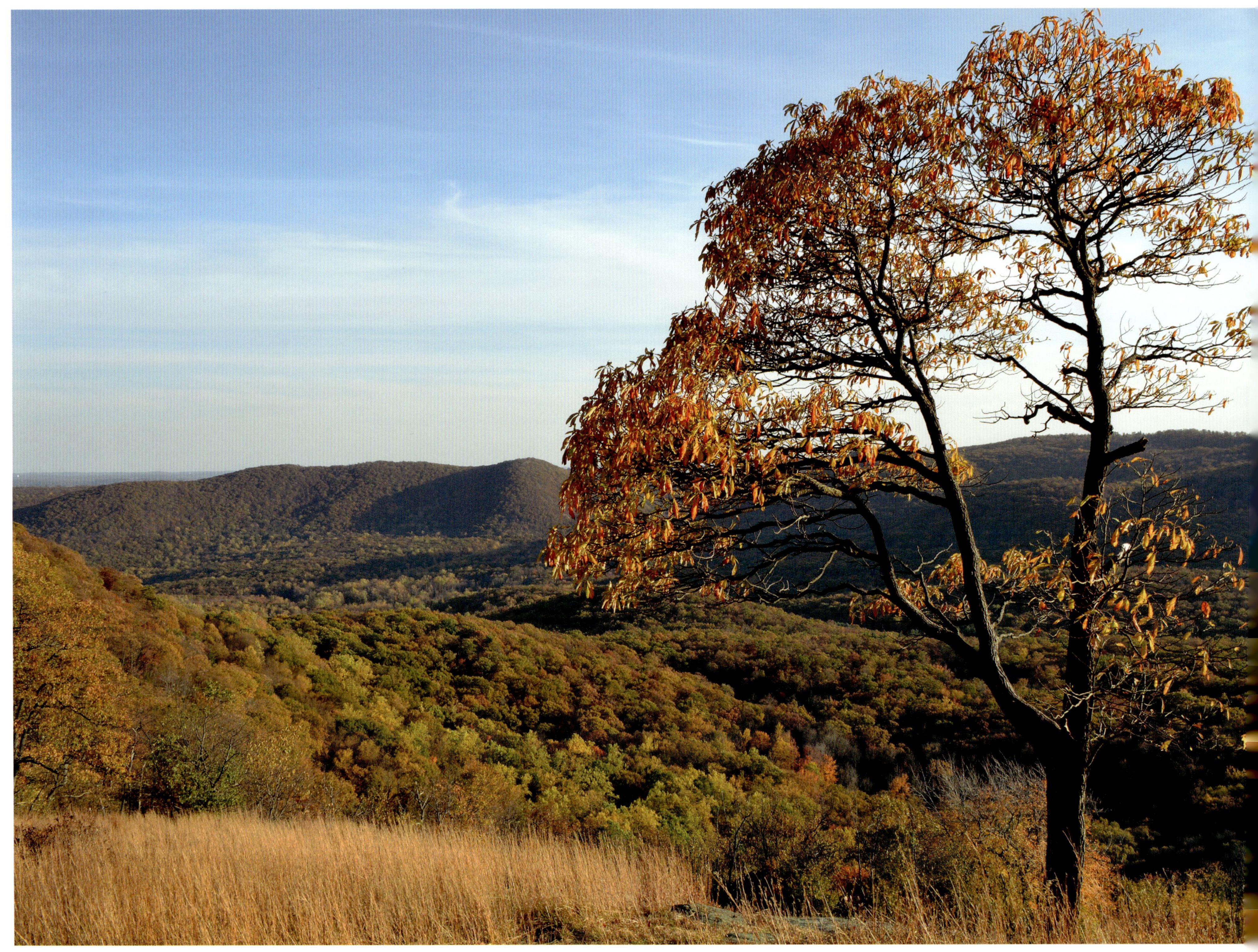

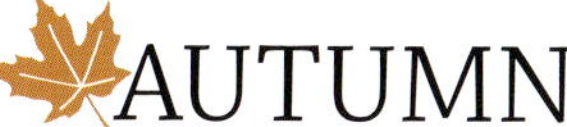

AUTUMN

New York, like the rest of the Northeast, puts on some of the most dramatic fall displays in the country. Each October the landscape becomes awash in a sea of color like a painter's palette. The most vivid scenes are to be found in the vast, uninterrupted tracts of forest in the Hudson Highlands, Taconics, Shawangunks, and neighboring Catskill Mountains. A perfect fall day is spent hiking in one of the valley's many state parks, and later stopping by a farm or orchard to partake in the season's tasty delights. Ulster County, in particular, is especially noted for its apple orchards, many of which still contain heirloom varieties far superior in taste to the fruit found in supermarkets.

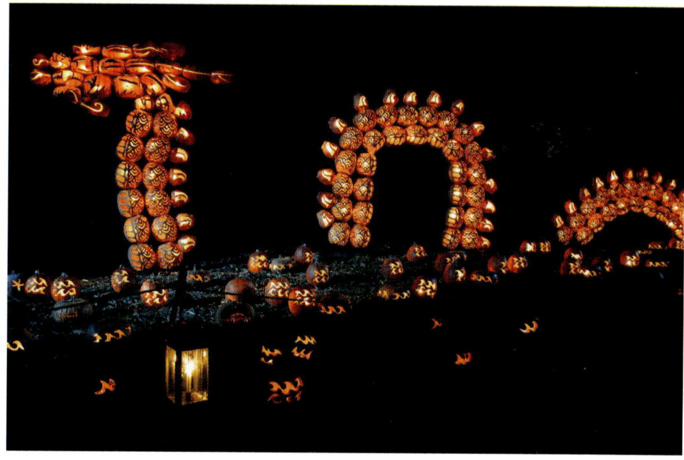

This page:
The Great Jack O'Lantern Blaze
(Van Cortlandt Manor)

Opposite page:
Bear Mountain
(Bear Mountain State Park)

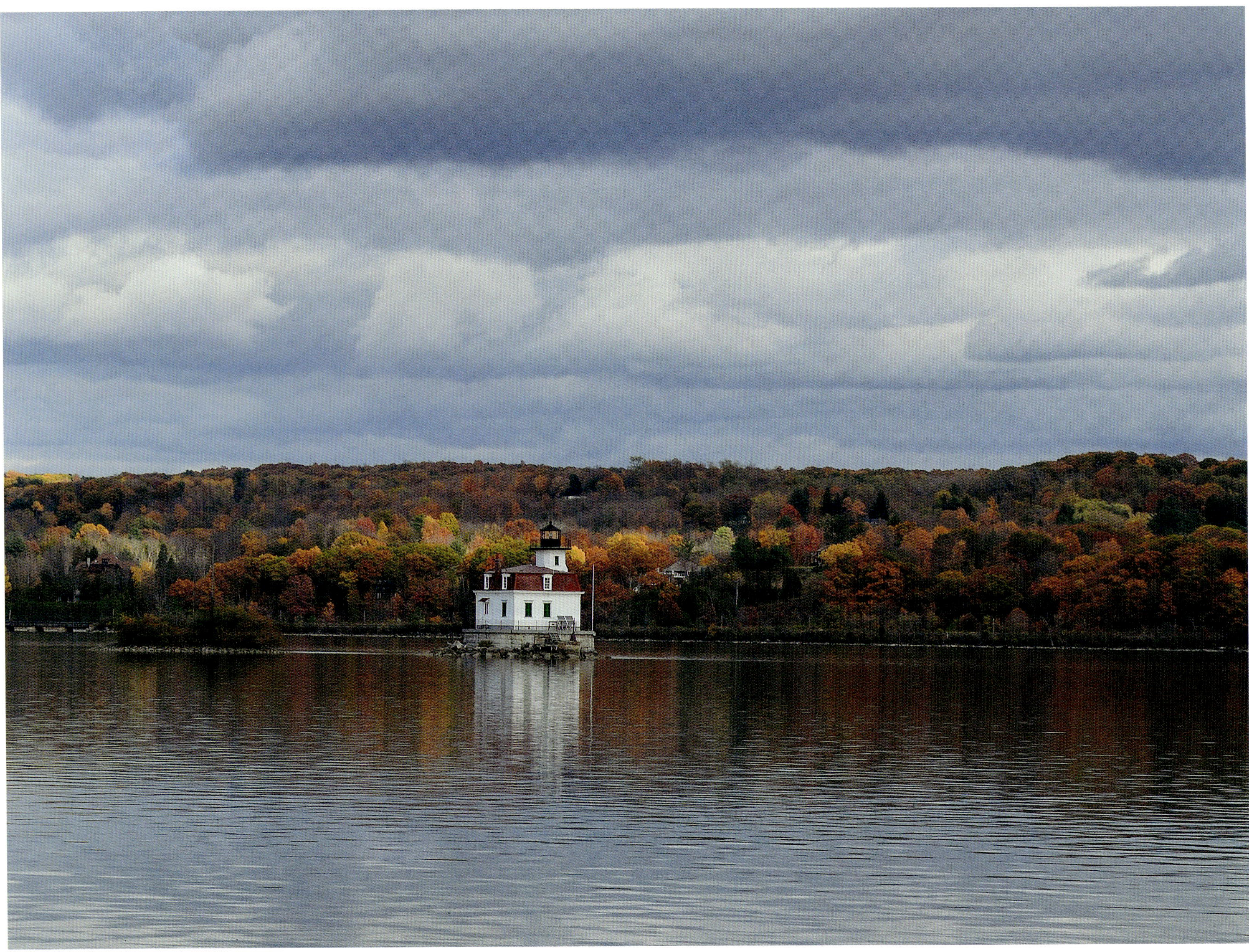

View of Esopus Meadows Lighthouse (Esopus Meadows Preserve)

The Esopus Meadows Lighthouse was constructed in 1871 atop the foundations of another nineteenth-century lighthouse that was demolished after being damaged by flooding and ice. The current structure is the sole remaining wooden lighthouse on the Hudson today. On the western side of the channel, its primary duty was to warn travelers of the expansive mud flats that clog the river near the town of Esopus.

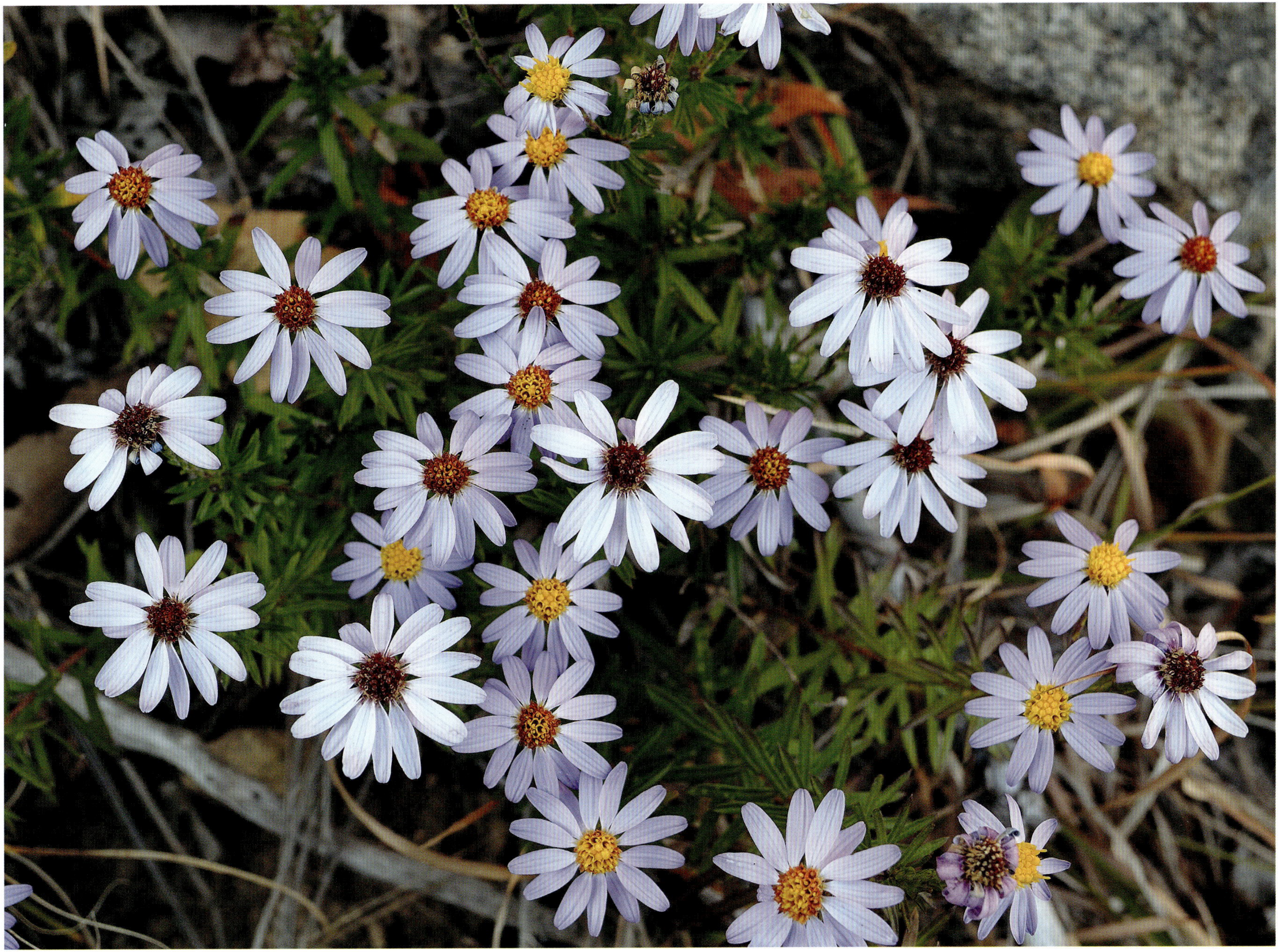

Stiff asters on Storm King Mountain (Storm King State Park)

When most other plants begin wrapping things up for the year, asters first make their appearance. Blooming in late August, and depending on the species, sometimes continuing up until the end of October or November, these flowers put on a show rivaling the foliage of senescing trees. Though 150 distinct aster species inhabit the US, many look nearly identical to one another, making identification tricky. Surveying the forests and fields during the fall is one activity sure to keep you busy for countless hours. How many types can you find?

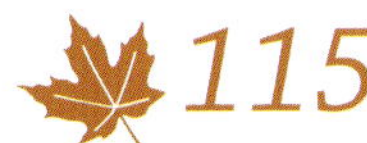

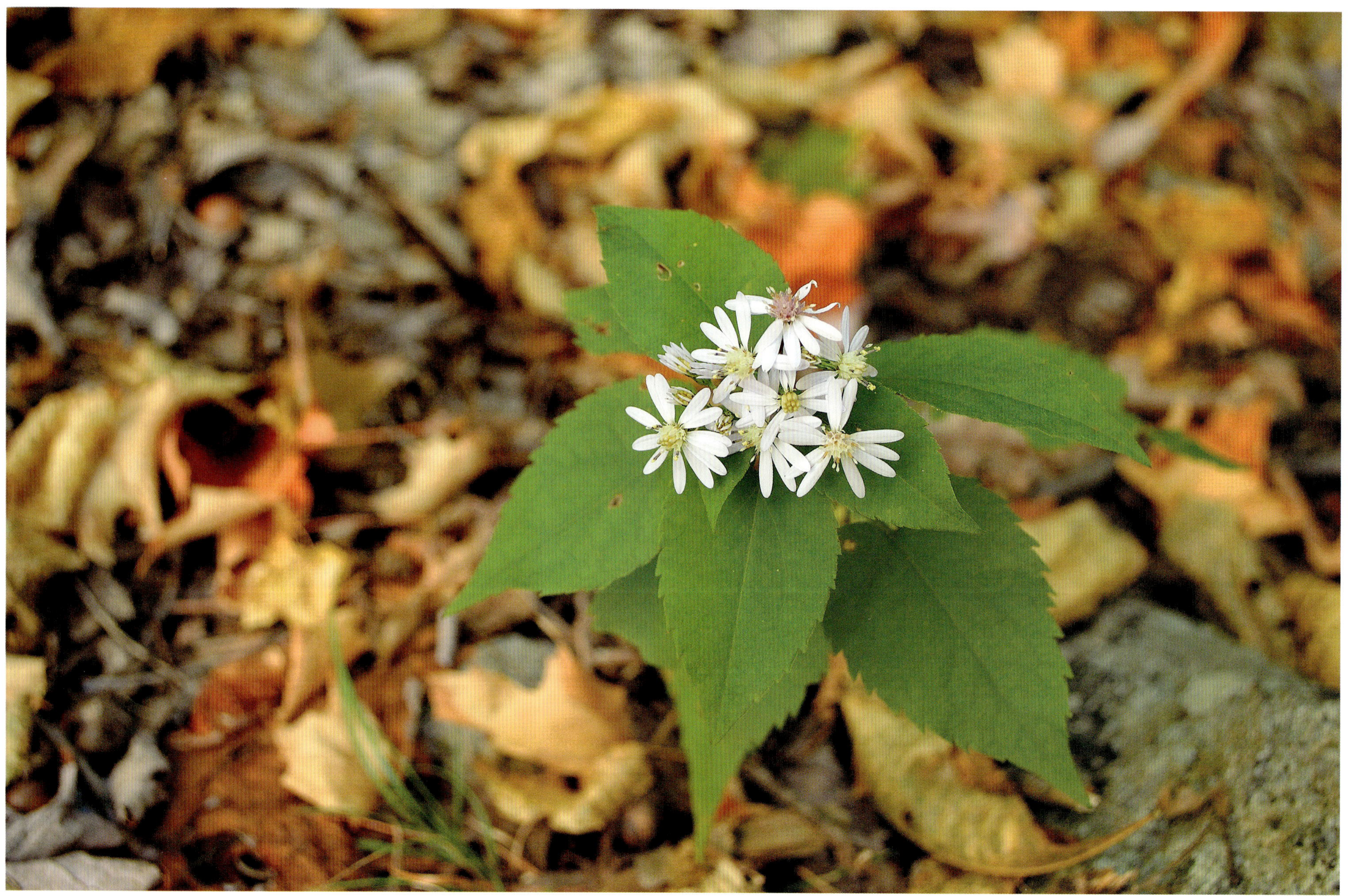

White wood asters (Fahnestock State Park)

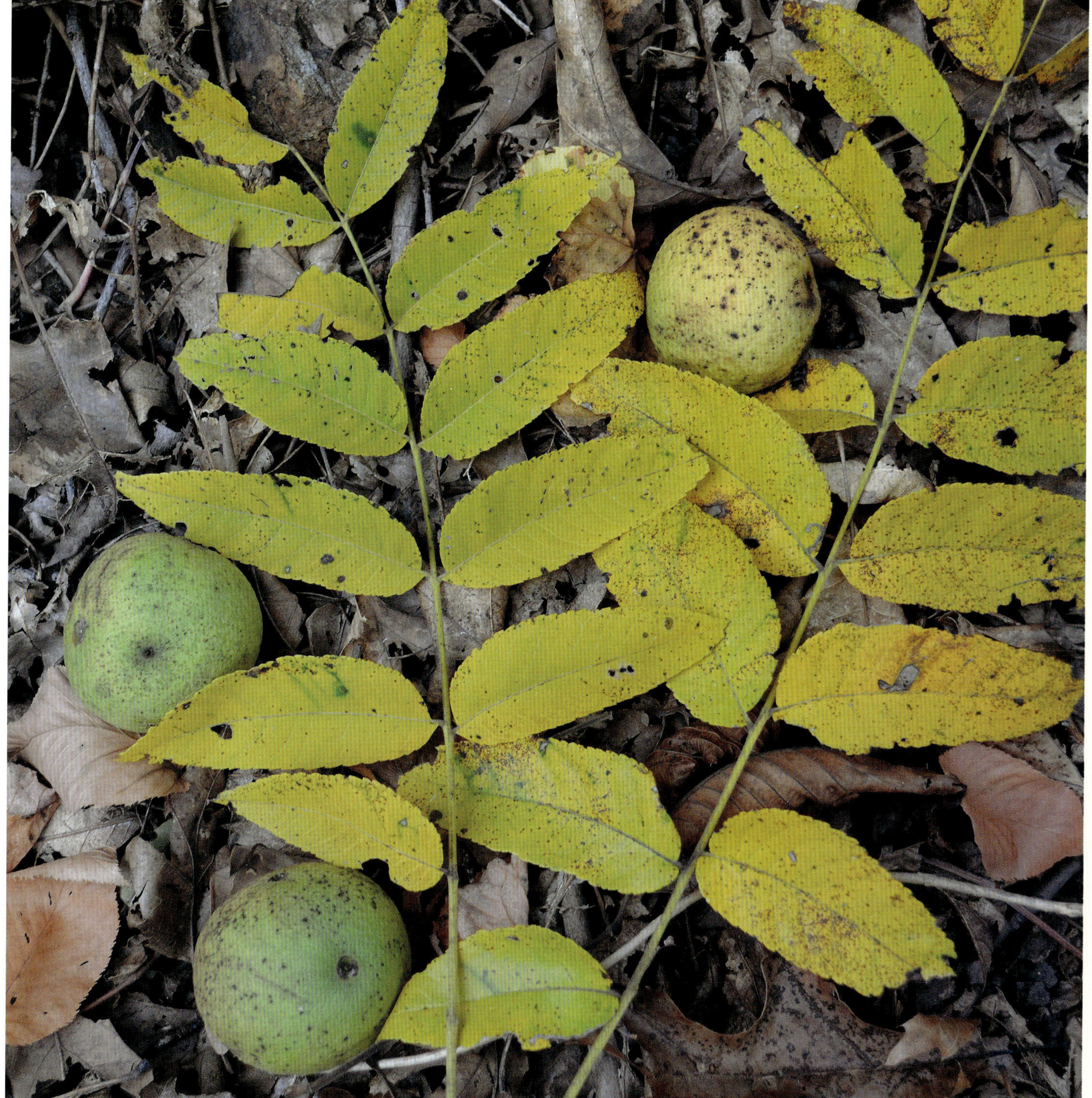

Black walnut (Bear Mountain State Park)

Anyone who has ever looked beneath a black walnut tree has probably noticed that few plants grow there. This is not due to a lack of sunlight.

Black walnut is an "allelopathic" species, meaning it produces a substance that alters the growth of other plants. All parts of the tree contain a growth-inhibiting substance known as juglone. This natural herbicide is released via decomposing leaves and nut husks, though live roots will also discharge small quantities as well. Juglone is weakly water soluble. This ensures the chemical doesn't easily leach from the soil, thereby helping to reduce competition.

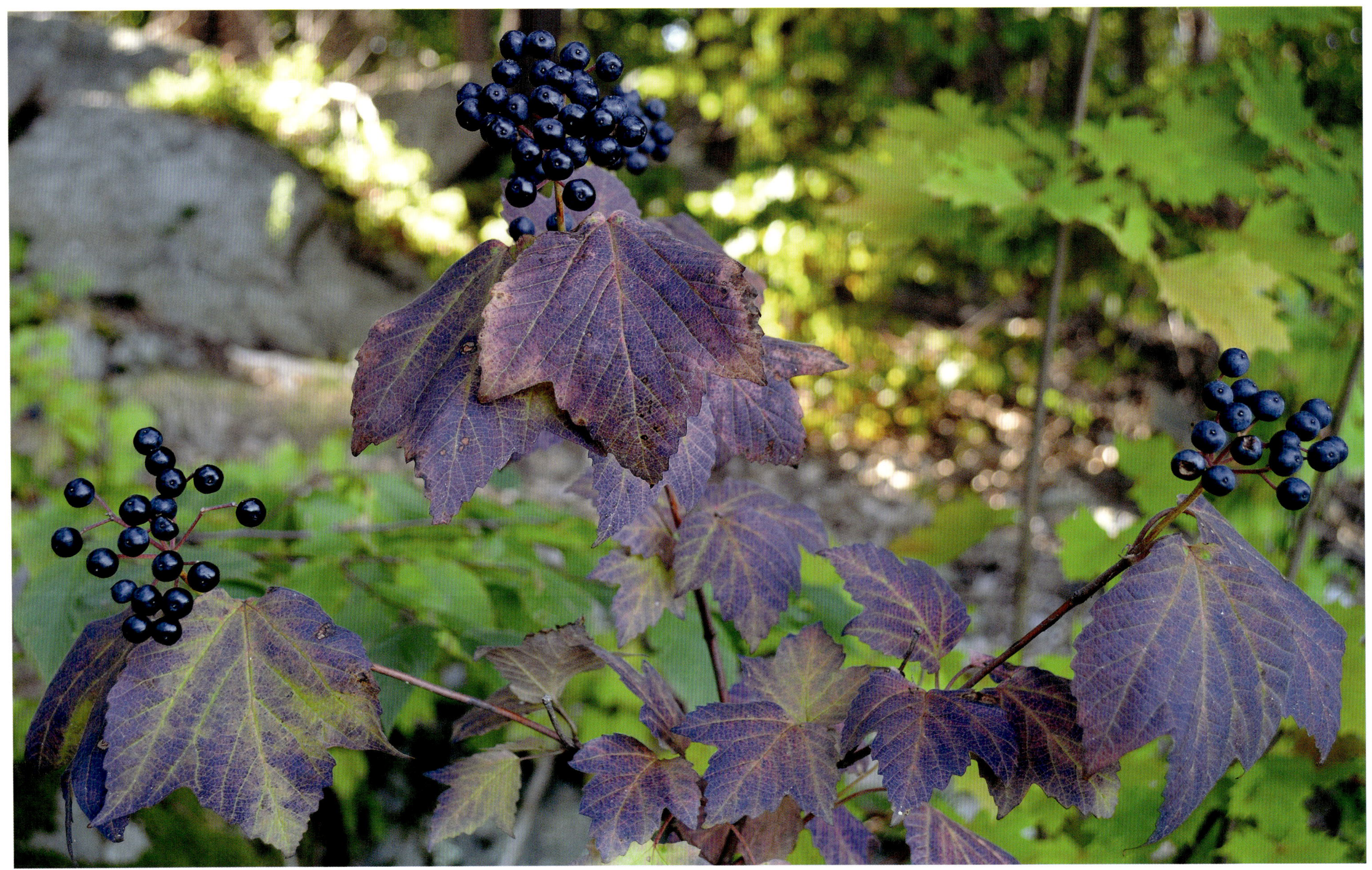

Maple-leaf viburnum (Schodack Island State Park)

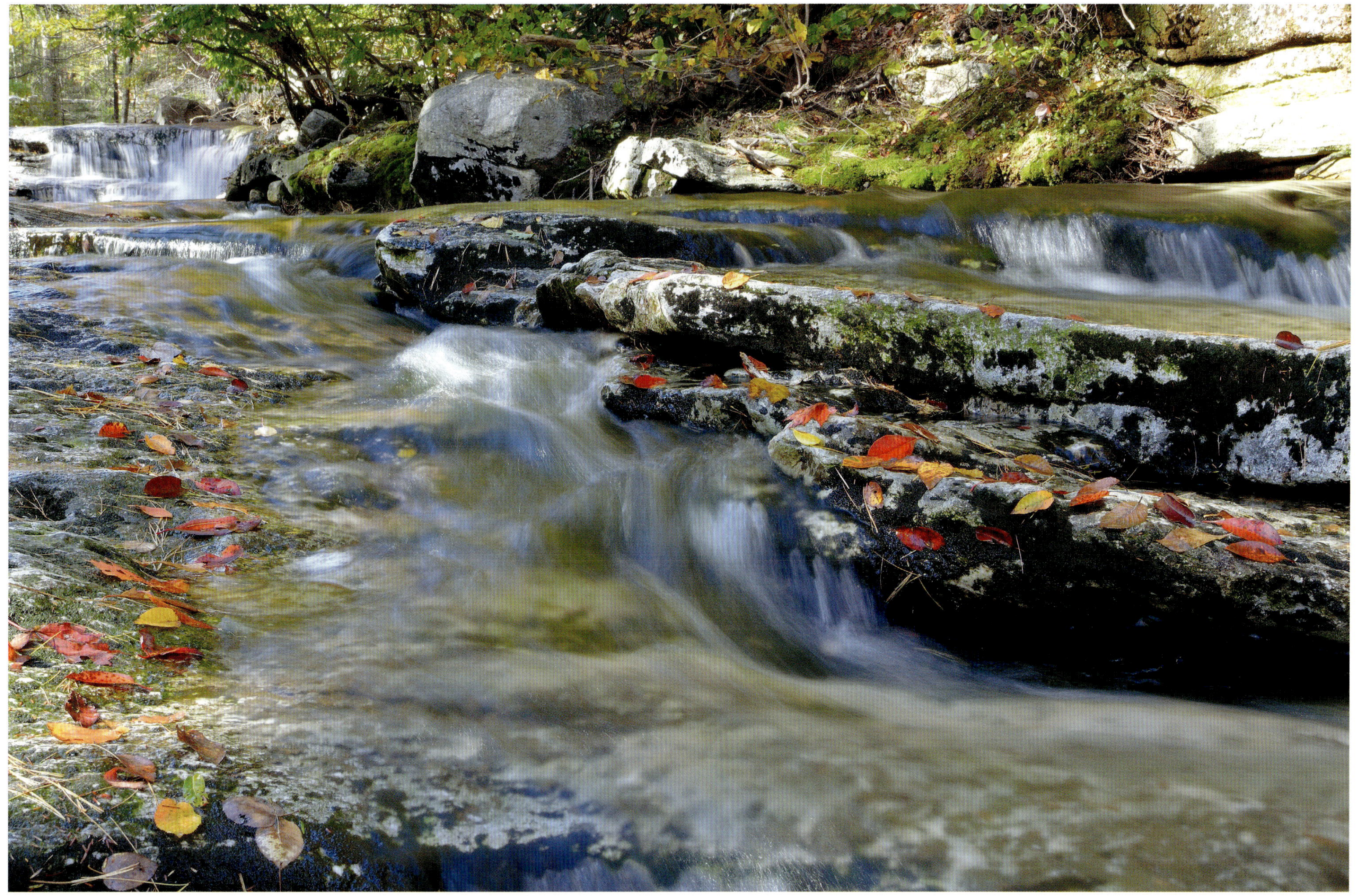

Peter's Kill (Minnewaska State Park)

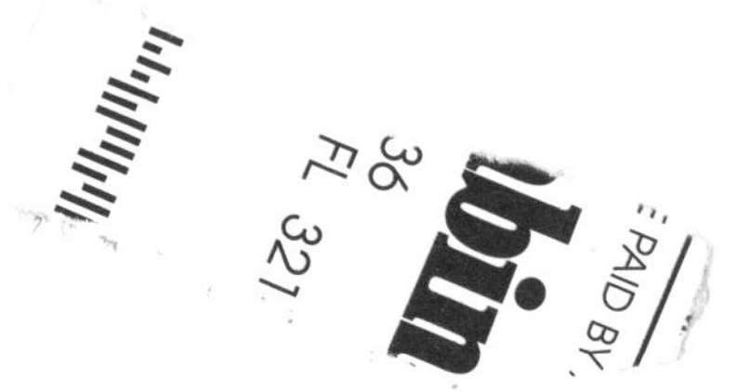

The ubiquitous white rock known as Shawangunk conglomerate, which is studded with quartz pebbles and predominates across the Shawangunk Ridge, was originally gravel dumped by several massive rivers flowing to a shallow sea in western New York during the Silurian Period (430 mya). Slowly the gravel became cemented together after being buried in quartz-rich groundwater for eons. On certain rock outcroppings erosion has weathered the binding agent and the pebbles have loosened. You can pick one up and know you're holding something that was shaped just as the first creatures climbed out of the seas and began to colonize land.

The Shawangunk Ridge is also the premiere destination in the Hudson Valley to glimpse traces of much more recent geological history. The last glacial period, which ended about 12,000 years ago, left its mark across the region, even on the highest mountain peaks, as ice was miles thick in places. While the topography of the entire region clearly shows the power of glacial ice sheets and is dotted with innumerable associated features like rugged ravines and canyons, moraines, kettle ponds, teardrop-shaped hills known as drumlins, and out-of-place boulders, or glacial erratics, the Shawangunks display the more subtle features that have disappeared in other places due to weathering. Shawangunk conglomerate is extremely hard and resistant to erosion. Stone outcroppings planed and polished by the ice have changed very little since the ice retreated north. Grit and boulders trapped underneath the glacier etched fine grooves and striations, along with larger crescent-shaped chattermarks, into the bulldozed stone. These marks reveal the exact direction of the glacier's movement on a southwest course.

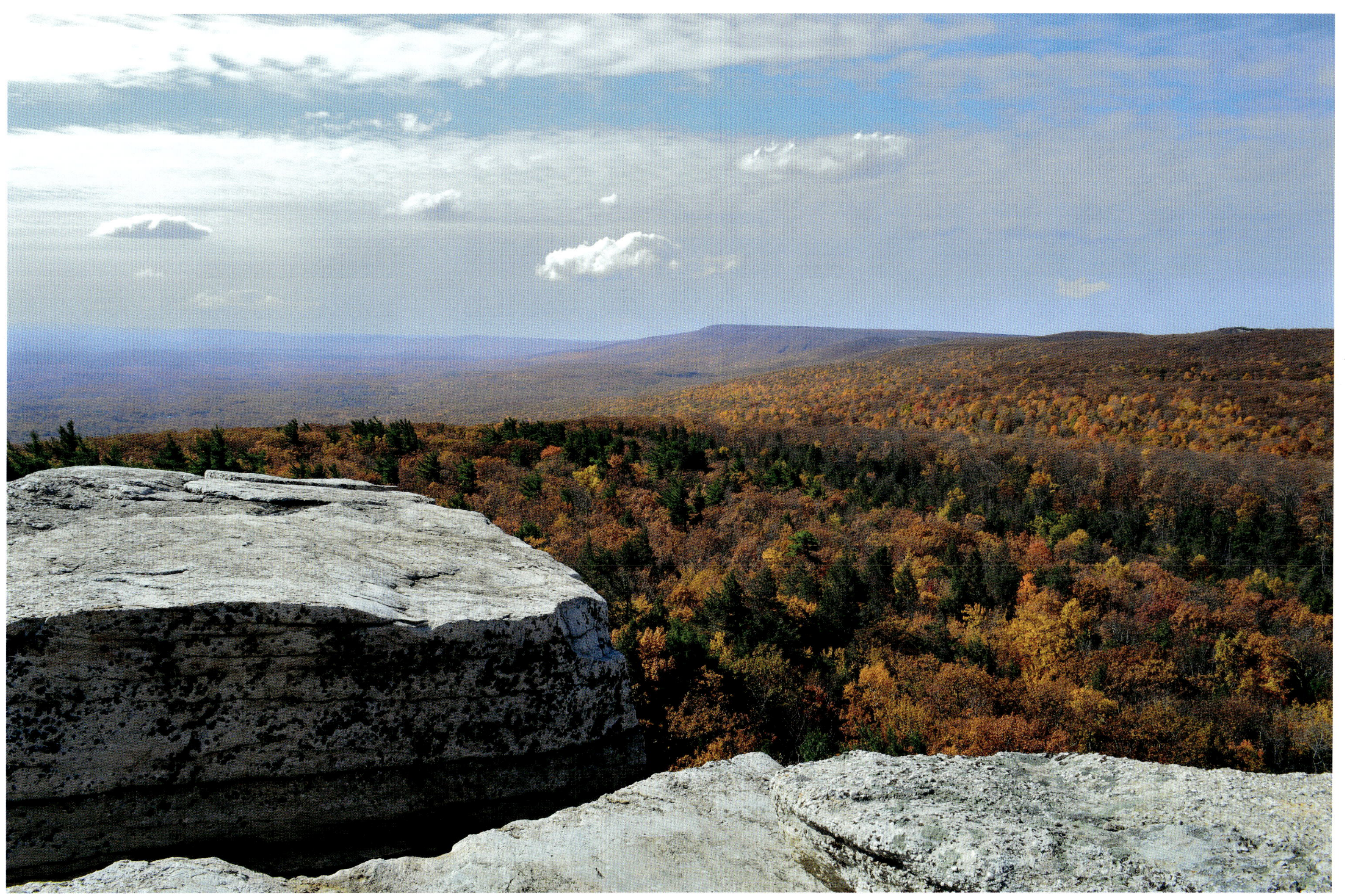

Gertrude's Nose (Minnewaska State Park)

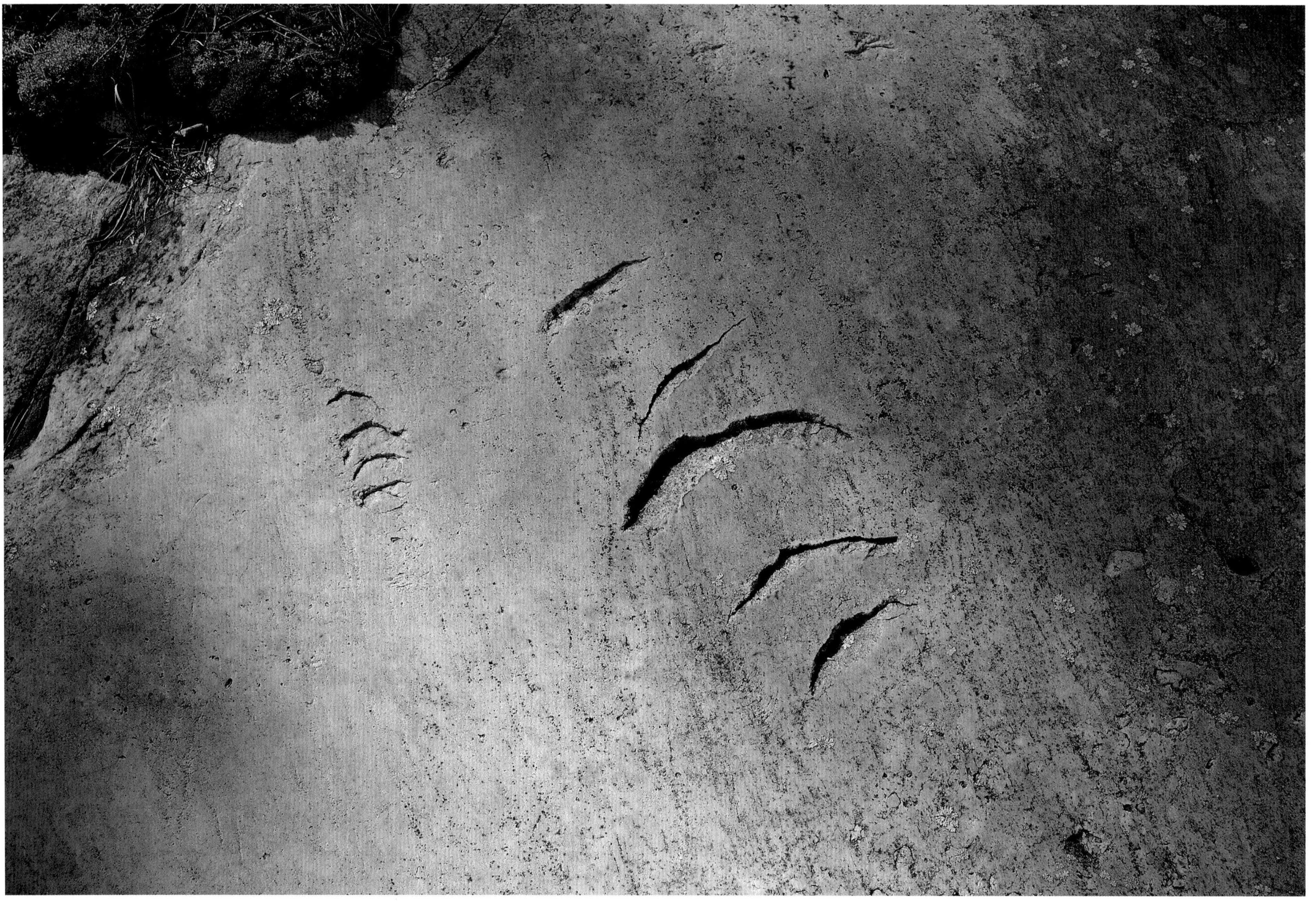

Glacial chattermarks
(Minnewaska State Park)

The linear pattern of crescent-shaped marks in the stone were created by a boulder trapped underneath a glacier of the last Ice Age. Unlike pebbles or small rocks that are drawn smoothly along by the ice and end up producing thin, continuous lines, more friction is exerted by larger debris, and will thus only move periodically. When the advancing glacier eventually exerts enough pressure to counteract the friction, the boulder quickly gives way and forcefully jumps forward, chipping the underlying bedrock where it lands.

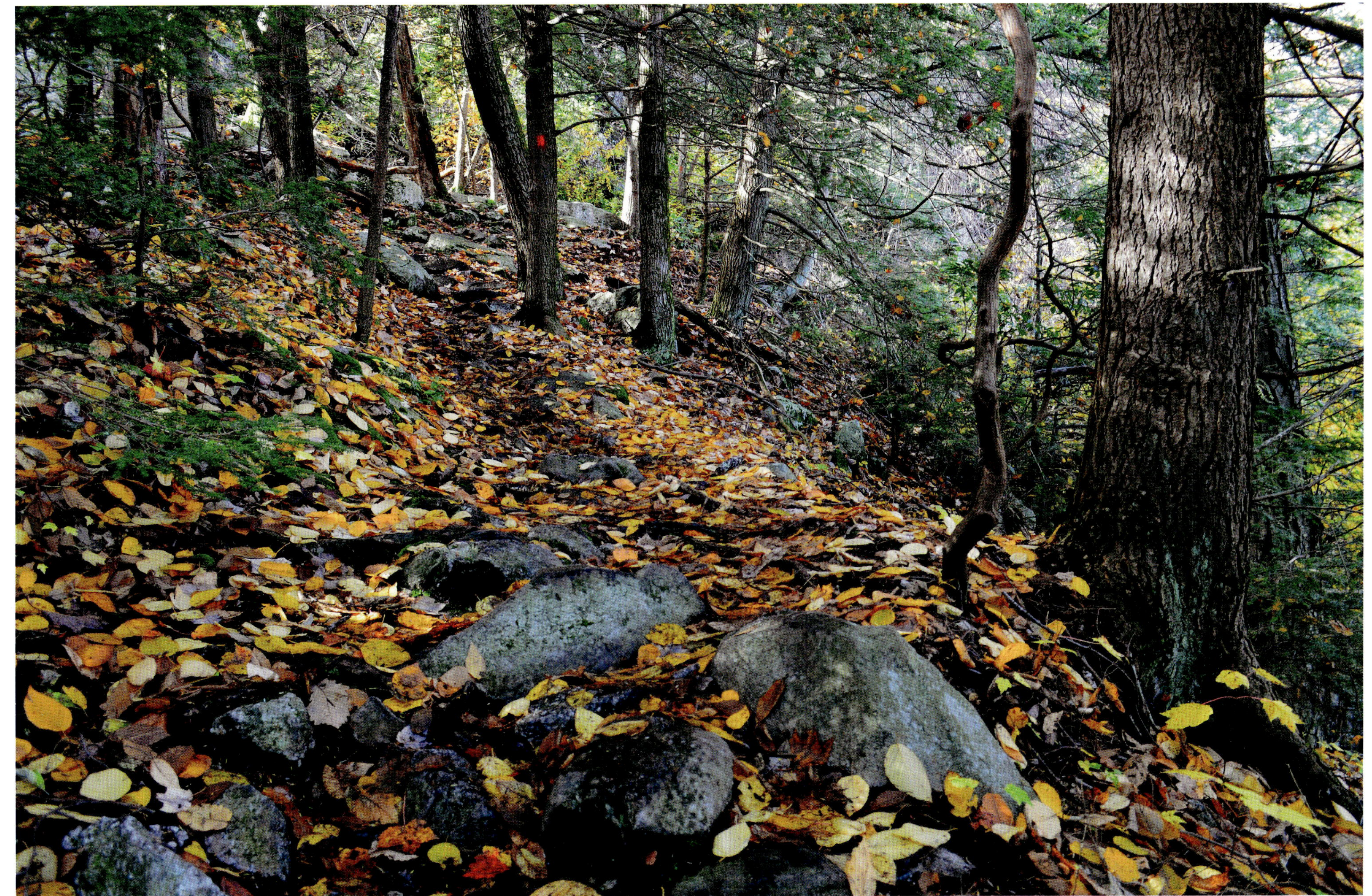

Millbrook Mountain (Minnewaska State Park)

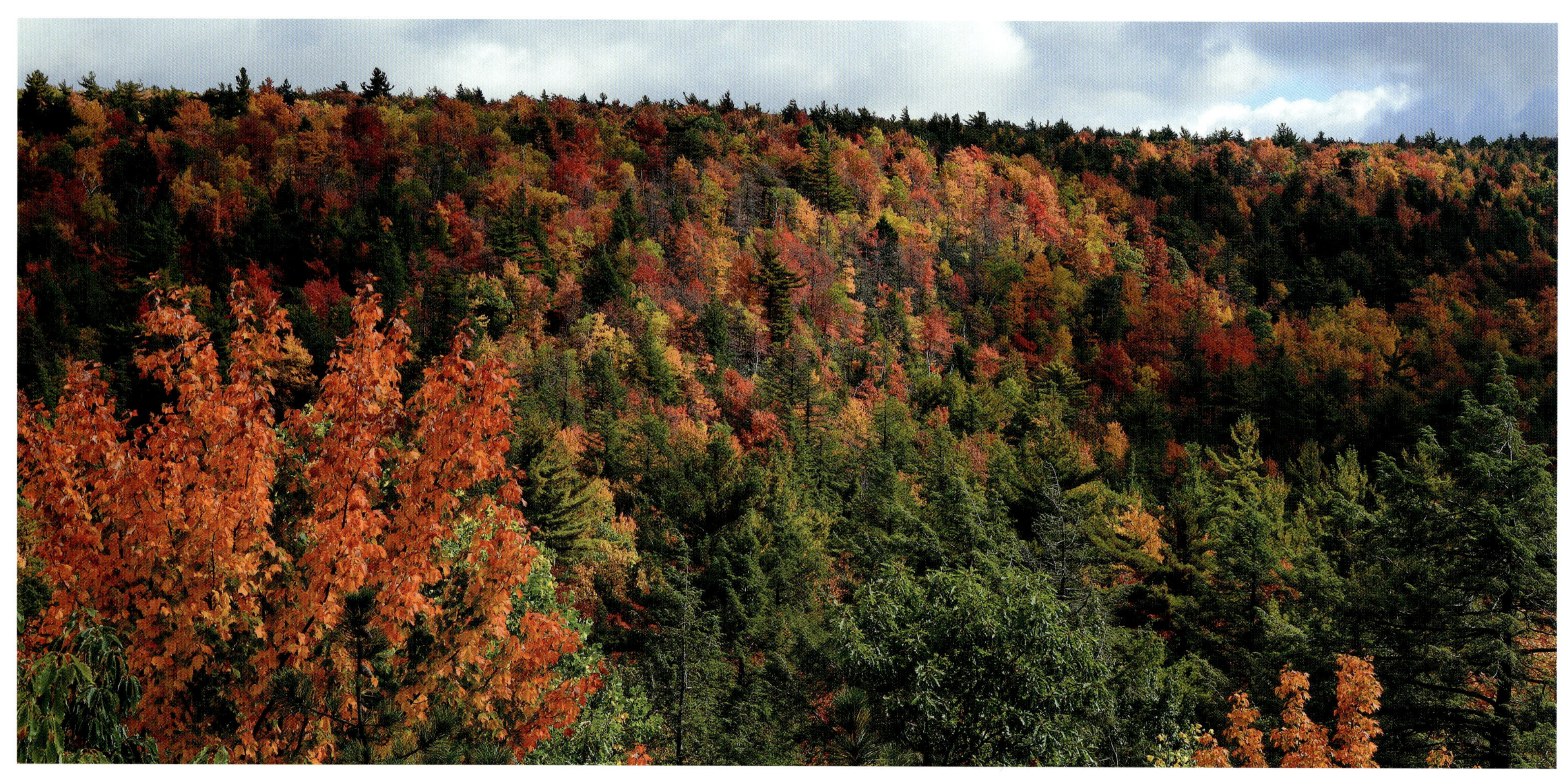

Autumn in the Shawangunk Mountains (Minnewaska State Park)

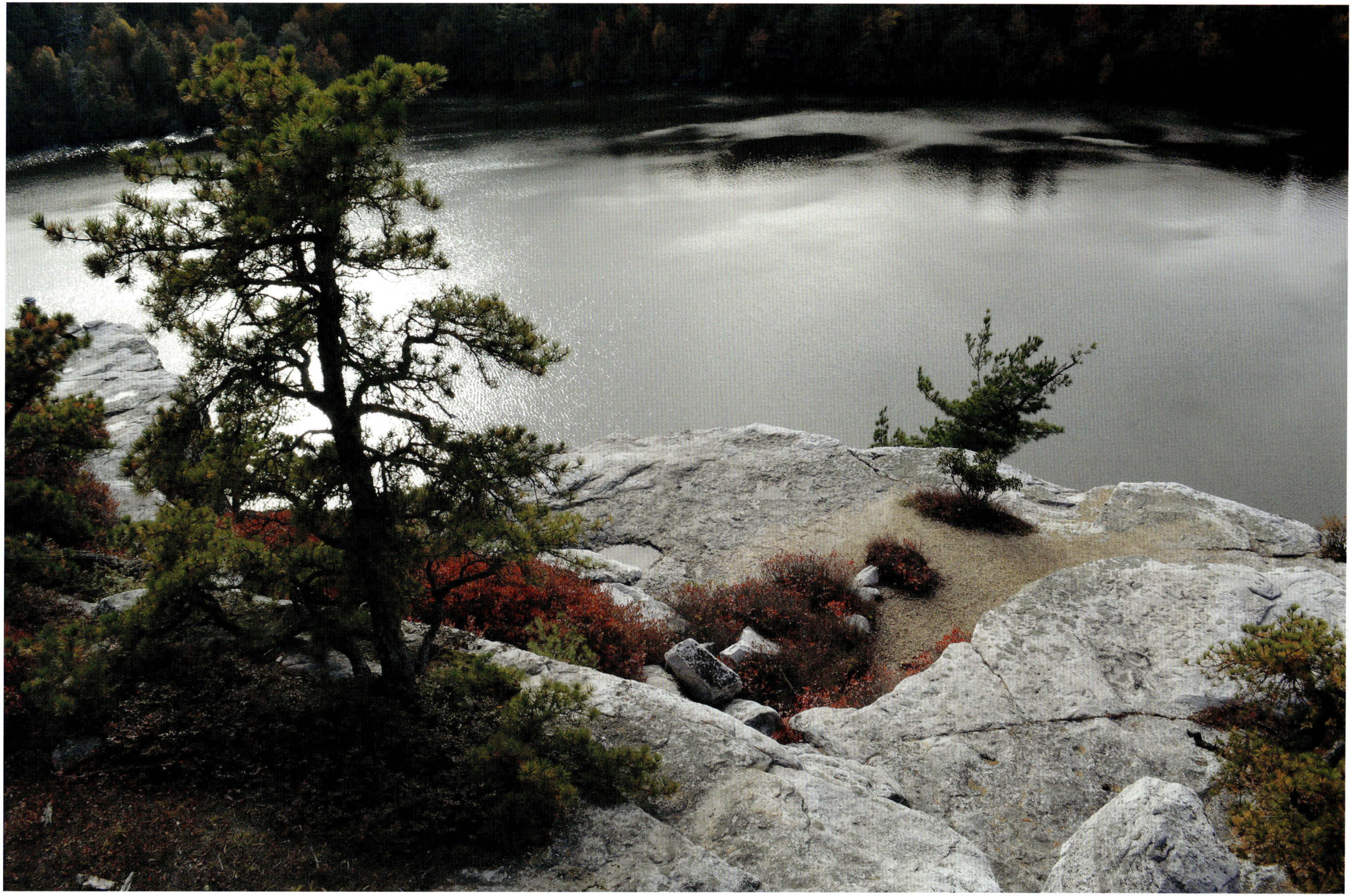

Lake Minnewaska

Once known as Coxing Pond, Lake Minnewaska was named by Alfred Smiley after his purchase of a 2,200-acre tract of land containing the lake in 1875. Wanting a more Native American-sounding name to appeal to guests who occupied the two hotels he and his brother had constructed near the lake, he chose Minnewaska, though it did not come from the language of any local tribe. By 1986, both hotels had been destroyed by fire. A year later, New York State acquired the property and transformed it into parkland.

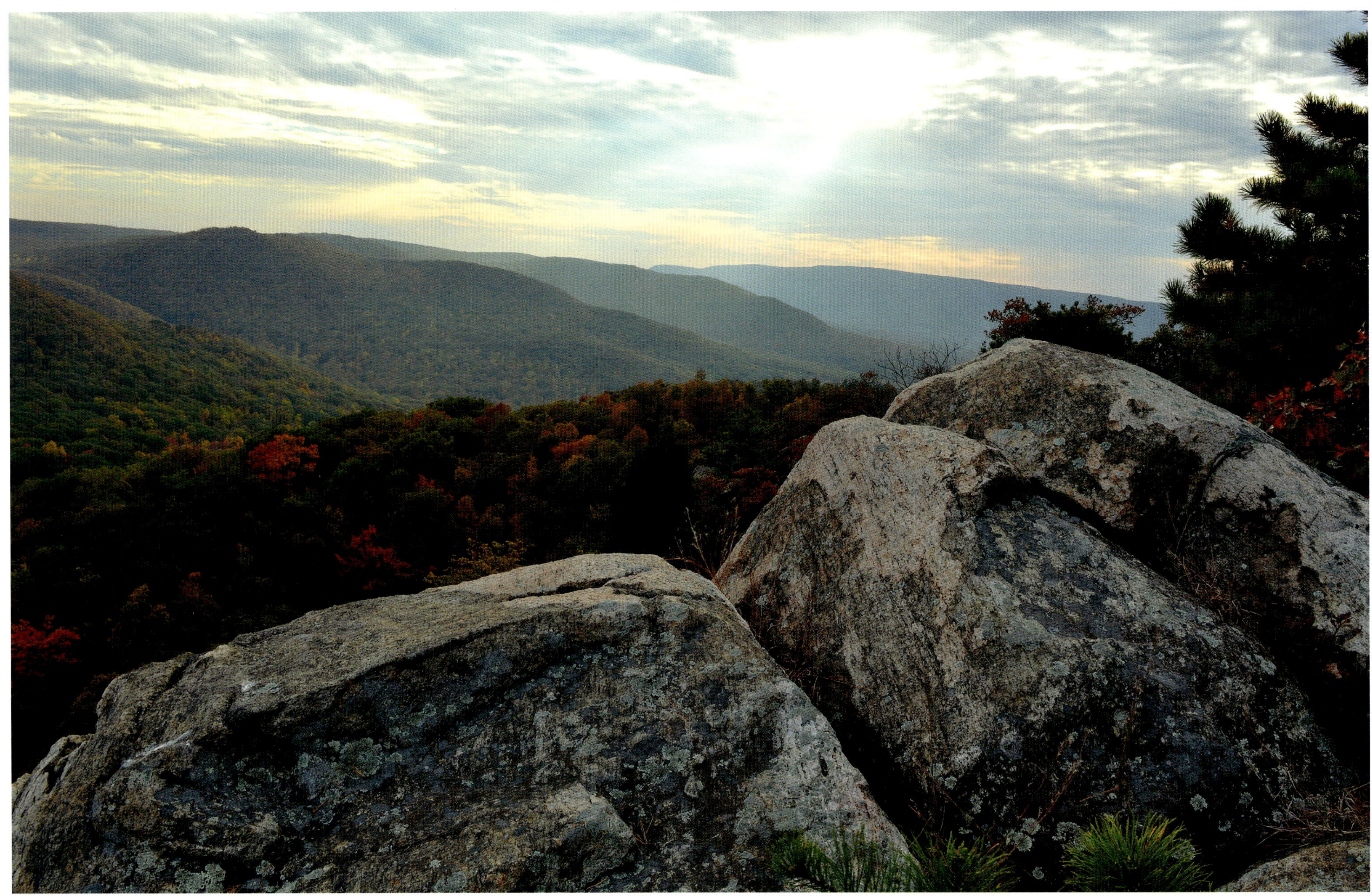

Storm King Mountain

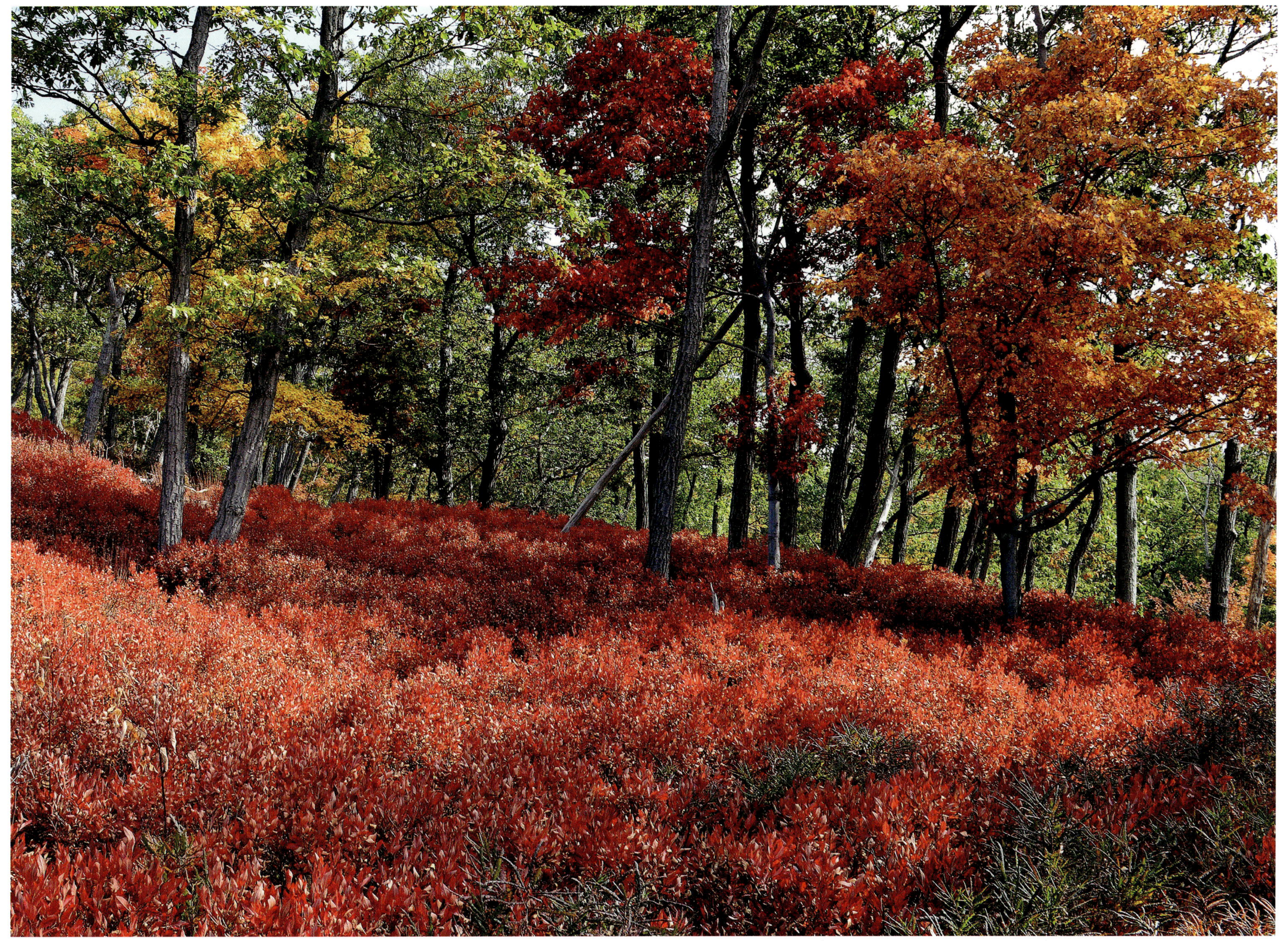

Crimson understory of huckleberry bushes atop North Point (Storm King State Park)

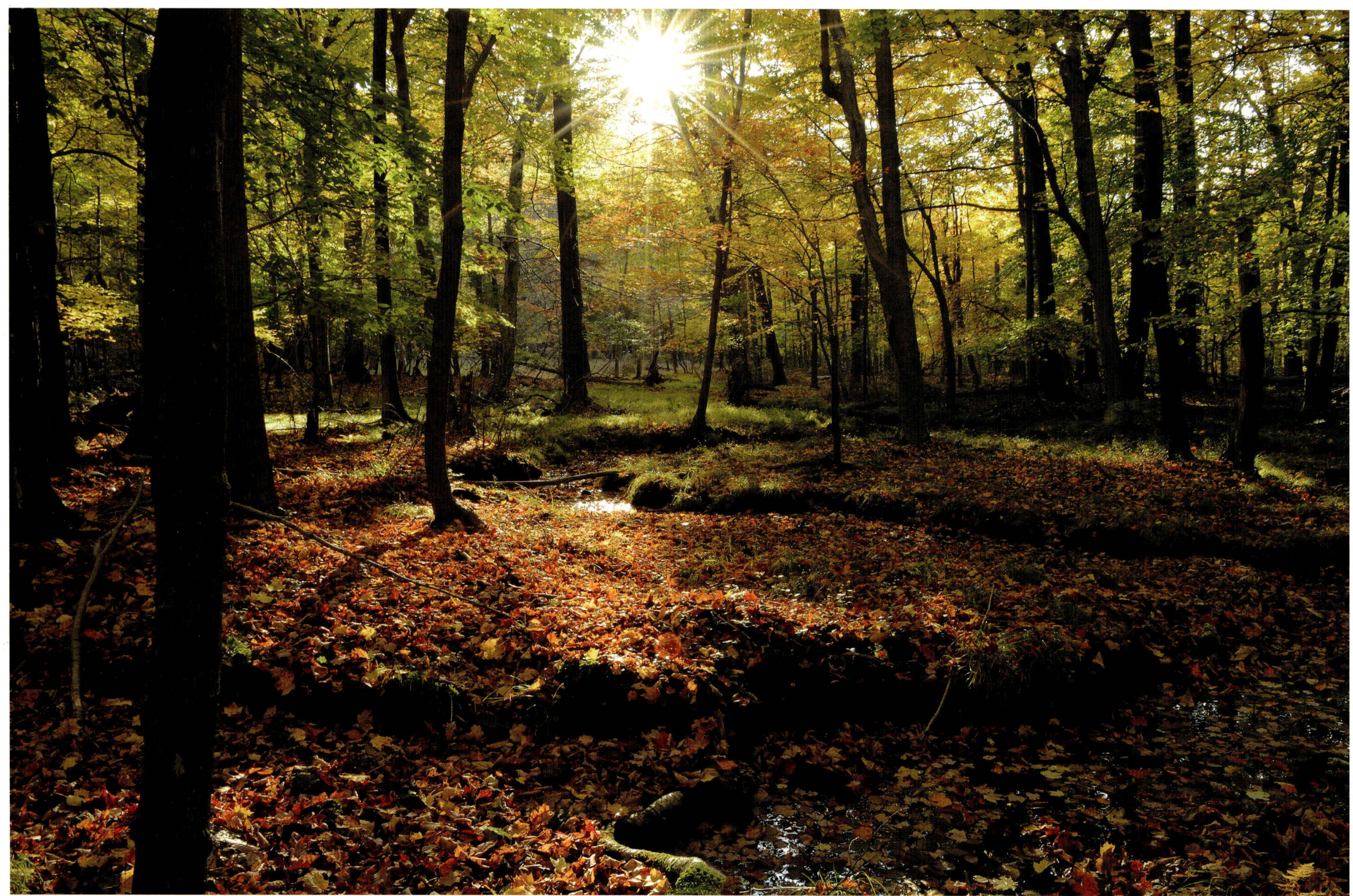

North Point sunset

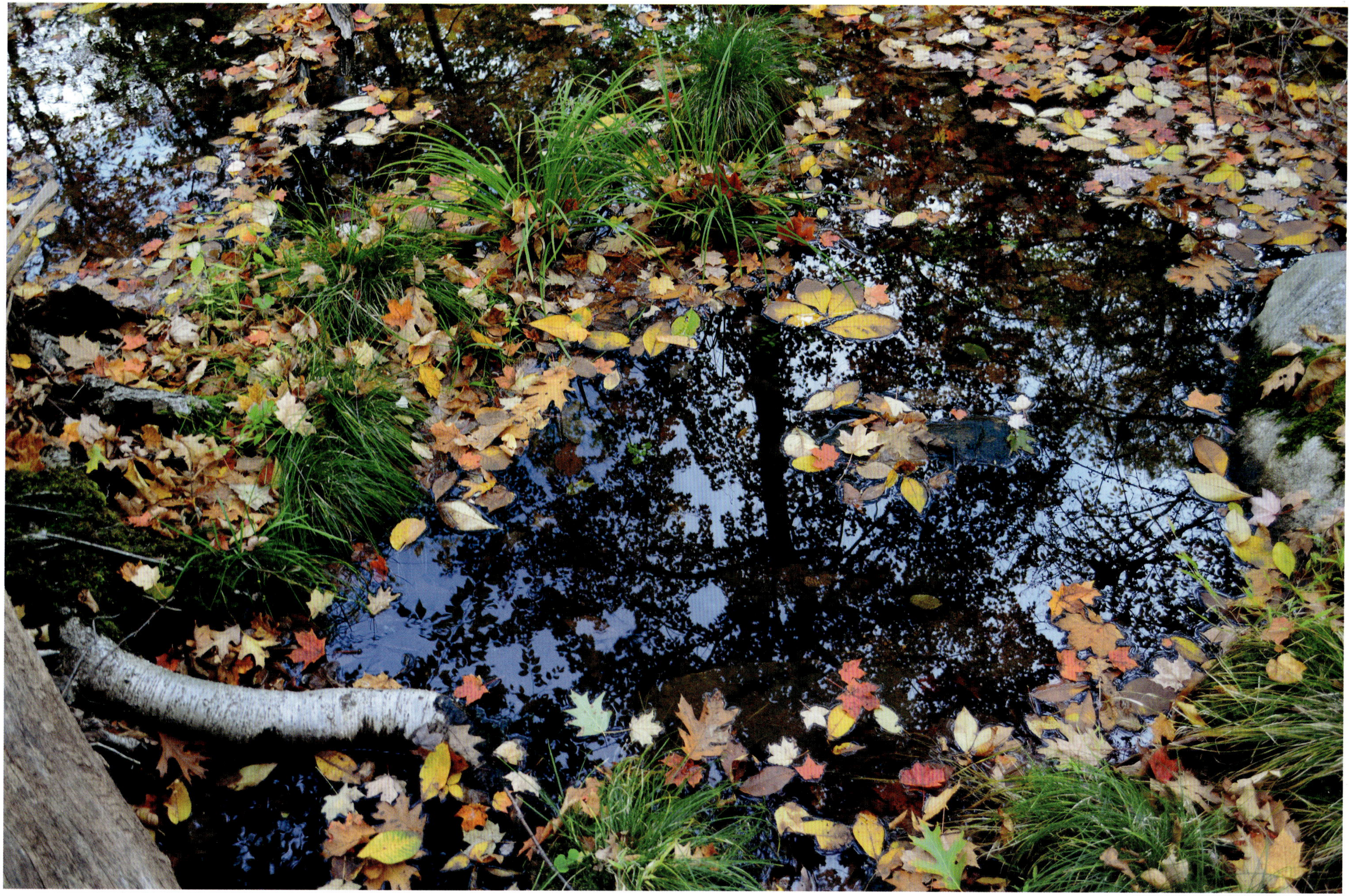

The changing of the leaves is driven not so much by temperature as by length of day. Longer nights stimulate cells in the abscission layer of the leaf near the juncture of the stem to divide, forming a corky barrier that cuts off the flow of nutrients to the leaf. As the green chlorophyll begins to break down, accessory pigments—the carotenoids and xanthophylls, which produce vivid oranges and yellows—are revealed. Reds and purples come from anthocyanin, a pigment formed from sugar trapped in the leaf once the link to the stem has been severed. Dry weather often results in subpar leaf displays due to limited sugar production that aids in the manufacture of anthocyanin.

Colors of fall (Four Mile Point Preserve)

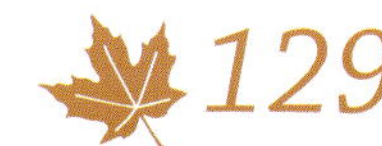

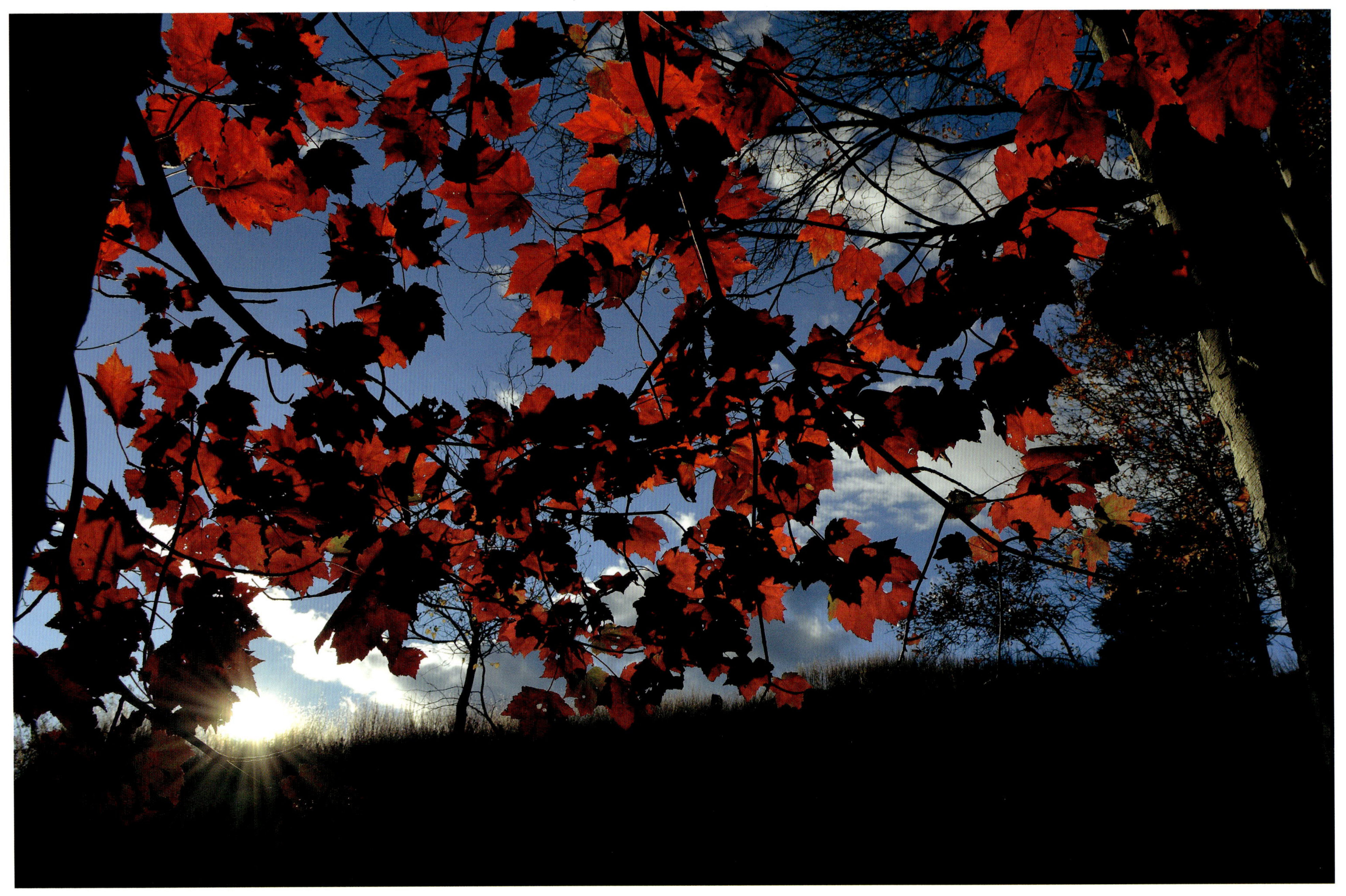

Red maple sunset (Storm King State Park)

Prized for its exceptionally brilliant crimson and occasionally lemon-hued leaves in the fall, this tree serves as a native ornamental. Apart from its vivid color scheme, red maple is ideal for landscaping as it grows well in a variety of soils. This is the most common tree in the country, which makes sense considering its uncanny level of adaptability. In the wild, red maples can be found equally thriving among soggy low-light swamps, rich well-drained woodlands, and thin, sunbaked soils of exposed mountain slopes.

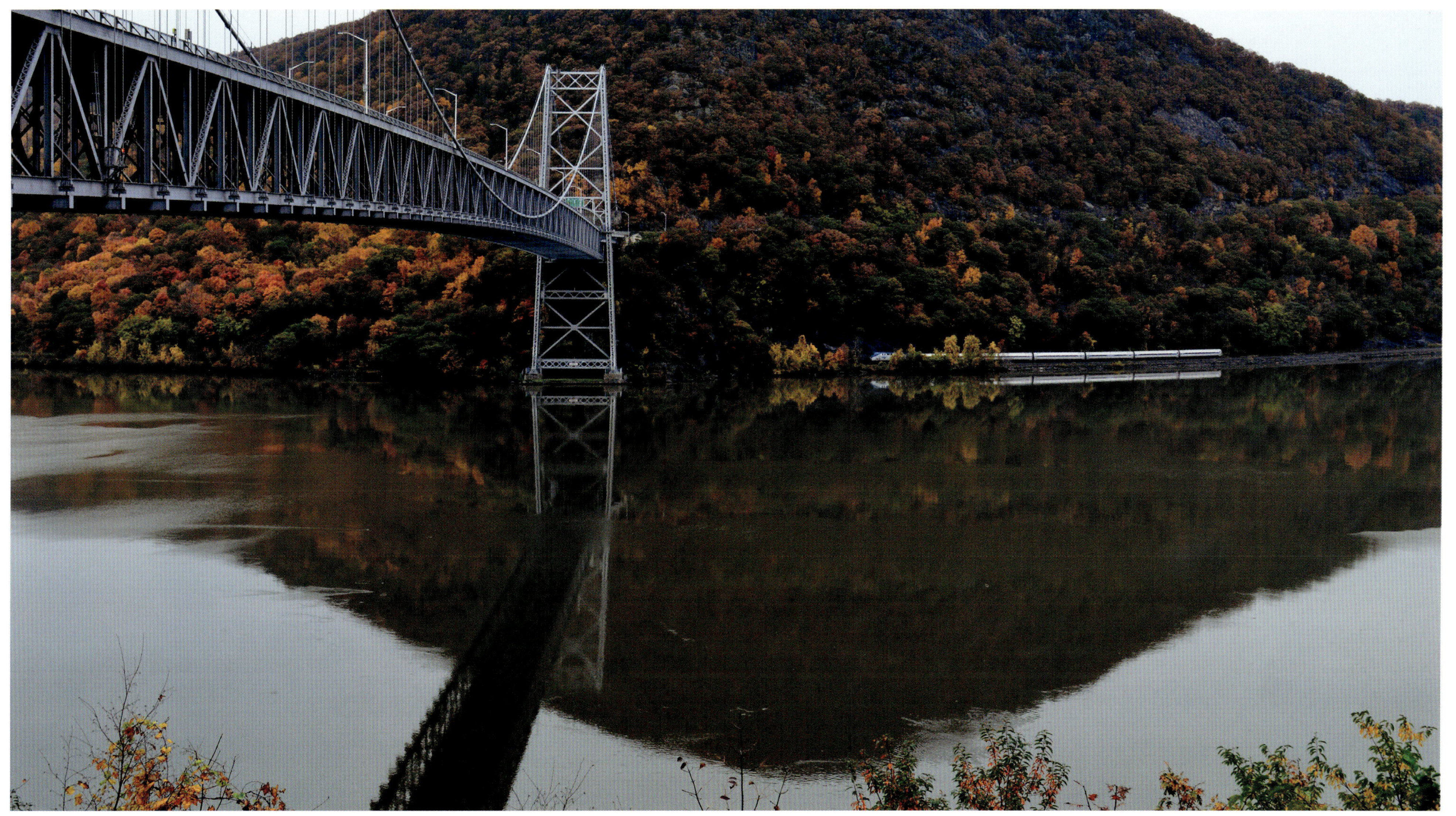

Bear Mountain Bridge (Trailside Museums & Zoo)

The lower Highlands are also historically significant. Bear Mountain Bridge forms a wall that separates two Revolutionary War fortifications on the western shore of the Hudson, similarly to the "Great Chain" that stretched across the river from Fort Montgomery to Anthony's Nose in the 1770s. The massive chain, with links two feet long and weighing sixty pounds, was constructed to keep British ships from passing northward in their attempt to sever the New England colonies from the rest of the country. Fort Montgomery lies to the north of the bridge and Fort Clinton to the south. Together, these twin forts were flanked and overrun by British and Hessian Forces in October 1777. Many American militia members slaughtered in the siege had their bodies thrown into "Bloody Pond," the waterbody now known as Hessian Lake at the base of Bear Mountain.

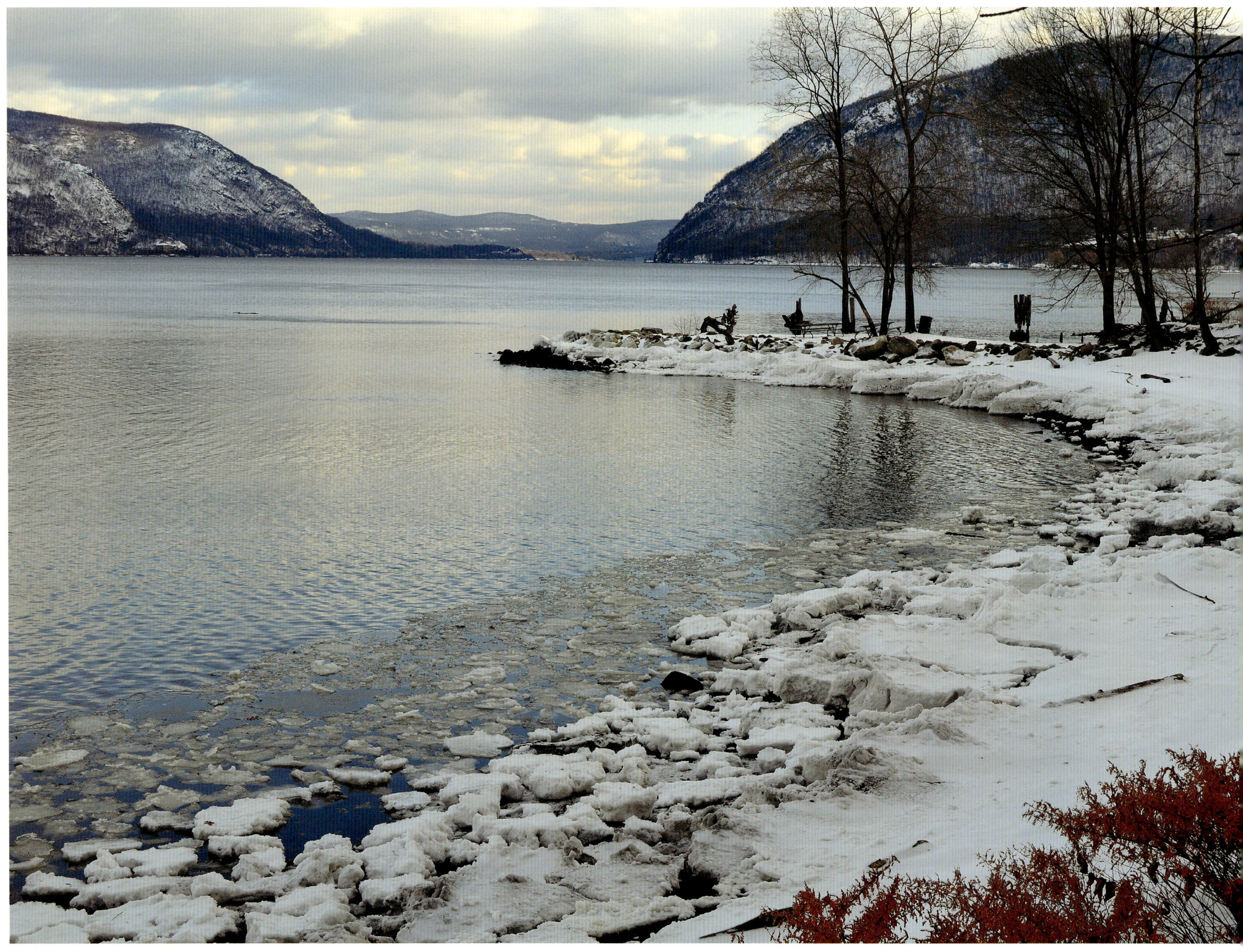

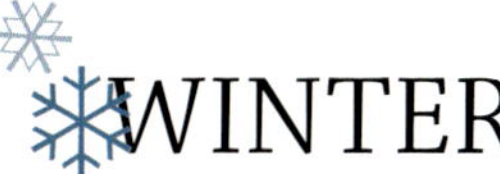

WINTER

Even in winter the Hudson has its charms and supports diverse outdoor activities. Wildlife watching is enhanced, as eagles and harbor seals are greatly contrasted against the bright ice floes they're apt to rest on. When captured in a long-exposure photograph, chunks of ice floating north or south, depending on the tide, leave trails that look like the silky rings of Saturn. Harsh beauty also graces the shoreline, where formidable heaps of ice, jagged and congested, provide a scene reminiscent of the arctic-lying Hudson's Bay. In the upper reaches of the river, ice yachts can sometimes be seen furiously racing along the frozen surface in protected bays left undisturbed by the icebreakers clearing the deep-water channels.

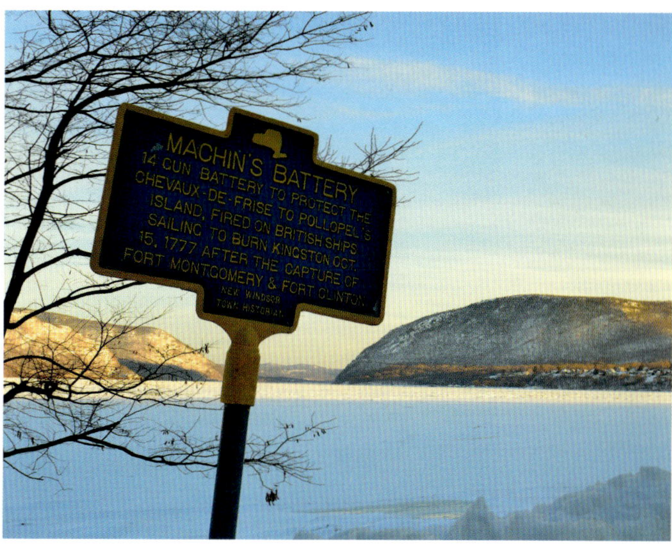

This page:
View of "Wey-gat," Dutch for Wind-gate, marking the northern entrance of the Hudson Highlands (Plum Point)

Opposite page:
Winter at Plum Point

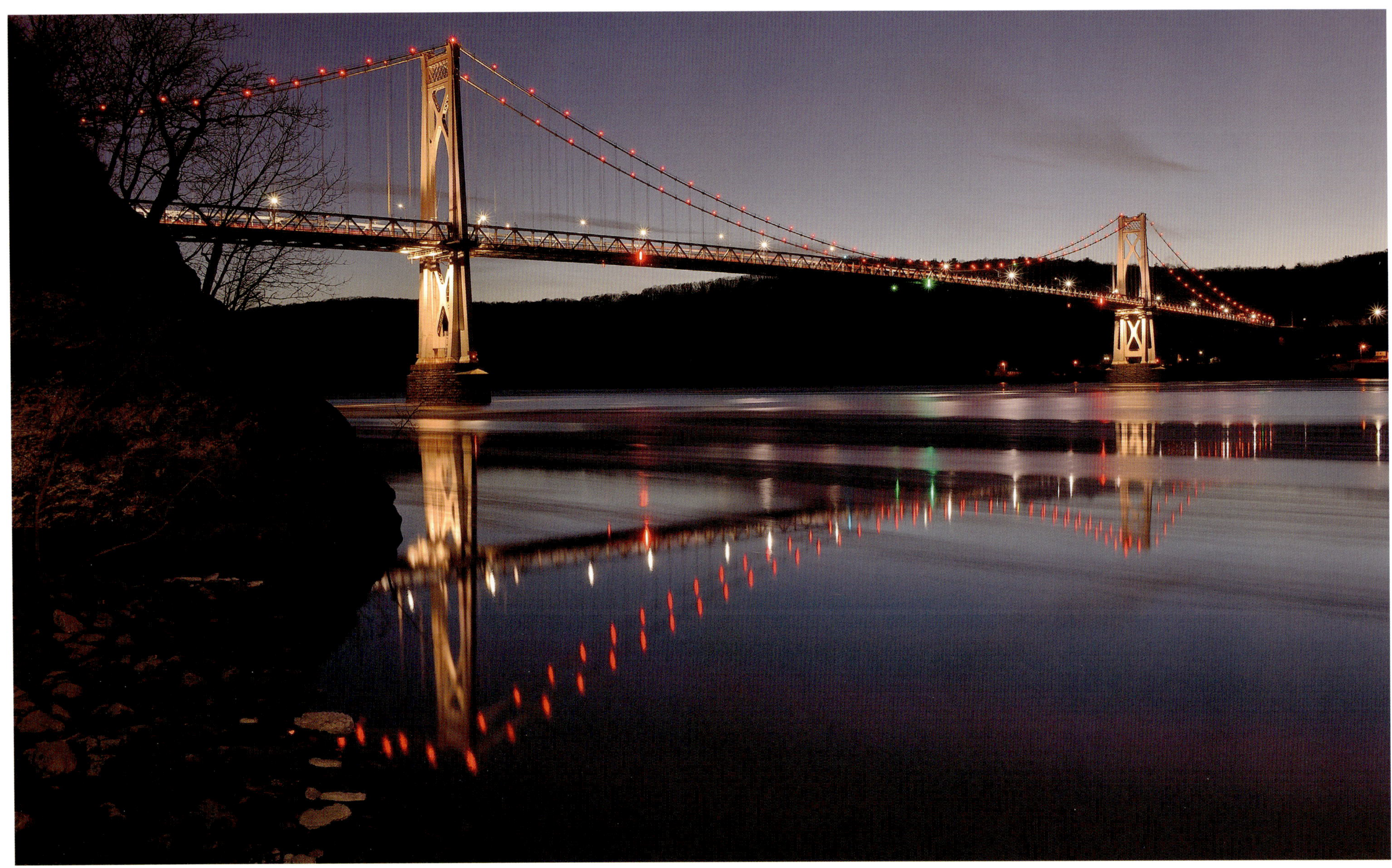

Mid-Hudson Bridge (Waryas Park)

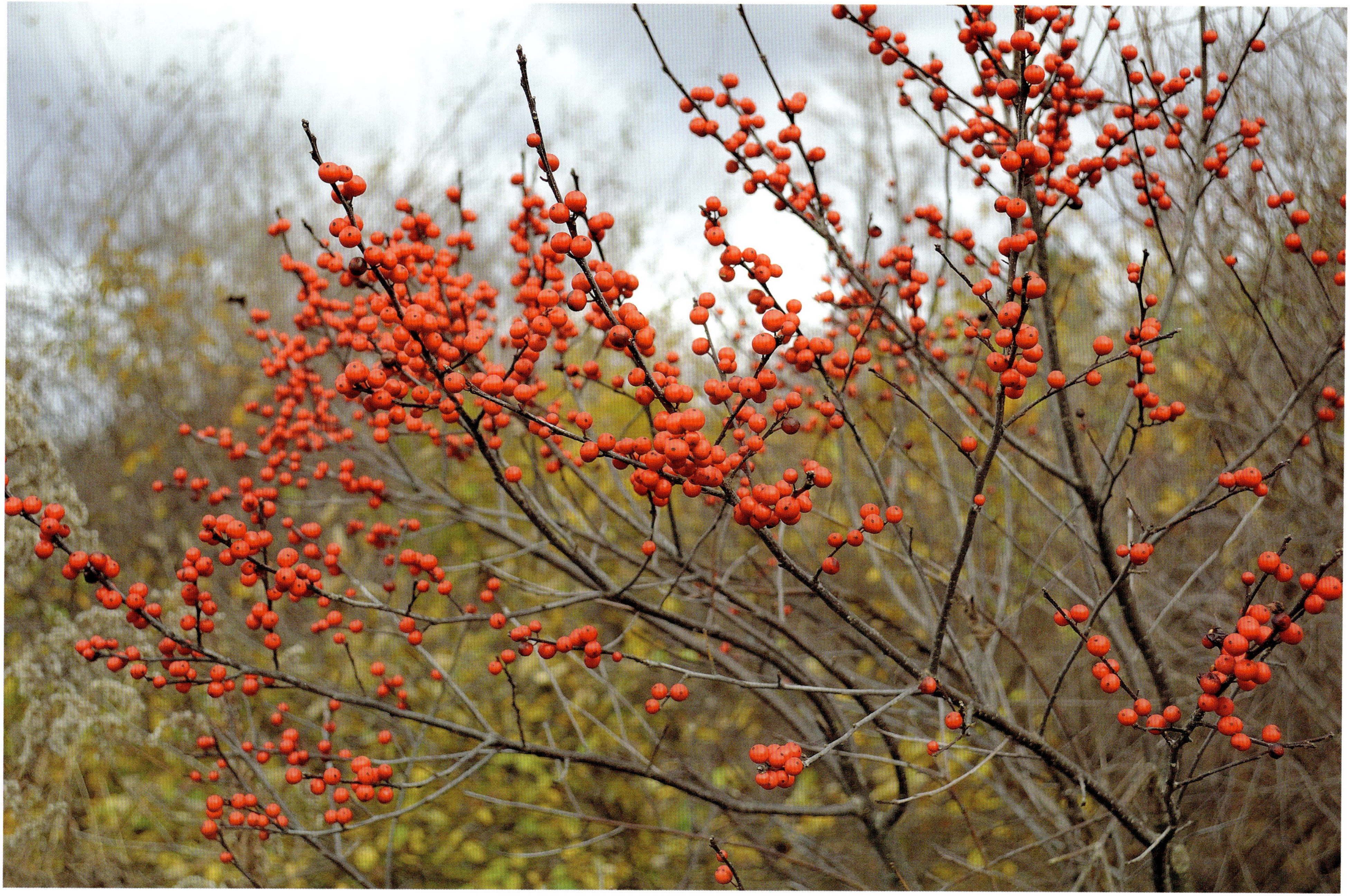

Winterberry (Mills-Norrie State Park)

When the showy autumnal leaves have fallen from their elevated perches, winterberry or swamp holly, becomes one of the most dramatic outdoor sights. This medium to large shrub typically inhabits shady wetlands. Its bright berries are consumed by more than forty-eight species of birds. Cottontail rabbits and deer browse the twigs and branches in the colder months when their preferred food sources become scarce.

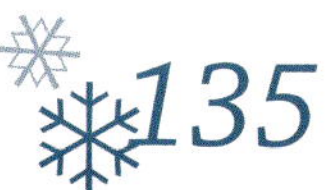

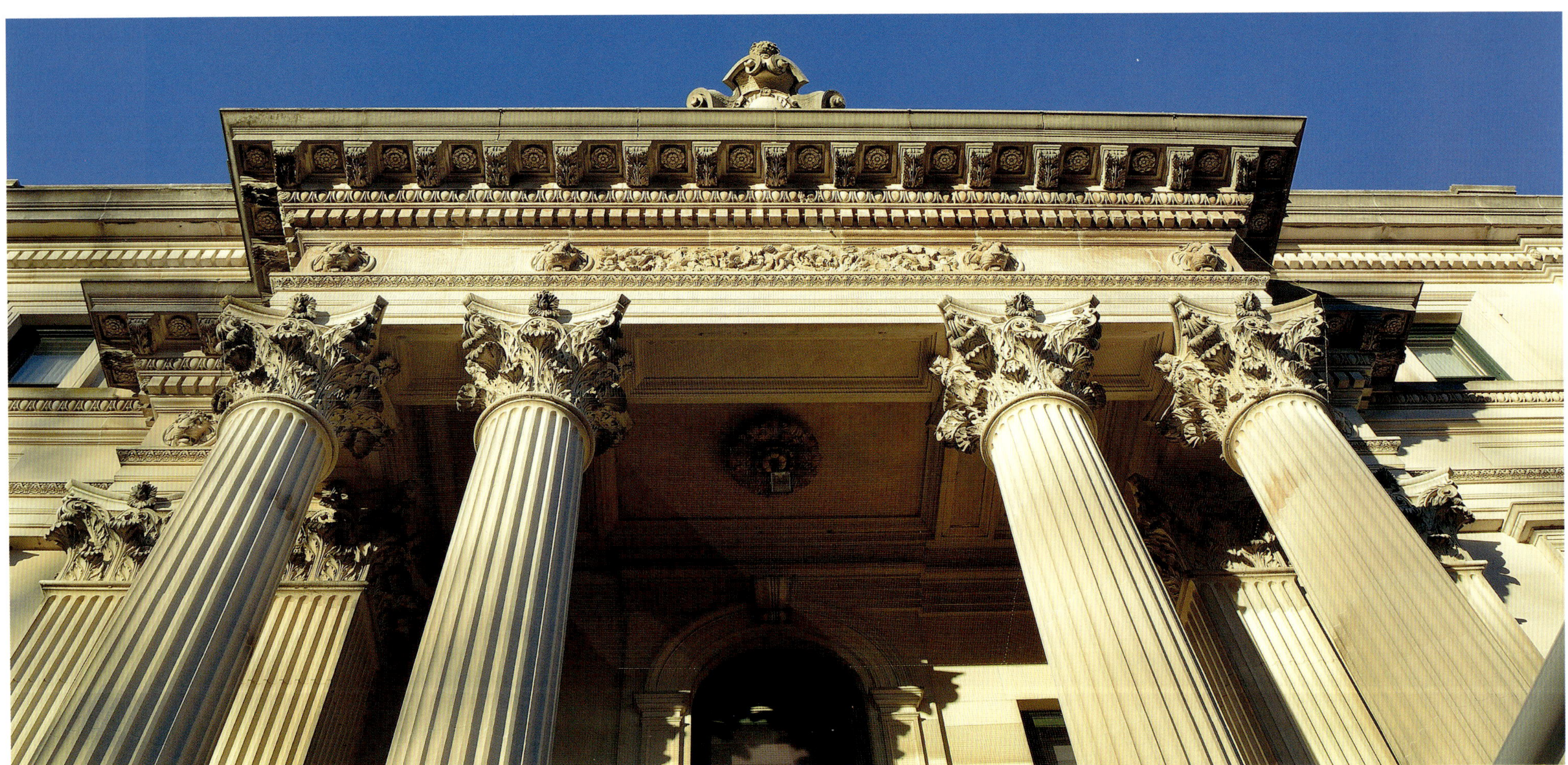

Vanderbilt Mansion Façade
(Vanderbilt Mansion National Historic Site)

Vanderbilt Mansion is one of the finest examples of Gilded Age architecture in the region. The fifty-four-room mansion boasts a lush interior adorned with fine moldings and extravagant paintings, along with priceless, centuries-old antiques, some acquired from ancient castles and palaces of Europe. The estate was commissioned by Frederick Vanderbilt in 1896 and completed two years later. Frederick was the grandson of Cornelius Vanderbilt, the famed captain of industry who through adept investments in steamboats and rail lines became one of the richest men in the country. With a nearly $2.3 million price tag, few people could afford such a palatial residence that heavily relied on the craftsmanship of scores of imported European artisans for completion. Situated atop a scenic bluff overlooking the Hudson River and Catskills to the northwest, the mansion and grounds offer exquisite views of the dramatic landscape. In 1940, the estate was donated to the National Park Service.

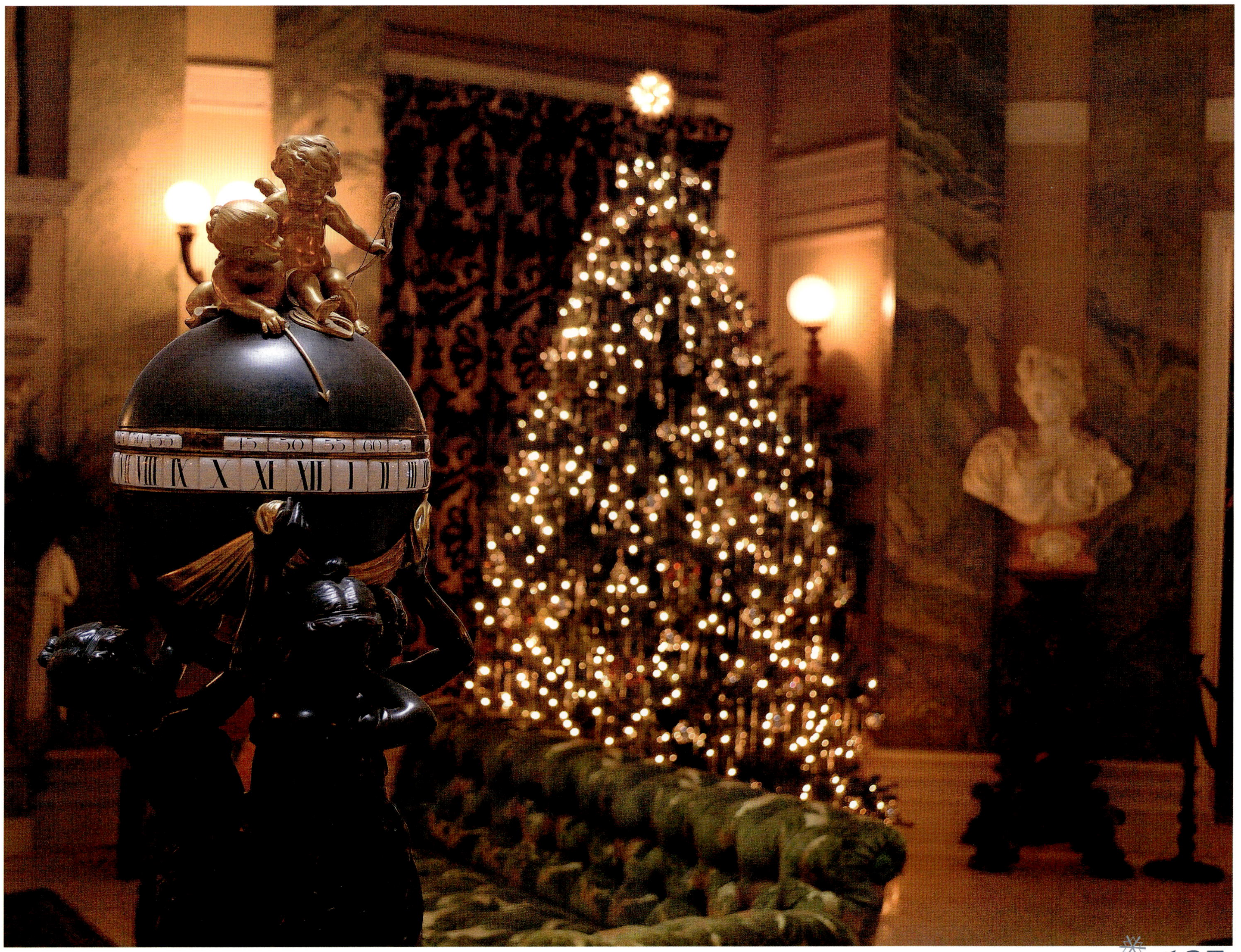

Foyer (Vanderbilt Mansion)

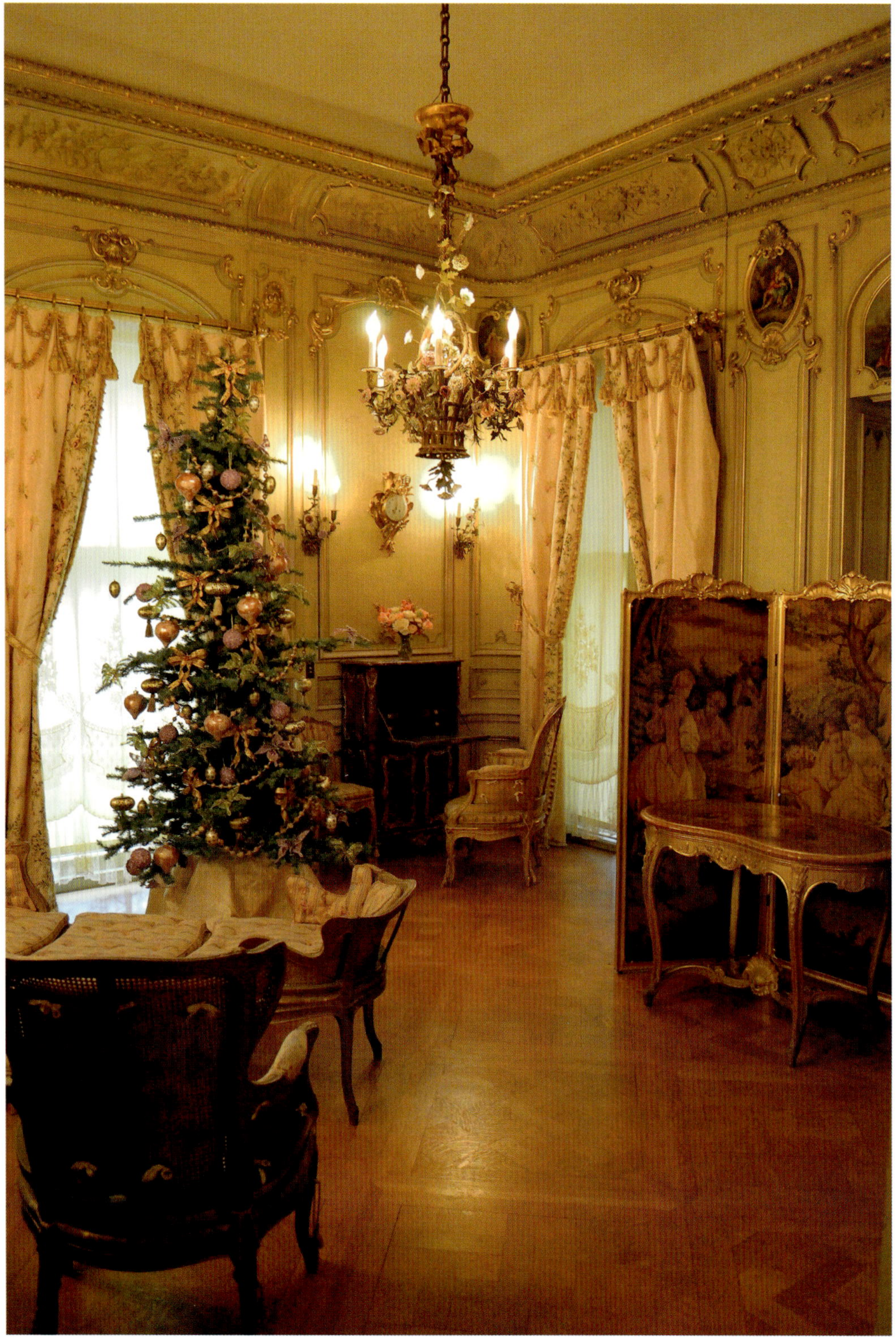

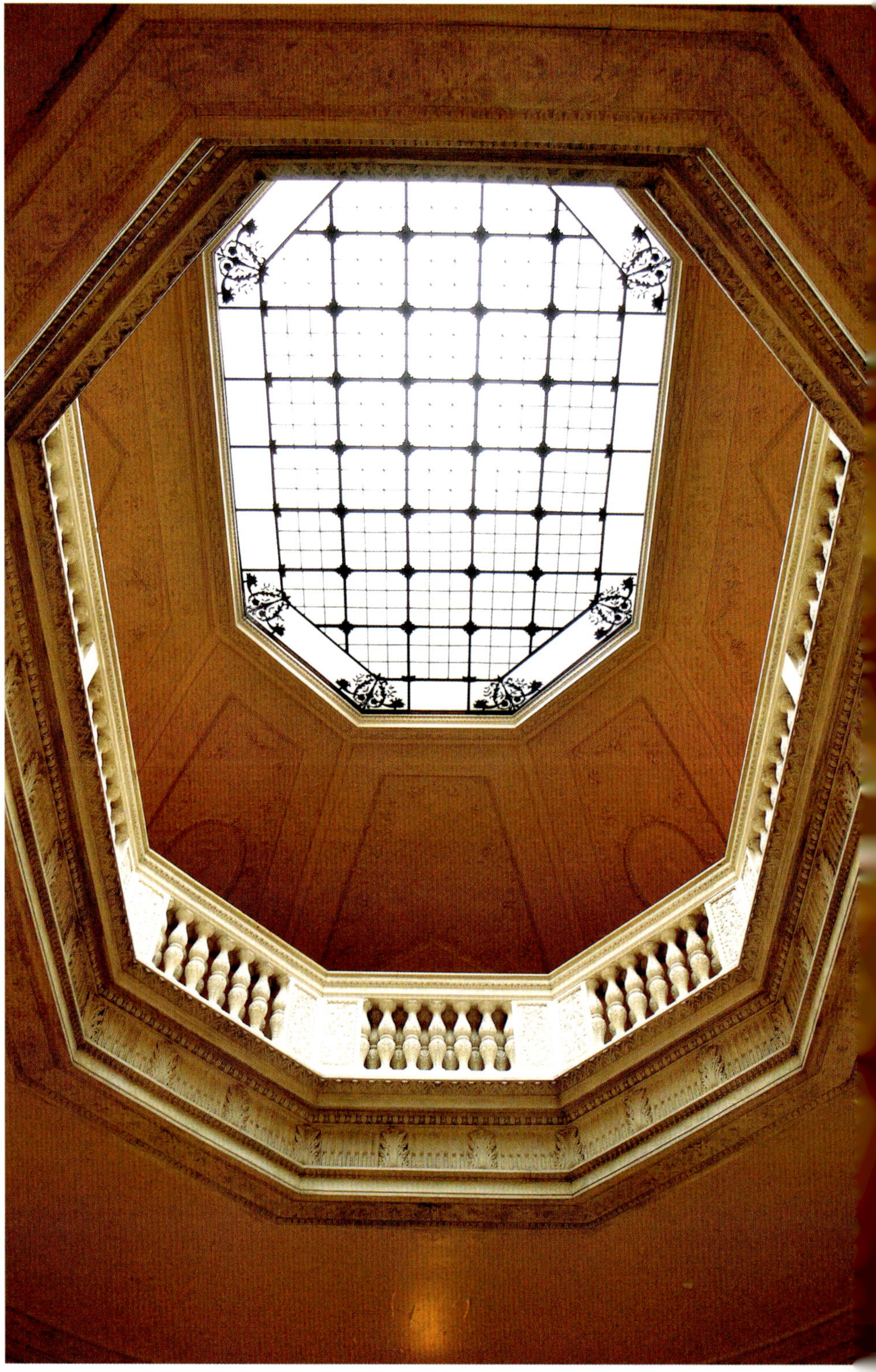

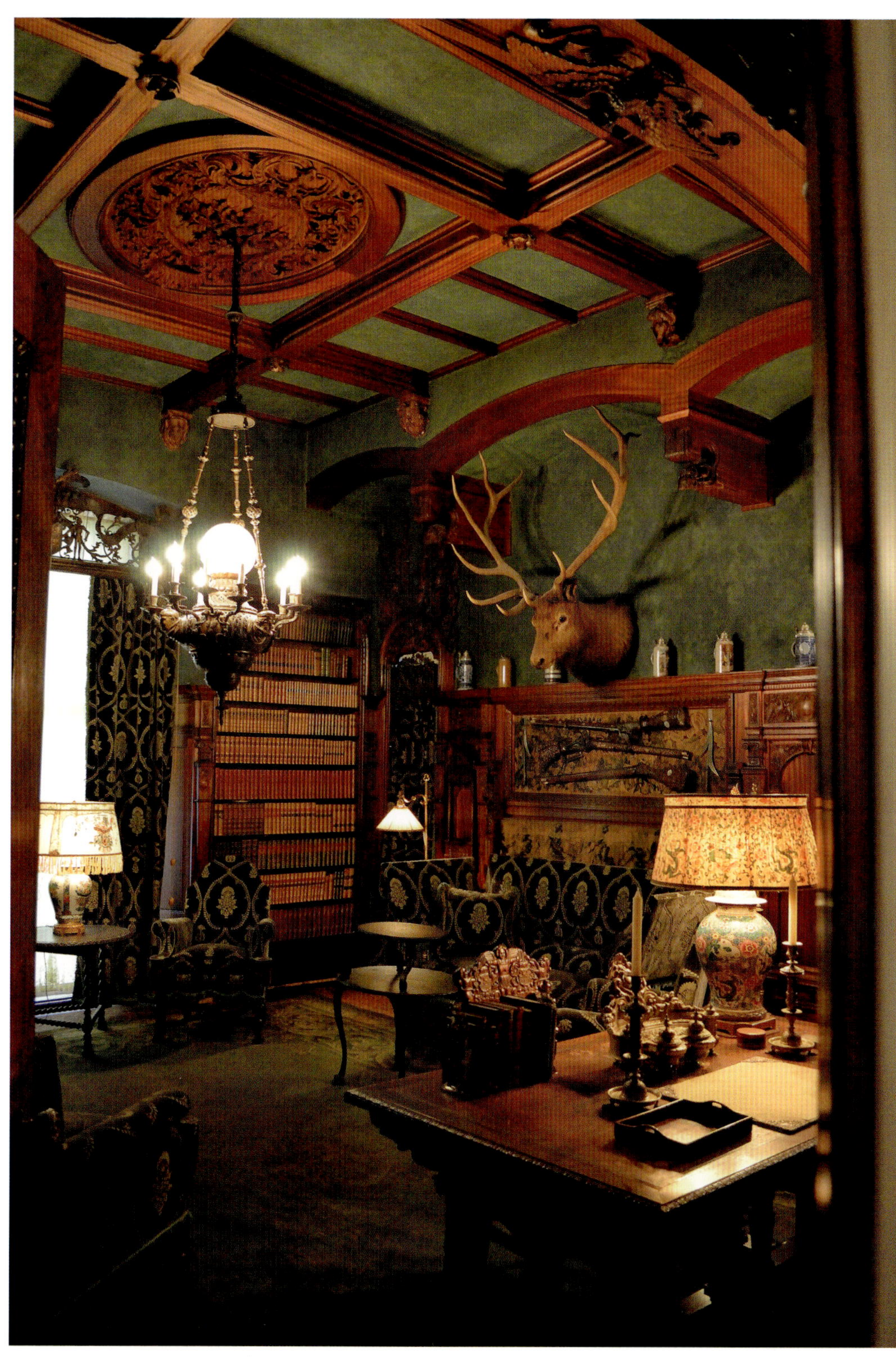

From left to right:
Gilded Room (Vanderbilt Mansion)

Skylight (Vanderbilt Mansion)

Sitting Room (Vanderbilt Mansion)

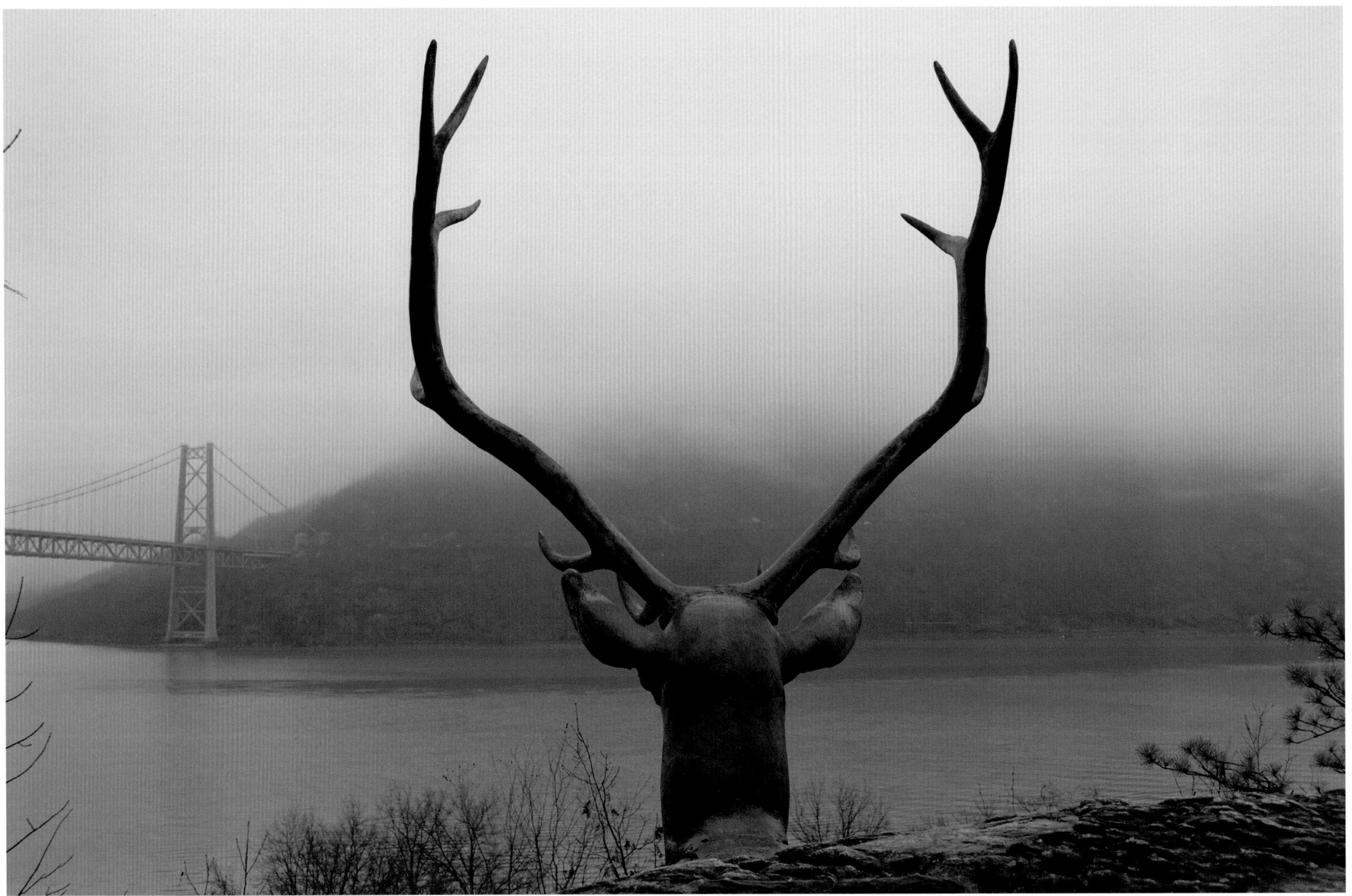

Elk Head Statue (Bear Mountain State Park)

The Hudson Highlands are especially rich in lore. There's certainly no shortage of tales detailing the supernatural beings that supposedly haunt the area. The most famous of these creatures is the "Heer of the Dunderberg," who's said to reside at the summit of Dunderberg Mountain, marking the southern boundary of the Highlands. If you look into the mist of a stormy Highland scene today, you may just be able to make out the ghosts and imps that Irving said were ubiquitous in the region.

"It is certain, nevertheless, that strange things have been seen in these highlands in storms, which are considered as connected with the old story of the ship. The captains of the river craft talk of a little bulbous-bottomed Dutch goblin, in trunk hose and sugar-loafed hat, with a speaking trumpet in his hand, which they say keeps about the Dunderberg. They declare that they have heard him, in stormy weather, in the midst of the turmoil, giving orders in Low Dutch for the piping up of a fresh gust of wind, or the rattling off of another thunder-clap."
—*The Storm Ship*, Washington Irving

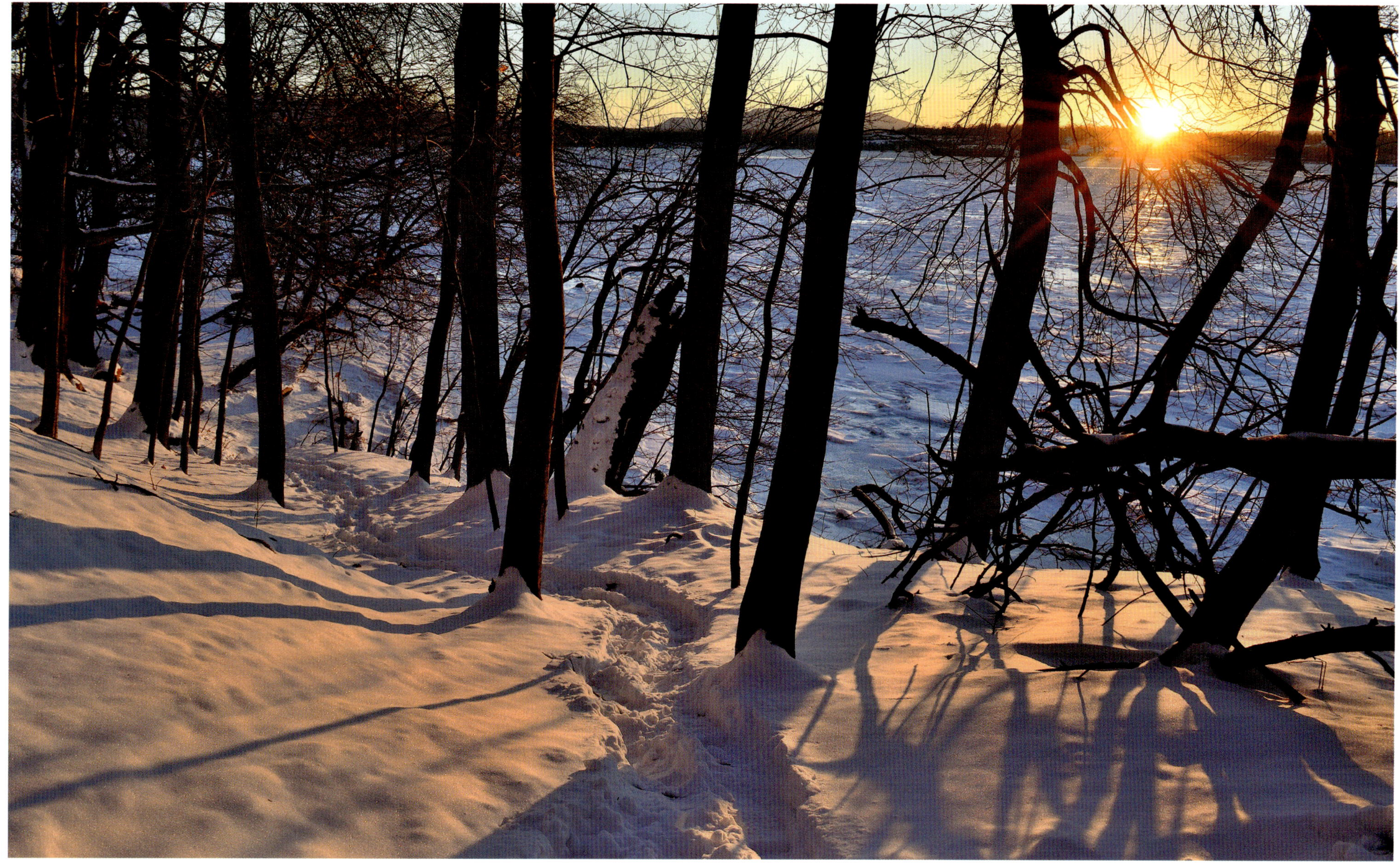

Evening at Denning's Point

Ever wonder how Anthony's Nose got its name? Well, in *A History of New York*, Washington Irving comically describes how the mountain just east of the Bear Mountain Bridge received its odd appellation during the reign of Peter Stuyvesant in the mid-1600s:

> "It must be known that the nose of the trumpeter was of a very lusty size. . . Now thus it happened that bright and early in the morning, the good Antony, having washed his burly visage, was leaning over the quarter-railing of the galley, contemplating it in the glassy wave below. Just at this moment, the illustrious sun, breaking in all its splendor from behind a high bluff of the highlands, did dart one of its most potent beams full upon the refulgent nose of the sounder of brass—the reflection of which shot straight away down, hissing-hot, into the water, and killed a mighty sturgeon that was sporting beside the vessel! . . . When this astonishing miracle came to be known to Peter Stuyvesant, and he tasted of the unknown fish, he, as may well be supposed, marvelled exceedingly; and as a monument thereof, he gave the name of Anthony's Nose to a stout promontory in the neighborhood; and it has continued to be called Anthony's Nose ever since that time."

If that sounded a little unbelievable, perhaps there's more merit to this story recorded in 1836 by Freeman Hunt:

> "General V. is the owner of Anthony's Nose, (on the river), as it is called. He gave me the origin of that name. Before the revolution, a vessel was passing up the river, under the command of a Capt. Hogans; when immediately opposite this mountain, the mate looked rather quizzically, first at the mountain and then at the captain's nose. The captain, by the way, had an enormous nose, which was not unfrequently the subject of a good-natured remark; and he at once understood the mate's allusion. 'What,' says the captain, 'does that look like my nose? Call it then if you please Anthony's Nose.' The story was repeated on shore, and the mountain thenceforward assumed the name, and has thus become an everlasting monument to the memory of the redoubtable Capt. Anthony Hogans and his nose."

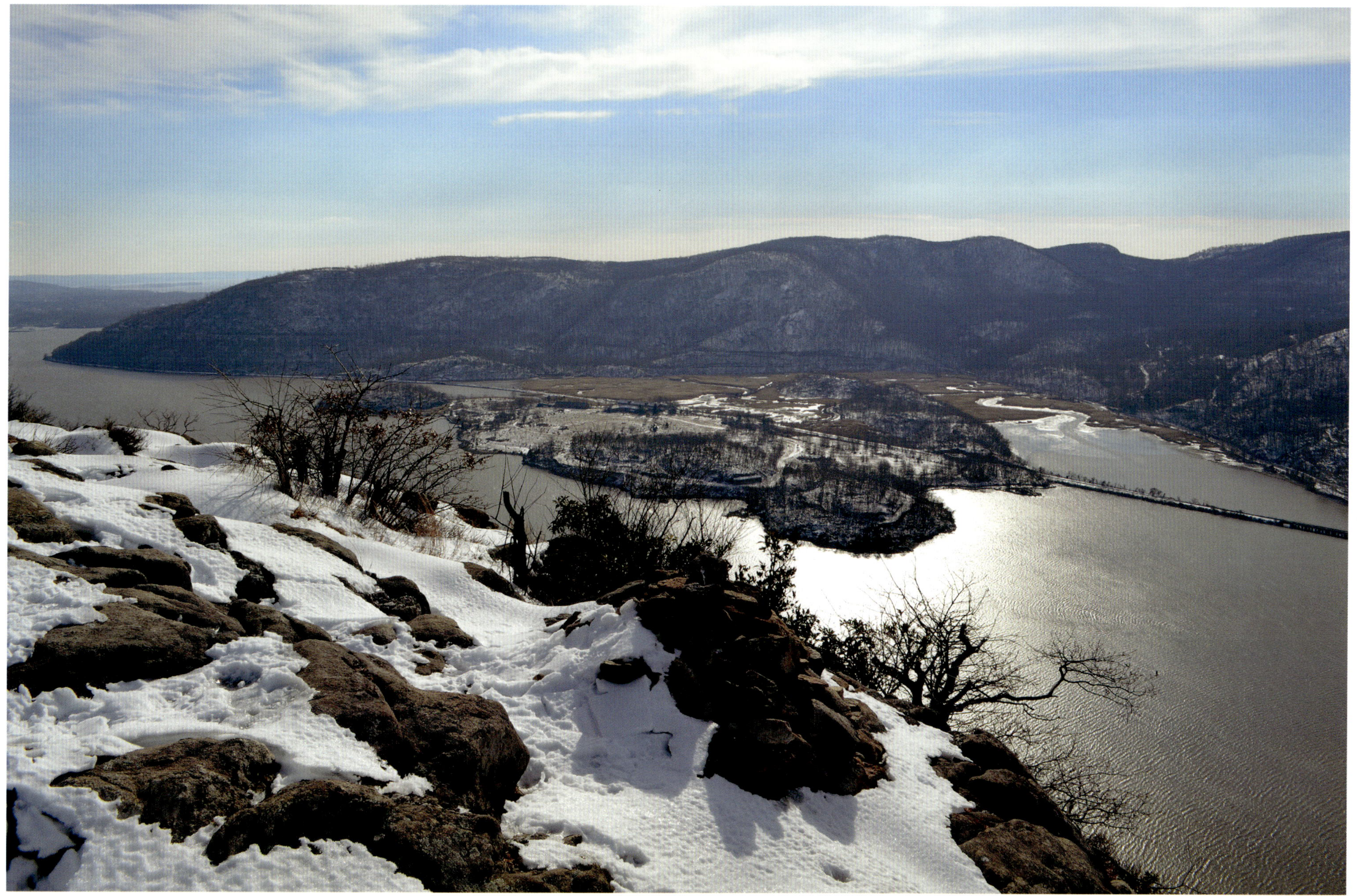

Anthony's Nose (Hudson Highlands State Park)

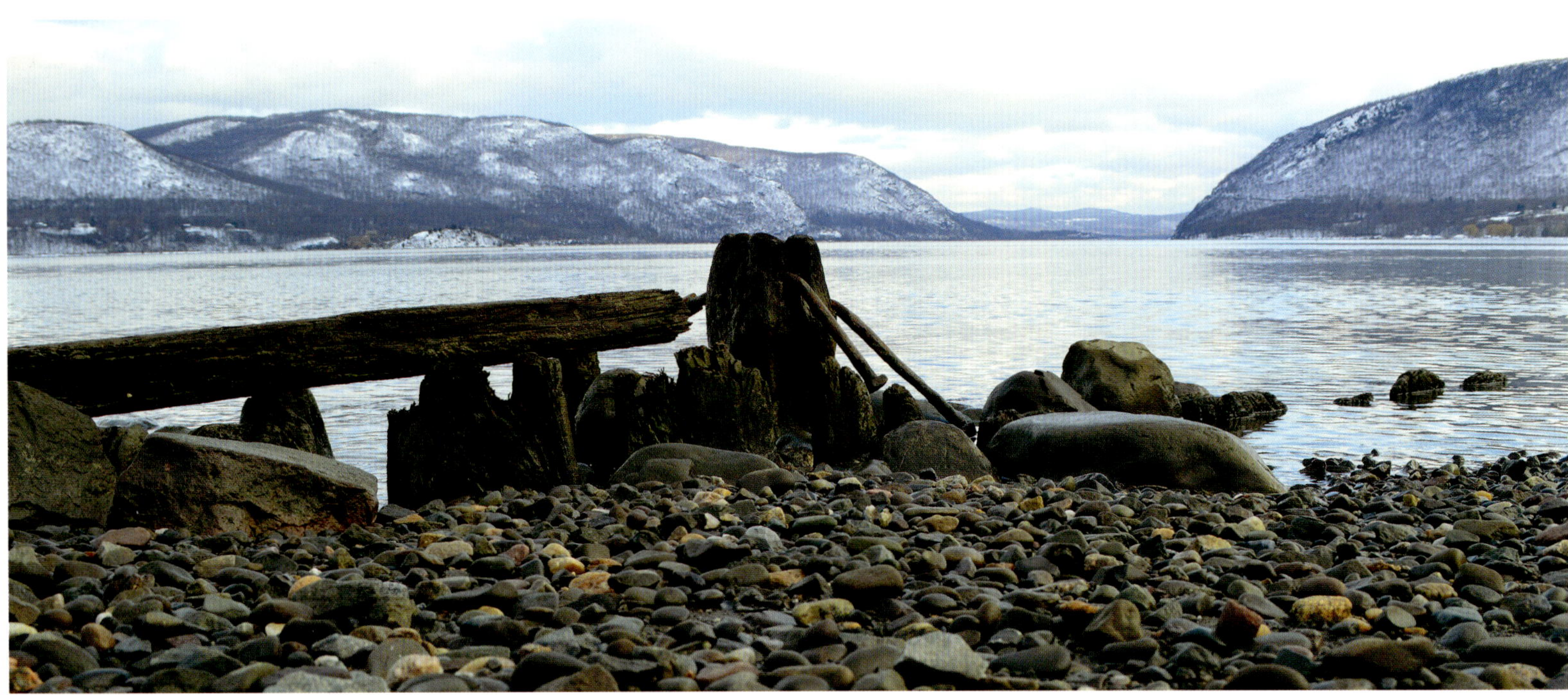

Cornwall Bay (Plum Point)

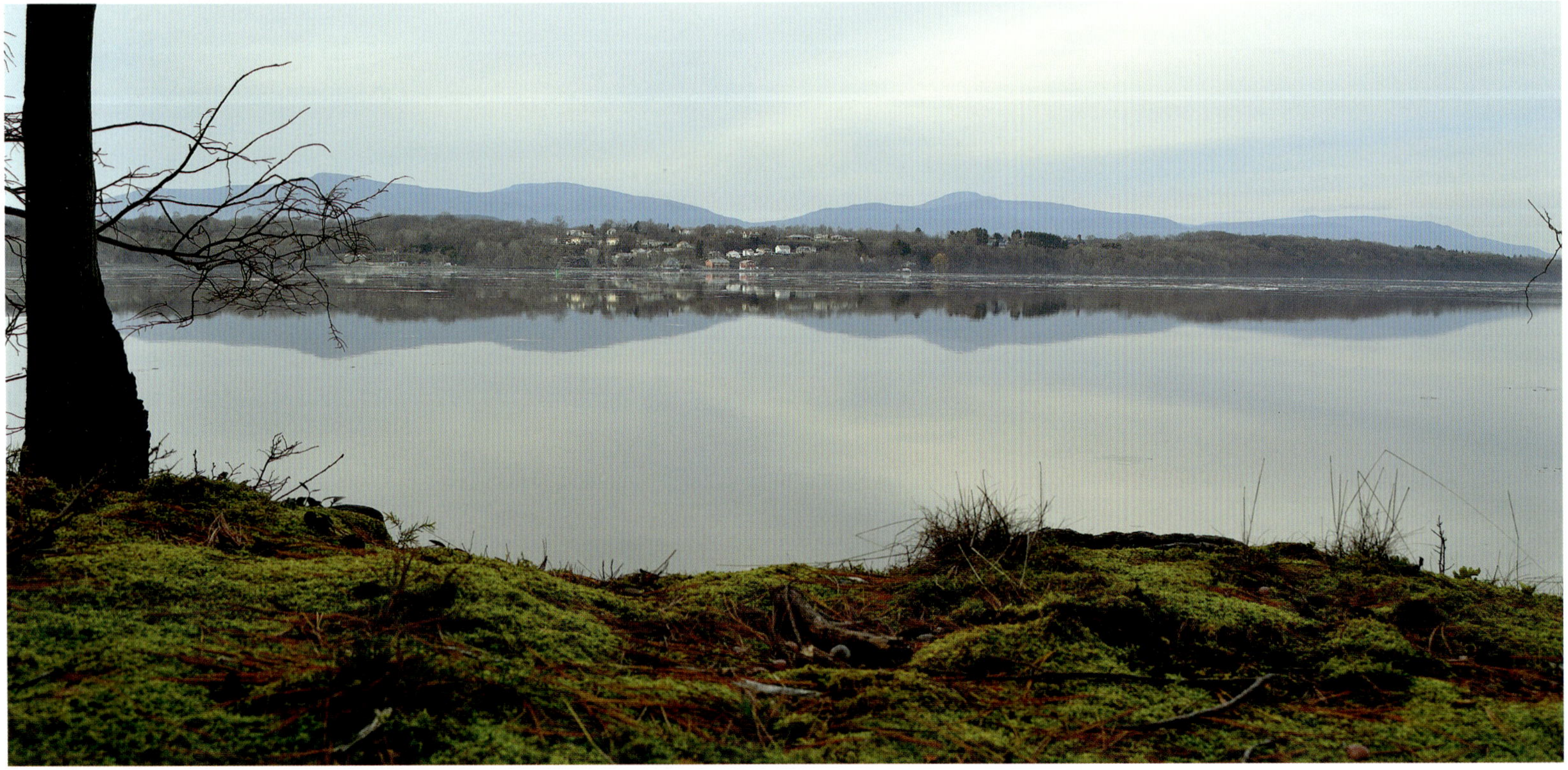

View of the Catskills from Cruger Island (Tivoli Bays Wildlife Management Area)

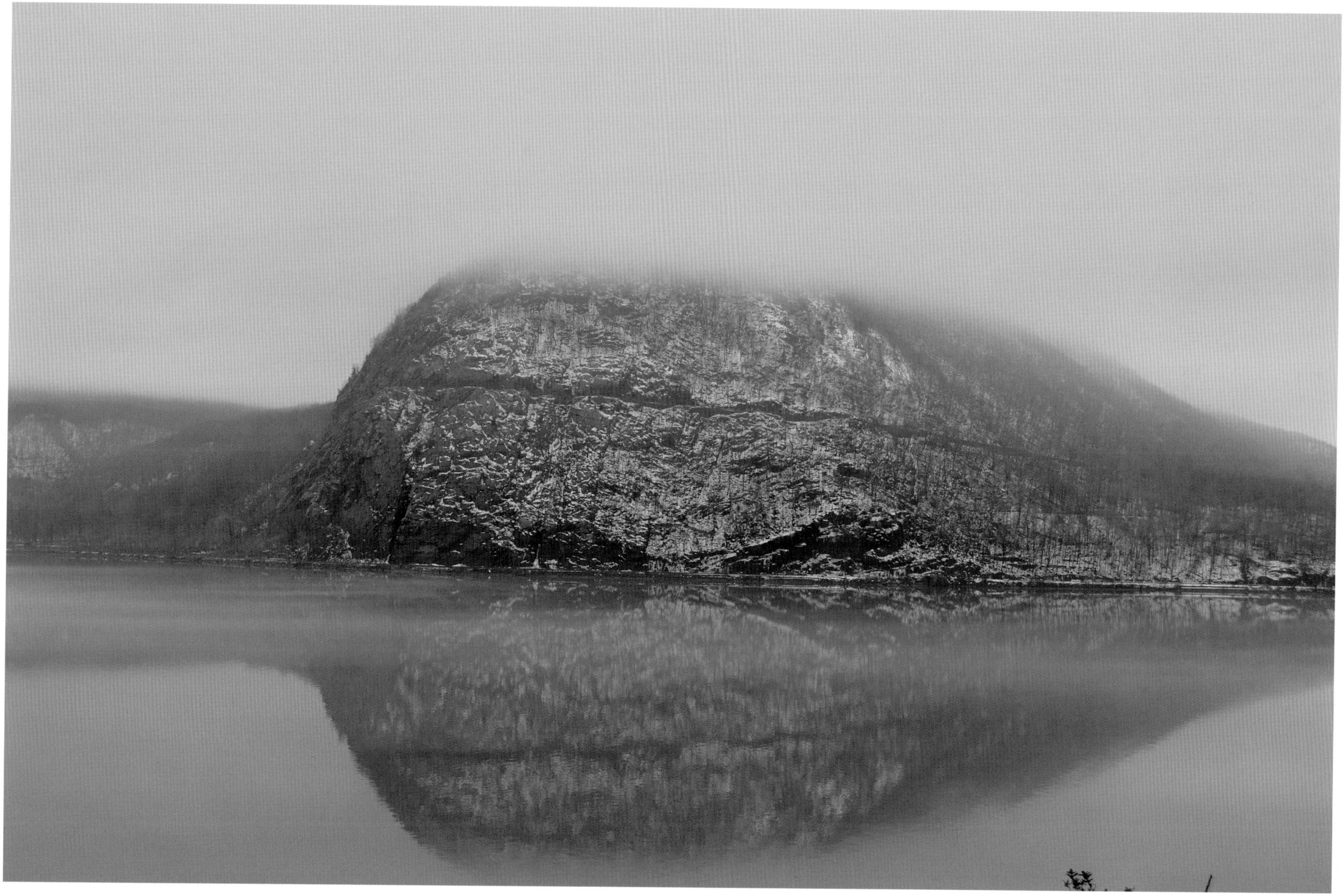

This national landmark was almost irrevocably scarred by a Con Edison power plant proposed in the 1960s on the mountain's northern slope. The nascent environmental organization, Scenic Hudson, fought valiantly to preserve the natural landmark. After an incredible seventeen years of tedious litigation the group prevailed. Storm King has since been acquired for parkland and continues to grace the northern gate of the Highlands in its current form, as it has done since the end of the last Ice Age.

View of Storm King Mountain (Hudson Highlands State Park)

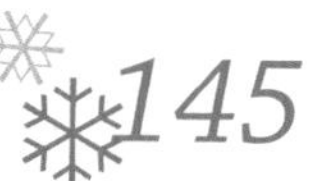

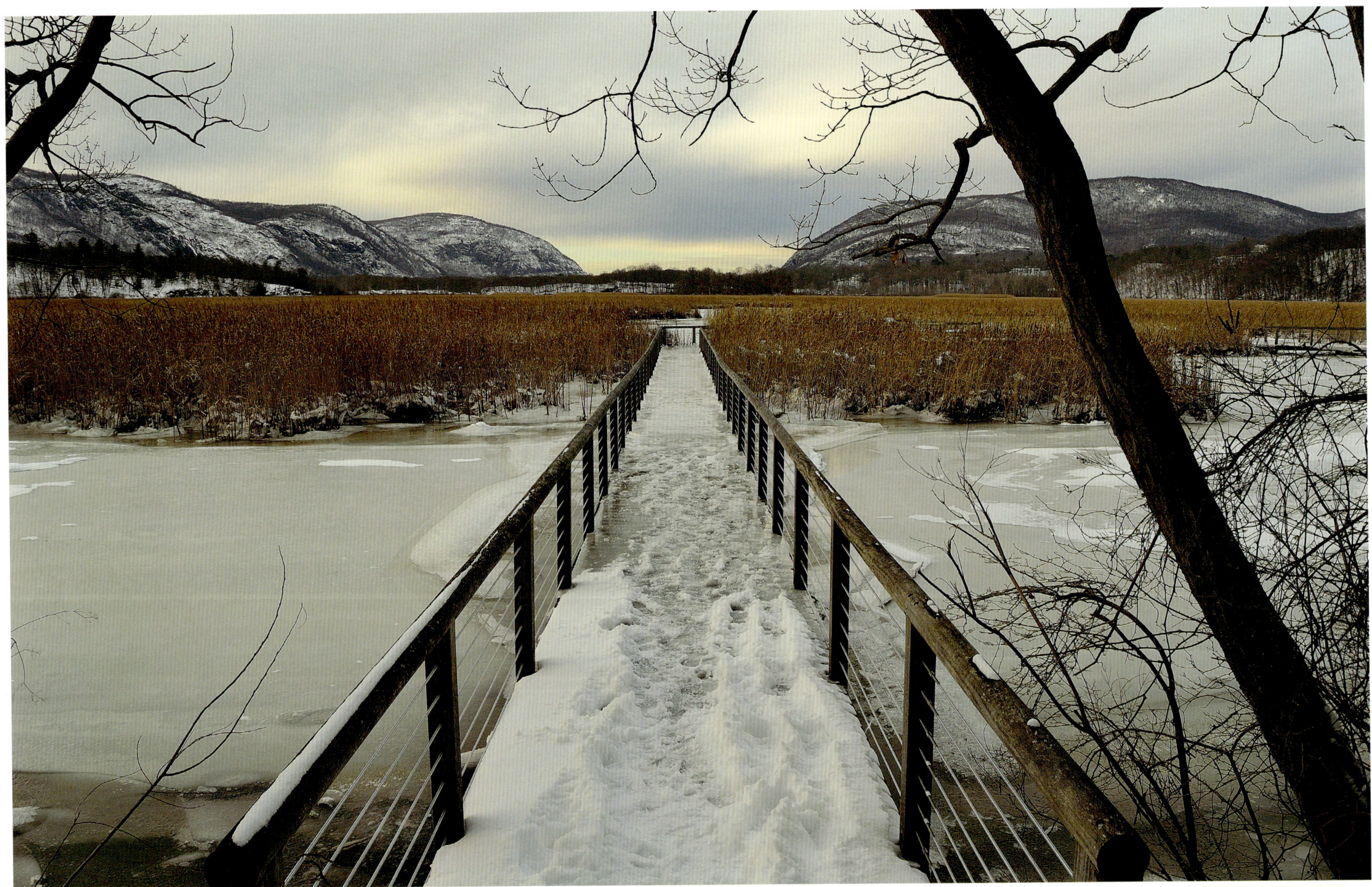

Constitution Marsh boardwalk

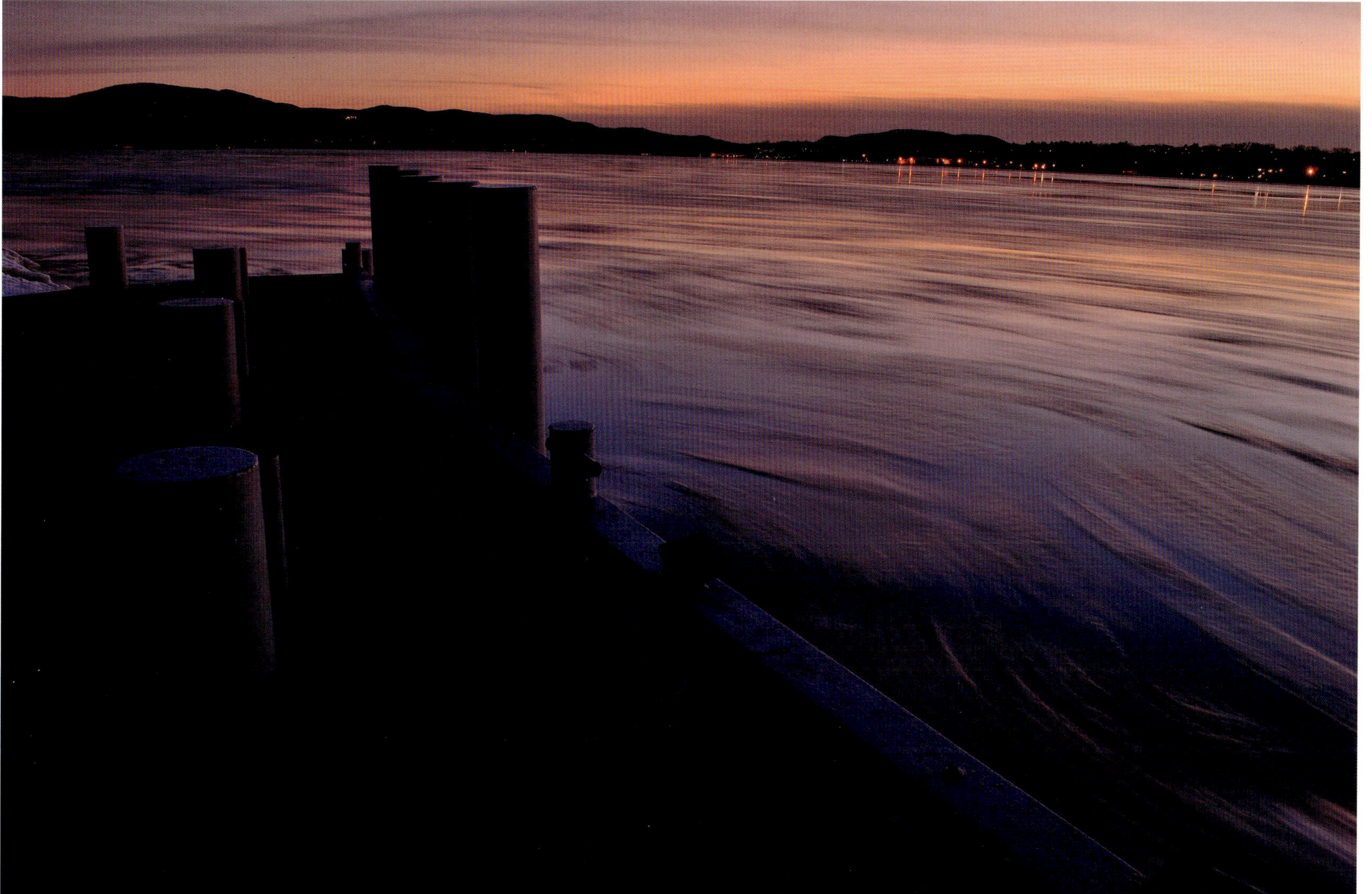

Ice floes at
Long Dock Park

The Hudson River is a tidal estuary. From New York City to the Federal Dam at Troy, 153 miles inland, two high and two low tides rhythmically raise and lower the Hudson's waters each day. The greatest tidal range (the variation between average high and average low tides) occurs at Troy (around five feet), while the smallest range occurs at West Point (around three feet).

Tidal flow in the Hudson is best described as water sloshing around in a bathtub. The upper portion has the most extreme tides due to a combination of factors. Water that would normally continue moving north with the incoming tide finds an impenetrable barrier at the Federal Dam, and so the energy of the tide is reflected back, causing the water in the immediate area to swell significantly. The second factor at play is the topography. The narrow upper Hudson constricts the flow of water, forcing it higher.

While the Hudson has been called an "arm of the sea," saltwater isn't propagated through the entire length of the river. The maximum extent of the salt front rarely ventures past Newburgh, although drought and high levels of precipitation will push it farther north or south, respectively.

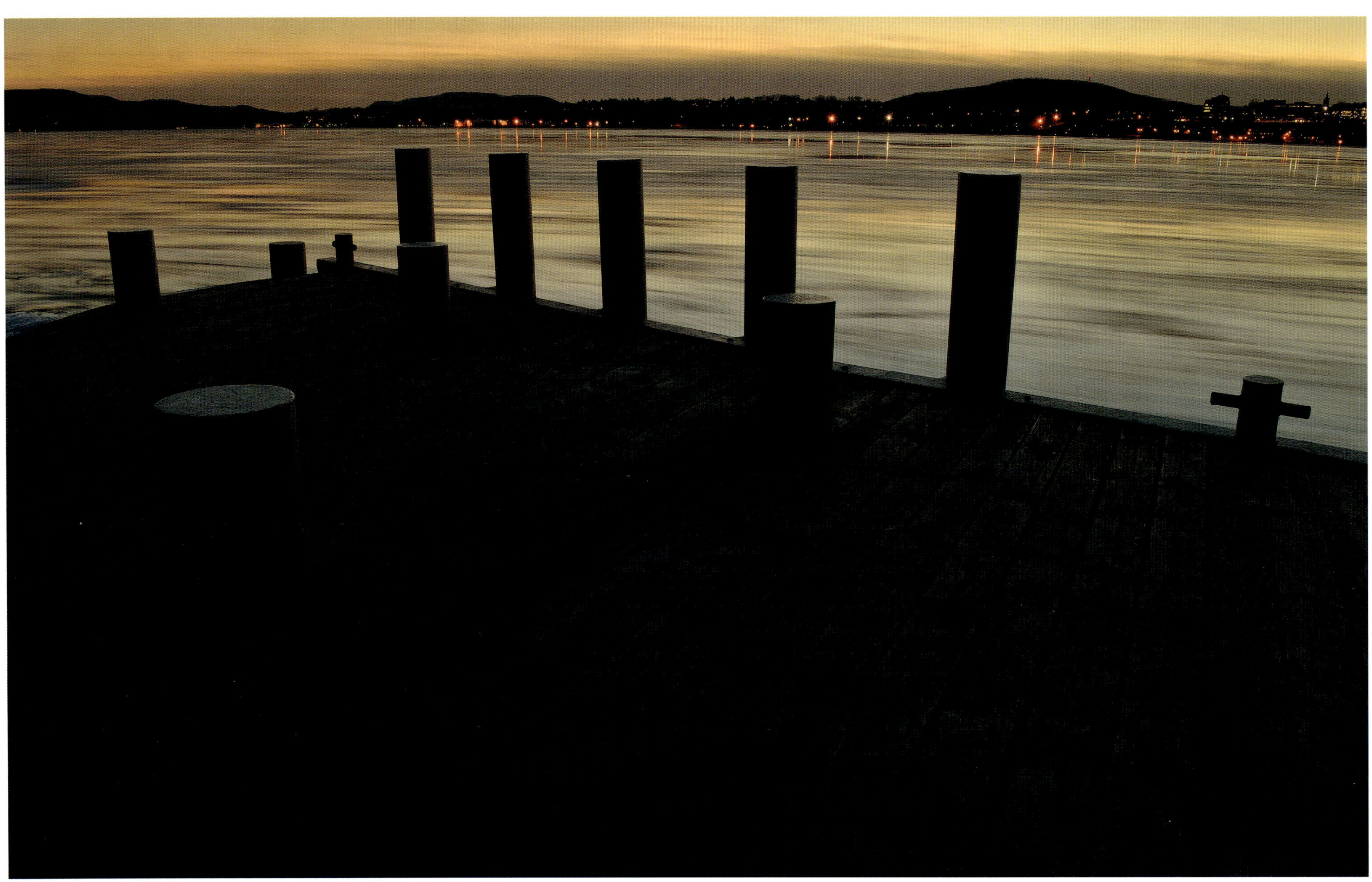

Twilight at Long Dock Park

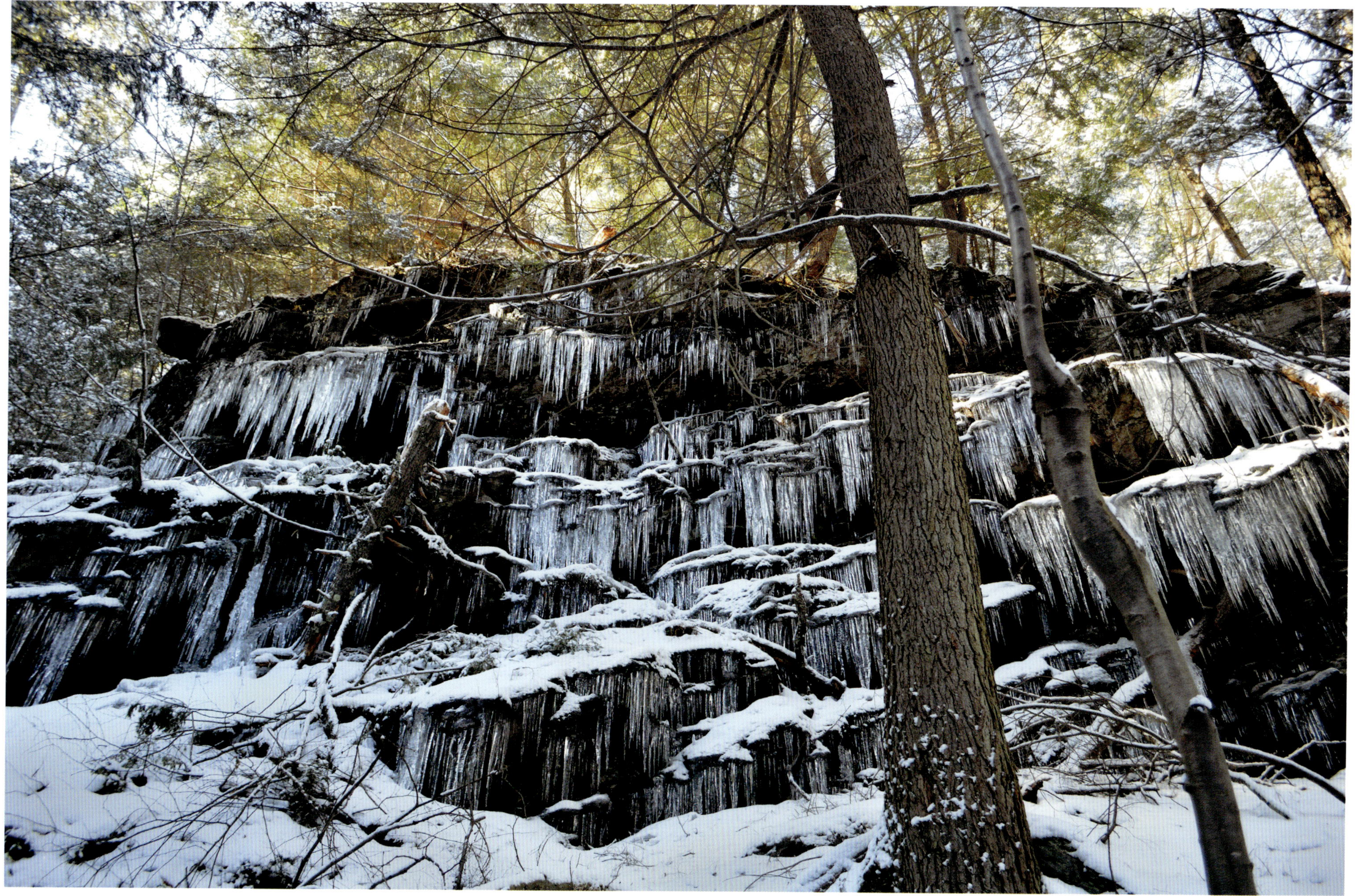

Icy morning (Dover Stone Church Preserve)

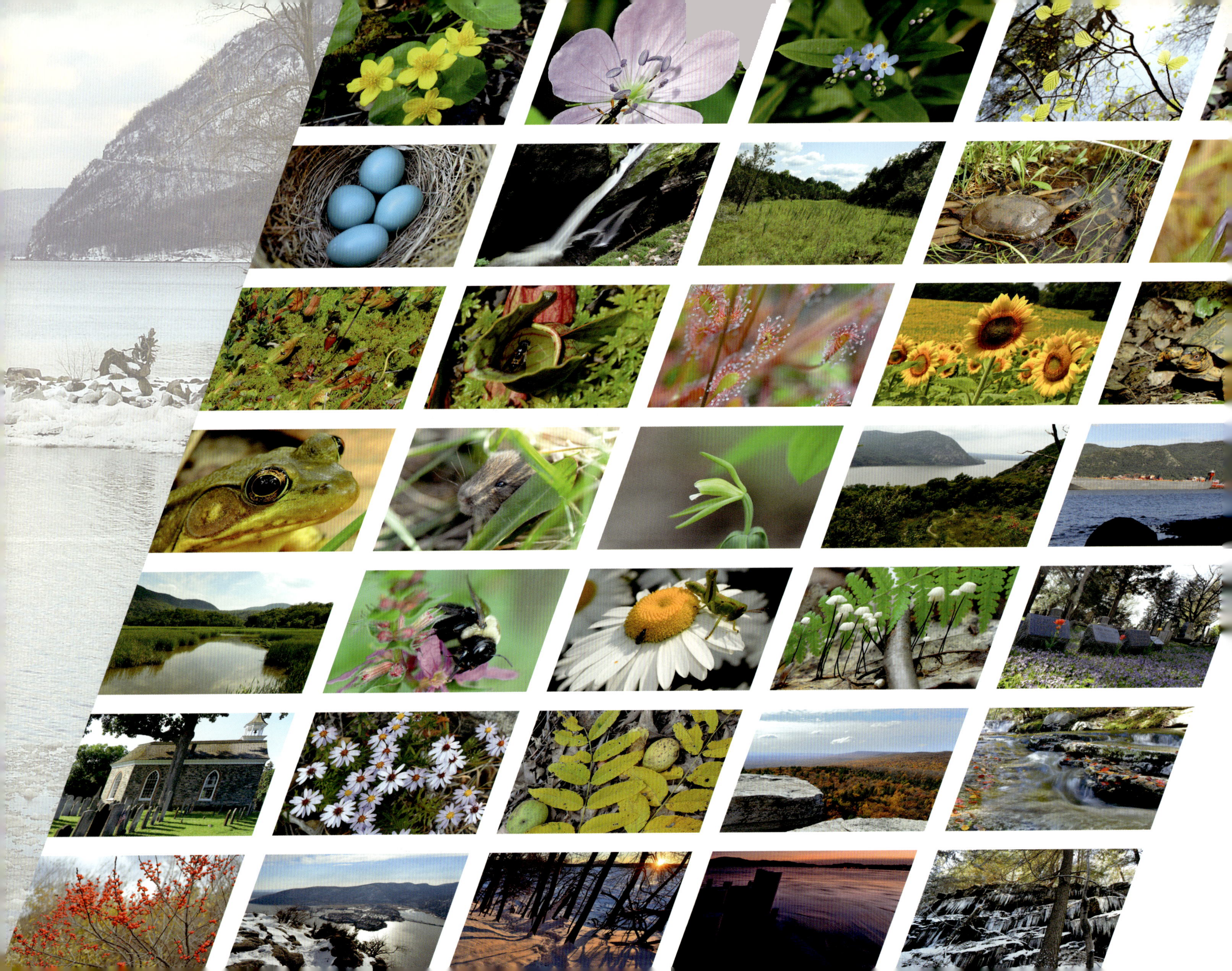

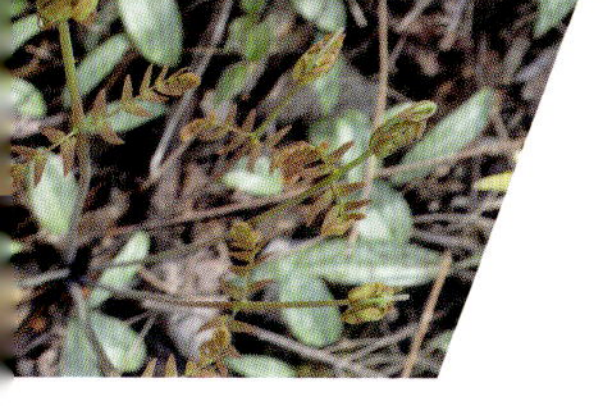
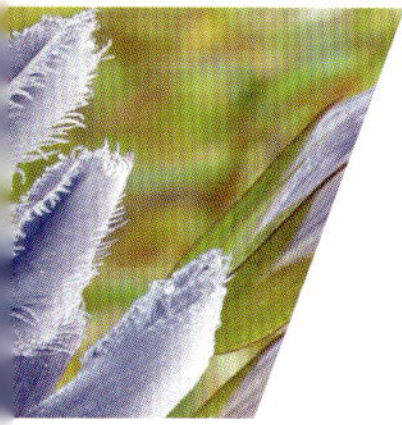
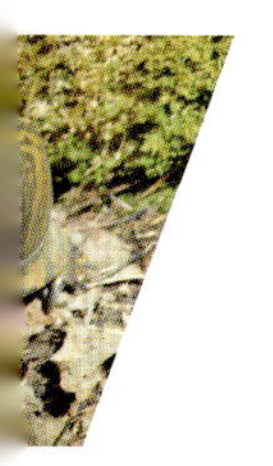

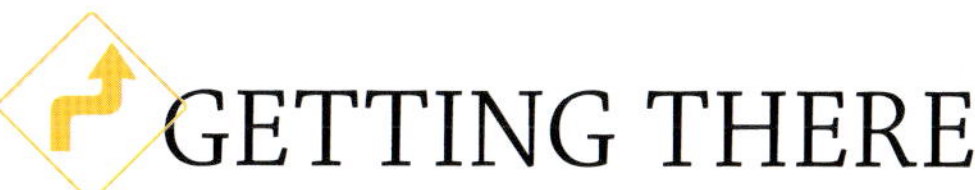

GETTING THERE

Listed approximately from south to north.

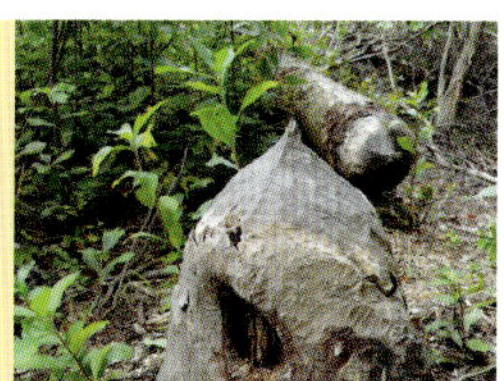

STERLING LAKE

115 Old Forge Road, Tuxedo

The parking for this pristine, sapphire-hued lake is along Old Forge Road. From the intersection of Long Meadow Road, it's a half-mile to the parking area on the left. The Sterling Forest visitor center is directly across the road. From the parking area, cross the street and head west following the blue-blazed trail, which takes you on a 4.1 mile loop around the expansive Sterling Lake. Signs of beaver activity can be viewed at the northern end of the lake, approximately the half-way mark of the loop.

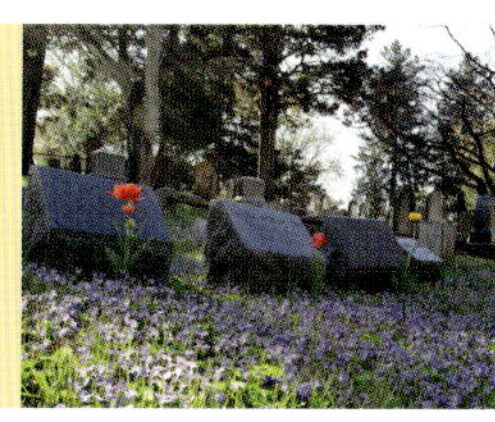

SLEEPY HOLLOW CEMETERY

540 North Broadway, Sleepy Hollow

From the main entrance of the cemetery off North Broadway, there are multiple roads and carriageways one can take to explore the historic grounds. Hours: 8:30–4:30.

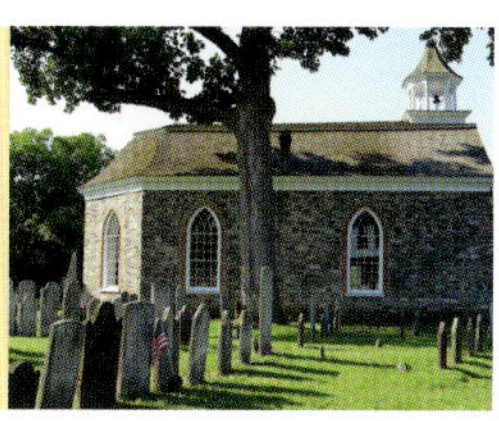

OLD DUTCH CHURCH

430 North Broadway, Sleepy Hollow

Though adjacent to the Sleepy Hollow Cemetery, the Old Dutch Burying Ground and accompanying church are not affiliated with the cemetery. Park along the roads inside the Sleepy Hollow Cemetery and walk to the site. Gates are promptly locked at 4:30.

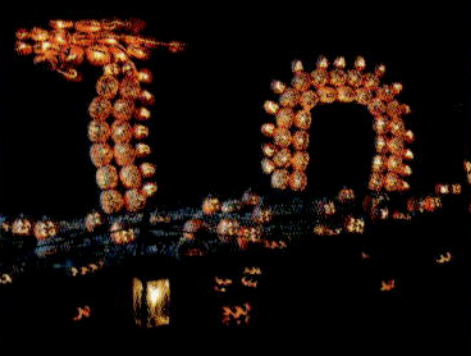

VAN CORTLANDT MANOR

525 South Riverside Avenue, Croton-on-Hudson

Historic Hudson Valley offers tours of this colonial residence once owned by one of the region's most prominent families. The Great Jack O'Lantern Blaze is held on the estate's grounds, usually from late September through early November. See their website for more information, hudsonvalley.org.

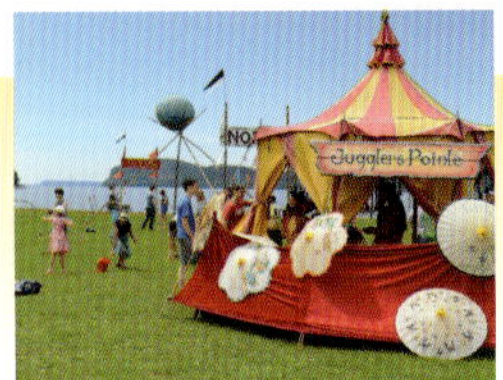

CROTON POINT

Croton Point Avenue, Croton-on-Hudson

This Westchester County park is at the western end of Croton Point Avenue. There are multiple parking areas along its length. Scenic roads and footpaths provide stunning views of the expansive three-mile-wide Haverstraw Bay.

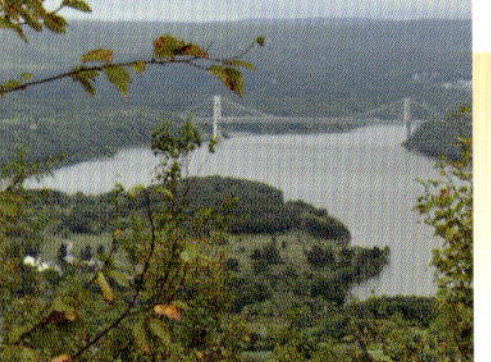

DUNDERBERG MOUNTAIN

Route 9W, Tomkins Cove

One of the best spots to view eagles during the winter months in the Hudson Valley is at the foot of Dunderberg Mountain. In the evening, as the birds retreat to their roost sites on the eastern face of the mountain, it's easy to get close-up views as they cross the Hudson, flying directly overhead. To watch the nightly show, park next to the massive anchor monument along Route 9W in Tomkins Cove. The anchor is a quarter-mile south of the intersection of River Road. The main trailhead for the numerous Dunderberg hiking trails is very near this intersection (a large pull-off for the trails is along the shoulder of the southbound lane of Route 9W).

To access the trailhead, walk south along Route 9W for a few hundred feet. Follow the blue/red-dot-on-white blazes for a quarter-mile. When a junction appears, bear right onto the red-dot-on-white Ramapo-Dunderberg trail. Proceed for approximately 1.25 miles to the summit. Glimpses of a grassy meadow will appear through a dense patch of small birches, regenerating from a decade-old forest fire. Bushwhack out to the meadow for excellent views of the Bear Mountain Bridge and lower Highland amphitheater.

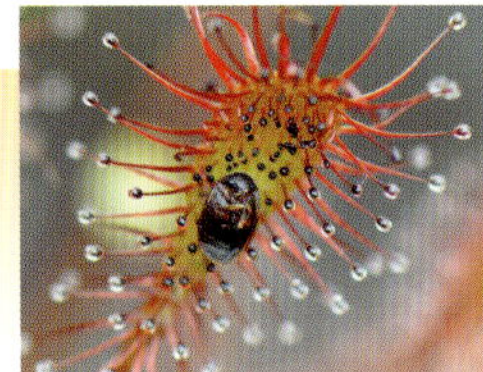

PINE SWAMP

Seven Lakes Drive, Tuxedo

The easiest way to access Pine Swamp is from the parking area on the shores of Lake Skannatati. From the intersection (traffic circle) of Seven Lakes Drive and Kanawauke Road, take Seven Lakes Drive north for eight-tenths of a mile. A sizable parking lot is on the left. Follow the Long Path (aqua) for around 1.25 miles, turning right onto the Dunning Trail (yellow). Pine Swamp will appear on the right in about a half-mile.

Actually a bog, Pine Swamp is ringed with dense quaking mats of sphagnum moss. Among the mats and along their edges grow carnivorous pitcher plants and sundews, colorful wildflowers (wild azalea, sheep laurel, steeplebush), along with cranberries and blueberries. *Note: bogs in our area are rare habitats and extremely sensitive. Sphagnum mats damaged by excessive foot traffic take many years to fully recover.*

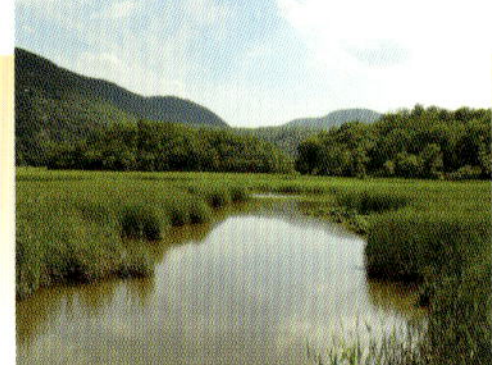

IONA ISLAND

Iona Island Causeway, Tomkins Cove

From the Bear Mountain traffic circle, take Route 9W southbound for 1.5 miles. The Iona Island Causeway is on the left. Access to the island beyond the railroad tracks is prohibited. An elevated wooden platform frequently used for bird watching overlooks the marsh next to the large pull-off by the railroad crossing. Several rare plant and animal species thrive in the marsh. Colorful arrays of wildflowers can be observed along the causeway beginning in the latter half of summer.

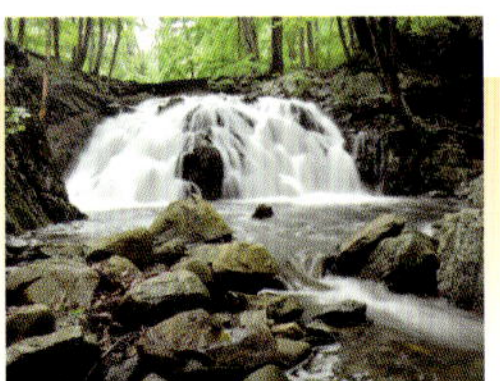

DOODLETOWN BROOK FALLS

Route 9W, Tomkins Cove

Parking for this waterfall is along Route 9W, one-tenth of a mile north of the Iona Island Causeway. A moderately sized pull-off is located on the shoulder of the north bound lane. The trailhead is adjacent to the small concrete bridge that spans the brook flowing into the marshland surrounding Iona Island. Take the blue-blazed trail uphill for approximately a half-mile until the falls come into view on the right. Follow the unmarked trail that will soon appear to reach the waterfall.

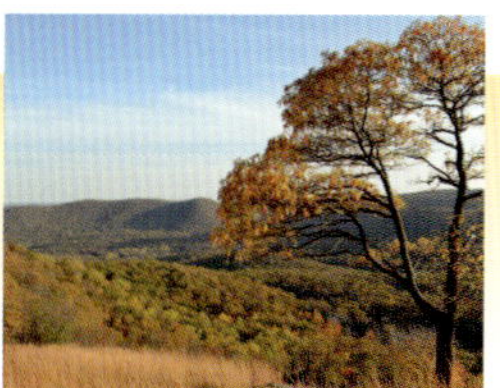

BEAR MOUNTAIN

Seven Lakes Drive, Tomkins Cove

Extensive parking for the most popular portion of Bear Mountain State Park is located behind the Bear Mountain Inn (3020 Seven Lakes Drive, Tomkins Cove). To reach the summit, go south on the Appalachian Trail, which wraps around the southern end of Hessian Lake, just north of the Inn, for slightly over 1.5 miles. Driving to the top is also possible via Perkins Memorial Drive (closed during winter). An observation tower stands at the summit, giving unrivaled views of the lower Hudson Valley. New York City, only thirty miles distant, is visible on clear days.

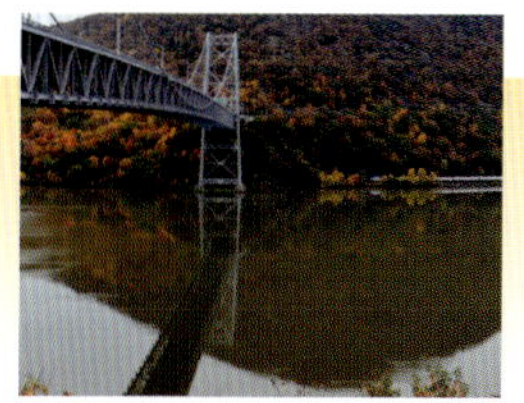

TRAILSIDE MUSEUMS & ZOO

Seven Lakes Drive, Tomkins Cove

Park behind Bear Mountain Inn (3020 Seven Lakes Drive, Tomkins Cove) and walk to the north side of the inn, following the white-blazed Appalachian Trail north along the shores of Hessian Lake. It's a third of a mile from the parking area to the southern entrance of Trailside. Several small museums, a zoo stocked with wildlife native to the region, and the remains of a Revolutionary War fort await visitors in what has been called an "outdoor nature laboratory." Visit Geology Point and the lawn behind the Historical Museum for scenic vistas. Open daily 10:00–4:30 (closed Thanksgiving & Christmas).

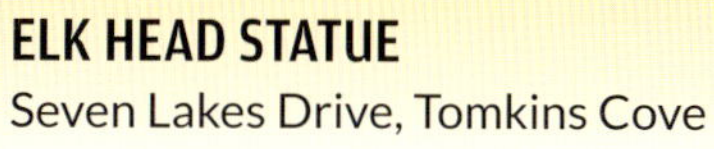

ELK HEAD STATUE

Seven Lakes Drive, Tomkins Cove

This life-like bronze statue overlooking the Hudson is located one-tenth of a mile from Trailside's southern entrance along the walkway leading down to the Bear Mountain Dock.

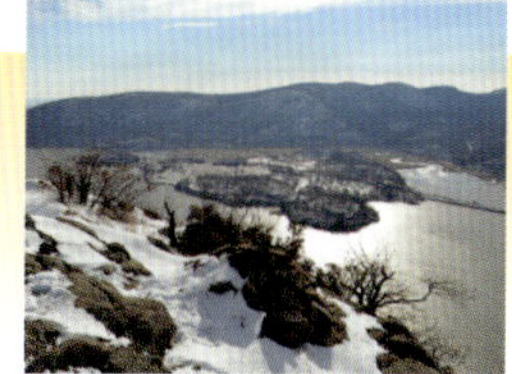

ANTHONY'S NOSE

Route 9D, Cortlandt Manor

The trailhead for this rugged hike is along Route 9D almost exactly at the Putnam/Westchester County border (it's well-marked by large county signs), a quarter-mile north of Bear Mountain Bridge. A small pull-off on the shoulder of the northbound lane serves as the parking area. From the trailhead, take the white-blazed Appalachian Trail uphill for about a half-mile. At the junction, bear right and follow the blue-blazed Camp Smith Trail to the dizzying summit of Anthony's Nose. The mountain's near-vertical western edge directly overlooks the Bear Mountain Bridge at the main viewpoint. The round-trip distance is 2.6 miles.

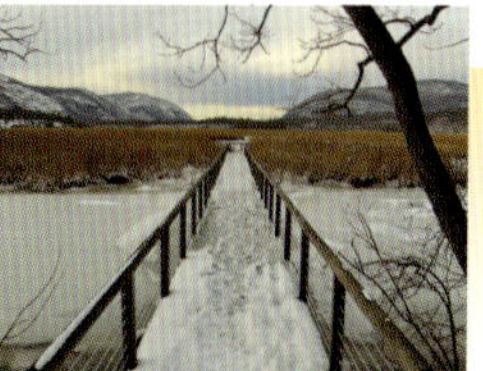

CONSTITUTION MARSH

127 Warren Landing Road, Garrison

A small parking area for the marsh is at the intersection of Indian Brook Road and Warren Landing Road. From here, follow Warren Landing Road downhill for one-third of a mile to the visitor center operated by the Audubon Society (open 9:00–5:00 Tuesday–Sunday, April–October). Behind the visitor center is a blue-blazed trail that leads to a boardwalk extending into the heart of Constitution Marsh. The 270-acre marsh is filled with an exceptionally diverse array of life, from prevalent cattails and showy wildflowers to wily snapping turtles and majestic eagles. Spectacular views of West Point and the surrounding Hudson Highlands can be glimpsed from the trail and boardwalk. This popular bird-watching destination is approximately two miles round-trip from the parking area.

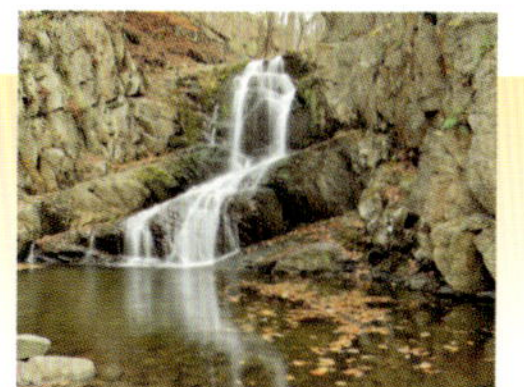

INDIAN BROOK FALLS

Indian Brook Road, Garrison

Parking for the falls is the same as for Constitution Marsh. From the parking area, walk east along Indian Brook Road for 700 feet, passing under the bridge that spans Route 9D. In another fifty feet, on the right, is a small pull-off. The green-blazed trail begins here, leading to Indian Brook Falls in less than a quarter mile.

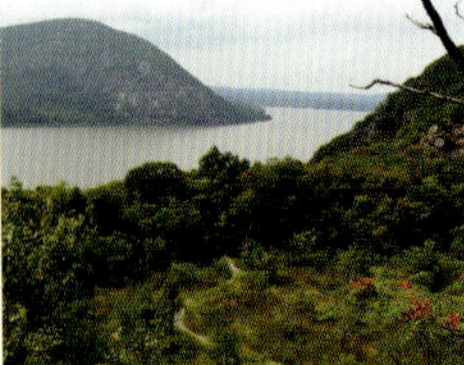

BULL HILL (MT. TAURUS)

Route 9D, Cold Spring

Access to Bull Hill is along Route 9D directly across from the Little Stony Point Citizens Association (3011 NY-9D, Cold Spring). The parking area is usually full on weekends, so it's often necessary to park along the road. From the trailhead, take the Washburn Trail (white) to the summit of Bull Hill, 3.6 miles round-trip.

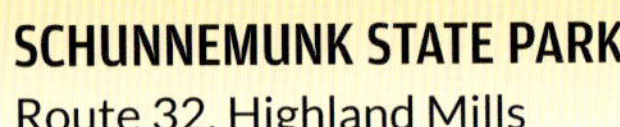

SCHUNNEMUNK STATE PARK

Route 32, Highland Mills

While this 2,700-acre park boasts several excellent hiking trails, the most prominent is the Long Path, extending 357 miles from New Jersey to approximately Albany. Parking for the trail can be found along Route 32 near the intersection of Evans Drive. From the pull-off, walk north on Route 32 for two-tenths of a mile. After passing under the railroad trestle, the aqua-blazed Long Path will appear on the right, just before you reach Falls Lane. The trail ascends Schunnemunk Mountain, offering pleasant eastern views of the Hudson Highlands and Mid-Hudson Valley. Numerous orchid species are found in the park; the pink lady's slipper is the most commonly encountered.

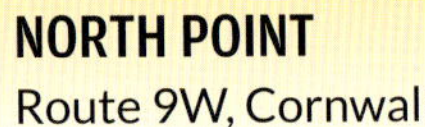

NORTH POINT

Route 9W, Cornwall

From Bear Mountain traffic circle, head north on Route 9W. At the exit for Routes 293/218, it's another 2.3 miles to the small unmarked parking on the right of 9W (just before a sharp left as you're going downhill).

At the parking area, take the white-blazed trail. After crossing the intermittent stream, the trail transforms into a woods road. Around a half-mile from the trailhead a junction will appear, with the woods road continuing downhill and a blue-blazed trail steeply ascending the hill on your right. Bear right, following the blue trail for a quarter-mile to the summit of North Point.

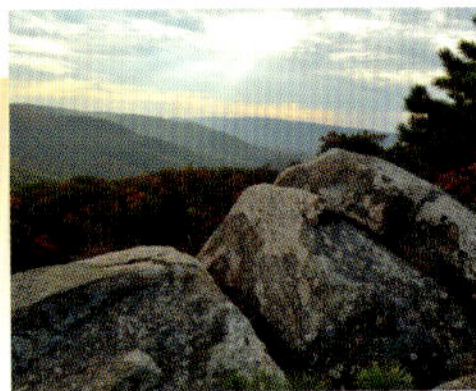

STORM KING

Route 9W, Cornwall

From the Bear Mountain traffic circle, head north on Route 9W. At the exit for Routes 293/218, it's around three miles to the trailhead. As you proceed downhill, an extensive U-shaped pull-off providing sweeping views of Storm King Gorge and the Hudson will appear on the right along 9W. There's a trail junction at the northern end of the pull-off. Take the route marked with a triple orange blaze until you reach the yellow trail, turning right, and following it to the summit. It's about a mile from the parking area to the top. Scenic vistas are scattered along the way. The hot, south-facing slopes are dominated by drought-tolerant shrub oaks, tall native grasses (mostly little and big bluestem), and colorful fall asters.

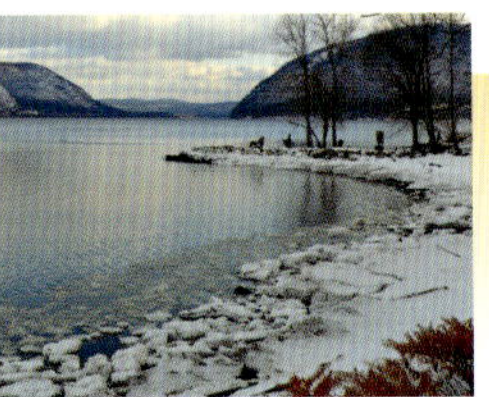

PLUM POINT (KOWAWESE UNIQUE AREA)

Plum Point Lane, New Windsor

This riverfront park offering sweeping views of Cornwall Bay is at the end of Plum Point Lane, off of Route 9W northbound. The park's long and easily accessible shoreline, complete with sandy beaches, make this site ideal for kayakers and anglers (no swimming permitted). Multiple trails throughout.

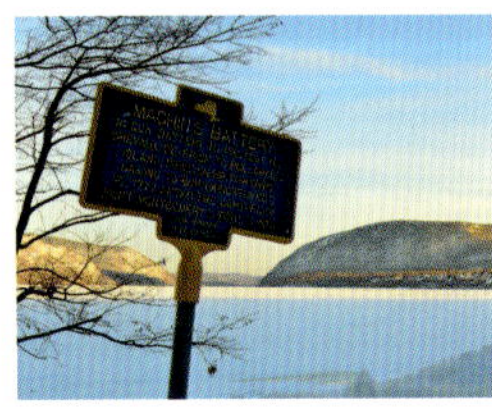

Machin's Battery, also found here, is adjacent to the Interpretive Center, overlooking the southernmost beach.

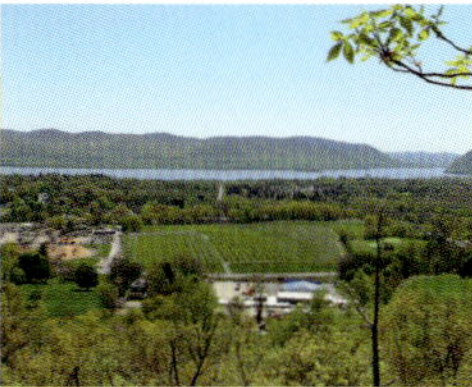

SNAKE HILL

98 San Giacomo Drive, New Windsor

Parking for this little-known preserve, managed by Scenic Hudson, is just north of the tennis courts in the San Giacomo Park, along San Giacomo Drive. Heading east toward the powerline crossing, follow the unmarked footpath briefly through a grassy meadow, part of the utility right-of-way, to the paved road. Take the road uphill. At the top, expansive eastward views can be found by following the several unmarked footpaths that lead to the edge of a steep, rocky cliff.

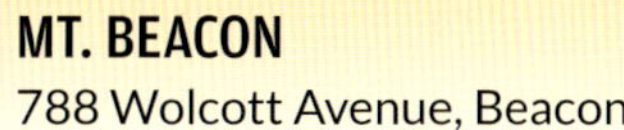

MT. BEACON

788 Wolcott Avenue, Beacon

From the Scenic Hudson parking area along Route 9D/ Wolcott Avenue, take the steep-sloped Red Trail. At the set of stairs, marking the start of the Red Trail, it's one mile to the remains of the defunct casino/incline railway near the first summit. A west-facing overlook at the edge of the casino's concrete foundations provides dramatic views of the Newburgh-Beacon Bridge that spans the Hudson, from this height resembling a thin, silvery ribbon, beyond which rises the sawtoothed Catskills on the distant horizon. To reach the fire tower, continue east along the Red Trail until you come to the intersection with the White Trail. Bear right on the White Trail and follow it for one-third of a mile to the base of the newly refurbished sixty-foot fire tower. On a clear day, a gaze southward will reveal the Tappan Zee Bridge and faint outlines of the Manhattan skyline. The hike is 4.5 miles round-trip.

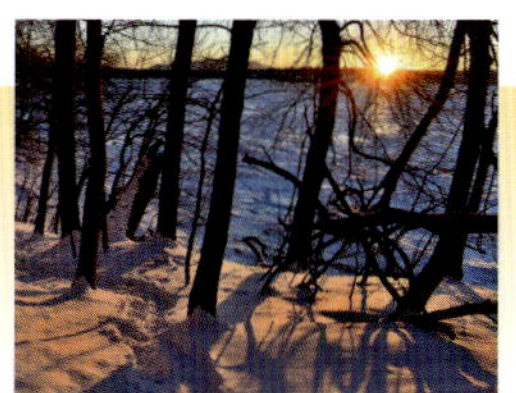

DENNING'S POINT

Denning's Avenue, Beacon

A large parking lot for this riverfront park is at the end of Denning's Avenue. From the lot, follow the unpaved road to the bridge spanning the railroad tracks and bear right, continuing down the road. Take the first left and proceed to the trailhead. A mile-long loop trail spans the peninsula, providing spectacular views of the northern Hudson Highlands. Denning's Point is closed from December 1–March 31, as the park serves as a winter roosting site for bald eagles.

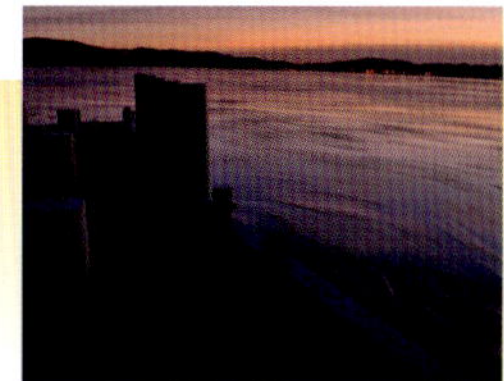

LONG DOCK PARK

23 Long Dock Park, Beacon

This elegant Scenic Hudson park sits atop a former brownfield site. Modern installations blend utility with art, such as the sculpture-like pier, constructed with a kayak launch running through the center. Limited kayak storage on site. Trail system links up to the nearby Denning's Point.

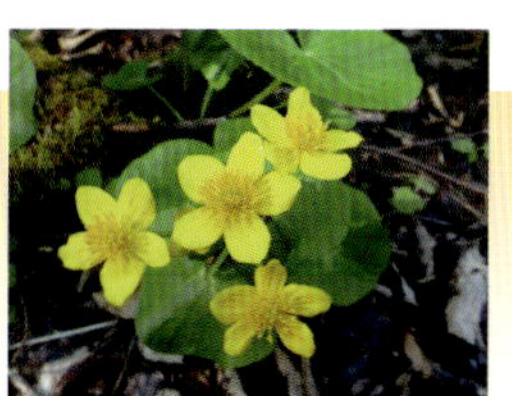

GREAT SWAMP PORTION OF THE APPALACHIAN TRAIL

Route 22, Pawling

The small parking area for the "AT" is off Route 22 in the town of Pawling. A short, unmarked dirt road that leads to it is several hundred feet south of the business Native Landscapes (991 Route 22, Pawling, 12564). From here, follow the path that leads across the railroad tracks and onto the nearly half-mile-long boardwalk. If the lot is full, parking can be found along both sides of Route 22 at the expansive pull-offs 400 feet north of Native Landscapes.

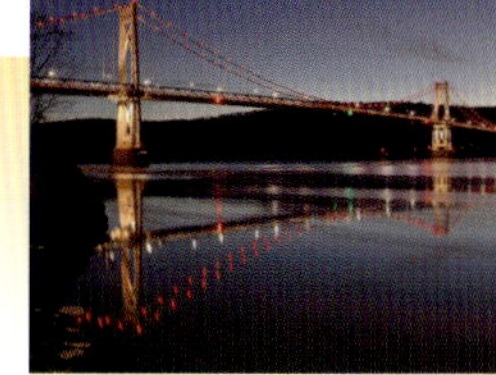

WARYAS PARK

Main Street, Poughkeepsie

A small parking area is at the western terminus of Main Street. From here, proceed to the promenade along the Hudson and walk south for a short distance. The pier at the end of the promenade provides unrivaled views of the Mid-Hudson Bridge and Walkway Over the Hudson.

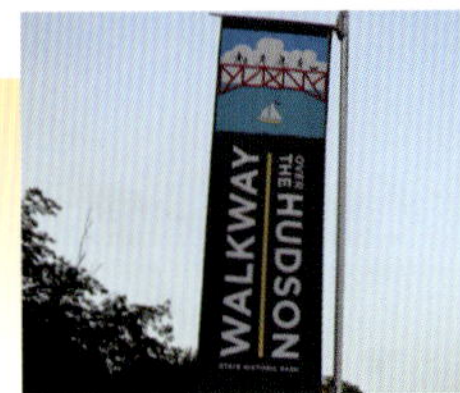

WALKWAY OVER THE HUDSON

Walkway East
61 Parker Avenue, Poughkeepsie

Walkway West
87 Haviland Road, Highland

There are two access points to the park, one on either side of the Hudson. Both have spacious parking lots. The 1.28-mile walkway is open from 7:00 a.m. to sunset. Biking is allowed.

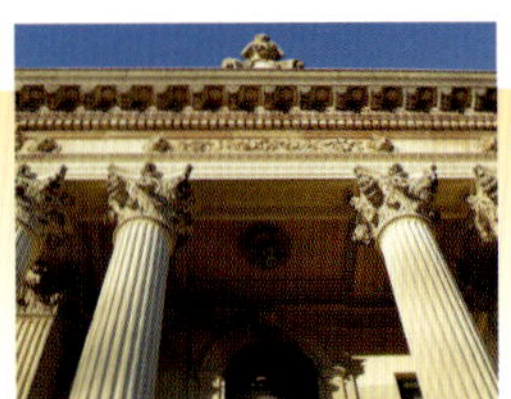

VANDERBILT MANSION

81 Vanderbilt Park Road, Hyde Park

Tours of this iconic Gilded Age mansion are offered multiple times per day throughout the year (closed Thanksgiving, Christmas, and New Year's Day). For a listing of tour hours, visit the National Park Service's website, nps.gov. The grounds are open year-round, sunrise to sunset. Historic architecture, spacious gardens reminiscent of an Italian villa, well-manicured lawns peppered with stately trees, romantic mountain vistas, and scenic riverside trails ensure this national park provides something of interest to every visitor.

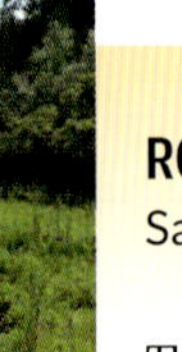

ROGER PERRY MEMORIAL PRESERVE

Sand Hill Road, Dover Plains

This small preserve managed by the Nature Conservancy is along Sand Hill Road two-tenths of a mile off the intersection with Lime Kiln Road. (Note: a parking area is at the entrance; however, the gate is normally locked. Park along the road.) The Roger Perry Preserve has only one trail, a half-mile, red-blazed loop that passes through several pure white sand pits created from the weathering of soft limestone outcroppings studding the preserve. These unusual features lend a beach-like atmosphere despite being nestled in the leafy Taconic Mountains.

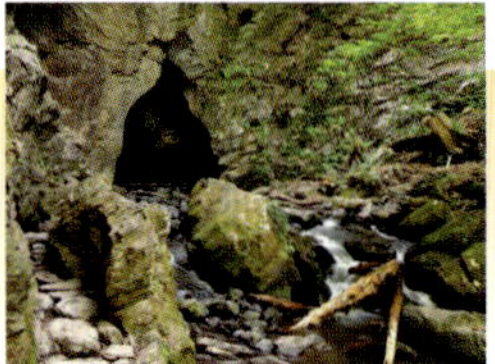

DOVER STONE CHURCH

Route 22, Dover Plains

Ample parking can be found at the Dover Elementary School (9 School Street, Dover Plains) when school is not in session. Alternate parking is allowed at the Tabor Wing House (3128 Route 22), Fresh Co. 22 (3156 Route 22), and Four Brothers Pizza (3189 Route 22). From the school, cross Route 22 and walk north for 250 feet until the blue and yellow Dover Stone Church historical marker comes into view. Immediately turn left, following the narrow lane to the trailhead. From here, it's an easy four-tenths of a mile to the church.

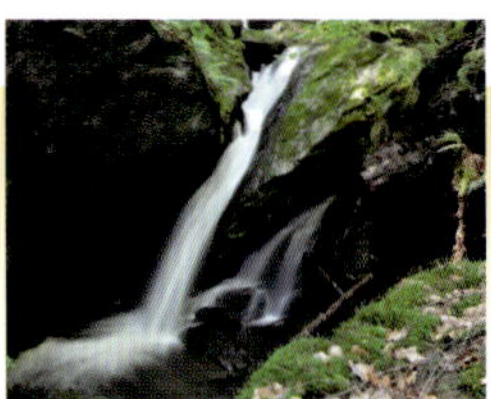

SASSACUS FALLS

Route 22, Dover Plains

This waterfall is approximately 300 feet upstream from where the brook flows through the Stone Church. To reach it, one must undertake a difficult and treacherous bushwhack up the steep and craggy slopes of West Mountain.

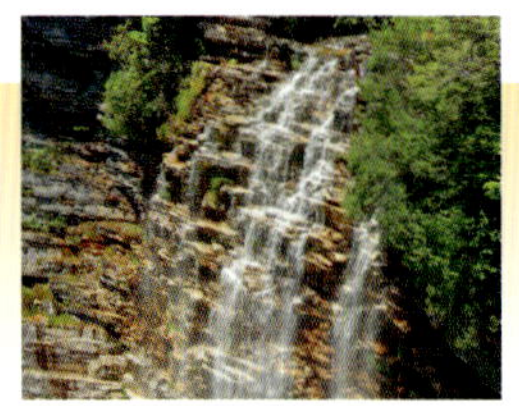

VERKEERDERKILL FALLS

400 Sam's Point Road, Cragsmoor

This spectacular waterfall is at Sam's Point Preserve (recently acquired by New York State and incorporated into Minnewaska State Park). Take the Verkeerderkill Falls Trail (aqua), 5.5 miles round-trip.

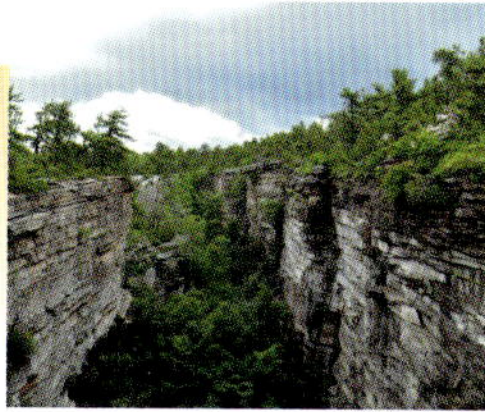

GRAND CANYON OF THE ELLENVILLE ICE CAVES

Berme Road, Ellenville
41° 42' 47.41" N, 74° 21' 44.27" W

Heading west on Route 52 in Ellenville, turn right on Broadhead Street, which soon becomes Berme Road. Follow Berme Road for one-tenth of a mile and turn right again, entering Berme Park. Parking is behind the tennis courts.

The only way to reach the "canyon" is through difficult bushwhacking. Begin by following the Smiley Carriageway located a couple hundred feet east of the parking lot. Stay on this for about 1.25 miles until reaching Shingle Gully. Proceed uphill following the intermittent stream. From here, it's mostly rugged bushwhacking. Permits are no longer issued for this section of the backcountry. To visit the area, one must now join a docent-led group hike, occasionally offered through Minnewaska State Park. Dates of scheduled hikes are listed on the park's webpage: nysparks.com.

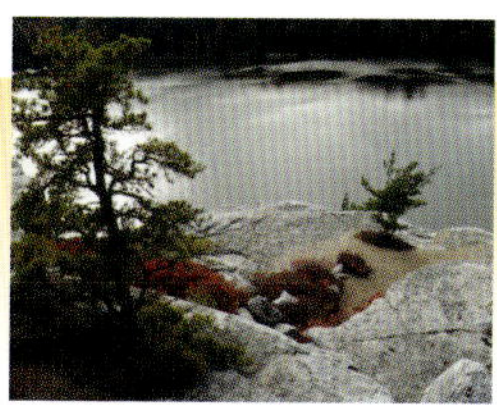

MINNEWASKA STATE PARK

Route 44-55, Kerhonkson

Lake Minnewaska

At the park entrance, drive uphill to the upper parking area. The red-blazed Minnewaska Carriageway is an easy two-mile loop that encircles the lake atop high scenic bluffs. In addition to shimmering lake views, the route affords crisp panoramas of the Catskills to the northwest. Swimming is permitted in designated areas in summer.

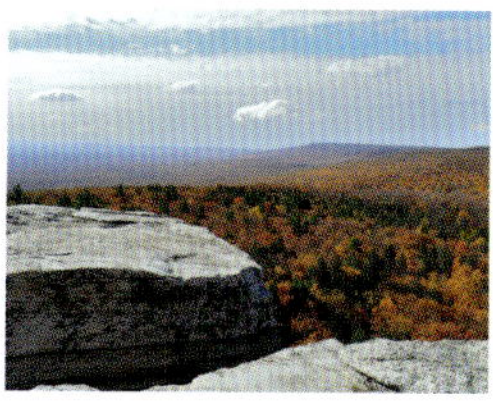

Gertrude's Nose & Millbrook Mountain

From the upper parking area, follow the trail maps to hike out to the red-blazed Gertrude's Nose trail, which later becomes the Millbrook Mountain trail. The shortest route that journeys out to both sites is approximately eight miles.

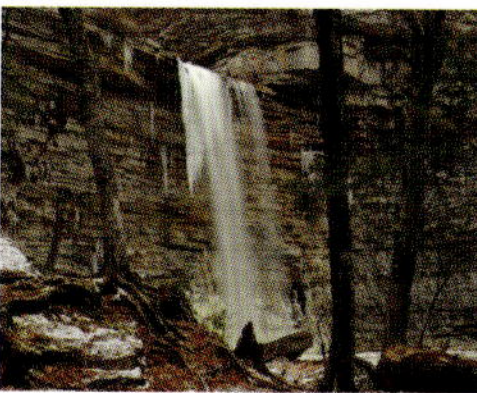

Awosting Falls

From the lower parking area, take the red-blazed Awosting Falls Trail for a quarter-mile to reach this impressive sixty-foot waterfall.

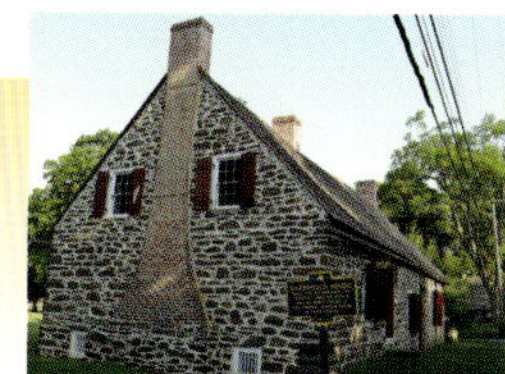

HASBROUCK HOUSE

94 Huguenot Street, New Paltz

This historic residence is on Huguenot Street, one of the oldest continuously inhabited streets in the US. Seven stone dwellings built during the early 1700s are open to the public. Historic Huguenot Street offers tours. Visit their website for more information, huguenotstreet.org.

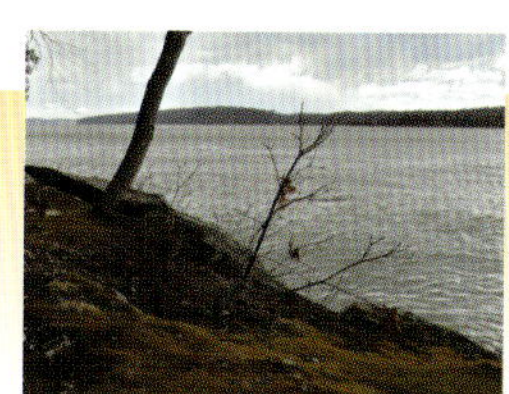

BLACK CREEK PRESERVE

Winding Brook Road, Esopus

Access to this Scenic Hudson park is along Winding Brook Road. The parking area is on the left, a few hundred feet from the intersection of Route 9W. Trails lead through dark hemlock stands, past vernal pools, and finally to superb views of the Hudson and Esopus Island. The eponymous Black Creek is also a popular fishing destination.

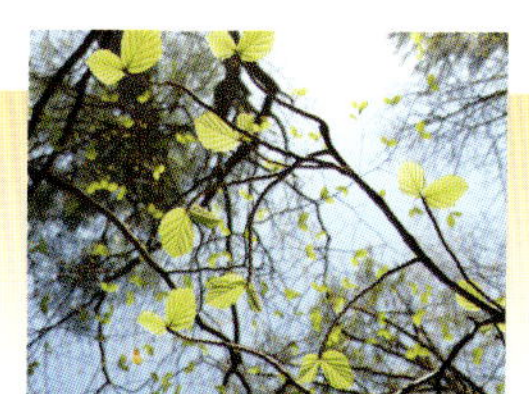

MILLS-NORRIE STATE PARK

Old Town Park Lane, Staatsburg

One of the many parking areas scattered throughout the park is at the western terminus of Old Town Park Lane. Located along the water, this spot is perfect for fishing, launching kayaks, or more languid pursuits such as relaxing in a gazebo that graces the Hudson shoreline, or perhaps on one of the stone benches that line the white-blazed riverside trail. There are multiple trails throughout. Mills Mansion, a Gilded Age estate, is in the northern portion of the park and open to visitors.

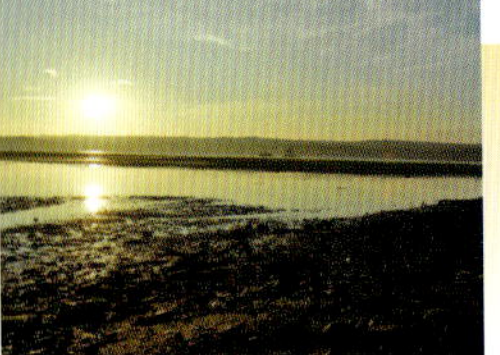

ESOPUS MEADOWS PRESERVE

269 River Road, Ulster Park

To reach this tranquil park managed by Scenic Hudson, take Route 9W north to the intersection of River Road. Make a right and continue 1.3 miles. The parking area will be on the right. Three hiking trails meander throughout the preserve, with some of the best scenery found along the Blue Trail that skirts the murky Hudson. Exquisite views of the Esopus Meadows Lighthouse and glimpses of the historic Mills Mansion can be seen from the sandy shores of this riverside trail.

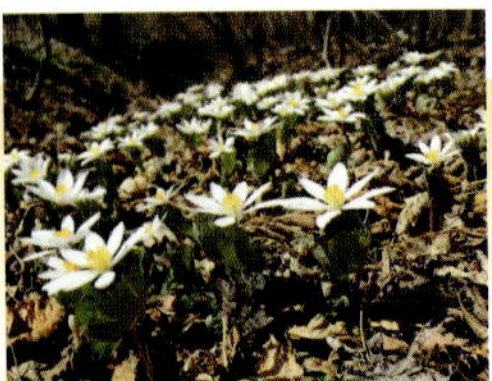

TIVOLI BAYS

Cruger Island Road, Tivoli

Parking for the Tivoli Bays Wildlife Management Area is toward the end of the unpaved Cruger Island Road, less than a quarter-mile from the intersection of Annandale Road, which bisects Bard College. Walk down the access road to the several hiking trails that branch off. Maps are available online: www/dec/ny/gov.

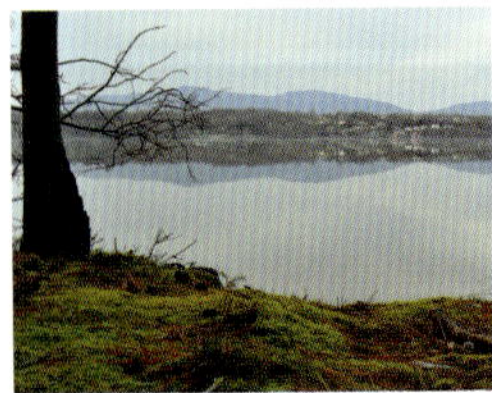

To reach Cruger Island, take the access road for a half-mile until it makes a sharp right at the bottom of the hill. Continue straight ahead on the causeway that leads into the marsh. (Note: the causeway is in poor condition, muddy, and partially submerged during high tide.) In four-tenths of a mile it will bring you to railroad tracks. Just beyond the tracks lies the island. Public access is restricted from January 1–September 30.

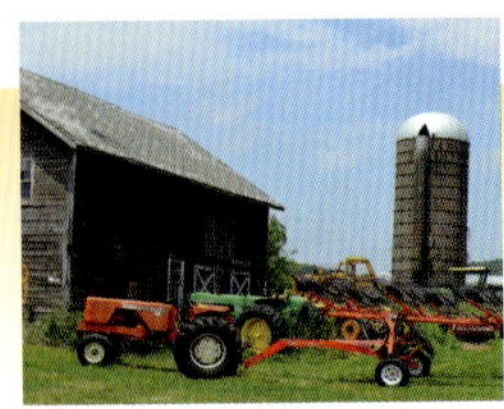

ANCRAM

Some of the best pastoral scenes of southern Columbia County can be seen driving along NY Route 82 and County Routes 3 and 7 in the town of Ancram.

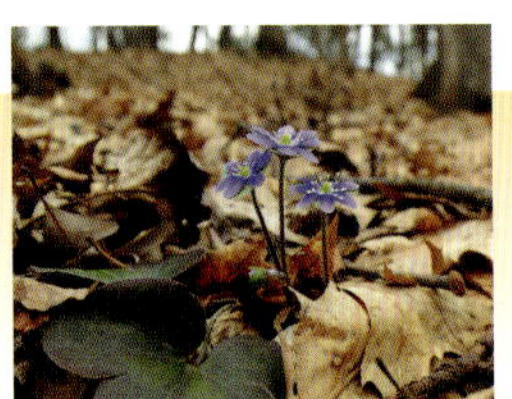

RAMSHORN-LIVINGSTON SANCTUARY

84 Dubois Road, Catskill

From the parking area, walk along the Old Farm Road for a half-mile. This will lead to the red, white, and blue trails. Each has a rich assortment of spring ephemeral wildflowers. A kayak launch is located toward the end of the Old Farm Road.

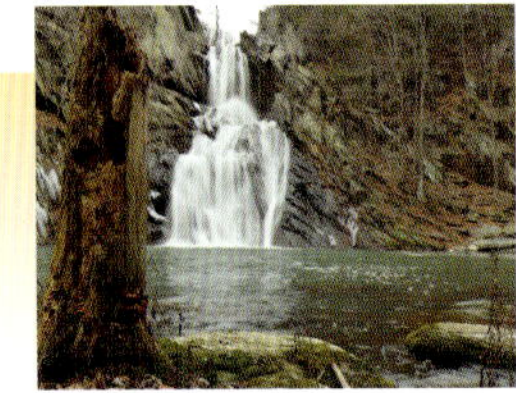

HIGH FALLS

540 Roxbury Road, Hudson

From the parking area, take the Green Trail to the Upper Blue Trail and walk to its terminus. Before coming to the end of the Upper Blue Trail, an impressive waterfall appears across the creek, but this is not the main gem. When the trail ends, keep following the Agawamuck Creek to the plunge pool at the base of the 150-foot High Falls (reaching this spot requires negotiating your way over innumerable slick, moss covered rocks). Alternatively, a pleasant overlook of the falls can be reached by taking the Green Trail to its end. These stunning sights can be reached with minimal effort—the three trails that comprise the park total only 1.2 miles.

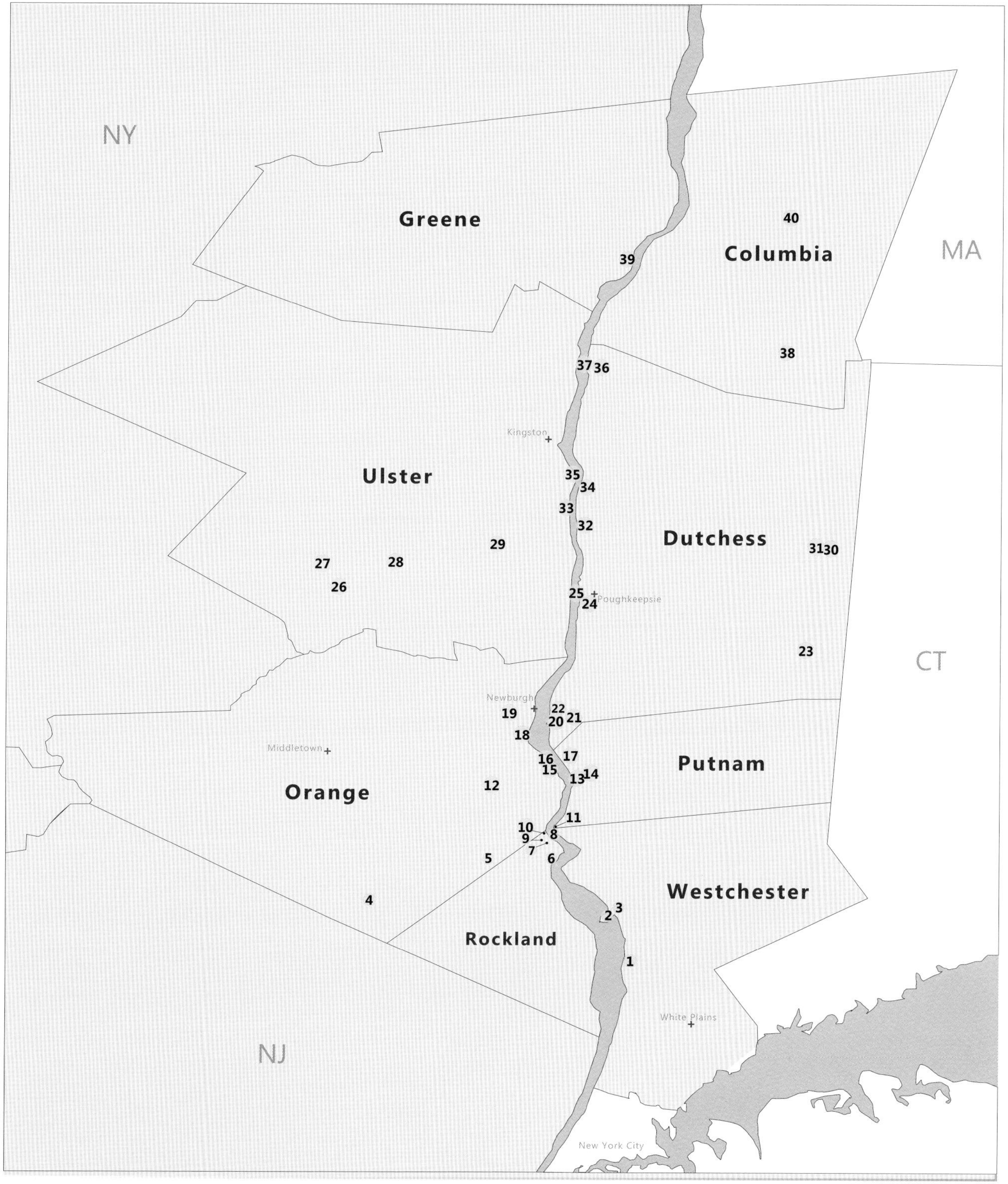

Hudson Valley Destinations

1 Sleepy Hollow Cemetery & Old Dutch Church
2 Croton Point
3 Van Cortlandt Manor
4 Sterling Lake
5 Pine Swamp
6 Dunderberg Mountain
7 Doodletown Brook Falls
8 Iona Island
9 Bear Mountain
10 Trailside Museums & Zoo
11 Anthony's Nose
12 Schunnemunk State Park
13 Constitution Marsh
14 Indian Brook Falls
15 North Point
16 Storm King Mountain
17 Bull Hill
18 Plum Point & Machin's Battery
19 Snake Hill
20 Denning's Point
21 Mt. Beacon
22 Long Dock Park
23 Great Swamp
24 Waryas Park
25 Walkway Over the Hudson
26 Verkeerderkill Falls
27 "Grand Canyon" of the Ellenville Ice Caves
28 Minnewaska State Park (Lake Minnewaska, Awosting Falls, Gertrude's Nose & Millbrook Mountain)
29 Hasbrouck House
30 Roger Perry Preserve
31 Dover Stone Church & Sassacus Falls
32 Vanderbilt Mansion
33 Black Creek Preserve
34 Mills-Norrie State Park
35 Esopus Meadows Preserve
36 Tivoli Bays
37 Cruger Island
38 Ancram
39 RamsHorn-Livingston Sanctuary
40 High Falls

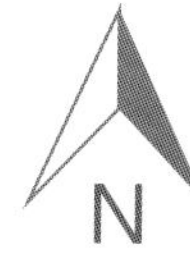

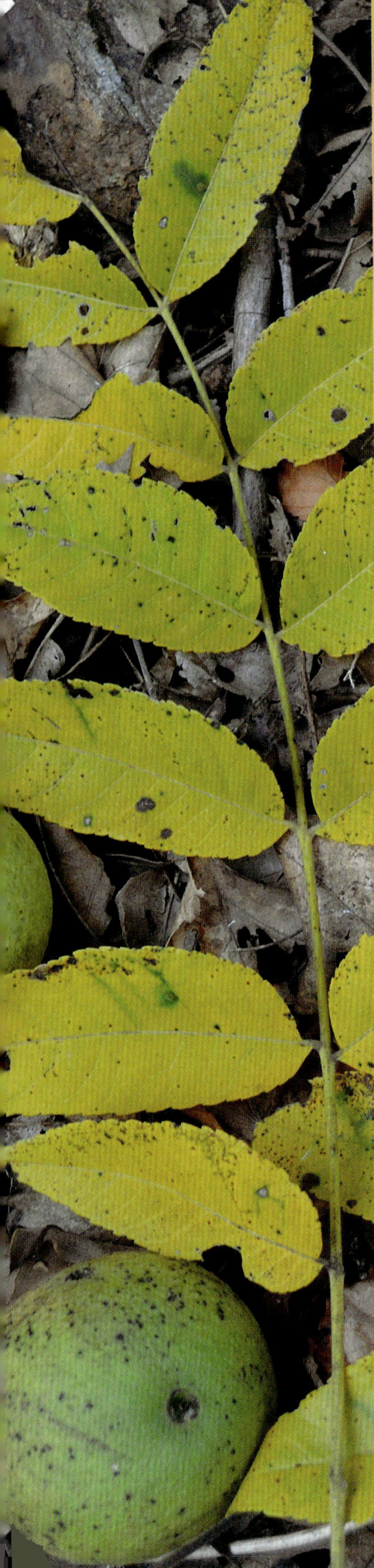

ACKNOWLEDGMENTS

This book is the culmination of many years of hard work and long days traipsing across the fields and forests, up the mountains, and down into the bogs and wetlands of the Hudson Valley. I thank those who joined me on countless hikes and other expeditions, putting up with my frequent and sometimes lengthy photography breaks along the way. Your company made the experience more enjoyable.

Some of the remarkable images of wildlife and plants would not have been possible without the invaluable assistance of numerous individuals in environmental agencies throughout New York State. For providing important leads on the whereabouts of certain species or offering useful facts that I included with some of the photographs, I gratefully thank Edwin McGowan, Elaine Brown, Jesse Jaycox, Amy Bloomfield, Emily Underwood, Kelly Farrell, Stephen Stanne, and Stephen Young.

Appreciation goes out to the team at One Nature, LLC, most notably Bryan Quinn and Emilie Potter, who helped create the map.

And to those who graciously offered support and guidance in a variety of ways, I offer my unwavering esteem: Shawn Marshall, Ailin Walsh, Andrew Jaouen, Christina Haering, Stancy DuHamel, Kathy Laura and Michael L. Adamovic, and, of course, Meagan Clark.

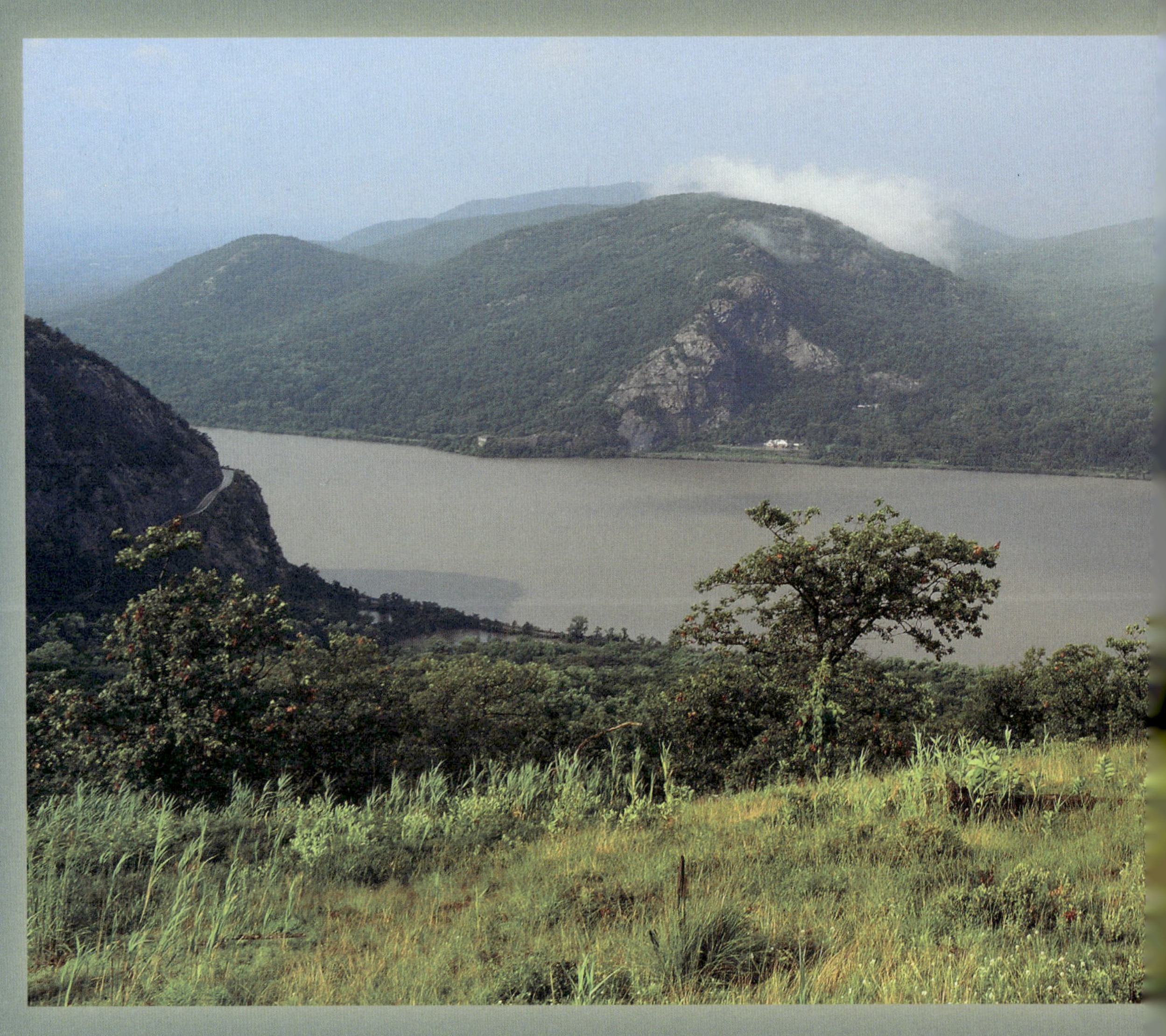